Writing That Matters

A RHETORIC FOR THE NEW CLASSROOM

W. T. PFEFFERLE, PH.D.

PRENTICE HALL
UPPER SADDLE RIVER, NEW JERSEY 07458

Library of Congress Cataloging–in–Publication Data

Pfefferle, W. T.
   Writing that matters : a rhetoric for the new classroom / W. T.
Pfefferle.
      p. cm.
   ISBN 0-13-862020-2
   1. English language—Rhetoric.   2. Report writing.   I. Title.
PE1408.P455   1999
808'.042—dc21
                                                      98-24399
                                                         CIP

Editorial Director: Charlyce Jones Owen
Editor-in-Chief: Leah Jewell
Director of Production and Manufacturing: Barbara Kittle
Senior Managing Editor: Bonnie Biller
Senior Project Manager: Shelly Kupperman
Manufacturing Manager: Nick Sklitsis
Prepress and Manufacturing Buyer: Mary Ann Gloriande
Director of Marketing: Gina Sluss
Creative Design Director: Leslie Osher
Interior Designer: Seventeenth Street Studios
Editorial Assistant: Patricia Castiglione
Cover Art: Don Carstens Photography
Cover Designer: Joe Sengotta

For permission to use copyrighted material, grateful acknowledgment is made to the copyright holders on page xviii, which is considered an extension of this copyright page.

This book was set in 10.5/13 Sabon by Seventeenth Street Studios and printed by R. R. Donnelley & Sons–Harrisonburg. The cover was printed by Phoenix Color Corporation.

© 1999 by Prentice-Hall, Inc.
Simon and Schuster/A Viacom Company
Upper Saddle River, New Jersey 07458

Printed in the United States of America
10 9 8 7 6 5 4 3 2 1

ISBN 0-13-862020-2

Prentice-Hall International (UK) Limited, *London*
Prentice-Hall of Australia Pty. Limited, *Sydney*
Prentice-Hall Canada, Inc., *Toronto*
Prentice-Hall Hispanoamericana, S.A., *Mexico*
Prentice-Hall of India Private Limited, *New Delhi*
Prentice-Hall of Japan, Inc., *Tokyo*
Simon & Schuster Asia Pte. Ltd., *Singapore*
Editora Prentice-Hall do Brasil, Ltda., *Rio de Janeiro*

Contents

Preface

To the instructor

I'm one of you. I've been doing this job for almost fifteen years. It's a job that is equal parts joy and misery. Sometimes I feel like I'm moving through a class easily, like a drop of water slipping down the side of a glass. Other times the glass breaks and the water spills all over my new pants. Teaching comp is a lot like being married. It takes plenty of love and even more imagination!

To be a teacher of writing often means staying out of the way. I've taught remedial students, traditional students, adult students, honors students, foreign language students, and so on, and I've never met anyone who didn't have *something* to say. Let them find their voices and their messages. They need our help, but they have their own brains, and sometimes theirs are more lively than ours!

Don't allow the "keeping of the grade" to be your sole duty in class. You and I both know that grades are necessary. We have to fill in some piece of paper at the end of each semester (and sometimes at midterm). So we know *someone somewhere* wants it. But remember that if you're going to play the role of "helper" to your writers, removing yourself from the "gradekeeper" role sometimes is imperative.

I've wrestled with the role of grades all of my career. When I started teaching I let grades protect me from students. Because I was young and insecure about my abilities in the classroom, I allowed grades to be my hammer. When I wanted to punish a student, I did it with a bad grade. When I wanted to assert my authority, I did it with grades. It's silly to me now. Grades are rather unimportant as they relate to our writers improving as communicators. Of course grades are important to them as *students*—as they move through college, earn scholarships, maintain academic viability—but grades should mean nothing whatsoever to them as writers. Try to see your role as an instructor of writing and communication. Interact with your writers. Show them some things you know. Help them find their own areas of interest. Encourage them to write and to keep writing. The grades are something else entirely, important in one way, but sometimes intrusive.

Many of the concepts that I hold dear (especially workshopping and conferencing) can only really work if you are open to them. The Support Group (Chapter 13), in fact, discusses step by step how these very important and useful tools can help us with our writers.

My ideas are good. But so are yours. If you see a better way to set up the assignments in the book, do it. Sometimes personalizing the tasks to your special needs can make a great deal of difference to your writers. I had a teacher in college who always talked about Maria Callas, Dwight Eisenhower, Elvis Presley, and communism. For him, those examples were timely. But each year he used them, they got more and more out of date and less and less useful for his writers. So, make this book something of your *own* whenever and however you can.

I don't think anything matters more than helping your writers communicate better. Be their partner. Be there for them. Hold workshops and conferences and office hours. Make it pleasant and enjoyable to visit with you. Don't "summon" students to a conference. Invite them. Try not to "make" them do so much. "Let" them. Give them the opportunity.

Obviously, some of our writers will need more encouragement, and maybe your "gradekeeper" status will come in handy. But I believe most of our developing writers will come along just fine without threats. Many of them want to write better; they just may not know it yet.

They're the horses. The work is in the water. Show them the way to the river.

W. T. Pfefferle

To the writers

I call you writers because the word "student" just doesn't cover enough territory. You *will* be learning about writing, but most of what you'll do this semester is write. Here are some things I want you to know at the beginning.

Writing is great. It can be fun, beautiful, thrilling, and it's one of the best tools to have when living on this planet. And, whether you like it or not, there is no way to avoid it.

If you want a simple reason to become a better writer, ask some other students who have been in college for a while how many essays they've written. Over the course of a four-year college career, you may write as many as 50–75 essays. Essays don't just happen in English classes. Think about tests and assignments: Many are essay questions. Over the next few years you will be asked to discuss and argue and make points in a more and more mature manner—most of them through writing.

In this class, we're going to explore ways to write. We're going to develop a language of mature and intelligent prose. We're going to discover ways to uncover the neat and fascinating ideas within your brain. And we'll help you find a way to explain your thoughts and ideas to others, so they can understand them, too.

Next, let's talk a little about that person up at the front of the room. Your instructor wants to help you. That person up there doesn't do this job for money. Ask for help when you need it, or when you're unclear. I'm an instructor, too, and I'm not perfect. I can't tell when my writers need help. Sometimes I can see their faces "squinch" up, or their heads shake. But, usually, if my writers don't say anything, I just keep going. I like to know when my students need help, and I bet your instructor does, too.

Your instructor has a lot of folks to take care of, so you'll likely be given a great deal of responsibility. Take advantage of this. *Listen*. Get your assignments. Do them on time. Work hard. It's not a joke. Somebody is paying for you to be here: you, your folks, a rich uncle, the state, someone! Get your money's worth. Be involved. Ask questions. Offer help when you can. There are always ways to get "around" work and just "get by." If that's your style, then I really can't do anything for you. I hope that your instructor and I and this book will energize you and that you'll be eager to play the game that is set up in the pages of this text.

Your success in this class is up to you. Your instructor has all the tools necessary to help you do your work, but in the end, it's you who's sitting there pecking away at that computer late at night.

If I could, I'd come to your class, wherever you are, and tell you how amazing your time in college can be. I would tell you that what *I* learned in college was that first-year comp (*this* class) is the best, most important, most useful, and coolest class there is.

Most of all, I'd just tell you to live it up. Life is short. Writing is great. To really communicate with the world is the greatest thrill we can expect on this planet, and I don't want you to miss out. This book was not written because I wanted the cash, or because I had to do it to keep my job. I wrote it because I wanted you to have a blast with the stuff that's inside. Keep an open mind. Have fun.

THE STEPS IN THIS BOOK

Each essay we will work on during the semester has its own chapter. You'll discover each of the following sections in a chapter.

SOMETHING TO THINK ABOUT

I talk about things at the opening of each chapter. Think of it as a lecture. I'm a firm believer in getting our minds together before starting off on a new journey. If I came by your house and told you we were going on a car trip, I'd also tell you how far we were going. I wouldn't just expect you to know we were going to drive to Portland, Oregon, and be gone for seventeen days. You might get in the car thinking we're going to the 7-Eleven down the street. To be fair to you, I'd try to get you thinking about Portland, Oregon, first. "Nice trees. Lots of coffee shops. It's in the Northwest!" That way when we get in the car (or when we start our essay), you've got an idea about what's coming.

GETTING STARTED

As I read, the question I ask most often is "so what?" When students write me essays, I'm always asking myself "Why am I reading this? Why is this worth my time?" Well, now that I'm about to ask you to work for me, I believe I owe you the same kind of consideration. I will try to show you different ways in which each essay's construction is beneficial to you, not just in this semester, but in your future.

WARMUPS

If you've never been swimming before, I wouldn't throw you in a lake. Instead, I'd start you in a pool, in the shallow end. I'd let you swim a bunch. Short swims, long swims. Likewise, I think it's a great idea to try some ideas out. So I've given you some small writing assignments inside each chapter that will allow you to try out these essay ideas before you write the real essay. (The real essay is a pretty big grade, usually, so these little warmup exercises are perfect for getting ready.)

This book is as small as I could make it. I only ask you to do things that I've seen help other writers. Your instructor won't be assigning work just for the sake of "giving you something to do." Everything we do in this book is valuable, and the warmups are essential parts of preparing you for the bigger writing to come next.

THE ESSAY ASSIGNMENT

This is the real thing. This is the essay assignment that the entire chapter leads up to. Your instructor will probably be involved here in helping you narrow the assignment down to something to write about. My assignment is good as it is, but your instructor may have some valuable and helpful ideas. He or she is trying to help you and is working hard to make this essay assignment one that will help you get better as a writer and meet the needs of your particular course.

SAMPLE ESSAYS

Most of the essays (usually two or three in every chapter) are written by people I've taught. They aren't fancy or famous writers, just nice people who have worked hard in my classes. These aren't the "best" essays I've ever seen, but in virtually every case they represent a very good approach to the assignment. I'd suggest that reading these samples is a great idea, because in all cases the writers have successfully grasped the lesson I'm trying to teach. However, you are your own writer, with your own mind. I'm sure your instructor will warn you not to simply imitate these essays. That would be a terrible idea. The essays in this book are genuine, original pieces that were sweated over by their authors. I want you to write your own, in your own style. There are many right ways in which to take on these essay assignments. The samples are merely a couple of examples that have worked. You should definitely read them (and my comments about them, and do the questions I assign after each), but you should always keep in mind that at some point you'll be writing your own essay.

You'll also find an occasional "professional" essay. Each was written by a writer out in the real world, and I've included them not so much as models but as "jumping-off" or starting points. When your instructor asks you to read these professional pieces, he or she is most likely trying to get you to start thinking, reacting to text, and formulating your own ideas in "response" to the text you're reading.

One of the tricky things about reading professional essays is in not becoming intimidated by them. Those writers have been writing for many years. They've been through this class and others like it; they've written in the real world, worked with a wide variety of other writers and editors, and for the most part are working at the height of their powers. The good news is that they've likely sat at their desks, in front of their computers or blank sheets of paper, and gone through a writing process very similar to the one you're going to be introduced to this semester.

I love to read a really great professional essay like the ones I've included in this book. But sometimes I feel discouraged because the writing is often so much better, more complicated, and more sure of itself than my own essays. You'll likely feel that way, too, but fight against it. Imagine how one day you'll be able to write as well, as persuasively, and as beautifully as those more advanced writers, and then those essays will be a goal to reach for in your thinking and communicating.

QUESTIONS

These are questions specifically about the sample essays. Just like the earlier section of "warmups," these are often writing tasks or assignments that you're asked to do.

The questions will often refer you back to the essay you've just read and ask you to comment on some of the essential essay elements our writer has worked on. Sometimes you'll be asked to rewrite a bad section of text or to explain what you think this sample essay writer should do next.

WHILE YOU'RE WRITING/WORKSHOP QUESTIONS

This is a section of hints and ideas for you to consider as you're actually working on your essay. Your instructor will have you on some kind of schedule, and some or all of these steps should be very helpful in managing your time as you work through the assignment.

Think of it as two checklists: one that you can use as you work on your essay, the other a help when it's time for the class to meet in workshop and share a peer-reading of essays in progress.

W. T. Pfefferle

Acknowledgments

When I was twelve I went to the "free school." I can remember that place better than I can remember most of the houses I've lived in during my life. No walls. No chairs. Beanbags on the floor. A big kiln in the corner for making pots. All the teachers had long hair, men and women. It was the 1970s, after all. This kind of school, also sometimes called the "new school," had a short heyday in North America, but some of its concepts still live on.

Much of what I do in the classroom to this day comes from my year and a half at the free school. (My limited time there ended shortly after my parents discovered that we didn't have chairs or desks in the free school, and I suddenly found myself at some other school, quite a bit more traditional.) But the "free school," and one teacher in particular, Peter Lanyon, remain in my heart and my mind. Peter Lanyon drove a Toyota Landcruiser and wore sandals and was the first cool man I ever knew. He was a "hippie," I suppose, in that time or any other. But he treated us as if we mattered and, more important, treated us as if our *ideas* mattered. It was freeing and wonderful and invigorating, and it was the first time I loved school.

It was there where I first felt "empowered" as a student and as a human being, and in fact "empowering" students is my principle educational goal now as a teacher. I would give anything to go back to that time and do it all again. I grew as a student and as a human being faster and more assuredly in that short span than at any other time of my life.

I can remember the first time I thought teaching was a good job. I was a sophomore in college, doing okay work in a great Shakespeare class taught by the late John Doebler. He made us come to his office once a semester so he could be sure we were alive and kicking and thinking. I went there one spring afternoon, and his office was startlingly different from the rest of the fluorescent classrooms and hallways of the huge Language and Literature building on the campus of Arizona State. He had a thick rug on the floor, soft lighting, jazz music playing on a small stereo. I was very impressed.

I sat in a nice leather chair, and when I saw the small refrigerator behind his desk, I knew I was in the presence of someone who was living a good life. I don't have any memory of what we talked about, but I do remember that office and how at ease he was in it. He was a guy who seemed to be comfortable in his own skin. After that day, I started to listen in class.

He loved Shakespeare. He loved the plays. He loved what those plays taught him, and he tried to teach that same stuff to us. We often didn't get it, but that never seemed to dissuade him in the least from going on.

Years and years and years later, I called his office and told him my name. It had been about 14 years since I had been an insignificant member of one of his hundreds of classes. "Pfefferle" I said. He paused a bit and said, "You were the one who liked my refrigerator." The next time I got an alumni newsletter, I discovered that John Doebler had passed away.

Around the same time, I met Marianna Brose. She was another English professor at ASU. She taught an intro to literature class that was made up of people like me, a psychology major at the time, taking some lousy intro class to satisfy a humanities credit. We had a big, dull, poorly edited book of poems, stories, and drama. I don't think any of us ever read a thing out of it. But Marianna did. She read out loud every class. Long pieces of text. Some of us snoozed. I know I did. She was an old lady (we thought). She was reading stuff written by dead people. I looked out the window most of the semester.

She never grew tired of reading. Toward the end, she read some John Keats to us. She told us to close our eyes and listen. She read "Ode to a Nightingale" and asked what we thought about it. Nobody said anything. She read the whole poem again. Then she asked what we thought. Again, nothing. Then she read it again. The whole thing. By now I was listening. When she finished, and when she asked what we thought again, I said "Wow," or something like it. That last line about being awake or asleep stuck in my head. I probably didn't understand much of that poem, but Marianna read it again for us. And from that day on, I listened.

I met Steve Carter on the very first day of my first teaching gig. We were picking up our textbooks and syllabi for our first classes. We laughed casually, chatted for a few minutes, and ambled off to our respective rooms, neither one wanting to admit that we were in way over our heads. I saw Steve the next day and the next, and now we've been pals for twelve years. Even though separated by hundreds of miles for the past decade, we keep in touch constantly. I would never say it out loud, or anywhere near him, but I think of him as my brother. He's smart, funny, loyal, and has an immense capacity for compassion and friendship. I hope I've given him as much as he's given me.

Dave Phalen comes from the same state as my wife, and he thinks that means he can flirt with her on the phone. It doesn't. I met Dave the same year I met Steve, and the three of us get together once a year in a sort of manly bonding ritual involving a lot of big lies about how great we could have been if the *world* hadn't kept us down. He's as fine a friend as he is a father to his three wonderful daughters, and that's saying a lot. In this book's last 96 hours, he did yeoman's work via e-mail and Internet Relay Chat, helping me put final touches on the manuscript. His crisp eye saved scores of small mistakes and several major ones. I owe him, and I don't say that very often.

I was a student of the novelist Frederick Barthelme for a couple of years. It was in the day when people were still allowed to smoke in America. In our grad class, Barthelme would smoke. He'd light a cigarette, smoke it for a while, then drop it to the linoleum floor, lighting another as he ground the first one out. He'd tell us stories about famous people he'd met. Every story would end the same way. He'd regale us with a wild story of debauchery and madness and then he'd say the famous person's name again. "Jim Morrison? He was short." Every story. Everyone was short. We loved it. We thought it was arrogance.

It wasn't actually. It was an accurate way of viewing the world. People are people. Human. Short, fat, bald, whatever. Just people. He taught us to view the world as it really was, not as it was taught to us by media or by fame or even by our own imaginations. We all wanted to be like him. None of us made it. We became teachers, carpenters, computer programmers, plumbers and so on, but we all remembered what it was like to sit in that class full of cigarette smoke and hear a guy who saw the world for what it was.

Dave Roberts was my first director of composition. He let me teach composition when I really shouldn't have been doing it at all. I was a grad student with lots of other stuff on my mind, and teaching young writers and young minds was beyond my abilities. He met with each of us once a week or so to see how things were going. I'd tell him some horrendous mistake I'd made in class and he'd tell me what I might want to do next time it came up. He lent me heavy comp books that he had read and highlighted himself. He encouraged me to hang in there, to keep teaching, to try out all these different crazy ideas that he taught us about. He taught me an appreciation of the earlier comp teachers, whether they were from the 1960s, or from the eighth century. He taught us that the key was in the class itself. Much of what I do to this day comes from those short meetings I had with him.

Mary Jo Southern had faith in my ideas and she was instrumental in helping me shape this book. Her unerring eye helped me see through some things in the early stages. Her validation of my ideas and the premise of this book meant a profound amount to me.

During those last hard months, Leah Jewell, Patricia Castiglione, and Shelly Kupperman worked hard in the trenches to get the project done. They answered countless silly questions, and some sensible ones, always with keen attention. If I bugged them (and I know I did), they never let it show.

I was treated like a superhero of composition research during a brief visit to Texas Tech University. I was the guest of comp director Fred Kemp, but everyone in the department made time to welcome me and answer my questions. Joanna Castner, Linda Myers, and Pat Tyrer all opened their classrooms to me, and Pat additionally acted as "cruise director" for my visit.

Karen DeVinney is a fabulous colleague. She doesn't pry, she's always ready for lunch, and she never talks about her dissertation. What a joy to be around. She's a person first. She also read several sections of this book on that last crazy weekend, and I'm indebted to her, too.

I want to thank the various friends through the years, who have accepted me as I am. I've lived a remarkable and thrilling life because of all of you, played lots of tennis and hockey as a boy, played in lots of bad bands in lots of bad bars as an adult. To those pals, I say thanks.

I first met my in-laws, G.O. and Bonnie, about fifteen years ago. I don't think I was much in the "son-in-law" department then, but they have always treated me with unselfish measures of love and kindness. Their home has always been my home, too, and I'm proud that we are all family.

My mom made me do English in the back seat of the car on vacation. She had this horrible little green grammar book from the seventh grade or something. Awful. Awful. Ruined many of my vacations with the thing. But she always encouraged me to read (even if it was just hockey and guitar magazines). She bought me books instead of toys sometimes, and once I even made her cry when she gave me a ceramic set of characters from the Winnie the Pooh stories. I wanted a truck or something, you know? Anyway, she never gave up on me. She always wanted me to read and to write. When my high school teacher told her I didn't write like I was "supposed to," that I was trying to be like Ernest Hemingway, she asked him "What's wrong with that?"

My wife lets me talk on and on. I rattle ideas through my head all day, and when she comes home from work, I rattle them off to her. She listens, or pretends to, even when she's tired or ready to say something herself. She's watched me go into my office (wherever it's been) over the past twelve years and given me the space and the encouragement to keep writing: short stories, songs, my first book, this book, long rambling e-mail letters I send all over.

Had she not "let" me, this book never would have gotten written. I should have taken her dancing more often, but I never did.

I always wanted to write a book of poems for her. Dedicate it to her. Write "for Beth" on a page by itself. Something romantic, you know? I always love seeing dedications like that. She's the greatest wife there ever could be and she deserves at least that. But, a textbook? Please! If I ever do write something sweet and funny and kind and pretty, I'll dedicate it to her. I don't want her waxing sentimental over a textbook, you know? Until that day though, this book—like everything else I do—is for her.

Credits

A section from *Zen and the Art of Motorcycle Maintenance*, Robert M. Pirsig. © 1974 Robert M. Pirsig. By permission of William Morrow and Company, Inc. See page 84.

"La Donna Nord: An Oasis in a Fast-Food World," Linda Bergstrom. © 1997 Chicago Tribune Company, all rights reserved, used by permission. See page 107.

"Pizza Hut vs. Papa John's: So Which One Makes the Better Pizza?" Scott Joseph. © 1997 *The Orlando Sentinel*, used by permission. See page 110.

"How Safely Can We Fly?" J. Mac McClellan. Originally appeared in *Flying*, May 1997. Reprinted by permission. © Hachette Filipacchi Magazines. All rights reserved. See page 142.

"Making the Case for Smoker's Rights," Robert Samuelson. © 1997 Washington Post Writer's Group. Reprinted by permission. See page 216.

"Safe Sex and the Singles Club," Ellen Goodman. © 1987 Boston Globe Newspaper Company / Washington Post Writer's Group. Reprinted by permission. See page 218.

"The Party's Over at 'Party Schools,'" Editorial. © 1997 Chicago Tribune Company, all rights reserved, used by permission. See page 220.

"A Town Takes On Road Rage," Editorial. © 1997 Chicago Tribune Company, all rights reserved, used by permission. See page 221.

"Trust," Andrew A. Rooney. © 1982, 1986 Essay Productions, Inc. Reprinted with the permission of Scribner, a Division of Simon & Schuster from *And More By Andy Rooney*, by Andrew A. Rooney. See page 231.

"Fish," Frederick Barthelme. © 1983 Frederick Barthelme. Reprinted with the permission of the Wylie Agency, Inc. See page 290.

"At the Swings," Henry Taylor. © 1985 by Henry Taylor. Reprinted by permission of Louisiana State University Press from *The Flying Change* by Henry Taylor. See page 298.

1

Why Write?

Something to think about

Let's begin at the very beginning. If you're holding this book in your hands, then you are at the entryway to a long semester of freshman composition. I want to make you feel at ease. "Why write?" is a reasonable question, and if I had a simple answer for you I'd give it right now and be done with it. But I don't. Why we should write is a complex query that deserves a lot of different answers. Let's start with this one.

We can't avoid writing or composing

As a college student, you will be doing your fair share of writing. But you will practice the basis of writing—composing—every day in every way. We compose—put ideas together and express ourselves—every time we write or speak. Putting words on paper with some kind of instrument is traditionally understood as writing, but we compose every time we talk on the phone. We compose our thoughts when we're talking things over with our dads. When we leave a note on the refrigerator for our roommate, we've composed that, too. We've negotiated dozens

1

of little interchanges with people over the past 24 hours: the 7-Eleven clerk, the person at the video store, our boyfriend, our girlfriend. Each of these little moments involves composing. Whenever we are faced with a circumstance where input is needed, we must think about the situation and choose some words and ideas and concepts. We compose our response and then we get our chance to tell the world (or whomever) what we think.

We can't avoid those opportunities.

WE WRITE OR COMPOSE TO INTERACT WITH THE WORLD

The only way we get through this world is by interacting with people. And whether we do that through talking or writing, it all involves the composition of our ideas into thoughts we share with others, be they listeners or readers. We have to share common land with others. They have their lives; we have our own. But we bump into each other at the oddest times and in the oddest places.

Next time you have an argument with a clerk at a store about what's on sale or what's not, think about what you're doing. You have a point of view—that sweater was on the table marked 30 percent off. It's not your fault that someone put it there incorrectly. Now, what are you going to do? You want the sweater. You want the 30 percent off. Do you want to leave it behind, or pay the extra money? Nope. If you're going to get that sweater at that price, you're going to have to interact. Now, do you want to interact in a good way, or a bad way? Here's the bad way: "Hey, gimme that sweater." Do you think this will work? No, I don't either. Think for a moment before you interact.

Before you talk to the clerk at this mythical sweater store, you have to consider some things. First of all, you are a person with a complex past and background. You believe in some things, such as truth in advertising, and based on this you believe that if a blue sweater is sitting in a store, on a table marked 30 percent off, no matter how that sweater came to be there (dropped out of the sky by the sweater fairy, perhaps), it's 30 percent off.

Now look at the clerk's side. The clerk made a mistake putting that sweater there, and now he realizes it. He knows that the 30 percent you save will come out of someone's pocket, the store's or maybe his own. The clerk's not a bad person. He doesn't want to keep you from happiness. He wants to make his $6 an hour and then go buy a nice sweater for himself sometime.

The interaction is much more complex than it first looks, isn't it? During it all our minds spin and whirl, and we think of things to say. We're composing little sentences in our heads, preparing words and language to help us through our interactions. We are not writing in the traditional sense (words on paper), but we are certainly composing. And we have loads of these interaction opportunities every day, with each one requiring some kind of preparation and composition: some a little, some a lot. In this book we prepare you for every kind of interaction, from simple ones like the above example to much more complex and involved ones such as position papers.

I believe our brains are doing the same thing, whether it is getting words together for a simple sentence we're going to speak to the sweater seller, or getting words together for a complaint letter we're going to write to the sweater seller's boss. Talking to the clerk is an opportunity for us to compose and express our ideas; writing a letter to the boss is the same thing. The two different compositions differ only because one's on paper and one's not. They require the same kind of effort and ability from us.

Think of it this way. Just because it doesn't happen with pen and paper, or a computer keyboard, doesn't mean we're not in the act of composing. We have to deal with the world in some way, and we do it mostly through talking, writing, and physical action. The act of writing happens to be the most tangible, real, and long-lasting form of those communications.

WE WRITE TO MAKE SENSE OF THINGS FOR OURSELVES

Writing helps me by focusing the jumble of ideas in my brain. For example, I have a couple of options when I go grocery shopping. I can go without a list and just roam the aisles. I have fun and get some neat food and some stuff I've never tried before. It takes me a long time because I'm just wandering around, and when I get home and want to have a meal I realize all I have are eggs, Twinkies, sunflower seeds, a bag of potatoes, and red shoelaces. Now, if I go to the grocery store with a list of food I need for the week, I go aisle to aisle with a plan and get what I need at home that week. I move more quickly because I know what I'm looking for, and when I get home and want to make a meatloaf, I've got all the ingredients.

That's how I use writing. In my head everything is piled together: good ideas, bad ideas, phone numbers, schedules, things I want to buy, my parents' anniversary, friends' birthdays, and so on. It's out of focus and confused. What I want to do with writing is bring order to the chaos. By making lists or writing things down, I can separate the junk from the good stuff.

WE WRITE OR COMPOSE TO MAKE SENSE OF THINGS FOR OTHERS

Just as we write and compose to help ourselves, we write or compose when we have to explain things to others.

We're always being asked to think about things. We face situations that need our response all the time: "What do you think about your teacher?" "What do you think about the dorms here?" "What do you think about the President?" Usually, for a question like this we have a pretty quick answer, the kind that comes off the top of our head. "My teacher's lame," or "My dorm stinks," or "The President must be out of his mind." That kind of answer is pretty easy to come up with. It's a reaction. We barely compose it in our heads and simply speak it. It's rather informal, and we hardly ever put too much thought into that kind of answer.

But what if someone asks you "What could be done to help your teacher do his job better?" or "If you had $500,000 to spend on refurbishing the dorms, what would you want to do first?" or "In the upcoming election, what kinds of qualities do you think the ideal presidential candidate should have?"

You'll want to answer these with more care. In fact, when I answer such a question, I start with a quick "off the top of my head" answer, and then begin exploring it. As I do that, I start composing. I start trying to bring order and focus to otherwise messy and chaotic ideas. "Hmmm, I do hate the dorms, but what would I do to fix them up? Let's see. Carpet? Nah, it's okay, I guess. How about paint? Yeah, paint all the rooms! Okay, what's next?" Answering this way puts you way ahead of most people.

We live in a multimedia age and—for whatever reason—the skill of writing seems passé. But keep in mind that everything from movies to video games to television shows to online resources is "written" in some way. Just because pens and pencils and "penmanship" are out-of-date concepts doesn't mean the act of writing has gone away. To write well is to communicate well. To communicate well is to reap success in the world.

How are we going to write?

One of the reasons many freshman writers are nervous about this class has to do with how writing was introduced to them. When you go through grade school and high school, most of your writing is graded and used against you in some way.

In fact, as it is taught, the whole notion of writing is as a piece of product. Write me an essay! It's a thing. You make it, usually in one sitting, and then turn it in. There's a starting point. The teacher says, "You owe me an essay on the Civil War." There's an end point. "It's due by Friday."

You write it, turn it in, and get it back a few days later. "Hmmm, I got a B." That's usually the end of the story. Your essay on the Civil War goes into the trash and is forgotten forever. Or if you're like some of my students, you retype it and hope to be able to use it in some other class, somewhere, eventually! (Why waste all that work, right?)

WE CARE ABOUT THE PROCESS MORE THAN THE PRODUCT

With this background, many developing writers think of essays as products. They don't think of the process that gives birth to the essay. We're going to examine the process all semester long as you work on various sections of this book. Your essay is not a thing; it's a journey. Think of it as a trip to Las Vegas. You figure out how you're going to get there. You pack some clothes. You hop a train or a plane or drive your car. You get there. Have some fun. Lose some money. Fall in love with a blackjack dealer or a desk clerk. You go back home.

That's a process. You learn from all of it. Your memory is not just about Las Vegas or of one moment in time. Your memory is multidimensional and rich with images and ideas.

Now, if you were in Las Vegas and a friend took a picture of you standing in front of a casino, that would be a product. You could hold that "thing" in your hand. You could look at it and keep it forever as tangible proof you were there, but it's lifeless and stale and contains only the tiniest bit of the actual journey. The actual trip can't be caught on film. An ordinary essay is a grainy snapshot of one moment in time. An extraordinary essay is a rich, inventive, creative document that contains time and space and dimension, beauty, and love.

Okay, all of that may seem a little crazy. Believe me, I hear students tell me every semester they think it sounds crazy. But those same students at semester's end tell me they now know what I was going on about. The journey is worth it.

I'm not going to lie to you; there is work to be done. There are indeed start points and end points to all of our writing. (After all, your semester does end, right? I mean you don't have to stay in this class forever.) But during the course of our semester, your essay will be given the chance to "live" a bit, to be in process, to be under construction. We're not just going to treat it as a thing. We're going to see it as a work in progress. We're all going to help you along the way, too—me, your instructor, and your classmates.

You will be helped to learn a great deal about writing because all of your class at one time will be working on similar essays. Of course, your topics will be your own, but for ease of instruction and to share the learning with fellow writers, we'll be working through a series of essay types: personal essays, issue-oriented essays, essays about problems and solutions. In short, we take on as many different essay types as we can, helping you practice writing in varied and challenging ways.

WE'RE GOING TO OPEN UP OUR ESSAYS TO OTHERS

Two concepts that you'll hear a lot about in this book are the "workshop" and the "conference." The workshop is a gathering of fellow writers. It so happens that you are surrounded by writers right now. Everyone in your class is a writer. We all will struggle along over the course of this semester trying to get better at writing. We'll all write essays, and all have trouble, and all figure things out every once in a while. Your instructor will help you with the workshop device. He or she will get you talking to one another about your essays. You will share good and bad things and maybe even read parts of your essays to each other. There's no better way to learn than by doing. The next best way to learn is hear what other people are doing.

The conference is different. The conference is a one-on-one meeting with your instructor. Think of it as a meeting between an editor and a writer. A good conference isn't about grades! A conference's goal is to talk about the work or the text you are writing. You both have exactly the same goal in a conference—to make that essay better. Let your instructor know you value the help. Let him or her be a part of the process of making your essay better. The biggest advantage teachers have is the number of essays they have seen. At this point in your development, you may have written a handful of essays. Your instructor has probably written and read hundreds, if not thousands. That kind of experience can be very valuable. If I want to make an omelet for the first time, I wouldn't mind sitting down and chatting with a chef for a little while. After all, the chef has done it a few times, has had the struggles, has broken a few eggs. I bet I could learn something from him, don't you think?

WE'RE GOING TO EXPLORE HOW COMPUTERS CAN HELP US

Machinery sometimes scares us. But there's no easier or better way to write than on a computer. If you're using this book, I'd bet your instructor has some interest in how computers and computing can help you as a writer and a researcher. I've been using computers ever since I got an Apple IIe in 1979. It was horribly expensive and didn't really do much in present-day terms, but it was an amazing development. After I used that for a while, I got a dedicated word processor made by Sony. It didn't have any games or graphics or other programs. It did word processing. I hammered at that thing and its full-page display for about five years. The machine was a behemoth, incompatible with everything else on the planet. But I wrote thousands of pages of every kind of writing on it. I got through college with that machine. I wrote a novel on it once. I wrote love letters and poems and heartfelt pleas to my mom to "send money" on it. It didn't do anything but process words, but at that it was a champion machine. It was during that time that I first realized the power of computing. The abilities I suddenly had—to edit text, to move it around, to save it, to delete it—astounded me. I began to "see" words and text in a different way.

I really began to understand that kind of editing power when I started teaching. Students would bring in their handwritten drafts of essays to my office. They'd be messy (the essays, not the students), long yellow pages of paragraphs. I'd gotten used to copy, cut, paste, and move commands, but these essays were unfixable, it seemed. I couldn't move that horrible first paragraph very easily. I could cover it with my hand but that wouldn't last. I could draw arrows on the sheet of paper showing my writers where I thought their paragraphs might work better, but it was not the same as actually reordering the text, and all I did was make the mess messier.

I don't remember where I got the idea—it surely isn't my own—but one day I got the scissors out and began cutting up student essays. Don't like that paragraph? Cut it with scissors. Suddenly, it was gone. Want to move something? Cut it out and tape it to a clean sheet of paper. Cut another paragraph of the original out and paste it underneath. It was messy and my students hated seeing their essays cut apart like that, but it was working. I was able to show my writers how I saw essays, how I edited them. Most of my writers had never imagined that their writing was malleable in that way.

When I began teaching, I didn't have any students who used computers to compose essays; those who had computers only saw them as game-playing machines or devices that people "worked" on. As I sat there cutting apart people's rough drafts, it began to occur to me to ask "Have you got a computer?" If the writer said "Yes," I sent him or her home right then. "Well, go put this essay in it right away."

Now you may or may not be a computer convert. Don't freak out if you're not. This book works perfectly well for writers who aren't online yet. (You don't see any wires or cords hanging from it, do you?) If you still write on paper and have to get your sister or boyfriend or mom to type for you, don't panic. All of the stuff we do works just as well for you as it does for your more technologically inclined pals.

However, your instructor and I will try to encourage you to experiment with the big machines. Undoubtedly, your college will have some kind of free computer lab (or labs) where for the price of a couple of floppy disks you can get up and running on machines that will do more for you and your text than you've ever imagined. And these labs, even if they're just staffed with student workers, are always full of people who can help you with those tentative first steps. "Where's the 'on' button?" "What's a mouse, and what do I feed it?" That sort of thing.

WE'RE GOING TO OPEN OURSELVES TO THE JOYS (AND FRUSTRATIONS) OF THE INTERNET

With the accessibility of the Internet, with its glorious e-mail and World Wide Web especially, we find ourselves with more options than ever for transmitting and sharing our writing. You can write something about a topic you're interested in and make it available to hundreds, thousands, sometimes millions of readers. Talk about pressure! The connected or "online" world makes the need for communicative skills even greater. Our words and ideas can be flying around in midair, faster than ever before. Your great-grandparents waited weeks for mail to cross the country, months to cross the ocean. Now, we send our thoughts around the globe in seconds.

Chances are that your school has some kind of Internet connection for you. You probably can send and receive e-mail, either on your own computer or on a computer in one of the labs. If you're fortunate, you're already online, perhaps on your own computer. Maybe you've tested the waters on one of the many fine commercial services: America Online, CompuServe, Prodigy, and so on. Or maybe you have a direct dial-up connection to an Internet Service Provider (ISP). Either way, whether you're a novice or an expert, I'm going to show you some ways that you can utilize computers as part of your writing process.

Regardless of what tools you use to write, you will be writing more this semester than perhaps ever before. And that's a good thing. You'll be plumbing your own soul and heart and brain in ways you've never tried. All through it, your instructor and I are going to talk to you and help you.

Let's go.

2 The Writing Process

I should have listened to Mr. Brookes

For a lot of you, writing probably seems like a bad thing. Maybe you think it's as bad as going to the dentist, or taking a test, or mowing the lawn. It's something you know you have to do, but not something you ever really look forward to. Well, that's probably because of the way writing has been presented to you so far in school. For one thing, your writing has always been graded by someone, right?

When I was in high school, my whole class feared Mr. Brookes because he had a red felt pen that he used when he marked our papers. He was a master at filling the white space of our papers with his marks. We didn't know what the marks were for because we never read them. We thought that a lot of red was bad and that was the end of it.

I know now that Mr. Brookes was trying to help us. Mr. Brookes wrote in red to catch our attention and make sure we knew he read our work and cared about it. But I was too stupid to see that. I saw a lot of red and I threw the essay in the trash. I thought Mr. Brookes and I were enemies. After all, that's how school sometimes seems. The teacher stands up front; the students sit. The teacher tells us when to start; we can't leave until he or she says so. The teacher assigns; we do the work.

But evaluation is simply a way in which the teacher helps you. Mr. Brookes was trying to help me the whole time. I didn't see it until years later when I first started to teach. Teachers are on your side in this venture of writing. They guide, they correct, they suggest, they evaluate, and they assign, all to help you discover more and better ways of expressing yourself through writing.

Writing is an opportunity

One thing I know about writing is this: It's an opportunity. It's a chance to tell the world (or just your friends) how you see things, what matters to you, and what you think should be done. I think your writing is going to help the world. Miscommunication is a part of many of this era's troubles. When the world understands you, the world becomes a better, safer, more understandable place. When communication breaks down, so do relations between people. What about divorce? The most commonly offered reason for divorce is irreconcilable differences. What happened? A couple couldn't communicate their way to staying together. What about intolerance and hatred, even racism? Those are all miscommunications of the highest order.

So here's how we're going to operate. I recognize that you have things to say. I value what you have to offer me, and so does this class and your instructor. We will all begin knowing that at times we will miscommunicate. But with a built-in support group like a bunch of fellow writers, we can get a handle on why we're miscommunicating.

When we miscommunicate it's not because we're bad, or because the audience is bad. It's just that we haven't passed along enough information yet. You're going to get to practice that this semester. Communication isn't happening until a reader or listener "gets it."

Here's a small example. If you were to write in your essay "There's nothing worse than being in a band," some people might say "Huh? I don't get it. Being in a band looks like fun." This is a miscommunication. What you really meant to say was something like "Being in a band looks like fun, but most people don't know about the long hours of rehearsal, the endless squabbling between band members, the sleepless nights bouncing around in the back of the van, the fights about money." That's better than the first sentence you tried because now you've explained fully what you meant, leaving less room for miscommunication.

The stages of the writing process

ROHMAN'S TERMS

The terms above were popularized by the very influential late 1960s composition scholar D. Gordon Rohman. We still use his terms today. Simply put, there are three stages of any writing process. Pre-writing is anything you do in preparation for the essay (getting the assignment, thinking about what you're going to write, picking a topic, etc.). Writing is that period of time when you are actually in the midst of the "real" work of writing an essay (writing sentences, writing paragraphs, making transitions, drafting, etc.). Post-writing is a period of time after you've completed a pretty good "draft" or version of your essay. Post-writing tasks involve fine-tuning your essay (editing, revising, proofing, etc.).

In talking of writing as a process, don't think we mean a simple step-by-step process. Writing is not like changing a tire or making raisin muffins, where you must do each step in turn, without variation. If you forget to put those raisins in the batter, and the muffins have been cooking for 30 minutes already, it's too late to have raisin muffins. You're going to have plain old muffins. But in the writing process, you can move back and forth through the stages, addressing your essay's concerns as they require your attention.

You don't have rigid steps to follow in a set order. There is some leeway, some elasticity. What many composition teachers say is that the writing process is *recursive*, folding back upon itself. What it means for us is that we can hop around the process if we need to. For example, if you start out on a paper and discover it's not working, there's no rule that says you have to slog along till the bitter end. You can go back and start again. Is your topic not good enough? Go back to the start and pick a new one. It's a very forgiving process.

OUR TERMS

In each of the three major stages, there are activities to undertake. They exist with lots of different names, but in this book I've tried to keep them as simple and as accurate as possible. We'll now look at each stage individually.

PRE-WRITING: TIME TO INVENT

Your writing process begins the moment you think about writing. It's that simple. When I tell you you're going to have to write an essay about some event that happened in your life, your writing process has begun. As I'm finishing my statement, your brain is starting to work: "What am I going to write about?" I wish it were a fancier explanation, but that's it. As soon as you begin to *wonder*, you are already on your way. It's this stage where the real "invention" or creation of your essay takes place. Many of the steps in this stage are simple ones.

- Listen to your instructor's guidelines about topics.
- Begin thinking of ideas and stories from your own experience that might fit this assignment.
- When you find something you're interested in, ask yourself and your instructor if your topic fits the assignment.

Let's say you're writing a personal experience paper. I tell you to write an essay about something that happened in your life. You instantly begin looking through the file cabinet of your brain. "What about that time I drank the sour milkshake? How about when my friend Kevin moved away to another town on my thirteenth birthday? What about when I fell off the slide and broke my arm?" As soon as you start thinking of these possible topics, you're inventing your essay.

Once you hit on an idea that sounds good, start to ask yourself questions about it. "What was I doing on the slide? How old was I? Who else was there? Was I goofing around? Who picked me up? How did I get to the hospital?" In a few minutes you've recreated the event in your head. If you still think this story or topic is worth passing on to another reader, get some paper out or sit down at your computer and write something. It's not an essay yet, so relax. You're just inventing, pre-writing. No one has to see it; this is just for you.

You start making lists, gathering memories so you can tell your broken arm story just as it happened. (Always remember, your reader wasn't there when it happened, so you owe us the whole story, bit by bit, so we understand it.) You ask your mom if she remembers it. If you've got a friend who remembers it, you ask her what happened. Once you're happy with this story as a topic, you go on to the next stage.

WRITING: TIME TO DRAFT

While you've already started making notes, writing out thoughts, maybe even pecking away at a keyboard, now it's time to actually write a draft. The fun thing here is that this draft is just a "first" draft or discovery draft. We call it the *discovery draft* because that's what a first draft is really for—discovery. You must find out from your initial draft if the ideas and plans you make in the pre-writing or inventing stage are going to work or not. Taking the ideas of invention and then putting them down on paper (or your computer screen) is an act of discovery. Because you will be writing this story or exploring this idea for the first time, you will be moving like an explorer through the text. What you will discover about your paper in this first draft will include the following:

- Do I want to write more about this?
- Do I know enough about my topic to keep pursuing this?
- Am I doing something that will be of interest to other readers?

Just like your earlier inventing or pre-writing work, no one has to see this either. You're still trying things out. Let's keep using our example from the previous section: a personal experience paper. You've remembered a story from your past and have spent a couple of days inventing it as a topic and gathering information about it. You've convinced yourself that the story is interesting and you want to tell it to someone.

In the writing or drafting stage, your job now is to write it out. But since we know we're still within the process, you don't have to worry too much about getting it perfect yet. You're drafting it, working with it, shaping it. This broken arm story sounds like something you might just tell a friend one day. So, how would you start?

> ▶ When I was about 8 years old I was playing with my friends in the playground. I remember it was cold that day, probably too cold to be outside. But we were messing around on the slide, and some of the big kids from fifth grade were pushing past us, trying to get to the top of the slide ahead of us. I decided to . . . ◀

And you keep going from there. Remember, in your first draft, you're still working things out. The key to the discovery draft is to write the whole thing. Get one solid piece of text finished. Start with when you walked onto the playground and stop with when you got released from the hospital. Tell a whole story so that it makes sense.

As we said earlier, this writing process is recursive. That means if at any time during drafting you feel uncomfortable about your topic, about your invention, you can go back and start again. Let's say you write your personal experience story about falling off that slide. You might try a discovery draft and find out that you don't have much to say. Well, the writing process is forgiving. You can simply go back and invent a new topic.

But if things go well, and if you've invented or picked a good topic, then you'll finish that first draft and you'll still be happy. The best thing to do now is to put the essay aside for a while, even if it's just a couple of hours. You need some distance from it to look at it with clear eyes. If you have someone around who might be interested in the draft, show it to that person. Ask that person to read it and tell you if it makes any sense or not. "Do you understand how I fell? Can you see it? Does the hospital scene seem scary to you like it did to me? Do you think I included enough dialogue when my dad was yelling at me for being a show-off?"

Just because this discovery draft is over doesn't mean you're finished drafting. In fact, most good writers spend a great deal of time writing draft after draft, trying different things, getting feedback from other people.

As you move through this book you'll find that most of your time writing an essay will be spent in drafting, building and rebuilding your essay. Don't leave this stage until you feel you've got a "final" draft. A final draft is rather different from a discovery draft. Your first draft is often completed just to find out if your invented topic is worthwhile. The final draft is one that you feel good about. It's complete. It's worthwhile. It's accomplished the goals set for it by this book, by you, and by your instructor. If it's a personal essay, it tells a complete story. If it's an argument paper, it has a thesis and support. It's got an opening, a body, and a closing.

When you're satisfied that your essay contains all the good information you've got in your heart and your head, then you move to the next stage.

POST-WRITING: TIME TO FINISH

This stage always surprises my writers a bit. They assume that the actual writing process is over once they've finished drafting. After all, I've just told you that a final draft is one you feel good about. But, that's not enough for the more mature and more demanding readers you will meet during and beyond your college years. Once you've got your essay written, there are some other ways to make that essay even better.

At this stage in the overall writing process, the heavy writing is over. The word *finishing* fits this stage. It can mean "to complete," but it also means "to polish." And after all, that's what we're looking for in a great essay: a completed and polished piece.

Finishing should take up the last part of your time. Think of it as a stage to revise and edit what's already written. You won't be coming up with new ideas (that's the job of "inventing"), nor will you be doing any serious writing (that's the job of "drafting"). What you will be doing is taking a last good look at the essay, checking to make sure that it has done the job you've set out to do. You'll be asking yourself the following questions:

- Does it meet the assignment?
- Does it meet my own standards?
- Have I done enough work? Have I been dedicated to the task and diligent about the work?

If you answer no to any of these questions, obviously you'll be going back to the writing stage and doing some more work. (Again, a handy feature of the writing process is that it's not linear or straight-lined. It's recursive. You can go back.) But even if you answer yes to all three of those questions above, there is still work to be done. Many people get thrown by the term "final draft." It sounds finished, right? It's not.

Too many developing writers are in a rush to get the essay out of their hands and off their minds. Even those who know it's important to proofread their work before turning it in often make the mistake of thinking that finding a few typos is the same thing as finishing a paper.

The message I give my writers is that the "corrections" are only a small part of finishing your essay. Of course you should get good at spotting and correcting errors. Typos, spelling mistakes, and simple surface-level errors have sunk lots of good essays. However, fixing those small things is "expected." You should automatically be doing that, whether with your computer's spell checker (not infallible, by the way) or with the help of a good reader from your class or your dorm.

But making corrections isn't all that's involved in finishing the essay. Sometimes essays only need a good proofreading and retyping on nice paper. But usually there are a number of other things that must be addressed.

Asking someone about your title can help you discover you've got a lame one. A friend might make a suggestion that will improve the entire paper, just by adding a catchier opening. Reading your paper aloud can give you a better perspective as well; hearing the words in the air makes you read more slowly than you would if you were reading silently. You'll be amazed and sometimes embarrassed at the little things you can catch this way. I always suggest to my writers that having someone else read their papers out loud can help them get a clearer perspective on how it sounds.

Maybe you can add a different title. Maybe "Broken Arm" (your first title) is too boring now that you've thought about it. How about "Nurse Johnson Saved My Life and Stole My Heart." (See, that silly broken arm story is more interesting than you ever thought!) Which of these titles would most make you want to keep reading?

Editing involves finer detail. Watch for that comma splice problem that sometimes plagues you. Correct your printed copy with a black pen. Get out that thesaurus if you've used a word too many times.

The point is you want us to care about your work. You've written the broken arm story five or six times during the last couple of weeks, and it's become an important part of your work in this class. Well, if you want *us* to care, *you* have to care. Give your best at every step. Think up the idea, shape it into form, and make the cleanest copy.

Rewrite the opening or closing paragraph. Maybe your friend read the essay and said, "Start with that 'thud' when you hit the ground. That's exciting." Or the guy next to you in class saw your closing and said, "I don't get it. What happened?"

When it's time to turn the paper in, you must feel satisfied that all has been done. As I said earlier, the paper must meet the assignment and meet your own standards, and you must feel as though you've given all the time and energy you've got to the project. If you don't feel comfortable about meeting these standards, you've not given yourself the best chance to succeed.

Still, deadlines come. Essays must be turned in, and every semester I have writers who want "just one more day!" They don't get that extra day, though, because there's another essay coming down the tracks and we all have to get on board. You might find yourself in the same situation from time to time, and all I can tell you is to do your best to meet the deadlines as they come. You'll likely get better at time management as you go, and you might ask your instructor specifically for some help with meeting deadlines. He or she will know how to help you finish your essays in time.

The shape of the essay

Essays are varied and wonderful things and I don't mean to suggest in this section that they all have the same shape. But I can show you a series of essay "parts" that do exist in some way in nearly every essay.

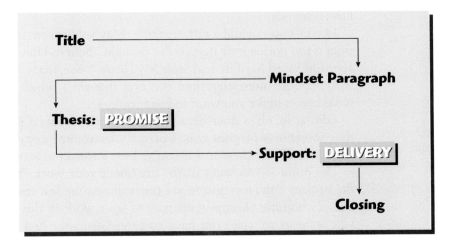

TITLE

Good essays have good titles. Titles are often underestimated by developing writers. Titles are not simply "names" for essays. For example, an essay about capital punishment shouldn't be called "Capital Punishment." That title is vague and not particularly evocative.

Evocative is what a title needs to be: suggestive, rousing, exciting, inviting, enticing. An evocative title will draw a reader into the essay; in fact, that's the job of the title.

An essay on capital punishment might be better served by a title like "Should Killers Live?" or "The Government Says We Should Kill This Man."

When you flip through the pages of a newspaper or magazine, for instance, what kind of text catches your eye first? Is it the small text of the article, or is it the large type of the title? Reader research shows that readers' eyes fall on the title first. We tend to make our mind up about reading an essay based largely on the title. If the title interests us, then we might enter the text. If the title does nothing for us, is too vague, is out of our area of interest, or is just plain confusing, then there's not much chance we'll ever read the essay.

If your reader doesn't read your essay, what have you written it for? A good title will make your essay stand out from the crowd, whether it is one of many in a magazine or in a stack of essays that your instructor is waiting to grade.

Titles are tricky. I think most of the essays in this book are pretty well titled. As you move through the book, ask yourself if the title draws you in or does nothing for you. After reading the essay, do you have a better idea for the title?

Let's assume we get our reader interested with a title. Once we've got them that far, we still have work to do

MINDSET PARAGRAPH

A good essay needs to be set up correctly. Too many developing writers simply "spring" their essay on the unsuspecting reader, before he or she is really in the mood.

I was in my backyard barbecuing one day and a neighbor walked over and launched in with this: "You know if we can't keep guns, this country is going to hell!" Now, I value anybody's opinion and his or her right to have one. But we didn't have much of a conversation that day because I wasn't ready to have that discussion. It was too abrupt. I said something like, "Okay, buddy. Whatever." And I went and talked to someone else.

My neighbor has every right to believe what he wants and to bring it up with me when he wants to. But I wasn't in the mood. My mind was not ready. He needed me to be in the same "mindset" he was. He had just finished talking to one of our other neighbors about gun laws. He'd been thinking about gun ownership and so on for ten minutes, debating, discussing it. I had just been cooking some meat.

What my neighbor should have done was get me in the mood, putting me in the right mindset first. He should have said:

> ▶ Hey, how is that meat coming? Good! Listen, I was just talking to Joe over there. You know he's a hunter. Yep. He's got a couple of rifles that he keeps in his house. He locks them up of course, and has the key in a safe place. What do you think about that? You think that's all right? You know what I think? I think that it's one of our rights to keep a gun if we want one. And I'm not talking about just hunting rifles and so forth. I mean handguns, personal protection guns. What do you think about all that? ◀

That's not the same as an essay, of course, but instead of coming up and blurting out his opinion and topic to me, he's eased into it. By the time he's presented the little story about talking to Joe, I'm prepared. If I'm interested in his topic and the issue at hand, I'll start chatting with him. If I'm not, then at least he's given me a good chance to think about the issue and decide if I want to invest in a ten-minute conversation.

That's what happens in our essays, too. We must get our readers ready for the topic. Whether it's an issue paper or a personal essay or research paper, you must raise the idea of the issue or topic first, before you line up on one side or the other.

"Mindset paragraph" is a phrase that I really like because I've struggled for years trying to get my writers to write really great opening paragraphs. I used to call the opening paragraph the "hook" paragraph, which is okay, too. After all, one of the things you must do in the opening section of your paper is get your readers interested by "hooking" them into the topic. Think of a big hook and a fish. Kind of gruesome, I know, but the theory is a good one.

The mindset paragraph opens every essay, bringing the topic gently and clearly into focus, allowing interested readers the chance to say: "Hmm, I'd like to hear more about gun laws," or "Wow, this guy went to Hawaii with his friends; I wonder what happened?" We should try to create an introduction that will make clear the issue to be discussed. It is not time yet to state our position, however, since many readers—particularly those who disagree with that position—may simply ignore the issue and stop reading. We won't even get the chance to talk to them before they tune out. The mindset paragraph simply gets our readers to start thinking about the subject, without trying to tell them "what" they should think.

THESIS STATEMENT: PROMISE

Now we're getting into an area that developing writers always struggle with. To clear out a crowded composition classroom, all most instructors have to do is holler out, "What's your thesis?" It's enough to send even the toughest students running for home. This kind of fear is largely unfounded and potentially disastrous. The thesis statement is actually a nice, fairly easily understood concept. It also happens to be absolutely essential to the success of any paper. You can't avoid it; it's the reason you write.

A thesis is the central, controlling idea of any essay or writing assignment. Your essay has to be about something, and that something better remain constant throughout the paper. "Central" means that your thesis is at the center of your essay. (This doesn't mean it appears in the middle paragraph; it just means that the paper and all its parts revolve around a steady center.) Think of a big wagon wheel. The hub is always in the center, the outside rim goes around and around. They never touch, yet they are connected. The thesis is your hub. The ideas of your essay form the rim around the outside, free spinning, but always connected back to the center.

"Controlling" suggests that the thesis controls everything else that goes on in the essay. If your thesis is "I let my desire to succeed get in the way of finding love and happiness during my high school years," then the rest of your essay, every paragraph, is controlled by that statement. You will write paragraphs to show your strong desire to succeed, maybe even telling where that desire came from. You will write paragraphs that prove you missed out on the social whirl of high school, passing up the friendship, love, relationships, and fun you saw other people having. You will write paragraphs to address how you're going to respond to these facts in the future. Did you discover that being number one was worth it? Or did you discover that a nice weekend in Key West was worth more? Regardless of your conclusion, all of these examples address the thesis, are indeed "controlled" by the thesis.

One of the terms that often gets mistaken for "thesis" is "topic." But they are really rather different things. If we can understand one, maybe we can understand both. Look at these examples below:

Topic: Fishing
Thesis: The new low-speed casting reels are changing the way modern-day fishers fish.

Topic: Cheese
Thesis: The long established methods of fermentation are being challenged by new cheese-makers.

Topic: Abortion
Thesis: Young women have the right to control their own bodies, especially in the case of unwanted or forced pregnancies.

How do we test these terms? Try asking the following two questions:

- What is your paper about? Fishing. (That's a topic).
- What does your paper do? It discusses the new low-speed casting reels. (That's a thesis.)

Your thesis is in charge—it's the hub of your essay. So that essay about cheese will not wander aimlessly, it will continue to address the thesis that says the old methods of fermentation are being challenged by new cheese-makers. In the essay, you can discuss the old methods of fermentation, the new methods of fermentation, and the things the new cheese-makers are doing. You can do all of this because your thesis allows it. Your thesis doesn't allow you to write a section about how dairy taxes are forcing some cheese-makers out of business. Why? Because that idea is not encompassed by your thesis.

Your thesis sets the path for your essay. Your reader will trust it and look for that thesis to be supported and delivered. If you wander from or go against your thesis, your reader will be left confused, and your essay will fail.

THESIS IN PROGRESS

Develop your thesis as early as you can. It's a prerequisite for the rest of the essay. It's the same thing as setting a goal. "We're going to get in this canoe and go down that river!" Even if you tip over a couple of times and even if you get wet and tired and sweaty and sunburned, the goal you set remains in your mind and drives you on. That's good! Set the thesis early to provide focus and direction.

But there's something you must understand. Your thesis is liable to change, to modify, to move as you learn more about your essay during the writing.

If your initial thesis or goal is "We're going down the river in the canoe," what happens if the river gets too low to canoe any more and you have to walk? You still need to get down the river; you just can't go in the canoe. So you pick the canoe up, rest it on your shoulders, and walk. The thesis has modified. You're still trying to do the same thing, but circumstances are changing how you can do it.

If something like this happens in your essay—say, you discover you don't want to write about falling off the slide and breaking your arm, you want to write instead about how wonderful nurses are—you must let the thesis move. The writing of an essay is a long journey. Be aware that amazing changes can occur as you go. Set a good thesis to get you going, but realize that to be a responsible writer means to let the thesis change if it needs to.

Of course if you *do* change the thesis, you have to be diligent enough to go back to the start of your essay and make sure the new thesis is indeed supported by what follows.

SUPPORT: DELIVERY

If a thesis is making a promise, then of course the promise must be delivered to the reader. Successful essays are promises that are delivered. If you don't do what you say you will do, or if you fail to support the point or idea you promise to develop, then the essay fails because the reader feels let down.

So, to deliver on the promise or to support the thesis, you must develop your essay through supporting ideas and concepts.

Let's talk about support or delivery in the context of an issue or position essay. (That's any essay where you express your opinion; it's not the only kind of essay we deal with, but it's great for proving this point about development.)

In the case of an issue essay, development often refers to proof or support. If the thesis of your essay is "TV hurts family life," then your audience is going to expect that you can prove that point. They will read on through your essay, looking for proof and examples. If you have that proof, and can show real and well-drawn examples, then your reader will trust you and you'll be on your way to an essay. However, many developing writers often state their claim or thesis or opinion and then never follow it up.

We may be lacking in this area simply because our developmental skills don't get much of a workout. We usually hang out with people we know, who have learned to trust us and respect us and who rarely question us about our feelings or ideas. If we say, "Tom Hanks can't act," most of our pals just say, "Yeah, you're right!"

But the rest of the world won't be that easy. When we say something like "Tom Hanks can't act," or "This cheeseburger is no good," or "Joe is the best man for the job," or "I think we all should vote for the Democrats," chances are someone is going to ask, "Why?"

What does "Why?" lead to? How about "Because . . ." And once you get that word in your vocabulary, you're making some strides toward understanding development or support. Your promise to tell me why I should vote for Democrats must be followed by supporting remarks or ideas that support your thesis, because as a listener or reader, I'm going to ask you "Why?"

Let's go back to the earlier thesis "TV hurts family life." That's a fine position to have, and a fine thesis to work with in an essay, but imagine this conversation:

You: "TV *is* bad for us."
Me: "What do you mean?"

You: "It hurts us."
Me: "Who does it hurt?"
You: "It hurts families. TV hurts family life."
Me: "Why? How?"
You: "Because."
Me: "Because why?"

That's where a lot of us stop. I hate to admit that often I don't have the energy to go past the "because" stage. But in writing, the most advanced and mature form of communication, we have to persevere.

Me: "Why?"
You: "TV hurts family life because it takes away the focus of family togetherness."
Me: "How?"
You: "Well, my grandparents always ate their dinner at the table and they didn't have TV. They'd talk to one another during the meal. By the time my parents were grown up, though, TV existed and instead of us talking together, we just watch TV."
Me: "So what?"
You: "Well, my parents knew what their parents were thinking and wondering because they shared their daily stories every night at dinner. As I grew up, we never shared our days. We were too busy watching TV. So when I had something on my mind, or when my Mom had questions for me, the TV always got in the way of our conversation."

What's happened here? The writer had to keep thinking of "because" statements. It's hard sometimes; we aren't used to defending ourselves too much. But in the above example, the reader (the "Me" character") simply keeps looking for an explanation. Look at the questions "Me" asks: What, Why, How, So What?

Each of those questions forces the writer to reconsider his or her point, and in answering those questions the writer keeps supporting and developing and delivering the meat of the essay. If you can ask yourself those questions, you'll be prepared before a reader ever gets to you.

CLOSING

Closings or "conclusions" are tricky. Many developing writers don't have enough respect for this part of the essay. Some writers have even told me "Nobody reads the ending anyway."

That's a scary belief. In reality, a good reader is going to use that last paragraph as a "send off," a place to begin their own thought process about your essay topic.

I talk a lot to my students about the "utility" of their writing. I always try to tell them that an essay is more useful, has more utility, if it continues in the mind of the reader even after the experience of reading is over. You know that when you eat a really good meal, hours later you may still have that meal on your mind. The flavors were so outstanding, the portions so large, the aromas so tantalizing, that you can almost taste everything still.

Powerful experiences have the ability to stick with us. Writing should do that. I get a kick out of entertainment. Entertainment is fun. I love watching *Blossom* in reruns. I have a couple of laughs as she and her pal Six get into trouble with something or other, but I hardly ever think about the silly show afterward. It never "stays" with me like a really good movie or a book.

Your essays must strive to be more than entertainment. Your essays must contain some element that engages or interests the reader. A good essay, in fact, comes right out and asks us to keep thinking.

Your essays should matter. Why bother if you're not going to write something that matters. For all of us, if we're going to take time and energy away from our everyday lives to sit down and write, I think we might as well make it worthwhile.

The closing of your essay is your last chance to make your point, complete your story, or convince the reader of something. Don't think of the closing as just a place to "wrap things up." It's your last scene! Think of it as a play. You're the last character on stage and the audience is waiting. They're wondering, "Well, why did we sit here for two hours?" Do you want to just wave and say "Bye bye," or do you want to give them one last good idea, one last reason to believe you, one last good reason to see things your way?

If you want your essay to mean something to the reader, you must strive to close your essay in such a way that it stays on your readers' minds. Here's a closing for the earlier example about television and its effects on families.

> At the end of the day we are left alone with our friends and our families and our experiences together. The outside world is shut out and we are left with those people who are closest to us.
>
> But I wonder, how close am I to my brother when the main thing we have in common is our TV schedule. I know we laugh at the same lines on "Mad About You." I know that he likes "E.R." more than me, and that I like "Law & Order" more than him. But I can't remember the name of

the class he's having trouble with in school, and I'm sure he doesn't know that a cool new guy asked me out this week.

It's not the TV's fault that this is happening; it's our fault. How much more would I know or could I do if I would just turn the TV off every once in a while? Would I have more time in "my" life? More time in my brother's life? Next time "Law & Order" comes on, I'm going to turn to my brother and ask him how he's doing. If he's got something to say, we're going to turn off the TV and talk to each other.

What are you going to do? There are always reruns on TV. There's no rerun for life. ◄

It's a great closing. It's powerful for a couple of reasons, the easiest one being the use of questions, some of them directed right at the reader. The reader has to answer those, and that gets the reader involved. When that paragraph ends the reader will still be thinking. That's the goal.

The controlling elements of the essay

The essay is yours, of course, but there are some elements that still control it and push it around. We recognize that we aren't just writing for ourselves and with that understanding comes responsibilities. We must meet the needs of people and ideas outside of ourselves. Here are four essential controlling elements of any good essay.

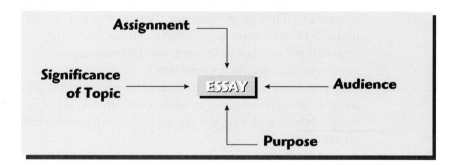

ASSIGNMENT

This is where all essays begin. This book contains a number of essay assignments that your instructor will probably use over the semester. Even if your teacher is following my assignments closely (Chapters 5–11), it's very likely that he or she will refine the assignment to fit his or her needs better. (I'd bet your instructor will often make my assignment better than it is now, tailoring it to special circumstances or needs of your class.)

When the assignment is made, the writing process begins. In fact, once your instructor says "Read Chapter 5. It talks about personal narrative essays; that's the first essay we'll write this semester," you've begun your own process. Why? Because your brain has started moving. But be careful; don't get out the good typing paper yet. Many developing writers spend too little time understanding the assignment and working toward the best topic they can find. I encourage you to ask questions about the assignment and to talk it over with your instructor and classmates.

All during the writing process of an essay, you should be referring back to the original assignment. After all, that's the journey your instructor has set you on. If your teacher says "Drive to North Dakota," that's the assignment. If instead you get a wild impulse and drive to North Carolina, you may still have a nice trip but you won't have completed what was asked of you. My best advice is to keep checking with yourself as you go. "Am I doing what the assignment asks? Am I still moving toward North Dakota?"

If you aren't, you'd better check with your instructor. (Or at least look at a map!)

AUDIENCE

Nothing matters more than your audience. If your audience doesn't get it, or buy it, or understand it, then your essay has not succeeded. In every essay we write, we spend a lot of time thinking about audiences and their expectations. There are some very simple ways in which audience matters.

Imagine you were writing an essay about a recycling plan to the mayor of a small city and an essay on the same topic to a class of fifth graders. Your language, word choices, and complexity of ideas would all be different. Your goals would be different. You might want the mayor to allocate funds to your recycling group; all you want the fifth graders to do is throw their aluminum cans into the proper receptacles after lunch period. Your essay, no matter how well you might envision it, is not ready to go until you have an audience in mind.

We're going to stay away from the term "general audience." If you write to a "general" audience, that suggests that everyone on the planet is perfectly suited to receive your essay. You know that's not possible. There is always some person or persons who are the right audience for your essay. There must be an audience you can imagine; otherwise, there is no essay.

An essay is a document that is directed to a real and specific audience. Many young, developing writers (that's all of you, regardless of your age) think a "general audience" is a viable reader of their work. I think it's a cop-out. You must know, and be able to tell me, who your essay is going to: people who like fish, your brother, city councilpeople, anyone who owns a cat, the mayor, people older than 60, guys who play in the NBA, people on your block, your roommate, people who own computers, people who don't own computers, the kid who cuts your lawn, all people who went to the Beck concert last week.

The simplest way to match up your audience with your paper is to ask "Who needs, wants, or would like to have this information?"

PURPOSE

Hand in hand with audience is purpose. The two seem almost inseparable. If we write something to someone, there must be a reason. Even something as personal as a diary or a journal has a reason. Maybe you're cleansing your mind and soul at the end of a hard day: "Just had my third date with Jackie. She still hasn't paid for a movie or a meal yet!" When we start writing outwardly, when our audience expands to include others, then purpose is clearly an even more important matter.

When you pick up the newspaper in the morning, or a magazine, or a book, or turn on the TV, you're looking for something. Entertainment? The score of a football game? What the local media thinks of a recent development on the subway system? Something! As you write your essays for this class, for any class, ask yourself "Why would anyone read this?" The key question any audience asks is "So what?" It may seem rude, but it's truthful. When you ask your instructor to read your essay, you are asking for time out of his or her day. I know the instructor assigned the essay and "made" you write it, but you must still provide a reason or a purpose to make the reader's experience of reading your work worthwhile. If it's not, if there is no answer to the "So what?" question, then your essay has not worked.

Let's look at a couple of examples. Read this paragraph and ask yourself if you see the writer's purpose.

▶ Being in Florida with my friends showed me that it was possible just to relax. My whole high school experience was so stressed, and so hard, that I felt like I had forgotten what it was like to relax and enjoy life. And I know that I was to blame for a lot of the hard times. I'm driven to be the best, and I've always wanted to be #1 at whatever I did.

> But, while we were in Key West we took in the sights, ate great food, went jet-skiing, and hung out. No competition. No rules. Just a bunch of friends enjoying themselves. I wasn't trying to win, or be the best jet skier. I was just trying not to fall down!
>
> I know that life after high school is going to be hard; I know that one day I'll work full time, and I know I'll always strive to do well. But I made a vow to myself on our last day in Key West to always find time to relax and enjoy the simple pleasures in life: the water, the sky, the sun, and the sand. ◀

What was that writer's purpose? I'd guess that he'd learned a lesson, and his purpose was to share it with someone else. Who is that someone else? I'll bet it was someone who identifies with the writer. He defines himself as someone "driven to be the best." Not everyone goes through high school that way. I know I didn't. In that short section of text, he does what he can to reach out and "connect" with readers who are like him, readers who will understand his actions, and who will gain knowledge and perspective through hearing that story.

SIGNIFICANCE OF TOPIC

While your audience will be wondering "So what?" about your essay, you should be, too. Every semester I ask my writers the simple question "Why did you pick this topic?" Many times the response is "I don't know," or "I thought you'd like it," or "Well, I wrote about it in high school."

These are not correct answers. I expect you to write about topics that matter to you. Nothing less is acceptable. Why waste your time writing in this class if you're not going to write about things that mean something? How many times will someone say to you "Please tell me whatever you want, personal or professional, about your life, about your dreams, about your plans"? It's a rare and special opportunity when you get to "tell it like you see it."

Do you want to waste that opportunity writing about a topic that doesn't matter to you? I don't want that either. In all writing assignments, all essays this semester, allow yourself the freedom to choose a topic that matters to you.

Writing Without Rules

The bad news is that this title isn't 100 percent true. But it's pretty close. This chapter is a really neat place to spend time during the early part of our semester, but you should feel free to visit it often. In it are some unjudged, ungraded writing tasks and assignments that you will be able to experiment with, use, and sometimes relax with.

Each of the steps below work exceptionally well in what we call the pre-writing or "time to invent" stage, as they all help you find and develop ideas. However, these skills are useful in many writing situations.

Brainstorming

Brainstorming is a great place to start when confronted with a new essay assignment. In fact, it's a good idea to talk to your teacher and your fellow writers right after an assignment's been made. When your instructor says "Any questions?" he or she really means it. If you've just been given an essay assignment, don't think to yourself "I don't quite get it, but I'll figure it out later." Your instructor and your peers need to talk the assignment over, get it straight, and make sure everyone understands it.

A great way to accomplish that is to simply respond to your teacher's question.

Teacher: Any questions about the assignment?
You: So, this is a personal essay? That means we can write about
            whatever we want?
Teacher: Well, yes, but it should be about a significant topic or subject.
You: Significant to me?
Teacher: Yes, but to others as well.
Another
Student: How will we know if the topic is significant to others?
Teacher: Well, let's talk about that . . .

And with that brief exchange, you've engaged not only yourself but your teacher and other students. When this class walks out of the room they're going to be a lot more informed about choosing a topic than a class who merely departs silently after the teacher says "Any questions?"

Brainstorming generally happens when any group of people talks about an idea or a concept. Usually, it involves people trying to get an idea "straight" or to figure out a plan.

You've probably sat around the kitchen table with your family, or at the local diner with your friends, and talked about plans.

"I don't wanna go to Wet & Wild. Let's go to the Wax Museum."
"Wax Museum? That's lame. Let's go to the mall!"
"The mall, are you kidding? It's so crowded, plus I don't have any
    money."
"Money? We don't need money if we go over to Dave Thompson's
    house. He's got a pool there; we can swim for free."
"Swimming? Wow, that's a cool idea. We could check out the public
    pool, too. There's one right down the street.
"And if we did that then we'd be around here in case Jennifer and her
    sister came back and wanted to go to the mall later."
"Cool, what are we waiting for?"

Thirty seconds have passed and a small group of friends has worked their way to the right choice for them on a hot summer afternoon. They were brainstorming.

It's a great word. A storm in the brain. What a cool idea. Think of your brain erupting with ideas. Lightning bolts of new things. Rumbling thunderous revelations. But just sitting by yourself and thinking about something specific can be brainstorming. Brainstorming can also refer to any sort of note-taking or listing you do as you search for topics or try to gather facts or information.

If your instructor says "We're going to write an observation essay," the following conversation might take place.

"What's an observation essay?"

"Is it about observing people?"

"Can you observe a thing?

"You know, I bet an observation essay has lots of description in it."

"I'd like to take my dad's video camera and tape everything so I wouldn't forget."

"Or talk into a tape recorder."

"Definitely gotta take a lot of notes."

In 30 seconds that group of writers has bounced a bunch of ideas off each other. I can remember one student bringing up the video camera idea in class one day and it was as if lights went on in all my writers' heads. That suggestion from a fellow writer helped everyone (including me) understand that to really write the observation essay (see Chapter 6) well required the writer to act like a video camera, taking in all the sights and sounds exactly as they happened. We figured that out one day when our brains were storming!

BRAINSTORMING ASSIGNMENT

Next time you're in a group with three or four friends, get out your notebook and raise some common-interest questions. Jot down notes as you go, just so you can observe how a good brainstorm will jump from idea to idea, but remember to stay focused on the conversation, too. Here are some simple places to start.

1. What is the best thing about this campus?

2. What's the worst thing about this campus?

3. When you're hungry, what's the best food to eat?

4. When you can't sleep at night, what's the best thing to do?

5. If you were given $5000 right now, what would you do first?

Free-writing

Unlike brainstorming, which can happen among a few or many people, free-writing refers to a very specific writing activity that a writer does essentially alone. The terrific writing teacher Peter Elbow developed the notion of free-writing in the late 1960s, but free-writing has taken on a life of its own since then, as teachers have modified it to suit their own classes and the needs of their own writers.

It's said that there's only one real rule in free-writing: Write without stopping. That's it: Write without stopping. And by stopping I mean stopping to think too much, stopping to worry about spelling or grammar, stopping to get a cheese sandwich. Don't stop. Get your pen started and keep it going. Your mission in free-writing is the same as in brainstorming—to generate lots of ideas.

The first writing my classes do is always free-writing. Sometimes on the first day of class I get there a few minutes early and write this on the board: "Hi, I'm writing in my notebook about whatever pops into my head. Why don't you try it out? We're going to start talking in about five minutes. Have fun."

I suggest you use free-writing during the early parts of every writing process or essay assignment. That's when you're usually the most open to new ideas and most ready to benefit from the remarkable and freeing exercise of "writing without stopping." It might take you a couple of times to get the hang of it, but it's a nice habit to get into. Let me share with you a typical first-day free-writing. This comes from a student of mine named Darryl; I think it's a terrific example, and something that you should be able to do on your own.

> ▶ Okay I'm writing in my book—I'm the second person here. Now another person is here. The teacher isn't talking. He's just sitting up there and he's writing with his head down. I think he's trying to make a point by not looking at us. Some more people came in and they're talking. Just like me they read the board and now they're shushing each other. My first class sucks already. But that girl from Carter is there so that's cool. There's like ten people here, twelve. I wonder how long we're supposed to write like this. I'm glad I brought a notebook with me. Some guy just asked me to borrow a piece of paper and the girls shushed him too. The teacher still hasn't looked at us. Maybe we're supposed to write all of our essays today. Okay, essay number one is always what I did on my summer vacation. At least that's what we did in Speech last year. I hope that this isn't like high school. Man, this room is quiet. Nobody is talking at all; I think they're all scared. The teacher just said: "Finish up in the next minute or so, okay?" Cool. Maybe this is my first essay. The End! ◀

Darryl thought that was silly, but just by writing by himself for a while he practiced this essential skill that he will work on in many more formal ways all semester. He asked himself questions, he talked about himself and his education. He mentioned some people he knew. He did some good speculation about what this class was going to hold for him. After that, he didn't have to wonder any more if he was a writer or not. All I had to do was say "Look at your notebook. You just wrote that, didn't you?"

The practice of writing and improving our writing is pretty simple. Do it. Just write. In fact, at this point in the chapter we really should write. Your instructor has probably assigned this chapter, or maybe you're getting a head start on your reading (good for you!). You've patiently read some stuff I had to say and I appreciate it. Let's do something for you.

FREE-WRITING ASSIGNMENT

Rather than talk more about free-writing, let's go ahead and try it. Get some paper and a pen or a pencil and make sure you've got about ten minutes to do this little exercise with me. In a few paragraphs, I'm going to show you a list of four words. Don't spend a lot of time thinking about them. Pick the one that hits you as being the most interesting and write it at the top of a clean piece of paper. If you've got a watch or a clock nearby, give yourself five minutes to write. If you don't have a clock, just write until you fill one side, single spaced, of a regular notebook or loose-leaf sheet of paper.

Remember our rule: Don't stop writing. Sometimes you'll get stuck with nothing to say as you write. Whenever I get stuck, I just write something silly like "All the king's horses and all the king's men," or "I got two turntables and a microphone," or some other song going through my head. I don't want to break my own rule, so I keep my pen moving. Pretty soon I think of something of my own to say and I write it down and keep going. I don't worry about making sense. I don't pick up a dictionary to check spelling. I don't pick up a handbook to check grammar or punctuation. I know that free-writing is about generating words and ideas. That's my goal; that's your goal.

Okay, the exercise is about to begin. Pick one of the four words below; put it at the top of a clean notebook or loose-leaf page and let's write for about five minutes or until you fill one side of a page. I'll talk to you once we're done.

- Winter
- Happiness
- Love
- Food

What should have happened? Well, you've only got the one rule. If you kept writing for most of the five minutes, then you did great. Free-writing is not something your instructor is going to grade. In fact, Peter Elbow urges writers to think of free-writing as unjudged, ungraded, and only for writers themselves to read. That means there's very little pressure.

You've got a page of ideas and words and sentences in front of you. If you're like Darryl (in the example earlier), some of your writing might be fairly informal and disorganized. But don't judge it like that. My only real criteria for free-writing is "Did it generate ideas?"

Let me show you a free-writing done by one of my writers in response to the same four-word assignment I gave you a few minutes ago. My student, Carol, had to pick from winter, happiness, love, and food. Here's what happened.

> ▶ Okay, five minutes? That means I have to go till 2:05. I'm going to watch the clock and get this over with. I forgot to pick a word. I'll pick food because I'm hungry. That burger did not cut it with me. I think I'm supposed to call my Mom tonight, too. Gotta write that down. I can even feel my stomach grumbling. I wonder if any one else can? That guy sitting ahead of me has some bad smell in his hair. Ugh. It's like bad cheese or something. Cheeseburger. Oh, I still haven't written FOOD down at the top of the page. FOOD FOOD FOOD FOOD FOOD. Glorious food. I've got one of those pudding things in my backpack. If I wasn't free-writing I could eat it right now. Why is pudding in a container different from pudding you make at home. This pudding in a can stuff is like a soft piece of chocolate plastic, and at home it's all nice and soft and whipped. If you could make good pudding and put it in a can you'd be a famous millionaire. FOOD FOOD FOOD. My friend Tammy ate a cheeseburger, and she weighs 104 lbs. She told me that herself, like she was waiting to hear how much I weighed. Forget it. I weighed 112 at the start of last summer, but I haven't gotten on a scale since and I'm not going to. Food is good. Food is great. The clock says 2:04. Good, almost done. I'm not hungry anymore. Tammy is over there and she's nibbling on her pencil end. I hope she gets fat from it. ◀

Carol did great. That's quite a few words in five minutes. If you write without stopping and keep at the job with good determination, you might have the same size writing experience. And if you don't, don't worry about it. Everyone works differently. The key is to do it!

All semester long you'll be faced with writing assignments. I believe that free-writing before each one is imperative. You may simply be free-writing around the topic: "What does this essay mean?" or "How will I write this essay?" You may be writing "I have to find a topic!" or "Is my topic any good?" Regardless, the act of writing is like any other skill. Do it to get better at it. When you're stumped and can't think of something to say or write, free-write.

There, we've done some writing now. I hope you all felt yourselves relax during that assignment. Let's go on to "looping," one more technique that we can use early in the process. It's based on free-writing.

Looping

Looping is actually a series of free-writings. What you do between steps is important, however. You begin with a single free-writing. We can use the free-writing about food that you've just read in the section above for our example. In that class, I asked all the writers to go back and read through their five-minute free-writing. I told them to read it and pick out the most "surprising" or "interesting" thing that they read there.

By doing this step, I am asking writers to pay attention to their own thoughts and ideas. After all, where else are they going to get paper topics from? Carol and the rest of her class read through their free-writings and picked out the most surprising or interesting thing. I told them to put that idea or sentence or word or concept at the top of a new page, and to free-write again. This time they were to try and focus only on this new concept or this new heading. This is why we call it looping. We start, then loop back to pick up one idea, loop around it to focus on it, and so on and so on. Here's what Carol did.

I HOPE SHE GETS FAT . . .

That is so harsh. Do I really think that? Tammy's my best friend here. Why would I say that? She doesn't brag about how thin she is, very much I mean? Am I fat? I'm not fat. I'm heavier than I was last year, but I'm okay. I did have to buy new clothes for this semester though. My old stuff was all tight and looked weird. I don't think Tammy's being mean when she talks about her weight. Maybe it's me who's a little too sensitive. Why would I wish that Tammy would get fat? Maybe so I'd feel better? I don't want her to get fat. I want to get thin. I wish I didn't come to class today. I should have gone running or something. I hate being fat. I feel so gross. I don't even like getting dressed for school anymore. Now I'm thinking bad thoughts about my friends because I'm so jealous. Maybe my problem is food. I'm always thinking about it and cooking and eating and eating out and taking people to the Burger King and sneaking food into the movie. This sucks.

That's a pretty good, focused, and insightful free-writing. This looping is going very well. The truth is, you don't always get so lucky and figure things out in a couple of five-minute writings. Usually, folks do a number of those on their way to finding an idea or a topic that they're interested in pursuing.

In the situation above with Carol, she was just exercising her mind, looking for what was going on in her head. She now knows that food, a person's weight, and envy are all topics that have been troubling her. As she moves through the writing experiences of the semester now, she has that knowledge to help her choose topics. If she is asked to write about a personal experience, she may choose a story about her weight and how it has affected her. If she is asked to write an issue paper, she may pick one about the health benefits of being fit. If she writes a paper in which she is asked to give advice, she may advise young girls to stay in shape during their early college years—a paper that Carol did eventually write in my class.

LOOPING ASSIGNMENT

Let's try looping. Remember, it's a series of small free-writings that narrow to a smaller focus each time. To practice looping, you can start with the question below. Write for five minutes, answering this question:

- Write about a number of things that you think will be the most difficult about college.

Once you've spent five minutes on that, go back and read what you've done. Pick one thing in particular, one idea or one sentence, and write it at the top of a new section of paper. Try to choose an idea that is especially surprising or interesting. Those almost always have the best chance of keeping your interest as you write. Write again using that as your topic.

Here's another example.

- Write about reasons why you like or don't like where you live (town, house, apartment, dorm, etc.).

Again, after you've written for a few minutes, go back and read what you've done and choose one idea, a surprising or interesting one. Write again.

All of this free-writing, brainstorming, and looping is designed to get you in touch with ideas and topics. All of them work beautifully within the pre-writing or "time to invent" period of the writing process. They also are helpful at other times in the process when you need to come up with new ideas, new examples, or new support for your essay.

Journal writing

This is not so much an assignment as it is a description of a type of writing you can use all semester long in a sort of ongoing attempt to increase your abilities and expand your mind. As you'll discover throughout this book, writers write, all the time, about different things. Many writers spend hours simply getting themselves ready for the real job of writing by keeping a journal or a diary.

Typically, writers keep an ongoing journal of ideas and notes. In my own journal, I usually keep ideas for upcoming writings for myself: something for my next class, a book idea, a letter I want to write to the makers of Snickers bars (why can't I find those peanut butter Snickers any more?). In my journal I can feel free. Just like our free-writing experiments, your journal is always a place just for you; it's unjudged and ungraded, so you can feel free to write the way you want.

What do professional tennis players do between tournaments? They play and they practice. They hit 2000 backhands with a coach or a ball machine. No one is there grading them or rating them or ranking them. They're simply doing the skill, knowing that at some point they'll need to hit a super topspin backhand over a rushing opponent.

So, what do writers do? They write. They write for themselves.

There aren't any particular rules for this either. Remember what we said earlier about free-writing. The only rule is write and don't stop. Well, the only journal rule is write and don't stop until you're tired. It's not punishment. It shouldn't be a chore. But you should do it for yourself and for your own improvement.

Before I go to class each day I sit down with my journal and just knock around a few ideas. Sometimes it's just ordinary babbling, "I think I need a haircut" kind of stuff; sometimes it's just a list of things I hope to do that day. A lot of the time I'm trying out things

I want to say in class. I'm composing on paper things I want to say out loud.

Funny, huh? Yet that's often how we write essays. We think them in our heads or say them out loud and then write them down. Writing and composing really are similar. (That comes from Chapter 1!)

Relax. Write. Make writing a normal part of your day and of your thinking process. Live. Breathe. Think. Write. Try it out.

Below are a number of journal assignments, and I feel a little odd giving them because they're only the very rawest of suggestions. After you get started on your own journal, if you take to the idea, you'll be ready to disregard anyone's instructions about how to write a journal. Writers who keep journals discover that it's a personal and wonderfully unique experience. Nobody can really help you with your journal except you. I don't mind getting you started, though.

JOURNAL-WRITING ASSIGNMENTS

- Take two facing pages in a notebook and title one "Diary," and the other "Response." At the end of a day, write down on the "Diary" page all the actual things and activities you did. Stick to the facts. Details. After you've got that done, go to the other page, the "Response" page, and write about each separate diary entry for a while. For example, if your diary entry was: "Went to school in Carla's car," your response entry might be

  Carla is really a slob. Her car is full of junk and paper and garbage and CDs and dirt. I saw a can roll under her brake pedal today and she just kicked it while we were rolling down the road. I thought for sure we were going to crash.

- Revisit some conversation you had recently with a friend or family member. Using your journal like a tape recorder, remember as much of the conversation as you can. Write it down like it's a play or a TV show. Put little stage directions in brackets like this:

  Mom [shaking head]: Your brother did the same thing at his age.
  Me [clapping hand to forehead]: I'm NOT MY BROTHER. How come you're always comparing me to him?! We're nothing alike.

- Write a pre-diary. A pre-diary is a diary of things you "want" to happen. This idea is similar to the psychological concept of "visualization." If you visualize yourself being successful, it's said to help your state of mind, allowing you peace and a positive outlook. Take ten minutes and write about some things that haven't happened yet, but that you want to have happen. Visualize some future great deeds, for example.

▶ I got the promotion down at the copy shop. Now I'm in charge of the night shift and I'm making a dollar more an hour. I'm feeling better about my chances at saving money now. I know that I can make it on my scholarship and my own earnings. I feel better about myself. I did very well on the history test. I found time to study on the weekend, even though it seemed hard, and the pages I read were worthwhile. I'm glad that I worked extra hard to get ready for it! ◀

In closing, use your journal for whatever helps you or pleases you. Like the other writing discussed in this chapter, you should consider this unjudged and ungraded writing as a time for you to experiment and grow.

4 Being a Writer

By this point you already know that I consider all of us writers. We've obviously written throughout our lives: at school, at home, and elsewhere. But I want to talk about some more practical concerns. You must think of yourselves as writers and take the responsibility of being a writer seriously. Suddenly, your ideas and dreams and beliefs are going to end up on paper and that is a remarkable difference from your ideas and words just being spoken in the air. Let's look at some things I'm going to ask of you during the semester.

Being open

First of all, being a writer requires a kind of openness. I want you to keep your mind open to imaginative thoughts and ideas. I stand in front of freshman writers like you every day during a regular semester and I see resistance . . . not just a sort of resistance to college or learning, a simple resistance of thought.

I say to them, "Think of a neat memory you have about being ten years old. Write down five sentences about it." I've had students actually groan. I had one student say—I can still picture his face to this day—"My head hurts already."

That's resistance to thought, to thinking. I don't understand why this happens. I get a kick out of using my brain sometimes. Someone says

"Remember when you were ten?" and I'm thinking about kissing Michelle McDonald at the skating rink and sneaking a cigarette with Alan Byl and playing house with Susan Deckeyser (the first girl I ever really "loved"). I love thinking. It's fun. I'm open to the idea.

Many writers come into this class with certain parts of themselves already closed off. You may be one of them. You may have a preconceived resistance already in your head: "I'll write essays, but I won't like it," or "I don't want to write a research paper," or "I hope he doesn't ask me to write about my summer vacation."

Loosen up the constraints on yourself, okay? Allow your mind to open. It's college, after all. I hope you're not here because someone made you go to college, but even if you are, why not get some fun out of it?

My father-in-law always says "Get the fun out of it." Of course, he always says it as I'm about to do something I hate to do, like go on an all-day antique shopping spree with my wife. But he's right. Get the fun out of it. I believe the exercises and assignments and the challenges that face you in the rest of this book and in this semester are wonderful and that there are moments ahead that will teach you about communicating better with the world.

It all starts with you being open to and ready for new experiences, new ideas, and new thoughts. They're going to come, and I want you to be ready to think and write about them.

Being dedicated

I think a writer needs to have dedication to the job at hand. I don't want to scare you about how hard the work we do is, but the truth is that it takes some time and attention.

Too many times my developing writers just go through the motions. You all know what that's like. It happens to all of us at some point. We have to go to a banquet when we'd rather not, so we get dressed up. We sit there. We eat the bad food. We listen to the bad speaker, smile when we have to, and finally, go home. The problem is, we don't have any fun and the people around us don't either. You might have heard someone say "It didn't look like you even wanted to be there . . . you ruined it for all of us."

Every semester I ask for a personal narrative essay and I get something like this.

> ▶ When I was six I had a pet frog named Barney. We played together in the back yard until one day my dad ran over it with a lawn mower. It made me sad. I was never the same. ◀

Well, I feel bad about Barney, too, and I never met the little green guy. But there's not much in that paragraph that makes me feel the writer is really into it. This "into it" quality is what I mean by dedication.

"Listen," I want to say to the writer of that paragraph, "You've decided to write about Barney the lawn-mown frog, so why not do it right? Let's get really involved. What's wrong with putting some energy into it?"

> ▶ When I was six my whole life revolved around the back yard. My mom was always afraid that I'd get run over by a car or a truck in the front, so when I got home from school she'd put me in the backyard with the high fence and swampy grass and I'd have to stay there until dinner. I hated it.
>
> One day when I was kicking stones around I saw something jump in a little pool of water. My eyes got big and I knelt down looking for whatever it was. Suddenly, out of the pool of water, red eyes bulging, green skin shining, a giant and beautiful frog leaped right on top of my head.
>
> I screamed, and ran around, knocking the thing off as I ran. But when I stopped running, there it was, right in front of me. His little darting tongue kept flicking out over and over again, just like I did when I'd get ice cream on my lips. He was cute. He was in the back yard, just like me. I decided he was going to be my friend. ◀

I haven't even gotten to the lawn mower scene; I swear you don't want to know about it anyway. But doesn't this section of text have more going for it than the first example? It's the same story; it's the same writer. The only difference is that the first section of text took about two minutes to write and the second one took about six. We all can spare the four minutes to improve an idea that much.

You've got to find time and energy to dedicate yourself to the writing and communicating you do.

Being imaginative

Being creative sometimes gets a bad name. Some folks think it's simply goofing off. Dreamers often look like they're doing nothing. But one of the most important things you can do as a writer is to daydream, walk around the park, think things over. Go outside sometimes and take a walk or a run and wonder what your writing or your essay needs next.

As you move through the book you'll find that each essay assignment includes a pre-writing stage, a time to invent. Take advantage of this time. Even though every semester I urge my students to follow their imaginations a little, too many of them stubbornly push ahead, writing without thinking, not giving their imaginations a chance.

Here's an example. In a simple writing assignment, I tell writers to compose a letter to a family member they want to thank for something. One writer shrugs her shoulders and writes "Dear Mom" on the top of the page, right away. Why? Is it a bad start? No. But this writer didn't do much thinking. She limited her options because instead of listening to my advice and thinking a bit about all the possibilities, she's just trying to get this writing over with. I said "Write to a family member," and in the next second she said to herself, "Family member, okay, Mom."

> Dear Mom,
>   You always took care of me when I was little. I can remember all the times you drove me to ballet and to soccer and you even drove my friends, too. You were the greatest.
>   Love, Jodi.

Maybe her mom is exactly the right person to write to. Maybe this essay will turn out wonderfully. That's not my concern at this stage. I'm not trying to help this writer with this one little, silly assignment. I'm trying to help this writer for the rest of her life, in every writing and speaking and communicating situation that arises. I'd bet somewhere down the road, it might be better for her to think of all the possibilities than to take the first thing that pops into her head.

On the same assignment, a writer on the other side of the room really hears what I say and thinks things over before writing this.

> Dear Three Bedroom on Clinton Avenue:
>   Well, old friend, it's been three long years since we all lived inside you, your high ceilings, your big backyard, your leaky shower head. But not a day goes by that I don't think a little about growing up there, under your protection and under your guidance.
>   I remember the night I was going to sneak out with Billy Brummer. Somehow you jammed my bedroom window tight. When I finally got it

open it made a huge noise, and I got caught. Mom and Dad made me go back to bed. It probably wouldn't surprise you if I told you all the trouble Billy got into that night. You did the right thing.

I think of all the storms you kept us safe from. Remember that year when the tornado was a few miles to our north? We stood under your strong, reinforcing beams and we carved our initials into the back of the door frame with the date. Hope that didn't tickle you. But the tornado never came and I don't think any of us every thanked you for that.

When Mom and Dad weren't there because of work, I always had you. I could bang a ball against your walls and you didn't complain or ever get tired. I could open and close and slam those kitchen cupboards looking for the last potato chips and you just let me keep going. When bugs came your windows kept them outside. When spring came we opened your windows and let the cool air blow in on us.

Why did we ever have to leave? Old friend, I live in a small little dorm room now. It's not even as big as my own bedroom once was. It's square. It's white. It's okay, I guess. But I wonder if I'll ever remember it like I remember you.

Thanks! Thanks for protecting me when I was a kid.

Your friend,
Ronnie.

Is a house a family member? No, not really. But clearly Ronnie's note expresses his sense that the house seemed to have humanlike qualities. What's the difference between his text and Jodi's? Ronnie took more time, investigated more ideas. He allowed his imagination to roam free. Had he settled on the first thing he thought of, probably his mom or dad, he never would have gotten the chance to explore this very neat idea.

Above all else, I encourage my writers to explore and to investigate and to let themselves feel freedom.

Being diligent

The bad news for some writers is that all of this writing takes some real work, some of it on your own. It means meeting deadlines, and asking questions, and being involved in class and workshop and conference and perhaps in the writing center.

Too many developing writers only write when they know they're supposed to. Many developing writers (and even students in general) assume that everything they should do will be assigned. This isn't the case. There are lots of things students or writers "can" do on their own to improve their own station in the class. You must take some of the responsibility for yourself about getting things underway and done on time.

I urge you to have a kind of diligence about your own class or, in this case, your own writing. Why not ask questions at the beginning of the process? If you'd like to write the personal essay about a friend but aren't sure if that's okay, why not ask? Just because your teacher hasn't officially told you to bring a rough draft to his or her office before workshop, doesn't mean you can't do it.

It's been my experience in almost fifteen years of teaching that most of my office time is spent reading, grading, or just listening to music or messing with my computer. You know what the real purpose of office hours is? It's for meeting students. There are some weeks when none of my students come by to see me. But there are always one or two students who visit on a regular basis. They bring rough drafts and they ask questions. They try to get ahead for the next essay. They confirm things they learned in class; they ask for further explanation. They write multiple drafts, even when they're not asked to do so. They write longer than they have to, more often than they have to.

These students—these writers—typically are my best students. By coming to my office, by working beyond the assigned minimum, they learn and do more. Their diligence pays off. Some of the synonyms for the student who is diligent include attentive, hardworking, and persistent. Those are all good qualities to have.

Habits

I wasn't the greatest student, not even in my writing classes. The main part of my problem was that I didn't have great habits as a student or as a writer. But I did learn from other students, and over the years I've discovered that nearly all of my best writers have had great work and writing habits. Here are a handful of habits to add to your own schedule as you get ready to start this course. All of these have worked for writers of mine.

IN-CLASS HABITS

Simply put, you must make sure you understand what your instructor is advising you to do on any kind of assignment, small or big. That means you must:

- Listen to the instructor *and* the other writers as assignments are discussed. The instructor may assign the next work to be done, but other students will likely ask questions that will further pin down the assignment. All of that questioning and answering is crucial.

- Take notes about what you hear and what you see on the board. Don't trust your memory. We all carry a lot of information around in our heads and it's easy to mix up "Read Chapter 9" from our psychology class with "Read everything but Chapter 9" from our English class.

- Ask questions for confirmation. If you don't understand something, find out what you've missed. There's no better time to clear things up than when the assignment or instructions are actually being given.

Doing these things offers a three-pronged approach to getting the assignment correct. How many times have you said to a teacher, "Oh, I didn't understand the assignment"? If the student or the writer gets the assignment wrong, that's the fault of the student. If something isn't clear in class, chances are it won't clear up in your head after you leave class. Your teacher likely will ask "Do you understand the assignment; are there any questions?" Those are real questions. If you have any confusion, clear it up while the teacher is still there.

WORKSHOP HABITS

As I mentioned briefly in Chapter 1, and will discuss at length in Chapter 13 (The Support Group), several times this semester you may get a chance to take part in a writing "workshop." This is a gathering of you and your classmates and your instructor. Writers get a chance to read portions of their essays to the assembled group, and we all get a chance to respond.

These are very helpful meetings that enable you to learn about your essay or writing in general. You play two roles in any workshop. You are there, of course, as a writer. During the course of the semester you should make sure you volunteer your work as the topic of discussion on several occasions. However, even if you aren't going to read and share your work, there is much to be gained by taking part in the discussions that go on around the essays of other writers.

The truth is, many students learn as much from participating in conversation about others' essays as they do in presenting their own work. This is because all during the workshop you will be hearing how other writers in your class are experimenting with the assignment that you are working on, too. Your instructor will be jumping in with comments and ideas that in many ways will help define the essay further and further.

For example, if your classmate Joanne reads her essay and the class decides they like it because it has a relevant quote from an outside source within the thesis, you'll learn that that technique is a good one. If, on the other hand, Leslie reads her paper and the group responds that the paper needs more background information, you'll know that it's important to include background information so your readers understand the ongoing ideas that make up the backdrop of any paper.

Two habits to develop for workshops are:

- Be ready to listen. (You can learn some things by listening.)
- Be ready to share your own work (You can learn other things by letting others listen.)

OUT-OF-CLASS HABITS

These habits are part of being diligent in your work. One of the things that separates great students from good or fair ones is the work done outside of class. Of course, it's clear that when we're in class we should be listening, focusing, and working on the tasks that our instructor has set out for us. But great college students know (or learn) that much of their work will come outside of class.

Most, if not all, of your essays will be written outside of class. You shouldn't look at this kind of assignment or challenge as a senseless intrusion on your time. Writing essays is the whole point of this class. In order to give these tasks their necessary time, it's crucial that you "block out" or "reserve" time in your out-of-class life so that you'll have the time and space to do the work. It's easy to understand that we must be in class every Tuesday and Thursday at 9 AM. It seems to be tougher for students to get the same kind of schedule together for their out-of-class work.

So, what to do? I'll tell you what my best students tell me. They plan their own schedule outside of class. If they have a regularly scheduled

Tuesday/Thursday class, then they set aside chunks of time on Monday and Wednesday, perhaps, to do the work. Or it may be four hours on Saturday afternoon or two hours after work on Sunday. Whatever you do, find blocks of time in your outside-class life for the writing and revising and reading that you will need to do to accomplish your tasks.

There's no room for flexibility here. If you're going to progress, you must work, and you simply cannot trust that your in-class time will afford you enough space to do all the thinking, reading, and writing that makes up this class (or many others).

A sample essay log

I've asked students to log their essay activities from time to time. By collecting these logs I can observe each student's writing process. It allows me insight into their habits and helps me know what steps of the process each writer needs help in.

The best ones often amaze me. Below is a log for one writer named Beth. Watch for how much work is done, and where, and when.

BETH'S ESSAY LOG ON DOMESTIC ANIMAL RIGHTS

September 7 (in class): Instructor tells us to write on an issue. He talked a while about issue essays. We free wrote in class for ten minutes on some issues or problems. I didn't come up with anything. [30 minutes]

September 7 (at lunch): My friend Leisa tells me to watch a TV show coming on that night about a woman who trains dogs for a living. [5 minutes]

September 7 (night): This TV show shows a woman from Alaska who trains dogs, but she only trains dogs who she finds in the pound or at the ASPCA. All of the dogs had been stranded or abused. [30 minutes]

September 9 (in class): Instructor asks us to share our topic ideas with our small group. I tell about the TV show and one of the guys asks if I'm more interested in the dogs or the trainer. I say I'm more interested in the dogs and the fact that they're abused. One of the girls suggests I think about talking to an animal shelter. [20 minutes]

continued ▶

September 10: I call the local animal shelter and talk to a woman who supervises hundreds of abuse cases. She tells me about an animal rights book that chronicles abuses in particular against domestic animals like dogs and cats. [15 minutes]

September 11: A rough draft is due in three days so I spend time in the library, finding that book and reading some of the chapters. I decide to write a paper about dogs and cats and their rights to a happy, healthy life. [2 hours]

September 12: I spend two hours writing different paragraphs for my paper. I spend most of the time writing my "feelings" down. "I hate it when dogs get hurt." "I hate it when dogs get abused." I even write about my own dogs and my love for them. [2 hours]

September 13: One day before the rough draft is due and now I've got to get settled. I write an opening paragraph that tells about my dog Joe, and about how much I loved him. Then I wrote a paragraph where I suggested that animals are sometimes our best friends. "Would you starve your best friend? Would you leave your best friend alone to fend for himself in a park, twenty miles from his home? Would you beat your best friend with a wooden stick if they made a mistake or spilled some food?" [1 hour]

September 14 (in class): In workshop, we all gathered and read our opening paragraphs. The class liked mine so far and one guy suggested I take out some of the occurrences of the word "hate." He said I sounded angry, and I guess he's right. The instructor said that I should feel comfortable being angry, but to be careful that I don't drive readers away with too negative or forceful language. [15 minutes]

September 15: I rewrote my opening, removing some of the hard language. [30 minutes]

September 16: I let my friend Laura read the essay and she almost cried. I'm getting to someone! [30 minutes]

September 17: I went back to the library and read some more of that book because I thought I needed some facts about the numbers of domestic animals who are abused each year. Found it in a different book! [2 hours]

September 18: Three days left and now I'm starting to finish the essay. I re-read it a couple of times and fixed some bad spelling mistakes and checked some grammar things in my grammar handbook. [2 hours]

September 18: After class today I went to my instructor's office and showed him my essay. He read the new opening and liked it a lot. He said that I had done my documentation of the dog abuse facts incorrectly and showed me a page in my grammar handbook that showed me how to fix the problem. He suggested I re-write my last paragraph because I didn't offer a solution or a "next step," for readers who might be interested in doing more. [10 minutes]

September 19: I called the animal shelter again and asked for that same woman. I asked her what I could do if I wanted to get involved more in solving the problem of domestic animal abuse. She suggested that there were some pamphlets and newsletters I could read that had suggestions; she told me about joining the local ASPCA; she told me about a walk-a-thon that happened twice every year for raising money. I re-wrote my conclusion of the paper talking about some of these suggestions. (Also had to look up how to give documentation credit to a person I spoke to in person or on the phone.) [3 hours]

September 20: I re-read everything, fixed some typos on the computer, printed it out, and let my friend Todd read it. (He already took this class!) He showed me a couple of places where he thought I was too emotional, and he suggested I tone it down a bit. I deleted a couple of sentences and then printed it out one last time. It's ready to be turned in. [2 hours]

Beth was a hard-working and diligent student who did all of the things I want my writers to do. Look at the ratio of her time in and out of class. She spent a total of nearly 16 hours outside of class thinking, writing, getting feedback, interviewing experts, and revising. Her actual class time during this assignment only amounted to about an hour and a half. That ratio is surprising, even to me. It probably shocks you.

I encourage you to keep your own log as you work on essays. They are helpful documents that allow you to verify that you're giving your best effort. If you find, for example, that most of your time on the essay takes place in class and that you have almost no outside time devoted to it, you can schedule "out-of-class" writing time for yourself for the next essay. If you go back and count your log hours and notice that you never made time for a conference with your instructor, then you can schedule one the next time an essay comes up.

A log will help you avoid making the same mistakes more than once.

The Personal Essay

5

Something to think about

We have to live inside our own skin. No matter what, we're stuck with ourselves. We bounce and bump around the world, but no matter how many friends and family members we have, at some point it always comes back to just us! We can have groups and family and neighbors and roommates, but the one constant is the self. Who's inside? "Just me," we cry. One person.

That's why personal writing is at the heart of any writer's existence. We may have goals and dreams to write about the world, to save the planet, to thrill and excite others with imaginary tales and wonderful plots. But the place where we must begin is within ourselves. Who do we understand? Who do we know? We spend a long time trying to figure out our worlds and the people in them, but self-knowledge starts it all.

So we must start within and work our way out. At this point you may be dreaming of writing about the Civil War, or sharks, or maybe just writing a poem. Well, all of that is available to you, but I believe you've got to know what's inside before you start writing outside.

Getting started

We all know a good storyteller. We've all got an aunt or a friend or a brother or someone from the neighborhood who can spin a good tale. The stories are always interesting, complex, funny, and surprising. Time flies as you hear them. Storytelling is a skill that is in high regard in our world. Not only do good storytellers make good guests at a party, they are also able to communicate in a lively, substantive way at work, at school, in the community, on television, in movies, and in books and magazines.

This first essay type asks that we tell a tale for our readers. We get to use our own lives as research material; we choose something from our own experience to tell others about. Sure, it sounds like fun, but there is also a responsibility there. Do we have a story worth telling?

The significance of our writing is all-important. The question that every reader asks as he or she reads our work is "So what?" If you're at a party and you're telling some story about going to the donut shop and the funny thing that happened to you there, at some point your audience is going to wonder "So what?" They are going to be listening to your story, and may even be enjoying the tale of how you got strawberry filling all over your shirt, but you're taking up their time and for that they expect a reward.

You may wonder why I'm "down" on writing that only entertains. After all, pure entertainment is certainly good enough for most TV shows, movies, and books. Entertainment, in fact, is often the only goal of these media.

But my reasoning works like this. If we get people's attention at a party by telling a funny or interesting story, then why don't we also take advantage of this opportunity to give them something extra? Let's make the story we tell worthwhile and significant. "But it's just a funny story" is not reason enough. Okay, see if this story helps make my point:

> For two weeks I'd been living back at my parents' house. I had lost my job; I was sleeping in a room with my little brother who was still in junior high. My mom made me get up every morning and do chores, just like when I was a kid. I hated it.
>
> Finally I got an interview. I stayed up the night before, reading my notes, laying my good suit out, and checking and rechecking the bus schedule for the next day.

continued ▶

When morning came I showered, shaved, dressed and then walked to the bus stop. I had plenty of time so I ducked into a favorite donut shop that was nearby and ordered up my usual: a couple of jelly-filled donuts.

I ate my donuts, read the front page of the newspaper, and then wiped my face with a napkin. I met the bus just as it pulled up, rode it a few minutes, and then made the tricky connection to a downtown bus. I walked in the front door of the office building with 5 minutes to spare.

My spirits were high; I had a sugar rush going from the donuts and when my name was called to enter the interviewer's office I felt great.

Right at the start of the interview, however, I felt something was wrong. I kept answering the questions, but the interviewer kept staring at me like there was something wrong.

My hair had been cut just the day before; this was my best suit. I had arrived on time. My résumé had been proofread a hundred times, but I kept losing confidence the longer I sat there.

We shook hands at the end and I left wondering what I had done wrong. As I walked toward the elevators I could see my reflection in the stainless steel mirrors. I had been right. My hair looked good, and so did my suit. I looked alert.

There was nothing wrong with me. Nothing except for the large red, jelly stain all down the front of my jacket and shirt.

As I got on the elevator I made a mental note to myself: "Next time, skip breakfast."

This story has a point. It means something. Sure it's funny and it's entertaining, but the writer is also telling about a lesson he learned. And there's nothing too fancy in there; it's written in pretty ordinary language. It's informal, yet it has a good message and a lesson. It's not just entertainment; it has an answer to the "so what?" question.

Let's talk a little bit about the elements that make up a good story. After all, we're going to have to write one soon.

HANS GUTH

Hans Guth, a terrific composition instructor, developed a helpful strategy called the "Five Storyteller Questions." These five questions are essential ingredients of any good story. Let's go through them one at a time, and I'll give you an idea of why these questions are important and how you can best answer them in your essay.

SETTING

Where and when your story takes place is always important. You must always keep in mind that your reader likely doesn't know you or anything about your story. Details that might be easily remembered by you will probably not even be known by the reader.

Imagine a story in which you were at a local lake in your town. You took a dare and stripped your clothes off in the car and ran from the car to the lake, jumped in, swam around, and then raced back to the car. Now that's a very different story if it takes place on a Saturday in the summertime at around noon with 500 strangers watching or if you did the same thing in the dead of winter at midnight with no one there but your brother. The difference in the setting is the difference between just a silly prank and a monumental breaking of the law!

You have a responsibility as a writer to re-create the scene in your story. Show us where we are. Tell us what time it is, how cold it is, where you were standing. In short, put us right there in the story with you.

CHARACTER

The people who populate your story are important, too. We need to know who they are and what their relationship is to you and something about them. If I tell you one of the characters is my sister, that's good. But if I tell you her name is Judy, that she's ten years older than me, and that she's got red hair, that's better. You're starting to see her and know her a little better. We often forget when we tell stories to fill in the blanks for our readers. When I write "My sister was there," a million memories and ideas pop into my head. I *know* her, and that sometimes becomes a problem for developing writers. I have to remember that my reader *doesn't* know her.

Because we know so much, however, we have to use a "selective" memory at times. Just because your aunt was there when your story happened, doesn't mean she has to be in the story you write for us. If your aunt had nothing to do with the story and was only there in the background, don't mention her. Now, I'm sure you love your aunt and all, but including her might actually confuse the story. Readers are always trying to understand. If you mention that your aunt is sitting in a chair, the reader will picture her, keep some space in his or her memory banks for her and inevitably be disappointed when she doesn't mean anything to the story.

BACKGROUND

This element is pretty much as it sounds. Background is anything that happened before this story that is necessary for the story to make sense. Take my sister Judy, for example. If I tell you a story about her and me, then it's appropriate that I give you some background on Judy and on our relationship. If I just say "sister," some of you might think, "Ah, that's nice. Sisters are great." Some of you might think, "Ugh, I hope she's not mean like my sister." Saying "sister" isn't as helpful as you think. You need to give background. If I tell you a story that has my sister in it, I'd better also tell you that she and I never got along, that she used to beat me up when I was little, and that she moved out of the house when I was only nine, so I don't even really know her. See the difference? Those details may have nothing to do with the story I'm about to tell you, but they are crucial in giving you background.

Background can be useful for many things besides describing characters. Let's say I tell you that when I was in high school my hockey team won the state championships. That may not mean much to you if you live in California or South Carolina. But if I lived in Minnesota where hockey is a fiercely competitive high school sport, bigger than baseball and football combined, then I'd better mention that competitiveness as background so you know how important it really was.

Background is anything your readers need to know for your story to make sense. If they miss the point of your story, it's often because they didn't have enough background.

HIGH POINT

You can also think of this as climax, although I don't really like the word "climax" so much. Many writers think climax suggests a BIG action. There are always lots of car crashes and funerals and high school graduations that make up many of our stories. But I try to warn writers as much as I can about using those types of stories because they're too "easy." They seem dramatic to us and we expect others to see the drama in them as well. Unfortunately, I have to tell writers every semester "*Your* graduation didn't mean anything to *me*!" And of course I add, "Unless you show me why."

And therein lies the problem. If we are too close emotionally to an event, we often forget that there are hundreds of little details that *made* it important. Because our mind can recall the events so clearly, we often forget that our readers simply don't know what's in our head.

A student of mine once wrote about his high school graduation. He was sure it was the biggest event of his life and in his essay he said things like "It was the biggest day of my life" and "I was so happy and proud." There's nothing particularly wrong with that, but a good reader needs and wants more. "Why was it big?" "What were you proud of?" It was the writer's graduation; he owed me an explanation. Yet his essay was vague and general and full of clichés. It ended "It was the most important thing

I had ever done." I kept making him rewrite it. "Try this again," I'd say. When he'd bring it back and it was the same, I'd ask "What's the 'so what?' answer in this essay?" He was frustrated; I was frustrated. I knew that his graduation memory mattered to him because he kept plugging away, rewriting it time and again. But I still didn't know why it mattered. There was no high point, no climax. I wanted him to explain to me why the story mattered. I explained Hans Guth's "high point" theory and asked my student to tell me what the climax of the story was. If he could prove to me there was a high point, I was going to let him turn in the paper. He sat there, reading the paper over and over and then pointed at a line. He told me that the high point was the moment when the principal handed him the diploma. I said, "Why?" He said, "Because that's when I graduated," and we both knew we were back at the starting point.

Finally, at semester's end, the student turned in the paper. I was frustrated but thought I'd read it one more time. In the closing paragraph, I nearly shouted out with joy:

> ▶ As I walked across the stage to receive my diploma, I spotted my dad in the audience. He was still wearing his shirt from the bakery and he was holding my mom's hand. He waved at me and smiled and I thought it was weird to see him smile. He was always so gloomy around the house. When he was home he was yelling at me to study, or to quit goofing off. I didn't know why he cared so much about my graduation, since he had never graduated. But there he was smiling. As we drove home from the graduation he took my diploma from me and looked at it the whole way home, reading it and holding it in his own hands. ◀

The writer had finally found the significance of his story. Do you see it? His dad had never finished high school. When the son finally achieved that goal, it was as if all the father's "yelling" had finally paid off. I saw this student right after grades had come out and I asked him if he knew he had figured out the essay. "Yes," he replied, "I know the 'so what?' answer now. My graduation meant something different to me than to most of my friends. To my friends it was a party. For me it was something I wanted to do to repay my dad."

The lesson about high point is simple: If your story, your essay, or a letter you write is going to matter for a reader, you must know why it matters for you. In this case the writer "knew" it was important, but it took him months to find out why.

LESSON

There is usually a lesson learned at the climax of a story. After all, part of the definition of the high point is that something must be discovered or learned. But when I say *lesson* in this context, I'm talking about a lesson that goes beyond this essay. A small or "local" lesson just relates to the story itself, while a big or "global" lesson (the kind we want at the end of our essay) goes past the particular story.

For example, in my student's graduation paper discussed above, his local lesson has to do with his father and that one story. He discovers that his father had hounded him all those years about school because his father had never graduated. That's the local lesson of that essay. However, not every reader will get the full impact of that small, local lesson. Your last job as a writer in this kind of essay is to try and "globalize" the lesson for us. Find a lesson that reaches more people.

For example, the global lesson to be learned in the graduation essay has to do with the expectations of others. My writer might have eventually written this.

> But what I learned from my dad that night went beyond graduation night. I learned that my actions mattered to others; I learned that other people depended on me. My success and my failure were connected to my family, my friends, and my co-workers. From that night on, I began to live life not just as a boy from a small town in Texas, but as a man who was a part of the rest of the world. ◄

While my student's local lesson was wonderful, this lesson goes past his own story and tries to attach itself to everyone. Not everyone has experienced the same father–son dynamic that makes his lesson so poignant. At the end of his essay, we try to find a global lesson that more readers can relate to. In the above paragraph, the goal is to show how the first lesson concerning his father leads to this last, larger lesson: "I began to live life not just as a boy from a small town in Texas, but as a man who was a part of the rest of the world."

That's a global lesson in the truest sense of the word.

Warmups

Since we talked earlier about what "warmups" can do for us, let me briefly remind you of their importance. As we get prepared to take on the main essay assignment, I want us to do some smaller exercises and writings first, to "warm up" our minds. Just as a runner wouldn't consider hopping out of bed and starting a marathon without stretching, we shouldn't take off running with the essay yet.

Let's ease into it with a couple of small assignments that will help us develop our abilities on some important elements we'll use later.

THE PHOTO ALBUM ASSIGNMENT

I love thinking about myself, and I imagine you're somewhat the same. Let's start our warmups with a treasure hunt. Find old photos of yourself, even those that make you want to cringe a bit: naked on a bearskin rug, with bad-looking hair, in your first suit. Gather four to six photos of yourself from different time periods. Put them in front of you and write three short free-writings about them. Remember, free-writing is just writing for yourself. The rules are to keep your pen moving and don't stop or censor yourself. You're just trying to get ideas down on the page. You can check for sense and make them pretty later on, if it turns out they're suitable for essays. (I've included some samples to help you get started.)

- What was going on in your world on the day of this picture?

  This was the day my folks took me to the family reunion. I'm wearing my new suit that I always hated. That's my creepy cousin Bruce standing next to me.

- Tell the first interesting story that happened after this picture.

  After this picture was taken, I headed over to the table where my other cousins were hanging out and we made up a spitting game to see who could spit the farthest into the duck pond.

- If a friend of yours were to see this picture and wonder why you have it, what would you tell her? Explain the significance of this photo.

  I think I still have it because my family doesn't get together very often. We all live in different states and only once every five years or so do we ever end up in the same place. It reminds me that I have cousins who I never see, and that although we live in different places, we all share a name and a family.

A LOOPING WARMUP

Here's a warmup in which you'll use the technique called looping. If you missed this information in Chapter 3, skip back and check it out.

- Do a four to six minute free-writing on one of the following topics: "A list of my favorite places, people, or events." Don't censor yourself. Your goal is to get as many items down as you can. If every once in a while an item seems to suggest an extra couple of sentences, then go ahead. But after a couple of sentences get your brain to jump to a new idea.

- Now, read over your list and circle one item that jumps out at you as the most interesting or surprising. This circled item becomes your new focus. Write it at the top of a new sheet of blank paper, or type it at the start of a clean screen. For example, if you were writing about places and came up with this list—Las Vegas, my bedroom, the back of Eddy's diner in Junction City, New Orleans, in my girlfriend's arms—then you would circle the one that jumps out at you.

- Write for four to six minutes using your new focus. Write only about that focus. Your goal is to come up with as many factual details or descriptions about that new focus as you can. Fill up a page if you can.

- Next, read your latest effort. Go through it carefully and find elements that are similar so you can group them together. For example, if during your free-writing or looping about the back of Eddy's diner you see that many of your descriptions had to do with smells, then circle and group all the smells: garbage, cabbage, cigarettes from the waitresses, gasoline from the Exxon next door. With that knowledge, you'll be able to capture that scene more vividly.

Your instructor might have some more warmups for you, and I hope you take the time to work on them, too.

The essay assignment

Write a multiparagraph essay that tells a story from your life. Your audience is this class. The paper should be long enough to deliver a "good" story, one that contains significance and Guth's Five Storyteller Questions. (Your instructor will likely give you some guidance about length.)

In your story you should try to re-create a crucial, essential scene—the high point of your story. Focus on a single moment or event. Avoid stories that cover a long period of time because they involve far too much material for your listener or reader to take in at one sitting. Strive for a story that has a general lesson that applies to many people, thereby satisfying a larger audience. Don't be afraid of using first person.

Sample essays

This is the first appearance of sample essays, so let me talk for a while about their importance and use.

Most of the essays in this book have been written by students in my classes over the years. They vary from good to exceptional essays. You will sometimes be seeing the final, best draft of essays and at other times the earlier, rougher drafts from when the writer was struggling.

I believe that sample essays are useful as models. As a writer, I hope you get some understanding of style and language and essay topic from these samples. I hope you read them and say "Hey, I've got a story like that" or "I see what she's doing."

The one thing that sometimes goes wrong with sample essays is that developing writers merely mimic or imitate the work shown as a model. After all, these sample essays are in a book! They are published. I must have picked them for a reason. But I want to tell you what I tell my own students every semester: Your own beautiful and interesting ideas are what we're really after. One of the things that sets all of these essays apart is that their writers came up with their own, fresh approaches to the assignment. They didn't simply try to do what others had already done.

Freshness is one of the qualities we will value in your writing. These models will show you some of the tricks and gimmicks "other" writers have used to tell their stories or prove their points, but it's important that you find your own way and your own style.

Here's an essay from a student of mine named Karen who was given the same assignment that I've described above. This draft isn't her final draft. There are still some things that could be done to make it stronger. But I wanted to start with it because it shares a number of elements with many personal essays.

FINDING CONFIDENCE

I had recently moved to a small town in Louisiana from Texas. I left all my good friends behind but I sincerely thought I had made some new ones. I met Kim and Heather in my new fourth grade class. Heather was very pretty and kind. Everyone liked her and the boys were constantly chasing her around the playground at recess. Kim was very thin and had long,

continued ▶

stringy brown hair. She wore glasses that seemed to perfectly frame her forever smiling face. We always got along well, although the other kids in school were always making fun of me. Even on the school bus I was the butt of all the jokes. I couldn't understand why everyone acted this way towards me. At my old school, my classmates were friendly to me and no one had ever made fun of me.

One day Heather, Kim, and I were standing on the playground during recess. The playground was a thin forest with pine and fir trees randomly sprinkled here and there, until you got to the edge of the school grounds, and then it was a thick, dark forest with snakes and other dangerous animals lurking deep inside. The school was brand new and badly planned; they had to build twenty portable buildings for classrooms to house the masses of students they hadn't accounted for. The portables were built on a corner of the empty playground that only housed one piece of playground equipment. It was built like an obstacle course with a tire wall that led to a wooden platform with a roof above it. There was a swinging bridge that stretched to an identical platform that had a large, metal slide attached at the opposite end. We were waiting in a long line for our turn to climb the tire wall when Kim came up with a great idea.

"Why don't you race through the course," Kim said to me. "Heather and I will wait here and time you. We can see who's the fastest."

"Yeah," Heather said. "It'll be fun."

So they stepped out of the line and waited for me to start. I remember Kim shouting at me to go and I took off as hard and as fast as I could.

While climbing up the tire wall, I almost knocked two girls over, but I kept going without even an apology. I became ruthless and determined to get to the end. I wanted to impress Kim and Heather with a fast time. I crossed the wooden bridge pushing people right and left, and even plowing right through them, knocking them down. The teacher who was on duty below the bridge blew her whistle at me and told me to slow down, but I wasn't going to lose any seconds off of the clock. The slide was just ahead and all I had to do was slide to the ground and I was finished. The bright hot sun had heated the metal slide and I could feel it burning through my jeans as I slid to the ground. When my feet hit the sandy ground, I looked around to find them. I didn't see them anywhere and then I realized, "Oh no, they wanted me to run back to them at the start!" Wiping the sweat from my brow, I ran back as fast as I could, dodging crowds of kids, and finally made it back to the starting line. They weren't there either. I looked all over the playground before I realized the race had all been a joke. I was so upset that I started to cry.

Why had they done this to me? I thought they were my friends. I had been a good friend to them; I helped them when they had needed help, and even shared my lunch with them. I walked to a secluded part of the playground while trying to hide my pain from the other kids. I sat against a tree, and wiping away my tears, tried to remember what I had done to cause them to ditch me like this. I watched my classmates across the playground running from tree to tree while being chased by others trying to tag them out. They were laughing and having a great time with each other. Why wouldn't they let me into their group? Why did they dislike me?

I took a deep breath to try and calm myself down. The smell of pine and fir trees was heavy in the air, as well as a dampness that never seemed to disappear. I started thinking, trying to figure out what I had done wrong to make them mad at me. I thought that they must be mad to ditch me like this. All at once the realization hit me, and hard. I remembered how everyone was nice to me at my old school in Texas, and now I knew why. I was too nice. I'd let them take advantage of me. If they had wanted help with their homework, I gave them the answers. They had all treated me as if I were their best friend so they could get the answers for that night's homework, even my best friend Katie. I had given anybody what they wanted so I could have friends and feel accepted. They had used me and I'd let them. My thoughts turned to the present and the jokes people made about me on the playground and on the bus. I was an easy target. They knew I wouldn't stand up for myself, and they took advantage of that. They would make fun of everything about me. I made good grades so I was a huge nerd; I was a little overweight so I got all the fat jokes. One time I caught impetigo so, of course, my new nickname was "Scabs." Kim and Heather probably didn't mean any harm, they just didn't know what my boundaries were because I hadn't established them yet. Naturally, they thought they could get away with this like all of the others did.

"I'm not doing it anymore," I told myself. "It's time I finally stand up for myself." That's what I had decided. I looked again at the kids playing tag, and this time they didn't seem so threatening to me anymore. It didn't matter to me what anyone else thought anymore, only what I thought of myself. Just then the bell clanged to end recess. I got up, brushed the dirt from my jeans, took a deep breath, and started walking to the classroom to give Kim and Heather a piece of my mind.

Two years later I was sitting in a sixth grade classroom back in Texas. I was the new student, again. I knew it was coming; all new kids got it. The jokes started all over again. I received respect from no one, and was teased as if I had no feelings. A girl I sat next to in class, Dana, seemed to be pretty popular, and as all the popular kids do she made fun of me also. One day we were paired up to do a worksheet full of fractions and I began to talk to her. "Why are you so mean to me?" I asked her confidently. All she could

continued ▶

do was stare at me with her big blue eyes. I went on to tell her to give me a chance, to get to know me before she judged me. I also told her what it felt like to be in my position. She began to understand my situation and became my friend. As time went on, the others began to accept me for who I was, and I didn't let them use or hurt me. I was finally included because I stood up for myself.

A CLOSE REVIEW OF THE SAMPLE ESSAY

Let's talk about the essay bit by bit and see if it's accomplishing the types of things that a good personal narrative requires. We're going to go into quite a bit of detail on this essay, something we don't do on all the samples. Because this is the first essay we are looking at together, I want to go slowly so you're comfortable with some of the key ingredients.

We'll start with the all-important first paragraph. In that paragraph something must be done to attract the reader. Regardless of the type of essay, readers are looking for something to convince them to stick around a while and read what you have to say. Let's see what this writer has tried to do. Here are parts of the first paragraph.

> ▶ I had recently moved to a small town in Louisiana from Texas. . . . I met Kim and Heather in my new fourth grade class. Heather was very pretty and kind. Everyone liked her and the boys were constantly chasing her around the playground at recess. Kim was very thin and had long, stringy brown hair. . . . We always got along well, although the other kids in school were always making fun of me. Even on the school bus I was the butt of all the jokes. I couldn't understand why everyone acted this way towards me. At my old school, my classmates were friendly to me and no one had ever made fun of me. ◀

What's going on in this paragraph? There's some background information given about the writer's recent move to a new town, and in the closing part of the paragraph, a revelation that things at the new school aren't as easy as they were at the old one. I'd suggest that we all have some experience with that sort of situation, being a new kid or a fish out of water somewhere. That's the idea or the beginning our writer wants us to have first. She's hoping we'll identify with her or feel empathy with her. If we've ever been in a similar situation, I'd bet we will find something in that paragraph to identify with.

In addition to that first point, the writer also begins developing some characters for us: herself, Kim, and Heather. The writer's descriptions of her friends are positive, and we're left with a good overall feeling about them, despite the hint of trouble in how the other kids treat her.

Let's move on to the next paragraph to see what our writer does.

> ▷ One day Heather, Kim, and I were standing on the playground during recess. ◁

That's a simple, but great opening line! One of the goals of this paper is to tell a story, a particular story. One story! Our writer here has taken that to heart, and despite the fact that she really could tell any story about the time she lived in this new town in Louisiana, she's picked one day in particular. That's an excellent choice. I encourage all my writers to find the smallest event they can. Don't write about a month, when you can find a single day that tells your story. Don't settle on one day, if you can find the important half hour where the story really took place.

Let's keep going in the paragraph.

> ▷ The playground was a thin forest with pine and fir trees randomly sprinkled here and there, until you got to the edge of the school grounds, and then it was a thick, dark forest with snakes and other dangerous animals lurking deep inside. The school was brand new and badly planned; they had to build twenty portable buildings for classrooms to house the masses of students they hadn't accounted for. The portables were built on a corner of the empty playground that only housed one piece of playground equipment. It was built like an obstacle course with a tire wall that led to a wooden platform with a roof above it. There was a swinging bridge that stretched to an identical platform that had a large, metal slide attached at the opposite end. ◁

Also in this paragraph we get some nice description of the surroundings of the playground. It's exactly this kind of detail that most young, developing writers avoid. In your own story, you can probably see the setting and what was there, and how things looked. Our writer here can do that, too, but she knows an important thing: Her readers weren't there! We often assume too much about what our readers can know. The truth is, giving description and recreating the scene as you saw it is very important to re-creating the scene for your reader. They've seen playgrounds before, but they haven't seen yours. There's a concept called "suspension of disbelief," and it's probably most well understood when you think of movies. When you go see a fabulous Hollywood movie with dinosaurs and jet boats and cities blowing up, you sometimes forget you're sitting in a theater in your home town. You get that sense of being "swept away" that movie directors and novelists and poets and artists count on. If the whole time you're watching a dinosaur march through San Diego (for example), you're saying: "Hey, this is a movie!" then the filmmaker hasn't really helped you suspend your disbelief. When that dinosaur is chomping on fine citizens, you should be on the edge of your seat, terrified, eyes bulging out, popcorn spilling on the floor. That's suspension of disbelief. The exact same principle is at work in an essay—only you don't get a 50-foot screen and surround-sound to help you. You've got to get that same job done with words.

How important is it, then, to recreate a scene? Very important. Our writer spends some of her time just telling us what the jungle gym looks like. We know what a jungle gym looks like, but she's going to take the time to recreate hers for us, so that we "see" the tires and the platform and the swinging bridge. If she doesn't take the time to do that, we may never get "into" the story.

Let's finish the paragraph now.

> We were waiting in a long line for our turn to climb the tire wall when Kim came up with a great idea.
>
> "Why don't you race through the course," Kim said to me. "Heather and I will wait here and time you. We can see who's the fastest."
>
> "Yeah," Heather said. "It'll be fun."
>
> So they stepped out of the line and waited for me to start. I remember Kim shouting at me to go and I took off as hard and as fast as I could. <

While the earlier "playground" section was descriptive, this last section gets back to the "story." It's sometimes a balancing act for a writer. You need to keep us going forward with the story, but you also have to keep us updated with background, and keep us visually excited with description. My favorite part of this section is the line: ". . . Kim came up with a great idea." Doesn't that sound like every "adventure" you ever had as a kid? And since this new information ends a paragraph, it leads us to want to go to the next paragraph—always a good writing trick! The action is in progress and we want to find out what happens next, so we read on.

> While climbing up the tire wall, I almost knocked two girls over, but I kept going without even an apology. I became ruthless and determined to get to the end. I wanted to impress Kim and Heather with a fast time. . . . When my feet hit the sandy ground, I looked around to find them. I didn't see them anywhere and then I realized, "Oh no, they wanted me to run back to them at the start!" Wiping the sweat from my brow, I ran back as fast as I could, dodging crowds of kids, and finally made it back to the starting line. They weren't there either. I looked all over the playground

before I realized the race had all been a joke. I was so upset that I
started to cry. ◀

Suddenly, we understand why this essay is important to our writer. It's
not just the story of a day in the playground. The concept of significance
is extremely important. As good readers, we are in a sense always asking
ourselves the question "So what?" When I read this paragraph, I understand why this story is still in the memory banks of our writer. Any good
reader will give a writer a few minutes of grace period. When you turn on
a TV program, you probably watch a few minutes before you decide
"Nah, time to switch," or "Yeah, I think I can put the remote down
now." With an essay, we're working on the same principle. At some
point, the payoff must come. For me, it happens in the paragraph above.

Despite the fact that our writer has done a neat job here of describing
things and telling a little story about being a kid, we still need something
big to keep us around. After all, when we invest time in an essay, we
expect some kind of return. The return or the payoff is this "significance." We learn in the paragraph above that this story means "something" to the writer; the story matters.

Let's look at material from the next two paragraphs. (As I've done
above in a limited way, I've cut some sections of text to speed things
along.)

> Why had they done this to me? I thought they were my friends. . . .
I walked to a secluded part of the playground while trying to hide my pain
from the other kids. I sat against a tree, and wiping away my tears, tried to
remember what I had done to cause them to ditch me like this. . . . ◀

Here our writer asks herself a question. It's her way of recalling the
troubling way she felt that day. We're watching the story through her
essay, and her question "Why had they done this to me?" is one that we
are likely to be asking ourselves.

This part of the paragraph is important as well because we're waiting
for the answer that will unlock this story's significance. Plus, if we're
still empathetic with the writer, and there's no reason for us not to be,
we simply feel bad for her and want things to turn around.

> I took a deep breath to try and calm myself down. . . . All at once the
realization hit me, and hard. I remembered how everyone was nice to me
at my old school in Texas, and now I knew why. I was too nice, I'd let
them take advantage of me. If they had wanted help with their homework, I gave them the answers. They had all treated me as if I were their
best friend so they could get the answers for that night's homework, even
my best friend Katie. I had given anybody what they wanted so I could

> have friends and feel accepted. They had used me and I'd let them. . . .
> Kim and Heather probably didn't mean any harm, they just didn't know
> what my boundaries were because I hadn't established them yet. Naturally,
> they thought they could get away with this like all of the others did. ◀

And there's where we get the answer. When the writer writes, "All at once the realization hit me, and hard," we have our high point. This is the moment that matters the most in the whole paper. It's the moment when the conflict or the struggle comes to its conclusion or climax. The story isn't over yet, but the moment of epiphany or learning has come for the writer.

And as she writes it, she gives us the lesson. She teaches us the lesson. She's taken a relatively small event in her life, found its meaning, and then found a meaning larger than the story itself. That last lesson, the global one, is one that can have resonance or meaning for all of us.

She's succeeded.

Another student sample

One of the toughest things for a writer to convey in an essay is emotion. The problem is that our strongest feelings are often too close to us for us to have perspective on them. The writer knew why this next story mattered and why its contents had an impact, but she couldn't express the emotion in any kind of way that would work for others. I sent the essay back several times until we got to this draft.

As you read it, watch for moments where the writer attempts to explain her feelings and emotions, and ask yourself if the emotions seem genuine.

In addition, be on the lookout for any weaknesses. I admit this is just a rough draft, and while the final draft ended up being an A paper, this draft has certain flaws. I'd like you to be on the lookout for them. Your teacher will probably want to have a discussion about whatever flaws you can identify.

GUS

> It was a humid and gloomy Saturday afternoon, the kind of day when
> you take a shower and then fifteen minutes later you feel like you need
> another one, the kind of day I hate. I work at an animal clinic and close

at noon on Saturdays. We were getting ready to wrap things up for the afternoon when we got a phone call from a family we knew. They were on their way to the clinic and had made the decision to put their cat to sleep. This cat was a gorgeous Siamese named "Gus." Gus and I had gotten to know each other very well over the past few weeks. He had been diagnosed with kidney failure and had been staying at the clinic. I was the one who had been treating and spending the most time with him. I became attached quickly. The day came when the doctors decided there was nothing left to do for Gus. His family was going to come and decide whether they would take him home to die, or leave him with us to be euthanized, or "put to sleep." I was hoping that Gus would go home with them, to die in his own home, not here at the clinic. I had never witnessed a euthanasia and was in no hurry.

When I was about ten years old my family had a Lhasa Apso with a neurological disorder. What ended up being the downfall of "Buster" was that every time my older brother and I would fight, Buster would attack my brother in my defense. I was the one Buster thought of as master. He and I shared some kind of mental bond. It was like he could feel my sadness, my happiness, my anger and vice versa. I knew he was just protecting me, but no one believed me. Buster loved to run and jump and he always was a good boy with me. He was a one owner, loyal dog and was punished for it. I never got a vote in the decision to put Buster asleep. I didn't even go to the vet that day; I refused to talk to my parents for weeks. This, along with my desire to care for and understand animals, ended up being the reason I decided to become a veterinarian.

When Gus and his family arrived, I stayed around long enough to say my good-byes and then quickly disappeared so I wouldn't have to witness the sad decision. As I was rounding the corner to cry, I ran right into the relief Vet who asked me to help him with Gus. My heart sank as I followed him to the treatment area. They had decided to put poor Gus out of his misery. As I watched the Vet unlock the metal box that held the sedatives and the Euthanisol, I was thinking this was wrong, all wrong. The Veterinarian who owned the clinic, the same man the family expected to be with them, was out of town. The man taking his place had all of the degrees that certified him to be a Vet, but should never have been allowed to become one. He was the most unfeeling man I had ever met; he had no regard for the family and how they felt, not to mention Gus. The family wanted to be in the room with Gus when he went to sleep. However, this iceberg of a man would not permit it. The Vet's biggest worry at this point was getting the whole thing over with. He kept complaining that this euthanasia was not scheduled and he had

continued ▶

somewhere to be. With every word he spoke, rage and sadness began welling up inside me. He walked over toward me with a needle full of Euthanisol and told me to hold Gus by his scruff and stretch his back legs out. This cat was in kidney failure. Any empathetic Vet could tell you this cat was not going to put up a fight. There was no reason Gus' last moments had to be ones of pain and torment. I started to protest but fell silent.

Gus' weak body began to emit the most awful howls and screams because of his position and the needle entering his leg. Inside I was shattered. I could feel all of the rage and hurt rising to the surface ready to be expelled. I wanted to take the Euthanisol needle away from this wretched man, and stick it into him, and tell him to contort his body into the ridiculous positions he made me put Gus in. Just as I was about to lay into the vet standing across from me, I felt Gus go limp. I looked into his eyes and they were empty. Gus was gone. The tears came flooding from my eyes but I did not speak. I did not move. I just stood staring at Gus' body.

I began to think about Buster, how I knew it was different for him. The Vet I had known all of my life, and my parents, were with him. He went the way he was supposed to, at ease and comforted. Suddenly I was not so mad at my parents anymore. I also realized that I should no longer flee from euthanasias but should be there to hold and comfort the animals as they go, partially for the animal's sake and partially for mine. I walked to the front of the clinic, tears still streaming from my eyes, and noticed the tears of the mother, father, and son. At that moment, I thanked God that they were not in the room when Gus left.

QUESTIONS

The questions below will focus on a couple of flaws within this draft. You'll likely need to read the question, reread the pertinent part of the essay, and then write your answer. When you're asked to write revisions, do them just as if the essay was your own and you were looking for a good grade.

1. Between the first and second paragraph there is an awkward and abrupt transition from the essay back to the story about the writer's dog, Buster. The information is important because it suggests the first time our writer thought about working with animals. However, it's out of place, not connected into the story very well. How would you fix its placement in the essay?

2. In addition, the entire story about Buster is confusing. It's a collection of details that don't entirely add up to a sensible story. Decide what details are essential and ditch the rest. Write your own version of the paragraph on a separate sheet of paper.

3. Treat the euthanasia of the cat by the relief veterinarian (third and fourth paragraphs) as a story all by itself. What details of the scene are unnecessary? What details are essential? What missing information is necessary for the story to have a more realistic feel?

One more sample

Let's finish up with one more essay. It's a nice example of writing about a specific person. Many folks who write a personal essay end up writing about one special person in their life, just as Renee does below.

This essay is not quite finished. Be on the lookout for things that might need more detail or explanation.

REMEMBERING UNCLE DAVID

Today I heard a song on the radio that brought back fond memories of someone who I grew up with.

I can see my Uncle David playing his bass guitar with the Johnny Mac Jazz Band for the residents at the Great Falls Nursing Home. The song he's singing is "Wonderful Tonight" by Eric Clapton. I can still recall the smells of medicine and death which are common among nursing homes. David is wearing his worn out Levi's, cowboy boots, and a tee-shirt, his sandy blond, shoulder length hair pushed back behind his favorite Atlanta Braves hat, his right pocket in the back worn away from his wallet, and a perfect outlining of a circle from his Copenhagen habit on the other pocket. I remember sitting around a small orange card table with my Grandma E. and my little sister, watching David sing away. I was eleven years old, and couldn't have looked up to anyone more.

David was my dad's youngest brother. He was only five years older than me, and he had always been my favorite uncle. Due to the closeness in age, he was more like my brother rather than my uncle. We were very close growing up. David and I saw each other several times a week, and shared every holiday together at my grandparents' house.

continued ▶

Easter was always one of my favorite holidays with David. When all the adults were hiding the eggs outside, he'd go outside, lurk around, and watch. When it was time for all the younger kids to go find the eggs, he'd stand to one side and point me in all the right directions. Every Easter David and I ended up with the most eggs.

I remember when David and I were fairly young, our favorite game was G.I. Joes. We use to sneak them to the park and blow them up with firecrackers. It's a good thing no one ever found out. I'm sure we would have been in a lot of trouble. David was a fun guy to be around. I never met anyone who didn't enjoy being around him. When I was twelve years old, my step-dad was transferred overseas to Guam. This would be our first move ever, and it was very far away from our family.

If anyone has ever experienced a move, they know that keeping in touch with family and friends is all you have to get you through the first few months in a strange place. Once you start establishing your new life, however, it doesn't seem as important to keep in constant touch. Most of us just assume that family and friends will always be there. I found new friends and made a new life for myself. I missed my old friends and our family, but mostly I got on with my life, having new experiences and enjoying our new life.

When we came back to Texas I was a new person, a woman. I met a great guy and we started to date. Now that I was older I didn't always have to go and visit family when my parents did. I'd find excuses to skip it. I'd rather go to the mall, or hang out with my friends, or see a movie with my new boyfriend. I saw Uncle David every once in a while, but he treated me like a kid still, and I was not a kid anymore.

I was out on a date with my boyfriend when I received the news. We were enjoying dinner at Red Lobster when someone paged me from my house. I returned the call and heard the news from my sister Laura. "Renee, I have terrible news. Uncle David was killed in a car accident." I was speechless. I didn't know what to say. I was in shock. I just hung up the phone and my date and I left immediately. When I got home everyone was in tears, but I couldn't cry. I was flooded with emotions; the thought of never being able to see or talk to him again was almost more than I could bear to think about. I just went to my room to be alone.

The sad thing is, I talked to David maybe three or four times over the last four years. At one point in our lives we were very close, but we lost contact and grew apart as we grew up. If I could go back in time and change the lost time I would. The death of my uncle made me realize the importance of keeping in touch with my family and friends, both old and new. They may be with us today, but they may be gone tomorrow.

Since David's death, I've taken the opportunity to keep in better touch with people I find important to me. I wish it didn't take the death of my Uncle David to make me realize the great importance for communication. Maybe if this would have dawned on me sooner, we could have been closer.

Now I try to call my grandparents at least once a month and send them a card to let them know how much I care. Each month I choose a few friends that I haven't talked to for a while and I give them a call. Because long distance is expensive, I've also been writing many people in my family and friends. It can be a hassle at times because I am so busy, but I know in the long run I'll feel better about keeping in touch.

QUESTIONS

1. How important is a clear physical experience of the person you're remembering or writing about? Does it influence the reader? Look back at this essay and see if Renee has done a good enough job - showing us Uncle David. If you think it's well done, then show us an example. If not, show us where it's not quite fully shown enough.

2. Find a number of moments in the story where dialogue could have been used. You don't have to write the actual dialogue, but make suggestions for at least four places in the text where actual words by the people involved would have helped you see the story better.

3. Is there any part of the story that confuses you? Ideally, we should feel totally comfortable each step of the way, even in short sections in which a lot of time passes. I think there's a confusing section right around the time the writer comes back from Guam. What's missing there? What needs to be said that would clear up any confusion?

4. What do you think of the lesson Renee teaches us? Do you buy it? That is, do you think she's really learned that lesson? Tell me yes or no and prove it to me.

5. How is this essay applicable to us as readers? What if we don't have a similar experience to Renee's? Has she made the lesson work for us, too? If so, where and how does she do it? If not, what must she do in the closing paragraphs to make us feel as strongly about her realizations as she does? (Write it in a paragraph.)

WHILE YOU'RE WRITING

While the essay is in progress, seek help from other writers, your instructor, and other readers whose opinion you trust. These are some of the things that you should consider.

- Start early. Start thinking. Daydream. Talk to friends, family. Read your journal, look at old photographs or home movies.
- Choose a subject that is/was significant in your life. You will always do your best work if you write on topics you care about.
- Try making lists. Choose some interesting ideas or thoughts from that list and make more lists: What do you know about this? Why do you care about this? What do you have to say? Use free-writing and looping to help you examine your ideas.
- What is your purpose? What do you want to say? Does the information you have support your purpose? Do you know who your audience is? Are you reaching them?
- Once you've decided on a topic, begin gathering information: stories, anecdotes, details, specifics.
- In what order will you tell your story? Would an outline help keep you on track?
- How should you start the essay? Should you start with some action? How about some description of main characters? Should you begin with the first thing that happened? Maybe you should give the background first. Whatever you do, make sure you build the essay from Guth's Five Storyteller Questions.
- After you have a draft that you like, read it carefully. Show the draft to someone and ask for help.
- Have you come to a workshop prepared, with a rough draft of your essay? Are you willing to let your colleagues help you improve your essay? Are you willing to help others see their good and bad points?
- Would a so-called general audience understand this? Would someone who doesn't know your subject understand? Are the stories you tell interesting and revealing? Are there enough details and specifics?
- Would a reader be able to see your subject? Would a reader be able to understand your subject's significance?
- Are you going to give yourself sufficient time to finish the essay, cleaning and revising for focus and significance?

WORKSHOP QUESTIONS

- Does the title make you interested in the essay?
- Does the first paragraph hook you with something fascinating or exciting?
- During the essay are you made aware of setting by the writer's descriptive terms and depictions?
- Do you know something about the characters? Can you visualize or picture the main characters?
- Are you confused by anything? Is there enough background?
- What do you think of the high point? Do you understand why it was a climactic moment for the writer?
- Does the lesson the writer describes seem appropriate? Do you think that you, given the same circumstances, would have come to the same conclusion or been taught the same lesson?
- Has the writer written about a significant topic? Has the writer made you see the importance of this topic?

The Observation Essay

6

Something to think about

We're watchers, aren't we? We're always watching what happens around us, taking it in. Sometimes we idly observe, like we were just watching some ordinary, but not very interesting, TV movie. Sometimes we really watch something like it matters: a high school football game, or our ex-girlfriend kissing some new guy at the mall. We watch, take things in, and observe the world around us at all times. (And, just to be clear, observing relates to seeing, hearing, touching, tasting, etc.)

Observing what goes on around us is unavoidable, but we sometimes don't pay enough attention to our surroundings. Have you ever just sat in a class and dozed off? Maybe you didn't fall asleep, but your eyes glazed over, or you were doing nothing but stare at the back of the head of the person in front of you. Of course you weren't listening to the teacher or the other students anymore. You were zoning out. When you were brought back to attention, back to life, weren't you amazed at how little you knew about what had happened while you were "gone"? Now, of course we're not alert and awake every moment of every day. Sometimes it's nice to let the day peacefully pass by. But as communicators in our world, we need to have our brains turned "on" as often as possible.

Anyone can go to the new Tom Cruise movie, pay our $8, and get in. But those of us who really watch it—really take it in, keep our eyes and ears open—we're the ones who actually "see" it. If you go to the movie and eat too much popcorn, or listen to the couple having an argument behind you, or get up and go to the bathroom eleven times, then while you've been "at" the movie, you really haven't "observed" as much as someone who watched it carefully. Being someplace only halfway attentive and being at the same place very involved are two different states of being.

So what? Sometimes it's not necessary to observe carefully and thoughtfully. Sometimes you just want to wander around the park, or mill around in a mall for a while. But there are other times, times that matter, when what's happening around you has a heightened level of significance, and you'll want to be awake and aware.

During a job interview, would you think it's important to watch the person who is asking the questions? Should you listen carefully for the next question? Watch the person's physical mannerisms? Pay attention to body language; listen for excitement (or boredom) in his or her voice? What about during a fight with your mom? You want to ignore her? I didn't think so.

Through careful observation we are better prepared to deal with the world. You want to cross the street? How about looking both ways? How about checking out the traffic signals? How about making sure your shoes are tied before you begin to run in front of that Ford Taurus? These may seem like small distinctions, but being aware of your surroundings prepares you for the events that come next. Making sense of those observations is a different act, no less crucial to your maturation as a writer, thinker, and citizen. Think of this assignment as your first attempt at "critical thinking," a widely praised educational goal that is at the heart of many college courses. To think "critically" is to go beyond simple perception.

The mature observer doesn't just see the pretty marionette show, he or she also sees the strings.

Getting started

With the personal narrative essay, we recognized that people who can paint a picture with words are valuable. When someone tells a good story we appreciate it; we feel as though we are there. We feel like the story is happening to us. But this essay takes us a little further. We're going to exercise some other skills we need as writers and communicators.

It begins with simple observation. Your first job in fact will be simply to go somewhere and watch what happens. You'll be asked to be an observer only, taking in the sights and sounds and smells of some "event." (Event is a funny word, perhaps; I mean event, occurrence, place, action, or even incident.) Your event, as you'll see below, can be anything you'd like. It can be an active event like a baseball game, or something as ordinary as sitting in a laundromat while your clothes dry.

Almost any place or event can work. Look at this short example:

> ▷ My eyes drift from one color to the next. Pink, green, orange, yellow, pink again. Different colors. Different shapes. The entire wall is decorated with this large sheet of paper. As I move closer to the wall I begin to see better, more definable shapes.
>
> From ten feet it looks like a giant drawing of a bowl, a crazy patchwork quilt of colors. At five feet I start to pick up words. Texas. Oklahoma. Arizona. Closer yet I see town names: Kansas City, Tulsa, Missoula. Now when I stand right next to it I see a remarkable spider web of lines; I recognize them as highways.
>
> Now I press my finger against the map and I peer in close, to the tiniest writing of all. That's my town there, at the bottom of my finger, the tip of my nail. I can see the dot where my town stands, and I can almost imagine the people I know inside that dot.
>
> I refocus my eyes out wider, past the big towns, the states, the borders, the entire country. When I can finally see the whole map again, my town is gone. It's just a blur. My little town, the town I grew up in, the place I call home, the place that sometimes feels like my whole world, is just one minuscule dot amongst thousands. ◁

The writer has spent several minutes staring at a map on his dorm room wall. He observed it at first just for what he saw—a piece of paper with colors on it. As he began to describe things further I'd bet you figured out it was a map before he even used that word. It's a short example. I'd like your essay to be longer than that. But our writer above has invested the right kind of energy and thought into his essay.

Two purposes of this essay

The observation essay has these two basic purposes:

1. to recreate the scene we've observed
2. to bring context or meaning to the scene for our readers.

In the example above, I think the writer took care of purpose 1 in the first three paragraphs, and purpose 2 in the last paragraph. Go back and reread the essay. Try to watch and pick out the moment when the writer is no longer focusing on the map as a physical object, but is now wondering about the map as a contextual object (an object with meaning.)

For example, in the second paragraph the writer writes: "From ten feet it looks like a giant drawing of a bowl, a crazy patchwork quilt of colors." That's description. In fact, the writer has used a *simile* to help him describe the shape of the United States.

The writer does something different in his last paragraph, the paragraph where I believe he's doing "context," not description. The sentence "My little town, the town I grew up in, the place I call home, the place that sometimes feels like my whole world, is just one minuscule dot amongst thousands" is not description. That's the writer figuring out what his observation means. That's what we call context.

Now, let's warm up by doing a couple of brief assignments. Just as in the previous chapter, do these alone or with others, if you think that can help. Ask your instructor if he or she has some good ideas to improve the assignment. I bet you'll get a cool idea.

Warmups

SOUNDS

- Wherever you are, begin taking notes about the sounds you hear. Pay particular attention to things that seem unusual or surprising. If you're in a loud place (cafeteria, airport terminal, etc.) make separate categories: Human noise versus machine.

BUSY SCENES

- Make sure you're somewhere busy, a cafeteria, or a mall, or a street corner. (Use your imagination and find a good, busy place.) Take notes on a sheet of paper about all the stuff you see. Get as much as possible. Don't try to describe anything too fully; just get it all down. Quantity is the goal here. Catch every visual you can. If ten people go past, get them all, even if it just means jotting down "Man with a White Sox cap. Lady walking a fat dog. Some kid with headphones . . ." After you've done about a full page of this, read it over. Pick a couple of the more interesting things you saw and write them on a clean sheet of paper, leaving a little space between them. Then write a little paragraph about each of them that answers the question "Why were they here today?"

CHANGE OF PERSPECTIVE

- Wherever you are, begin taking notes about some object. Focus on it, and begin describing its color, shape, size, texture. Write for five minutes and then move to a different spot. Now focus on finding something different about the object. Look for things you missed the first time. What things did you see that would be missed by a casual observer? What things did you see in the new perspective that changed the object's quality for you?

The essay assignment

Write an essay that recreates a vivid, interesting, and significant scene you have recently witnessed firsthand.

FIRST PURPOSE: OBSERVE

As I said earlier, there are two distinct purposes in this essay. The first one has to do with making careful observations of a scene. Below are a number of different options that you might consider when looking for a topic. (Obviously, I want you to find your own final topic, but the ones below are pretty good and might get you thinking. If you find something below that you really want to do, try it out with your instructor.)

- Choose an active location, a place you can observe on several occasions (the mall, a cafeteria, etc.).
- Choose an exotic or unusual place somewhere in your community. Observe this place at different times under different conditions, noting differences in your different observations (cemetery, pet store, etc.).

▪ Choose an ordinary place, a location where you find yourself many times during any given week or month (grocery store, your own room, etc.). Since the place should be rather familiar to you, look for and note things you've not paid much attention to before.

OBJECTIVITY

Regardless of your topic, attack this essay in the following way. When you're in the actual process of observing, take notes on what you see, hear, and experience. Try not to become a participant in the scene; it will hamper your objectivity, and definitely make it harder to record your observations. Keep your personal opinions and thoughts out of your notes. For now you're just capturing what you see and hear and experience. Don't judge. At this point you're only acquiring raw data. Your context will come later.

SECOND PURPOSE: PROVIDE CONTEXT AND MEANING

Our second purpose in this essay is to provide context. Remember the earlier example of the writer looking at his dorm room map? His first three paragraphs merely described the object. In his last paragraph he came up with "context" or "meaning." The map made him think about how small his little town was, compared to the vast size of the United States. That was a brand-new thought for that writer, one he wouldn't have had without the simple observation of his map. Your job is the same. Once you collect raw data about your trip to the mall, or your nighttime visit to the cemetery, or your hour spent taking notes in your tiny room, you must prove to us that what you've observed has importance and significance beyond the simple fact of its existence.

Finding the context won't always be easy. It will involve very mature critical thinking skills that are incredibly important to you as a writer, a student, and a human being. The truth of the matter is that many things interconnect in some kind of way. The writer of the short map essay had no idea he was going to find context in that little, colorful map. But he did.

It's my assertion that context is always there in the background waiting to be found. Why? Because we are connected to our own thoughts and to others through sheer proximity. Things I do affect you, and vice versa. One of the most startling and shocking proofs that I've ever received about our "interconnectivity" happened a couple of years ago as I was driving to school.

I was late, and got caught in the wrong lane. I sped up and cut off a woman in a red Honda. I felt bad, but I told myself it wasn't that big of a deal and I'd never see her again anyway. When I got to school there was a young woman in the front row with a huge coffee stain on a pretty red dress. She was dabbing at her dress with a wet paper towel and saying to the person next to her "He just cut me off, like I wasn't even on the road."

And yes, she recognized me. Luckily, she had a good sense of humor and we laughed the whole thing off. But that moment (and others) proved to me that meaning exists behind the smallest incidents. Even if meaning does not seem to be present on its own, our own perceptions bring meaning. Here's what my red-dressed student wrote that day in class.

> Ever since I was a kid I've been a show-off. I love the first day of school, of a new job, parties, etc. I want to show my stuff to the group. I remember getting a chance to dance on Soul Train when I was 16. I dressed up in my best clothes, and my hottest shoes, red velvet heels. As my brother Kenny and I walked to the studio to try out to be on the show, I stepped in a giant, black, oily mud puddle. My shoes were ruined. I didn't even try out.
>
> Today the same thing happened. I put on my best red dress for school, even though it's too dressy for a casual class. But I wanted people to remember me, to see me, as a proud African-American lady with style and class.
>
> All of that went south when a bad driver swerved in front of me and my coffee spilled all over my classy red dress. When I did get to school I was just another student with a great big stain.
>
> I laughed it off, though. Whenever I try to show-off, something brings me back to earth. Muddy shoes and coffee-stained dresses let me know that it's better to just be real, rather than pretend to be something more.

I'm still sorry I made her spill, but I'm glad that our little "accident" was so powerful to her. She unlocked a secret about herself that she would not have found any other way than by observing and paying attention and looking for meaning in a seemingly random, meaningless set of actions. She found the "context."

Well, let's give you a chance at all this fun. Your instructor will set the length of the essay or leave it up to you. Check on that before you start drafting.

Try to use the following steps to help you along your way:

- Get together a list of places that you could observe. Pick something that seems unusual or fun; don't kill yourself with a dull topic. If you think it's dull now, just imagine how dull it will seem after a couple of weeks of work. And don't forget how dull your poor reader will think it is, too!

- Gather information through note-taking, capturing specific details, using your senses, and so forth. You should act like a video camera, capturing both audio and video of the place, with the addition of smell, touch, and taste where applicable. We want to see it like you see it. (Pick a place you can observe multiple times; this is especially helpful if your first draft is short on details.)

- Recreate on paper the experience of observing your subject. Remember, the reader wasn't there. Treat your essay as a collection of thoughts or a presentation of your observations, without including judgments or opinions. Ideally, your essay will be awash with descriptions, details, observations, comparisons, and the like, so the reader can have the same experience you did.

- Go through the workshop and conference. Your principal goal should be to find out if an objective audience is experiencing your topic in the way you intended.

Sample essays

This is our first so-called professional essay. It's a small section out of a book written by Robert Pirsig called *Zen and the Art of Motorcycle Maintenance*. It's a fascinating work, first published in 1974 but widely republished ever since. In the simplest terms, it's the story of a motorcycle trip that a father takes with his son and two other good friends.

They travel around the country, and while they do, we learn a great deal about the father's way of thinking—his way of life. It's a very engaging and interesting story, rich and vivid with its detail. I teach it to classes whenever I can because it's really a book that makes a reader think and work and respond.

I've taken a bit of the opening chapter of that book and given it to you to look at below. Because this is the first professional sample we're examining, I want to reiterate what I said earlier. Don't consider them "models." I provide student essays in each chapter for that purpose. Those student essays were written specifically to meet the assignments these chapters describe. When I pull a professional writing from another source (as I will from time to time throughout the book), it's being put in front of you for different reasons.

I want you to see the "possibility" in this kind of writing, the potential. I think Pirsig is pretty good. He is doing many things in this essay that I think an observant writer must do.

Read it; enjoy it. Think about what happens in it and see if you can extract some of the ideas and spirit of the essay as you prepare to write your own.

(FROM) ZEN AND THE ART OF MOTORCYCLE MAINTENANCE

I can see by my watch, without taking my hand from the left grip of the cycle, that it is eight-thirty in the morning. The wind, even at sixty miles an hour, is warm and humid. When it's this hot and muggy at eight-thirty, I'm wondering what it's going to be like in the afternoon.

In the wind are pungent odors from the marshes by the road. We are in an area of the Central Plains filled with thousands of duck hunting sloughs, heading northwest from Minneapolis toward the Dakotas. This highway is an old concrete two-laner that hasn't had much traffic since a four-laner went in parallel to it several years ago. When we pass a marsh the air suddenly becomes cooler. Then, when we are past, it suddenly warms up again.

I'm happy to be riding back into this country. It is a kind of nowhere, famous for nothing at all and has an appeal because of just that. Tensions disappear along old roads like this. We bump along the beat-up concrete between the cattails and stretches of meadow and then more cattails and marsh grass. Here and there is a stretch of open water and if you look closely you can see wild ducks at the edge of the cattails. And turtles. — There's a red-winged blackbird.

I whack Chris's knee and point to it.

"What!" he hollers.

"Blackbird!"

He says something I don't hear. "What?" I holler back.

He grabs the back of my helmet and hollers up, "I've seen *lots* of those, Dad!"

"Oh!" I holler back. Then I nod. At age eleven you don't get very impressed with red-winged blackbirds.

You have to get older for that. For me this is all mixed with memories that he doesn't have. Cold mornings long ago when the marsh grass had turned brown and cattails were waving in the northwest wind. The pungent smell then was from muck stirred up by hip boots while we were getting in position for the sun to come up and the duck season to open. Or winters when the sloughs were frozen over and dead and I could walk across the ice and snow between the dead cattails and see nothing but gray skies and dead things and cold. The blackbirds were gone then. But now in July they're back and everything is at its alivest and every foot of these sloughs is humming and cricking and buzzing and chirping, a whole community of millions of living things living out their lives in a kind of benign continuum.

You see things vacationing on a motorcycle in a way that is completely different from any other. In a car you're always in a compartment, and because you're used to it you don't realize that through that car window everything you see is just more TV. You're a passive observer and it is all moving by you boringly in a frame.

On a cycle the frame is gone. You're completely in contact with it all. You're *in* the scene, not just watching it anymore, and the sense of presence is overwhelming. That concrete whizzing by five inches below your foot is the real thing, the same stuff you walk on, it's right there, so blurred you can't focus on it, yet you can put your foot down and touch it anytime, and the whole thing, the whole experience, is never removed from immediate consciousness.

Chris and I are traveling to Montana with some friends riding up ahead, and maybe headed farther than that. Plans are deliberately indefinite, more to travel than to arrive anywhere. We are just vacationing. Secondary roads are preferred. Paved county roads are the best, state highways are next. Freeways are the worst. We want to make good time, but for us now this is measured with emphasis on "good" rather than "time" and when you make that shift in emphasis the whole approach changes. Twisting hilly roads are long in terms of seconds but are much more enjoyable on a cycle where you bank into turns and don't get swung from side to side in any compartment. Roads with little traffic are more enjoyable, as well as safer. Roads free of drive-ins and billboards are better, roads where groves and meadows and orchards and lawns come almost to the shoulder, where kids wave to you when you ride by, where people look from their porches to see who it is, where when you stop to ask directions or information the answer tends to be longer than you want rather than short, where people ask where you're from and how long you've been riding.

It was some years ago that my wife and I and our friends first began to catch on to these roads. We took them once in a while for variety or for a

continued ▶

shortcut to another main highway, and each time the scenery was grand and we left the road with a feeling of relaxation and enjoyment. We did this time after time before realizing what should have been obvious: these roads are truly different from the main ones. The whole pace of life and personality of the people who live along them are different. They're not going anywhere. They're not too busy to be courteous. The hereness and nowness of things is something they know all about. It's the others, the ones who moved to the cities years ago and their lost offspring, who have all but forgotten it. The discovery was a real find.

I've wondered why it took us so long to catch on. We saw it and yet we didn't see it. Or rather we were trained *not* to see it. Conned, perhaps, into thinking that the real action was metropolitan and all this was just boring hinterland. It was a puzzling thing. The truth knocks on the door and you say, "Go away, I'm looking for the truth," and so it goes away. Puzzling.

But once we caught on, of course, nothing could keep us off these roads, weekends, evenings, vacations. We have become real secondary-road motorcycle buffs and found there are things you learn as you go.

We have learned how to spot the good ones on a map, for example. If the line wiggles, that's good. That means hills. If it appears to be the main route from a town to a city, that's bad. The best ones always connect nowhere with nowhere and have an alternate that gets you there quicker. If you are going northeast from a large town you never go straight out of town for any long distance. You go out and then start jogging north, then east, then north again, and soon you are on a secondary route that only the local people use.

The main skill is to keep from getting lost. Since the roads are used only by local people who know them by sight, nobody complains if the junctions aren't posted. And often they aren't. When they are it's usually a small sign hiding unobtrusively in the weeds and that's all. County-road-sign makers seldom tell you twice. If you miss that sign in the weeds that's *your* problem, not theirs. Moreover, you discover that the highway maps are often inaccurate about county roads. And from time to time you find your "county road" takes you onto a two-rutter and then a single rutter and then into a pasture and stops, or else it takes you into some farmer's backyards.

So we navigate mostly by dead reckoning, and deduction from what clues we find. I keep a compass in one pocket for overcast days when the sun doesn't show directions and have the map mounted in a special carrier on top of the gas tank where I can keep track of miles from the last junction and know what to look for. With those tools and a lack of pressure to "get somewhere" it works out fine and we just about have America all to ourselves.

On Labor Day and Memorial Day weekends we travel for miles on these roads without seeing another vehicle, then cross a federal highway and look at cars strung bumper to bumper to the horizon. Scowling faces inside. Kids crying in the back seat. I keep wishing there were some way to tell them something but they scowl and appear to be in a hurry, and there isn't.

Up ahead the other riders, John Sutherland and his wife, Sylvia, have pulled into a roadside picnic area. It's time to stretch. As I pull my machine beside them Sylvia is taking her helmet off and shaking her hair loose, while John puts his BMW up on the stand. Nothing is said. We have been on so many trips together we know from a glance how one another feels. Right now we are just quiet and looking around.

The picnic benches are abandoned at this hour of the morning. We have the whole place to ourselves. John goes across the grass to a cast-iron pump and starts pumping water to drink. Chris wanders down through some trees beyond a grassy knoll to a small stream. I am just staring around.

After a while Sylvia sits down on the wooden picnic bench and straightens out her legs, lifting one at a time slowly without looking up. Long silences mean gloom for her, and I comment on it. She looks up and then looks down again.

"It was all those people in the cars coming the other way," she says. "The first one looked so sad. And then the next one looked exactly the same way, and then the next one and the next one, they were all the same."

"They were just commuting to work."

She perceives well but there was nothing unnatural about it. "Well, you know, *work*," I repeat. "Monday morning. Half asleep. Who goes to work Monday morning with a grin?"

"It's just that they looked so lost," she says. "Like they were all dead. Like a funeral procession." Then she puts both feet down and leaves them there.

QUESTIONS

1. Using our goal of writing both observation and context, which parts of the essay address each of those goals? For example, the opening two paragraphs are all description and observation, but the third paragraph begins to provide context to the experience. Find at least three sections of text that you'd consider "observational" and three that you'd say were "contextual."

2. What addition to the text does the appearance of Sylvia make? It seems clear that the writer could have made his point with just the story of himself and his son. Why does he bring Sylvia in?

3. If you had the job of writing an explanatory paragraph at the end of this section that "summed up" the message of the piece, what would it be? Write it.

Student sample

Let's look at a sample essay written by one of my own writers, Andy. Andy struggled with the topic of this essay for a while. Simply looking at something and describing it wasn't one of the things he had ever done in a class before, and the reason for doing it just wasn't hitting him yet. He did what I advise many of my writers to do when they're stuck: Look at the first familiar thing and describe it! See how long it takes you to figure out what he decided to look at.

SIMPLE OBJECTS MEAN SO MUCH

Standing about ten feet away, I observed that this rectangular shaped object stood parallel to the floor in the center of my room. This object had four metal helpers to make it sturdy and to keep its two feet distance from the floor. The surface was perfectly horizontal. It appeared to have two layers or levels with some sort of cold metal framing.

As I halved my distance I could feel the cold coming from the semi-chilled, dark brown layer of steel. Each of the two layers was nine inches in thickness and six feet by six and one-half feet in size. There was no temperature nor a smell on these two layers. The bottom layer held a firm structure that only gave way partially, but the top layer seemed soft and consuming.

With a puzzled look on my face, I once again halved my distance. By this time I was in reaching distance of the object. I stuck out my right hand. I was right. The steel framing was very chilled. The temperature was less than comfortable. I began encircling this rectangular object that was located in the center of my room. I knocked on the bottom layer. Knocking from all areas of contact, I found that this layer was a very strongly springed invention with curved wooden edges. The firm layer was covered by a thin white piece of material. I again journeyed around the object.

This time I studied the top layer. The top of the top layer stood about two inches from my waist. As I tested this one in the same manner, I found that this layer was much less firm than the other. This layer, too, seemed to be built with springs, but much more padding, and the springs were smaller and coiled less. This layer was also covered in a white material though the material was greater in thickness. What would possess someone to create such an object? What goals did they have in mind when they decided to produce these? As these questions passed through my head, I found myself sorting through the various options for the answer. I figured that the answer must lie on top. I found myself putting first a hand, then a knee. The rest of the body seemed to follow me onto the object's surface. Within moments the structure was supporting my weight. I rolled from my stomach over onto my back. I completely sprawled out and covered all of the outer edges of the object. My body became suddenly relaxed. I reached over on the right and picked up a rectangular white object that was completely soft and comfortable.

   As I continued to lie on the object, I found myself forcing the smaller white object to change shape. I forced it under my head in more of a fat "U" shape. Now my head was being supported at the perfect height. No way could I put such a feeling into words. What had just happened was remarkable. I felt my eyes getting heavy. As they began to close more and more frequently and for longer periods of time, I felt the most satisfying feeling. The maker was a genius. The way that the combinations of those two objects took a complex human and put him into utter relaxation in order to recharge was incredible. That was it, a series of metal springs and cloth had provided the perfect environment for relaxation.

I remember reading that essay a few semesters ago and shouting out "It's a bed!" No big deal, obviously, but Andy had to stretch his imagination and his creative skills to describe something so ordinary. If he had said "bed" early in the essay, all of us would have instantly pictured our own bed or our old bed from our family's house. That's no good. This is Andy's essay, and he must do something to show us "his" bed. So to avoid us jumping into the essay with our own preconceived notion about what a bed is, Andy doesn't tell us what he's describing, he just describes it.

Now, what about context? Remember that's really the key to unlocking the significance of this writing assignment. Andy's doing a great job in the opening paragraphs about describing the object, but does he ever really give us the significance?

I think he does, but it comes late and it's a little brief. Look at some of the last paragraphs, again.

   ▷ What would possess someone to create such an object? What goals did they have in mind when they decided to produce these? As these questions passed through my head, I found myself sorting through the

various options for the answer. I figured that the answer must lie on top
. . . No way could I put such a feeling into words. What had just happened was remarkable. I felt my eyes getting heavy. As they began to
close more and more frequently and for longer periods of time, I felt
the most satisfying feeling. The maker was a genius. ◄

In his closing paragraph he wonders how a "bed" ever got invented
at all. When he climbs on top he instantly gets sleepy, convincing him
that whoever created the bed was a genius. His context section ends
there. Because he falls asleep, his essay is over. (Good trick, Andy!) I
think it's a cool little essay. However, what I'd ask Andy to think about
in a revision would be to use his current last paragraph to jump off on
some new ideas. He deals quite well with the first requirement for the
paper, the description. I think he comes up a little bit short on the
second—the context. Given more time and thought, I'd bet Andy would
provide some more interesting ideas about the "genius" who invented
the bed.

QUESTIONS

1. At what point in the essay did you realize what object it was he was
   describing?
2. Did you like the mystery of not knowing in the early section of the
   essay, or did the mystery get in your way of understanding?
3. Pick out three or four examples of some language that you'd say was
   good description.

Another student sample

Now here's another essay written by one of my students, Brandy. I'd like
to take credit for how this one came out, but truth be told Brandy did it
mostly on her own. The assignment I gave really made sense to her very
early in the writing process and the essay came together quickly. That
happens sometimes. Sometimes an assignment your teacher gives you
will "make sense" right away. Writing is a lot more fun when you know
what's going on. Read Brandy's essay, and then we'll talk a bit about
what she does that is so good.

BETTER LEFT FORGOTTEN

The steep, barren ground came to an end and green weeds took its place. Unsuspecting, I looked up and gasped at the sight that lay before me. Lines of overgrown bushes broke here and there where occasional gaps gave glimpses into what lay beyond: eight vertical feet of gray chain links topped with coils of barbed wire. Never had a nature walk turned so depressing or thought provoking with a single glance.

Someone's curiosity had matched my own. Around a turn and between the dry limbs of a dead bush I saw where the links had been cut and pulled aside. I dropped to my knees and crawled through the opening. Standing among the trees and overgrown grass sent chills up my spine. To my left stood a huge pile of sticks, tree limbs and leaves. A few beer bottles and cigarette packs stood out from the heap. As I walked toward the pile, something stirred from within. I backed up so as not to disturb whatever creatures called it home.

I found myself alone with the trees and all of mother nature. Man may have created that place, but it was in his absence that it had bloomed. Where trails once led through the grass, honeysuckle and morning-glory now climbed the tree trunks and blanketed the ground. As I walked I could not see my feet among the vines. Nature holds no ties to man yet we will always be in her debt. There among her tall cedars, she had watched the sleep of a town for over a hundred years.

The first tombstone rose from the sweet blossoms, the weathered writing that was etched into its granite surface long since illegible. The second and the third used the same mouse hole design: a rectangle with an arched roof. The familiarity of legible names that I saw on old street signs was not as shocking as the imbalance in the number of years these people had lived. Their ages ranged from a few days to seventy years. Births only half a century after the Revolutionary War, days before and during the Civil War, and deaths all in the span of ten years. Some of the smaller tombstones had no name. A simple "Beloved Daughter" or "Son" and the number of days they lived were all that was remembered. The fact that so many people died at such a young age came as no surprise. The problems of the 1870s were drought, tornadoes, illnesses and women dying in childbirth.

My heart dropped when I noticed all the tombstones that were broken in half and thrown around the cemetery. It was obvious that alcohol had its negative effect here among the dead just as it had among the living. The effort it must have taken to stack so many of the stones against one side of the gate troubled me not so much as a single metallic monument, looking so out of place among the others, lying on its side among the weeds with only a few beer cans for company. I doubt that those stones that have been moved will ever find their true resting place.

continued ▶

As I left the cemetery by means of an entire section that had been torn away from the fence, I stopped, picked up the cans that surrounded the one solitary stone, and hurled them as far beyond the fence as I could. With effort I righted the marker even though I doubted it marked anything other than a memory. Among its ornate scroll-work and flowers read a simple inscription: Beloved Child.

I've often meant to return to that secluded place, to clear a few of the modern signs from a place best left in the past; but intentions, like nameless children are often forgotten. Perhaps my time would be better spent planting more bushes in the gaps around the fence to hide it from others. Perhaps something like mending fences and planting flowers would be better than working on the inside. Then I might be able to forget the things I saw there. I could safely hide away the thought that someone else might one day stand above me while I sleep in some secluded place, trying to read a fallen marker above me that bears a stranger's name.

First of all, what works for me in Brandy's essay—and this wasn't even the final draft!—is that it's clear the subject matters to her. This observation essay could be done in lots of ways. You could go to the cemetery and say "There were some tombstones that were broken and lying all over." But to get to the next step, a moment of significance and insight, takes some real thought. Look what Brandy does: "I doubt that those stones that have been moved will ever find their true resting place."

Now the stones aren't just lying there. That's just observation. Observation plus context means the writer must wonder what it means that the tombstones are misplaced. Brandy did just that.

SURPRISES

Beyond the significance of her location, Brandy develops lots of good moments in the essay. My favorite line is the first one of the fourth paragraph in which, suddenly, we realize where we are. In an observation essay it is a beautiful device or "trick" to use. You are supposed to act like a camera, for example, so as you pan around from greenery to weeds to trees, if a tombstone should pop up, you'd report it just like Brandy did. "The first tombstone rose from the sweet blossoms. . . ." The tombstones are surprising. That they exist in this otherwise picturesque scene is really interesting and shocking. There's beauty, right next to death. Brandy even notices that contrast and brings our attention to it by describing the "sweet" blossoms around the tombstones, playing up the dichotomy.

CHANGING ANGLES

Also, the essay has a kind of movement or flow. It moves along as she (the narrator) moves through the scene. She is doing exactly what I asked her to do as she wrote her observation, to pick a spot, describe, keep moving, changing point of view, angle, and so on. And as her position in the scene changes, she sees different things and focuses on different parts of the scene. That's an excellent idea for you to work on in your own essay—move around and see how things change.

QUESTIONS

1. Keeping in mind that one of the goals of the observation essay is to recreate a scene, does Brandy do that? If so, pick out five examples (or sentences, or phrases) where she's described something so you feel as though you are right there with her. If not, find three places where Brandy could use some extra description to bring that moment to life.

2. One thing that I stress about this paper is doing "observation" first, then providing "context" later. Reflect back to the short map example early in the chapter. Remember how the first three paragraphs were nothing but observation, and then the last paragraph showed what the observation meant to the writer? Is Brandy's essay divided as cleanly as that? If you agree, where is the break in Brandy's essay? If you disagree, do you like Brandy's method of providing little bits of context as she goes?

3. It's very important for an essay to include essential information, without the addition of too much that is nonessential. Go back and read Brandy's paper. Are there sections of text you think are unnecessary to the purposes of her paper? Why aren't they needed?

4. React to Brandy's essay in a journal writing. Remember we talked about journal writing in Chapter 3. Writing a "reaction" to something you read is a great activity that allows you a chance to write freely about how the essay or article made you feel. You aren't trying to write your own essay, nor are you trying to rewrite Brandy's. You're just responding with your own thoughts to how this essay affected you. Use Brandy's essay as a jumping-off point. Open your journal or a notebook and "react" or "respond" to Brandy and the ideas in her paper. Let yourself have some freedom; if you start on a topic but stray after a while, that's okay. You aren't writing an essay or a test or a paper, so don't do the job like you're digging a ditch. Enjoy yourself. Imagine that Brandy has read her essay to you, then sat back for your reaction.

Tell her what you think. Tell her what it makes you think of. Tell her what memories of your own it brings to mind. Tell her your own story.

WHILE YOU'RE WRITING

While the essay is in progress, seek help from other writers, your instructor, and other readers whose opinion you trust. These are some of the questions that you should answer.

- Is the description of the object clear?
- Is the description of the object interesting and fresh (not just clichés)?
- Does the description come from multiple senses (sight, sound, touch, taste, etc.)?
- Is the description long enough to give the reader the sense of being there?
- Is there a transition from description to context? (That is, does the writer begin explaining why this observation is important? At the very least does the writer begin wondering what's so important?)
- Does the context make sense to you?
- At the essay's end, do you feel that the paper is complete?
- At the essay's end, do you feel as though you've taken a journey and that the journey makes sense to you?

WORKSHOP QUESTIONS

- Does the title make you interested in the essay? In this essay, with so much visual imagery and observation at our command, the title can be a very exciting and evocative phrase or idea. Has the writer missed something that he or she might have used?
- Does the first paragraph hook you with vivid and real description? Some confusion as the observation is being made is okay, but are you "too" confused by something that actually makes you lose interest in the paper?
- Getting from pure observation to the "context" section of the paper is our biggest writing challenge. In the best cases, the transition will be smooth. As you listen to the other writers, watch for that moment. If it's smooth and natural, how did they make that move? If it's jarring and obvious, like "Here's the context!" suggest other ways of making that transition.

The Evaluation Essay

Something to think about

What's good? What's bad? We tend to make these kinds of judgments all day long. When we stand at the counter at our local donut store, we point at the apple danish we want. We want a good one; it looks like a good one. If the man behind the counter reaches for a different one, we point our fingers at the glass and motion him to the one we want. "Over here," we say, pointing. "*This* is the good one."

The one we want looks "good." We can't taste it yet; can't smell it. We can't even compare its taste with others around it. For a collection of reasons, we think it's good. This isn't the kind of evaluation we think much about. No one usually questions our taste in danishes. For some of us, the "good" one is the biggest danish there. For others, it's the one with the most apple. Some like the one with the darkest crust color. We each might go to the same store and point at a different danish. Not often do we have to defend this kind of judgment or this kind of evaluation, so in many ways our formal evaluative skills don't get much practice.

When we pick out a shirt to wear in the morning, or some pants for a dinner, or a blouse or a hat at a store, we are making judgments and evaluations about these things. "That shirt looks better." "That shoe looks better." "This hat goes better with my shirt." It is not often that we are asked "Why?" The red shirt looks better to you because that's a color you like. Or it's a color that accents your hair. In those cases, the evaluation is coming from inside. Just because you think the red shirt is better doesn't mean everyone does. Your friend may say "It makes you look fat." Your sister may say "It doesn't match your pants at all!"

Evaluation is a very personal and often subjective thing. We aren't often asked to defend our choices on things like donuts and red shirts. If people don't dig your red shirt, and you do, you'll probably wear it anyway.

But there are times when our evaluations can't be so subjective, so personal. If you're asked to help pick the winning poem for your literary magazine's contest, you probably can't get by with saying "Well, it's better than those other ones." Someone is most assuredly going to ask "Why?" Then you've got to go further. "Well, I like this first one because it has more descriptive language."

Having a reason behind your evaluation is a major breakthrough. Giving support for why you like one poem or another means that you've entered into a mature evaluative process. It would be like saying to the donut man, "I'd like this danish, please; it appears to have the most apple, and for me, that's the most delicious part of an apple danish." Obviously, we're not going to do that, but that's the kind of attention and thought and support a well-founded and defensible evaluation must have.

Good and bad. You choose nearly everything you do during the course of your life based on these distinctions. Developing clearer guidelines and systems for these choices means you're becoming more mature, more complex. The chances improve that your choices will be less and less arbitrary, and more and more grounded in your actual preferences.

Getting started

The art of evaluation is being able to understand the thing being evaluated. You shouldn't try to evaluate a restaurant unless you have some understanding of restaurants. I don't mean you have to have a long food service history; I mean that if I'm going to trust your evaluation of a restaurant, I have to have a strong feeling that you know about restaurants.

In fact, one of the items of your finished evaluation essay requires that you identify yourself in some way as an "expert" in the field. Below is a paragraph from a writer who discovered he was an expert in something.

> ▶ Ever since I can remember, I've been going to restaurants. Neither my mom or dad did much cooking around the house, and so we

were always going out for food. My mom loved steak places. My dad liked Italian. I developed a taste for Chinese food. So two or three nights a week, all during my childhood, we would get in the family car in search of a new dining experience. Since I've left home I've had less money to support my "dining out" habit, but I still go out at least twice a week. ◀

What does that paragraph do? It provides background information about the writer establishing him in the field to be discussed. I feel better hearing a restaurant review from this guy now that I know he knows his way around a few.

So, what are you an expert in? How about toothpaste? You've been brushing your teeth for a long time, right? You've probably tried ten kinds of toothpaste. You stopped buying that one brand because you prefer the gel to the paste. You probably would rather have the cherry flavor than the plain. You probably find you brush longer when you use a larger amount of the stuff. You know what kind of toothbrush you like better, too, I'd bet.

We are often experts on things that we probably don't even realize. At the very least you're an expert in getting out of high school. Taking driver tests. Being a son or a daughter. You must have some kind of hobby. Play an instrument. Play a sport. Maybe you collected baseball cards. Maybe you used to build model planes. Couldn't you evaluate a model plane kit? Couldn't you evaluate the local basketball team? Couldn't you evaluate your dad?!?

The options are endless. Be creative as you try to find something to cover in this essay. If you can tell someone why the South High Destroyers basketball team was so bad last year, then you can do this essay.

AUDIENCE

Think of your audience for a minute. They will be more than pleased to hear you spout off on your opinion. But their first question will be "So, who are you?" If that answer isn't "expert," then your audience simply doesn't have the obligation to trust you. When I talked earlier about identifying yourself as an expert, I was trying to get the point across that you must in some way show your audience that you are someone to listen to.

How are you going to get your "expert" status across to an audience? Are you going to give them your background? Are you going to explain that you were the sports reporter for the South High newspaper and that you saw all 25 games the Destroyers played last year? Are you going to show them how you played junior high basketball?

Whatever you do, you must show your audience that you're comfortable with the evaluation of your topic.

CRITERIA

To evaluate, we have to use some sort of standards or guidelines. And each thing we evaluate has its own criteria. For example, we already determined that a good danish has a good crust, good filling, and is large. Those are criteria that we could use to differentiate between a number of different danishes. By applying the criteria to your topic or subject, you can determine the goodness or badness of whatever you evaluate.

There are two kinds of criteria. Let's look at them.

EXTERNAL CRITERIA

External criteria are verifiable criteria. External criteria can be tested or observed by anyone who wishes to make the effort. They are observational, not opinion-based.

The nice thing about external criteria is that they are difficult to argue with. If you say the new Chevy Cavalier gets 45 miles to the gallon, and that's the highest gas mileage for a V6 currently made, no one can reasonably say you're wrong. Using external criteria actually helps you gain the confidence of your reader.

If you can tell us that the electric Sunbeam coffee grinder was rated number one by *Consumer's Digest*, that will add weight to your evaluation. Part of that weight is the source of the rating or ranking, however. Most people recognize *Consumer's Digest* as an excellent, unbiased source. However, if the same Sunbeam coffee grinder was awarded "Grinder of the Year" by a flyer called "Joe's Digest," that might not have the same credibility.

It's tempting to use "any" good facts or stats to help us make our evaluation. But we must be judicious in what we present to our reader. Most of them won't know if "Joe's Digest" is credible or not, and then your evaluation based on the "Grinder of the Year" award won't be worth anything.

INTERNAL CRITERIA

Internal criteria are subjective criteria. These criteria depend on your personal preference. These things are almost always subjective.

Do you ever see kids arguing about baseball? "Barry Bonds is the best baseball player ever." "Is not, Ken Griffey, Jr. is." "Why?" "Uh . . . because he is!" Those kids are expressing their evaluations quite clearly. They're using internal criteria, which is fine. But they offer no support for that internal criteria. "Because" is not going to get it done in the more formal setting of the college essay.

When you use internal criteria, there are lots of ways people can argue with you. So, you must support your criteria fully with examples that show how you made your judgment. If you're going to say the Cavalier is the best-looking car on the road, you'd better back it up with something pretty convincing.

> ▶ The new Cavalier is built like a rocket ship, low to the ground. Its futuristic, curved design makes it look like the top of a sleek, sexy bagel, round edges, curving delicately into the dark, tinted glass. The headlights are low, and tapered. The doors melt into the frame, forming—when closed—an unbroken, sleek, elegant side view that will make pedestrians mutter: "What a freaking car!" It is, without doubt, the best-looking car on the road today. ◀

PURPOSE OF THE EVALUATION

Providing descriptive proof or support of your contention that the car looks good adds credibility to your evaluation. Oftentimes, *sounding* like you know what you're doing is as good as actually knowing. (I'm not making a joke.) An opinion that is clearly stated, then supported with clear evidence, is very persuasive. That's how you win people over. And in this essay, your evaluation has two purposes: to convince your readers that you are a worthy and credible evaluator and to convince them to come on board to your way of thinking.

This second purpose is a purpose of persuasion. Ideally, your audience should read your toothpaste essay and rush out and buy a tube. Or go test drive the new Cavalier. Or go see that movie. Or check out that Chinese restaurant. That's the power you hold in the evaluation essay.

A MINI-EVALUATION SAMPLE

Lots of folks struggle with the notion of expert. I don't want that to hold you back, so let's start out simply, by doing some mini-evaluations. A mini-evaluation is about a paragraph long. All you have to be able to do is judge the topic and provide at least one reason why you've made that judgment. Here's a little example of what I'm going to ask you to do.

> "Hawaii Five 0" is an excellent TV show because it has high drama. For example, on last night's episode Steve McGarrett was held hostage by the bad guys. Kono, Chin-ho and Danny spent most of the episode chasing around the islands looking for him. I found that suspense to be very satisfying!

Why is that a good evaluation? Let's break it down into its parts.

- It starts with the **evaluation:**

  "Hawaii Five 0" is excellent.

- It provides a **reason:**

  . . . because it has high drama.

- It gives an **example** that proves the reason:

  Kono, Chin-ho and Danny chased around the islands looking for the kidnapped Steve McGarrett.

You can use that model of evaluation + reason + example in your warmup exercises below and then later in your essay.

Warmups

- Write mini-evaluations for four of the following topics. Remember, I'm just asking for a paragraph for each one. Follow the *Hawaii Five 0* example above.

  - A TV show
  - A new CD
  - A class you're taking
  - Your high school experience
  - Your current living space (dorm, apartment, home, etc.)
  - A product of some kind you like
  - A recent eating place (restaurant, etc.)

- Now, let's carry on with a new exercise that builds on the first. Pick the one mini-evaluation of the four that you had the most stuff on and write three paragraphs about it. Think of it as a mini-essay. Here's a sample outline you can follow.

- Overall evaluation: *Hawaii Five 0* is a great show.
- First criteria: Because it's suspenseful. (give example)
- Second criteria: Because it's visually appealing. (give example)

- Okay, go back to your original four mini-evaluations and pick another one. Use the topic and write a persuasive note or letter to a friend about it. Your job in the letter is to get your reader to do something. If you wrote about toothpaste, encourage them, compel them to go buy some. If you raved about a new restaurant that you checked out, then write your note to encourage your friend to get out there and try it out! Keep in mind that as you're persuading, you're still going to have to prove your evaluation is sound and reasonable by showing examples, just as in our other warmups.

The essay assignment

Write an evaluation of something you feel comfortable judging. The topic can be just about anything that you think you have some knowledge of and experience with. You should feel as though you're an "expert" in the field. And remember that we defined "expert" fairly reasonably earlier in this chapter. If you have experience with and knowledge of something, you can consider yourself an expert.

BEFORE THE ESSAY

Because this paper proves to be a little tricky for some writers, the short sections below might help you arrange your thoughts and ideas in preparation for this essay. In fact, once you begin looking at the steps below, you'll recognize that an evaluation essay is a very active process, one that requires you to get out there and do a little work gathering the necessary information. Here are some things you need to do before you write your essay.

PICK A TOPIC

- Pick something you want to evaluate, something you think you have a little bit of knowledge about. Let's use a fast-food restaurant (my nearest Wendy's), for example.

SELECT CRITERIA

- Decide ahead of time on some criteria, some things that are important in the overall judgment of, in this case, a fast-food restaurant. My personal list would include quality of food, size of portions, cleanliness, and service. But regardless of topic, there have to be smaller criteria that can be judged as a part of the overall evaluation. I'm going to tell you, for example, that the Wendy's is good; but I'm also going to show you how that "good" evaluation came about. It came about because quality of food was "great," size of portions was "fair," cleanliness was "poor," and service was "above average." Each criterion I identify as important gets its own little evaluation (in separate paragraphs, of course). The overall evaluation is a combination of those smaller ones. Having the criteria ahead of writing time allows you to gather information more sensibly and easily. It's the same thing as having a grocery list when you go shopping. You know what to watch for and you're more likely to get it.

CRITERIA MATCH

- Perform a criteria match. That is, make sure not to leave out any criteria that a "normal" reader might be expecting. In my case, I'd probably better add cost as a criterion because I didn't think of it the first time. This is a hard step for some folks. I want you to feel confident about your own criteria; after all, you are the writer of the paper and it is your evaluation. But keep in mind that a paper is only worthwhile if it reaches an audience and completes a purpose. Someone reading your evaluation essay on toothpaste is going to want to know about taste. My fast-food readers—at least a good portion of them— might want "cost." Now, I could leave cost off, but that wouldn't be very reasonable. The goal in most writing is to reach people. If the readers are expecting something, it's childish or immature of me to leave it out. Doing a good criteria match sometimes means asking others for advice. Show your criteria to your peers or your instructor and see if they can come up with some criteria you didn't include.

GO TO THE SITE

- Go and evaluate your topic, keeping in mind that you are trying to do two different things:

  1. come up with an "overall" evaluation

  2. fed by smaller evaluations.

In my case my overall evaluation is of the entire Wendy's experience. To do that, however, I have to evaluate its food, service, price, also.

- When I walk in I might notice prices. If they seem high, then my overall evaluation is not so good. If after eating a burger, though, I find the taste to be excellent, the overall evaluation makes a comeback and is good. Then I note how clean everything is, and the overall evaluation goes up again.

- The prices, the taste, and the cleanliness are the small evaluations. They are a part of my essay. But I'm always thinking of the overall judgment of the place.

TEST SOMETHING

- It's very helpful in any kind of evaluation to actually test your topic. Imagine ways in which you can experiment with your topic. Our goal is to come up with our own empirical evidence, evidence that will be very helpful in convincing our readers that we know what we're doing. For this Wendy's paper, I'm going to time both the drive-thru and the counter service. I'm going to compare the speed of service at my Wendy's with two other places on the same street at roughly the same time of day, just for reference. This data will allow me to say:

  > On a weekday at noon, I found that both the drive-thru and the counter service at Wendy's were faster than comparable fast food places on the same block. In fact, it only took me two minutes from the time I got in line at the drive-thru until the time I drove back out of the parking lot. When you're talking fast food drive-thrus, two minutes is like lightning. ◄

NOTE EVERYTHING

- In addition to testing, I try to remain very aware of everything during my visit to the Wendy's. I take as many notes as possible, writing down everything I can see and experience. Now is not the time for disregarding something. Don't say "Ahh, I won't need that info." Take everything down. It's much better to discard something extra later on during the writing of the essay than to need something extra later on and not have it. Once I've had the entire Wendy's experience (and a good burger and fries!), I go home with all my notes.

AFTER YOU'VE GATHERED YOUR INFO

Now we're headed to the real writing work. We've got notes and ideas and a bellyful, so we can start.

TITLE

With the title, readers start to pick up on things. They begin to learn, but they only learn what you teach. If I title my Wendy's essay "Fast Food Done Right!" then the reader thinks, "Hmm, fast food. I like that. I'll keep reading." Then if I say "Wendy's" somewhere in the first paragraph, the reader thinks "Hmm, I didn't know he was going to talk about Wendy's."

It's a step-by-step process by which the writer delivers information and the reader processes it. We have to be aware of the tremendous responsibility that creates.

The title is a great place to get the reader interested, but you don't want to show bias too early. Calling the essay "Wendy's Stinks," or "Wendy's Rules" will turn off some readers immediately.

MINDSET PARAGRAPH

As in any good opening paragraph, we must raise the idea of our topic, fast food in this case. Forget evaluating for now. Nobody in your audience is ready for you to start doing that yet. Just get fast food on the minds of the readers.

▶ America is a fast-paced and exciting place. We race from work to home, from home to the gym, from the gym to the video store, from the video store to the bank, from the bank to the dry cleaners. FAST FAST FAST. And even though it's all happening at breakneck speed, we still want good service wherever we go. Nowhere does America's fascination with fast results and fast service show itself more clearly than in the world of fast food. We want it fast and we want it good all at the same time. ◀

That paragraph begins with a fairly understood and agreed upon idea: We live fast-paced lives. It moves through some simple examples that most of our readers will have some familiarity with. Then it delivers its topic, "fast food," in the closing line. Your reader is hooked and ready to know more.

THESIS STATEMENT: PROMISE

As with any essay, we need a thesis, but our evaluation essay has a split thesis. We're going to offer a simple or brief thesis early and a more complex one later. This is because an evaluation essay's thesis is the evaluation itself. In our example, if you have a great experience at Wendy's, then your thesis will be "Wendy's is good." I'd like you to try and offer a brief thesis as I do here, and then save the more complex and detailed one for later, once all of your criteria have been discussed.

> ▶ Luckily, one restaurant has found a way to couple our "need for speed," and our craving of good, inexpensive food. Wendy's wins out for my fast food buck every time, for its high quality food and excellent service. ◀

The early statement of your thesis need not be very lengthy, nor too detailed. That's because evaluation essay readers are typically eager for proof and support. They want you to prove your evaluation to them, and the only way to do that is to get to the middle paragraphs of your essay. The paragraph above is brief, to the point, and does contain an overall thesis. Later in this discussion we'll work again with this thesis, adding to it.

SUPPORT: PROOF

Next, we write the middle of the paper. In our example, we've just made a promise about the value of our topic. We must now deliver on that promise, or support that thesis. If we say Wendy's is good, we'd better start proving it now.

Compose mini-evaluations for each of the criteria. In my Wendy's paper, we'd be writing one paragraph that is an evaluation *just* of the service I received; one that is *just* about the quality of the food; one that is *just* about the cost of the place.

Though these paragraphs can be written very much as their own little assignments, we will have to bring them all together at some point with transitions. But each one should be written well enough to stand alone.

TRANSITIONS

When we talk about transitions, we're talking about how an essay's parts lead into and out of each other. We must write transitions as we go from idea to idea. After all, an essay is not just one long paragraph; different things are going on in it all the time. Those different things become paragraphs. At some point you've got to remember that your reader is out there waiting to be taken on a trip. You'll have to write transitions from paragraph to paragraph. Here's an example.

Let's imagine you're finishing a paragraph about the bad service you received while at the restaurant. Coming up after that is your "small" evaluation of the quality of food. You know these parts exist and that they all work together to feed the "overall" evaluation. But your reader needs to be helped along. Take a look at this sentence below:

> ▶ While I was very unimpressed with the rude service I received, as I reached my table and opened up the shiny container of a triple beef burger, the smell reminded me what I came to Wendy's for — the food. ◀

That sentence ends a paragraph about service and forecasts the upcoming paragraph about quality of food. Between each of your paragraphs you need the same kind of "bridge" or transition. You must help readers from point to point, from idea to idea.

ANOTHER (MORE COMPLEX) THESIS

As I mentioned earlier, our example contains a "split thesis." Early in the paper we offered an overall evaluation of the Wendy's experience. However, as we wrote the middle of our paper, the evaluation became more and more "sure" of itself. We used examples from our dining experience to prove that the evaluation was right, and now with all this extra information, our thesis is stronger and more complex. It's time to show it off.

Thesis statements modify or grow all the time in essays. Writers may start off writing one paper, but as they go through it they find different angles of interest that they hadn't considered before. It's always a good idea to make sure your thesis is really forecasting and controlling your finished paper. Writing a second thesis near the end is a way to make sure you've done your job well.

As we write this second thesis toward the end of our essay, we also recognize that our job is almost done. Our closing is also going to be needed.

Refresh your memory for a second about part of your purpose in this kind of essay: to persuade the reader to act on your evaluation. Let's see an example of a paragraph that handles that job.

> ▶ So when faced with little time, hampered by a small wallet, but still looking for a good meal, you can do a lot worse than a stop at a local Wendy's. I found the food to be substantial and tasty; those burgers won me over, but you might like the variety of lighter foods. In all of my visits I was made to feel welcome in the restaurant. Obviously the Wendy's corporation is doing a good job instilling pride in its employees as both restaurants were very clean. And I found that I could eat for a good price, too. It's easy to dismiss all fast-food restaurants as being the same, but Wendy's goes beyond in every category. It's a place I go even when I've got lots of time. I'll see you there! ◀

In the paragraph above we get three ideas:

- The evaluation: "Wendy's is good."
- Criteria reminder: The food is "substantial," for example.
- Persuasion: "I'll see you there."

The essay has done its job and served its purpose.

Sample essays

Let's look at a couple of professional essays. This first one comes from Linda Bergstrom, a staff writer for the *Chicago Tribune*. Her essay is a restaurant review. As you read it, imagine you're a reader in the Chicago area. You've picked up a weekend newspaper and are reading about a restaurant in your area that you've never had the chance to try. I'm going to break into the essay from time to time to show you some things Ms. Bergstrom is doing well.

LA DONNA NORD: AN OASIS IN A FAST-FOOD WORLD

At times, northwest suburban Golf Road seems to be no more than bumper-to-bumper traffic and an unending stretch of fast-food restaurants, strip malls and car dealerships. Although La Donna Nord in Hoffman Estates has a Golf Road address, it represents a respite for the harried traveler, a nice, quiet restaurant with quality Italian fare.

Let's start by noticing the good title. It identifies the restaurant by name and calls it an "oasis in a fast-food world." That last part is a nice preview to the first paragraph, which includes a brief thesis, a technique we've already talked about in this chapter. The brief thesis judges the restaurant favorably for its nice, quiet quality and its quality food. Like all theses or promises, we look for these to be delivered further in the essay.

On a recent Monday evening, it was almost too quiet; for a while, our party was the only one in the restaurant. And that's too bad; diners are missing the little touches that they may not find at the chain restaurants down the street.

continued ▶

> For instance, how often do you find a chef who worries over unfinished portions? That's how much La Donna Nord wants to please. (We liked our pasta; we were just full.)
>
> And do most desserts come with a mother's touch? Our waitress confided that her mom, Fran Barbanente, makes the tiramisu—and that she has some of the luscious dessert nearly every morning.
>
> La Donna Nord is run by Tony and Nicola Barbanente; other Barbanente family restaurants include Via Veneto and La Donna, both in Chicago.
>
> La Donna Nord offers a mix of traditional fare and specialties in its regional cuisine, which combines northern and southern Italian cooking.

This paragraph above summarizes the "style" of food the restaurant offers. Remember my Chevy Cavalier example earlier in this chapter? At some point in our evaluation essays we have to "define" our subject. In the Cavalier essay, we might say something like "The new Cavalier is a low-priced, entry level car, both sporty and functional." That helps the reader know how we are judging the subject. In this restaurant review we're told, "La Donna Nord offers a mix of traditional fare and specializes in its regional cuisine." That defines this restaurant as something different from, say, a pizza joint.

> An appetizer special was a winner. A portobello mushroom is stuffed with spinach and cheeses and finished under a broiler. It's a nice blend, with just a hint of garlic.
>
> The calamari is just as good. This appetizer is becoming almost commonplace and the preparation is often overdone. But La Donna Nord uses a light breading in its version, allowing the flavors to come through. Marinara sauce is served on the side.
>
> Another good way to sample La Donna Nord's marinara is in the linguine ai frutti di mare. The nicely balanced sauce, with slivers of garlic throughout, covers a generous sampling of seafood, including mussels, octopus and shrimp. The serving is large; take home the extras as not to offend the chef.
>
> Veal parmigiana offers a lighter touch than usual. The sauce is thin, with just a few tomatoes to cling to the accompanying linguini. The thin cutlets have a crisp coating.
>
> Salads are not included with entrees, but that just leaves room for dessert and the tiramisu. Soft, spongy ladyfingers are layered with mascarpone cheese and dusted with chocolate. It is rich without being overpowering, and the liqueur just blends in with the smooth, creamy cheese.

The above five paragraphs each take on a different dish. Each one contains its own mini-evaluation. This is an excellent technique, as the overall evaluation of any subject is built by a series of smaller mini-evaluations. And the writer really does a fabulous job of describing the tastes and textures and flavors. Sometimes evaluating is quite difficult because it's hard for us to put words to our feelings. But Ms. Bergstrom is very convincing; my mouth is watering.

> Dining at La Donna Nord is leisurely, and for good reason—entrees are prepared to order. Diners can almost see behind the wooden partitions that separate the L-shaped dining room from the cooking area. But there's always a fresh supply of bread, which can be topped with a simple but delicious mix of fresh tomatoes, fresh herbs, oil and garlic. And the servers do a good job of seeing to diners' needs.
>
> The room is small and the decor is simple. About the only decoration is a large wine cabinet that occupies one wall. Colored-glass chandeliers and wooden benches and chairs warm the room, with its tile floor and white tablecloths. Fabric shades offer a touch of color.
>
> An oasis can sometimes seem far away. Diners should visit La Donna Nord to drink in something a bit unexpected.

These are the last paragraphs of the essay, and you can clearly see that we're in a different part of the evaluation. Our writer is now focusing on matters other than food. We hear about the servers, the decor, the layout of the restaurant, even the furniture.

But compare this section to the more detailed section that discusses the food. Because fewer examples are being offered here in support, it would be safe to assume that this writer feels "quality of food" is more important than "decor." If that's her goal, then it's terrific. But do you remember her title and opening paragraph? The essay begins with the idea of La Donna Nord being an "oasis," a "respite for the harried traveler." Those promises are met only briefly.

QUESTION

If indeed the amount of information provided about the restaurant's oasis-like quality needs to be supplemented, where would you add information, and what kind of information would it be? (Feel free to be creative and make up a few details; write as if *you* were there.)

Another professional sample

Let's look at one more short review. It is a little shorter than the sort of essay you'll take on in this chapter. In my questions that follow this piece, you'll see where I think it could use some extra detail. It is still a very confident and neat little restaurant review from a writer for the *Orlando Sentinel*, a paper in Florida. As I was looking for essays for this chapter, this one jumped out at me because it does a couple of things I really like. For example, watch out for his "test" of the pizza delivery.

PIZZA HUT VS. PAPA JOHN'S: SO WHICH ONE MAKES THE BETTER PIZZA?

I placed the first call to Papa John's and ordered a large sausage and mushroom pizza for delivery. The person on the phone told me it would take 25 to 35 minutes for delivery. One minute later, I dialed the number for the nearest Pizza Hut and placed an identical order. The Hut's estimate was 35 to 40 minutes.

Both pizzas arrived simultaneously a mere 20 minutes later. There was an awkward moment on the doorstep as the two deliverymen eyed each other. I was afraid I was going to have to break up a fight, pizza boxes and warming containers flying everywhere. But luckily, they just got in their cars and raced each other down the block.

The two pies looked quite different. The Pizza Hut pizza appeared to have more toppings. What's more, they covered the whole pie – Papa John's toppings didn't quite make it all the way to the start of the crust.

I removed the pizzas from their boxes and served them to the assembled pizza panel. They were told the pizzas were from national chains, but they were not told which ones.

One member of the panel summed up the experience: ''Both toppings are pretty blah." Everyone agreed. And it was only by default that all the tasters chose Pizza Hut's pie over Papa John's.

The Pizza Hut pie was a little too doughy, but the toppings were better. Papa John's sauce was too sweet and the crust too ample.

There was a difference in prices. The Pizza Hut order was $13.24; Papa John's rang in at $10.80 plus-tax.

Although Pizza Hut's pizza was declared a better pizza, it still fell short of satisfying the panel. So in this war, there are no winners, only survivors.

QUESTIONS

1. Is there a mindset paragraph? If so, identify where it is and what it says. If there is not, what kind of information would a mindset paragraph for this essay include?

2. What's the point of the time trial? How does the writer use this information to strengthen his argument? How would you have used that same information?

3. Paragraphs 3–6 deal with the look and the taste of the pizza. Pick out what you think is the best "description" or "observation" from those paragraphs. Can you think of other, better ways to describe the look and the taste? What are some examples you can think of from your own pizza eating experience.

4. The price of the pizza is certainly an important item in the review. How is it used in this essay? Is there a better way to discuss the price rather than just telling the reader what each pizza cost? If so, write an example now.

A student working sample

Okay, this will take a little time, so make sure you've got a pen and some paper and about a half hour or so. We're going to go through this next sample essay and do some of our own revisions. The very nice Sarah has provided us this essay in progress and we're going to go through it, applying some of what we know of evaluation essays (and indeed essays in general) to it.

This essay needs some help. By working through it together, we're going to get a really good, firsthand look at the thing. (We did something similar in Chapter 5, if you remember.) Here's the title and opening paragraph.

POPULARITY OF TALK SHOWS

It is 3:00 PM, class is over and I am watching television. I have the choice between two talk shows: "The Oprah Show" and "The Ricki Lake Show." Oprah is a more serious host, while Ricki has a tendency to be quite obnoxious. Oprah's topic is "Should the government decide if we can smoke or not," and Ricki Lake is talking to teen prostitutes. Flipping back and forth between

continued ▶

the two shows, I have seen that Ricki's audience is already yelling at the guests, and Oprah's audience is remaining quiet while Oprah speaks. I decide to watch "The Ricki Lake Show," instead of "The Oprah Show," because Ricki's unusual show topics, obnoxious style of being a host, and rowdy audiences appeal to teenagers. Even though many people believe that "The Ricki Lake Show" is "trash," they still continue to watch for the entertainment that the above issues provide.

TITLE

Title first. What do you think? It fails one of our earlier standards for titles; it's just a name for the essay. It isn't even very accurate, is it? As soon as you get into the essay's first paragraph you discover the essay is about a couple of talk shows in particular. The essay's title suggests that the paper will discuss the popularity of TV talk shows. That doesn't appear to be the case at all.

What to do? Well, I always like to find some element of the essay's topic to get in there. Since it's about Oprah and Ricki, even a simple thing like "Oprah vs. Ricki" would be better. If you want to give it a little extra kicker, you could make it something like "Oprah vs. Ricki: A Talk Show War."

That's pretty good! Can you think of one? (Discuss it with someone else, maybe your class.)

MINDSET PARAGRAPH

Let's get into the first paragraph proper now.

> ▶ It is 3:00 PM, class is over and I am watching television. I have the choice between two talk shows: "The Oprah Show" and "The Ricki Lake Show." ◀

That's great. Look how Sarah has already created herself as a character. The use of "I" early on lets us know as readers that someone is going to talk to us. That's always very comforting. Also, she does a good job of further identifying her topic. She's got the choice between two talk shows that are on at 3 PM. Which show should she watch? Also, she seems to have familiarity with a couple of afternoon talk shows, so we get some sense that she's an expert. However, that's not overwhelming evidence yet. All in all, it's an okay start.

THESIS

Once we're in the essay, Sarah has to give us an idea of what's coming. She must forecast the paper with a thesis statement. The thesis is always the central, controlling idea of the paper. Looks like she provides us a thesis at the end of this opening paragraph (a good place for a thesis).

> ▶ I decide to watch "The Ricki Lake Show," instead of "The Oprah Show," because Ricki's unusual show topics, obnoxious style of being a host, and rowdy audiences appeal to teenagers. ◀

CRITERIA

In her thesis statement Sarah gives us a preview of how she's going to evaluate the worth of a talk show. In the sentence above she provides us with three elements that help her decide to watch Ricki instead of Oprah:

- Unusual topics
- Obnoxious host
- Rowdy audience

I'd guess these are going to be Sarah's criteria. She says she chooses to watch Ricki because she has these three things going for her. The implication is that Oprah does not. What Sarah must do in the rest of the paper is prove she's right.

SUPPORT: PROOF

The support or proof is the delivery of whatever promise our writer has made. Sarah has set up some promises; let's see if she's delivering on them.

> ▶ The first issue of obtaining popularity is that talk shows have to be creative when it comes to show topics. The show has to be able to keep our interest with original ideas for a subject. This is the reason we see shows about "Parents wanting to divorce their trouble teen," "Men who rule their wives," "Women who dress like sluts to get money," and "Men who sleep with their best friend's girl." Even though these topics repeat quite often, the show finds people with even more outrageous stories than the first time the topic aired. These subjects seem interesting to us because as ordinary, everyday people, we do not experience these strange problems. It also helps us realize that our problems are not as bad as we may think. ◀

Excellent start. She identifies clearly the criterion she's dealing with: creativity of show topics. So, she's delivered on part of her promise. She even gives us some examples of topics. Sarah goes on to tell us why "outrageous" stories are appealing to an audience. But, what's missing?

Well, Ricki and Oprah, for starters. She begins talking "generally" about talk show topics. That's not what this essay is about. If you're like me and have read through the opening, we know this paper is about two specific shows. There's a crucial element missing. The evaluation itself. Let's insert one sentence into the opening section of that paragraph so I can show you what I mean.

> The first issue of obtaining popularity is that talk shows have to be creative when it comes to show topics. **On any given week Ricki Lake does a far better job of offering creative topics than Oprah does. For example, recently Ricki has had topics like** "Parents wanting to divorce their trouble teen," "Men who rule their wives," "Women who dress like sluts to get money," and "Men who sleep with their best friend's girl."

I've bolded the section I added or changed. It helps the paragraph complete the evaluation of this particular criterion. Before, it was merely a collection of details. It was so vague, in fact, that it didn't even address either of the two shows in question.

Sarah has shown how Ricki's topics are good. What else must she do? She must show that Oprah's topics are not so good or as creative. Does she do that in the next paragraph or not? You decide.

> ▶ On the other hand, serious talk shows have the same topics that we see on the news every night. Although these subjects are important, we often become tired of hearing the same lecture or gossip over and over again. Honestly, how many times can we hear the names Amy Fisher, O.J. Simpson, and Paula Jones in one decade and still remain sane. ◀

Sarah is suggesting that some talk show topics are overdone and boring, but she never names Oprah, and she doesn't even express exactly what kinds of topics she's talking about. She begins to hint at some ideas by mentioning three public figures who have been involved in public scandals. Still, we have to get Oprah into the paragraph. You try it on your own page, and I'll do it below.

> **While Ricki's topics are exciting and fresh, Oprah often has boring and over-seen topics. Some of these, like the Paula Jones scandal or the O.J. Simpson trial,** are the same **issues** we see on the news every **day.** Although these subjects are important, we often become tired of hearing the same lecture or gossip over and over again. **That's**

why Ricki's show is better. Ricki avoids the tired and traditional "newsy" topics.

Okay, once again I've bolded the area where I've added or modified stuff. I'm not doing much; I'm just keeping in mind that I have to continue proving to the audience that one show is better than the other and why. Promise and delivery. Over and over again. The first sentence and modifications I added connect us (or makes a transition) from the previous paragraph. The second sentence I added completes the evaluation by stepping forward and making a judgment. The evidence or support was already in Sarah's paragraph, but she wasn't punching the reader with the evaluation.

Let's keep going. If Sarah is following the promise she made in her opening, we should be onto the second criterion now: "Obnoxious host." Let's see if she delivers.

> ▶ How a host lets the audience play along is another part of what separates good talk shows from bad ones. Oprah sets her show up so that she is sitting with the guest on the stage for a one on one interview. Ricki's audience is made to feel welcome at the show. That clearly makes for a better show. When the audience is allowed to interact, my ideas and thoughts are almost always shared by someone in the studio audience. And when someone shouts out "Leave him, girl, he's a fool," I sometimes jump out of my chair: "That's right!" When I watch Oprah, I become passive, like her audience. ◀

Okay. Is this about obnoxious hosts? No. But it's a good paragraph that does help in Sarah's evaluation. So, what do we do? We can simply add this concept to the earlier thesis. Remember our writing process is recursive, it lets us go back at any time. We need to fix the thesis of this essay by adding the concept of this paragraph, something like "Ricki's show is better because the audience is an active part of the show."

We've been doing quite a bit of work. Let's pause and make sure we're all still clear.

REVISED CRITERIA

We have to deal with the problem of Sarah's "promise–delivery." At the beginning of the essay here's what Sarah told us would be her criteria:

- Unusual topics
- Obnoxious host
- Rowdy audience

Well, the first one (unusual topics) was promised and delivered. Great. But what Sarah promised would be second (obnoxious host) doesn't exist in the paper at all. She promised something that she didn't deliver. She says "obnoxious host" in her opening paragraph but never deals with it again.

Instead, she gave us the paragraph about active versus passive audience that we *did* like. So let's substitute "active audience."

- Unusual topics
- ~~Obnoxious host~~ Active audience
- Rowdy audience

Now we have two criteria that deal with audience. Let's read this next paragraph to see how Sarah explains "rowdy audience." It must be different from the earlier section on "active audience," or there's no reason to keep it.

> ▷ The talk shows audience is one of the main contributors to high ratings. A loud audience may appeal to us as viewers because we usually find ourselves yelling at the stupid people on the show also. On Oprah's show, the audience does not get as involved as they do on Ricki's show. Oprah's audience always seems more serious and their appearance is a lot more clean cut and sophisticated. It is also rare that we will see a group of punk-looking teenagers, or teenagers at all in Oprah's audience. However, on Ricki's show almost all of her audience is teenagers. This fact contributes to the excessive rowdiness of Ricki's audiences. ◁

What about that? There are a couple of good examples in that paragraph. But does this paragraph really do much different from the previous one about the audience being involved? Not really. Let's dump it.

So Sarah has run out of criteria. But she's got another big paragraph coming up. We better see what it has to say.

> ▷ The final factor is that an exciting talk show must have a variety of guests. "The Oprah Show" of recent years has focused on celebrities like Tom Cruise, Tom Hanks and Roseanne, but this does not always guarantee excitement. This is because she always asks them the questions they have received a million times before. Ricki sometimes has celebrities, but her show has always focused on real people, like us. She turns her guests into the celebrities of the show. And with the entire world of nutty people out there, her guests are always varied and interesting. She makes the "Guy with Three Girlfriends" a star for a half hour. We laugh and have fun and get angry with him like each of his girlfriends do, and then there's a new star coming out the second half hour. ◁

In the first line of this paragraph we already see the problem. Sarah says "The final factor is . . . " That means there is another criteria, one that we were not given at the beginning. By hiding this otherwise interesting paragraph late in the essay, we take the chance that our readers will never know it exists.

The paragraph is so good, in fact, that it forces us to reinvent that opening paragraph by once again modifying the thesis statement, and thus our criteria list.

ANOTHER REVISED CRITERIA LIST

The criteria of "variety of guests" must be added. Our criteria list now looks like this:

- Unusual topics
- Active audience
- ~~Rowdy audience~~ Variety of guests

Okay, Sarah's done with her promise and delivery. She's got a closing paragraph for us.

CLOSING

> Even though serious talk shows like "The Oprah Show" are watched by many viewers, more and more people are tuning into shows like "The Ricki Lake Show." For me, the sum total of all this discussion comes down to one factor: I want to be entertained. Ricki entertains me. Her show topics, her choices of guests, and her rowdy and active audience combine for a rollicking good hour of fun and mayhem. Maybe if I wanted to learn something after a long day of school and work, I'd watch Oprah. But I'm looking for a "show," and Ricki always delivers. ◄

Well, that paragraph answers some of the problems. Sarah does a much better job at the end of the essay than she did at the opening. And this is often the case. We actually *learn* as we write, so it's not unusual for us to build up a head of steam and actually write "better" at the end. After all, we've figured out what we're doing.

I'd bet Sarah was reading as she wrote, checking back on stuff she did. In fact, I guarantee you she reread her essay before writing the ending. How do I know? Look at how carefully she re-presents the three main factors that she uses to decide on watching the Ricki show. They're all in the last paragraph:

> Her show topics, her choices of guests, and her rowdy and active audience combine for a rollicking good hour of fun and mayhem. ◄

That sentence, which acts very much like a "second" thesis in the paper, is convincing, clear, and much more correct than the first one she wrote earlier. Her paper has modified as she wrote, so now when she goes back to revise, she'll be more sure of herself, and she'll emphasize points that she covers well and delete ideas that she doesn't end up covering at all.

THE COMPLETE, REVISED ESSAY

Let's put the "new" essay together and take one last read-through.

RICKI VS. OPRAH: A TALK SHOW WAR?

It is 3:00 PM, class is over and I am watching television. I have the choice between two talk shows: "The Oprah Show" and "The Ricki Lake Show." Oprah is a more serious host, while Ricki has the tendency to be quite obnoxious. Oprah's topic is "Should the government decide if we can smoke or not," and Ricki Lake is talking to teen prostitutes. Flipping back and forth between the two shows, I have seen that Ricki's audience is already yelling at the guests, and Oprah's audience is remaining quiet while Oprah speaks. I decide to watch "The Ricki Lake Show," instead of "The Oprah Show," because Ricki's unusual show topics, her active audience format, and her variety of guests, all appeal to me. Some people call this "trash TV." But for me it looks entertaining.

One of the first criterion I use in determining what talk show to watch is the creativity of show topics. On any given week Ricki Lake does a far better job of offering creative topics than Oprah does. For example, recently Ricki has had topics like "Parents wanting to divorce their troubled teen," "Men who rule their wives," "Women who dress like sluts to get money," and "Men who sleep with their best friends' girl." While Ricki's topics are exciting and fresh, sometimes Oprah has boring and over-seen topics like: political issues, and AIDS awareness. These are the same issues we see on the news everyday. Although these subjects are important, we often become tired of hearing the same lecture or gossip over and over again. That's why Ricki's show is better. Ricki avoids the tired and traditional "newsy" topics. Honestly, how many times can we hear the names O.J. Simpson and Paula Jones in one decade and still remain sane. After a long day at school I don't know if I want to have anything heavy. Ricki won't fill me up.

How a host lets the audience play along is another part of what separates good talk shows from bad ones. Oprah sets her show up so that she is sitting with the guest on the stage for a one on one interview. This setup excludes the audience from being able to react on the spot. Halfway through the segment, audience members are allowed to line up at a microphone to ask a question, but for us viewing at home, it is as though we do not achieve the full effect of audience interaction with the guest or the host. Ricki, however, stands in the audience while the guests share his or her story from the stage. Being in the audience allows Ricki to involve the audience more actively in the show. All an audience member has to do is raise his or her hand and Ricki is right there with the microphone. The cameras are constantly switching from the guest on the stage to Ricki. This allows us to see the immediate reaction of the people around Ricki.

Ricki's audience is made to feel welcome at the show. That clearly makes for a better show. As I watch at my house, I'm always thinking of things to say or do. When the audience is allowed to interact, my ideas and thoughts are almost always shared by someone in the studio audience. And when someone shouts out "Leave him, girl, he's a fool," I sometimes jump out of my chair: "That's right!" When I watch Oprah, I become passive, like her audience. Oprah is in charge. She asks the questions. I start to nod off just like her audience because I'm not allowed to be involved.

I tune in as much to watch the audience as I do the host. A loud audience appeals to me as viewers because I usually find myself yelling at the stupid people on the show also. As I mentioned earlier, it is also interesting to see the reaction of the audience. The camera always seems to find the one person making the face that sums up what everybody is thinking. It also finds the person saying those words we have all learned to lip read. On Oprah's show, the audience does not get as involved as they do on Ricki's show. Oprah's audience always seems more serious and their appearance is a lot more clean cut and sophisticated. It is also rare that we will see a group of punk-looking teenagers, or teenagers at all in Oprah's audience. However, on Ricki's show almost all of her audience is teenagers. This fact contributes to the excessive rowdiness of Ricki's audiences. For example, a group of teenagers is more likely to start fights with the guests on stage than a group of yuppie older Oprah watchers. These fights appeal to us because we are more than likely simultaneously saying, "All that girl needs is a good butt whoopin'!"

The final factor that helps me in my choice is whether or not the show has a variety of guests. "The Oprah Show" of recent years has focused on celebrities like Tom Cruise, Tom Hanks, and Roseanne, but this does not always guarantee excitement. This is because she always asks them the questions they have received a million times before. If you're like me, you've

continued ▶

heard Tom Cruise on Entertainment Tonight and read what he had to say in some magazine. When Oprah asks him the same questions again, what's he going to say? The same thing. Ricki sometimes has celebrities, but her show has always focused on real people, like us. She turns her guests into the celebrity of the show. And with the entire world of nutty people out there, her guests are always varied and interesting. She makes the "Guy with Three Girlfriends," a star for a half hour. We laugh and have fun and get angry with him like each of his girlfriends do, and then there's a new star coming out the second half hour.

Even though serious talk shows like "The Oprah Show" are watched by many viewers, more and more people are tuning into shows like "The Ricki Lake Show." For me, the sum total of all this discussion comes down to one factor: I want to be entertained. Ricki entertains me. Her show topics, her choices of guests, and her rowdy and active audience combine for a rollicking good hour of fun and mayhem. Maybe if I wanted to learn something after a long day of school and work, I'd watch Oprah. But I'm looking for a "show," and Ricki always delivers.

Well, that's a lot of work, but I hope you see how this paper has evolved. What you've gone through is like a mini-conference. This paper is definitely better and much more focused toward the goals of an evaluation essay.

Another student sample

We've done a lot of work together on that essay above. You're on your own this time. Read the following essay and respond to the questions at the end. This, too, is an essay in progress and in need of a good deal of help. Remember as you read that we're looking at these sample essays to learn from them. Very few of them are perfect models. Good luck. Keep your eyes open!

THE DATING GAME

Okay, girls, I just wanted to let you know that I am officially an expert on dating. Countless evenings spent with members of the opposite sex have helped me attain this privileged status. Some of these evenings have been very enjoyable, with the conversation flowing as freely as the alcohol. Many more of those evenings have been awkward hours spent with boys who do not know how to do their own laundry, much less have an intelligent conversation with a girl. Can I share some conclusions about dating with you?

Ladies, I am trying to spare you some of the pointless, never-ending, dates-from-hell that I went on. Please read on for your own sake. One simple evening with a member of the opposite sex can leave a girl feeling so confused that she may never want to associate with a member of the opposite sex again, even if he does look like JFK, Jr. On the other hand, one evening with a member of the opposite sex could leave a girl so intrigued that she only wants more and more contact with males in order to figure out their mystique, to find out what makes their devious little minds tick. You girls know what I'm talking about, right? However, none of this confusion is necessary. The right attitude toward dating can turn your experience into a wonderful time. All you have to do is realize the follow-ing: there is no such thing as a perfect male (perfect females are another story), looks aren't everything, don't expect too much from the dates that you do accept, make sure that the guy pursues you, and finally, have fun on your dates. By following these guidelines that I have so graciously pre-sented for you, dating can be fun.

First things first; there is no such thing as the perfect male. If this is what you are searching for, you are bound to stay at home for an eternity of Saturday nights, dateless. Don't worry though; this is where a lot of us go wrong in our dating lives. No person is perfect, regardless of sex. Of course, we as females do not ever have to admit that we are even a smidgen away from achieving perfection. We just need to have a little room in our hearts to forgive the mistakes that we all make, male and female alike. Put your-self in a guy's shoes. Try to imagine how hard it would be for you to be a smooth talker when, standing in front of you, is the embodiment of perfec-tion (all of us females). A guy is bound to say the wrong things, forget to iron his shirt, and generally make a fool of himself when faced with this type of pressure. Remember that guys are used to hanging out with their beer-drinking, belching buddies. Refinement may be a little too much to ask for, so don't expect perfection. So, when that cute guy (you know, the one that was in your marketing class last semester) strikes up a conversation with you at the bar, do not turn away just because his eyebrows are not perfectly even. Give the guy a chance if he seems nice. A major barrier to enjoying the dating scene is the thought that every date must look like Chris O'Donnell or Fabio (depending on your taste) in order for it to be a good time. Many men are actually too good looking for their own good. They end up being so impressed with themselves that they cannot allow

continued ▶

appreciation of anyone else to enter into their minds. A conversation with this type of man will be less than stimulating.

The average looking guys have to make up for their looks by becoming genuinely nice people, fun to hang out with and talk to. These guys will listen to what you have to say and (hopefully) respect your views. Conversations will be more real rather than focusing on how perfect his pecs are. So realize that your next date does not have to be an Adonis to be fun. Still skeptical? Look at Claudia Schiffer and David Copperfield. She is a goddess, and he, a mere mortal being. Yet they have been together and happy for quite some time. Now that we have established that the search for a perfect male is not a realistic goal, it is time to broaden the guidelines a little bit. This leads me to my third dating guideline—don't expect too much from a guy, and you will most likely end up getting more than what you bargained for. Expect the guy to fall at your feet—Shouldn't he?—and you will be sorely disappointed. For some reason, guys have a strange way of knowing when we do not expect too much from them. This takes a little bit of pressure off of him. Suddenly, he is calling you, wanting to talk to you and spend more time with you. Amazing! We as women need to leave guys hanging, to make them wonder if we feel the same way that they do, or if we are not interested. So don't call him. And don't expect a call from him. If he liked you and the date went well, he will probably expect a call from you. However, when you don't call, this will leave him guessing, and he will most likely call you. If he doesn't, then he wasn't that interested in the first place and he is definitely not worth your time. Thus, the fourth criteria for maintaining good dating attitude is to make sure that the guy pursues you, and not the other way around. Your obvious conclusion should be not to go on dates with guys who leave all the work of dating up to you. If you call him all the time, and the plans are always up to you, the guy is not worth it. A guy that is worth dating will pursue you with phone calls and romantic plans.

Finally, remember that when you are single, the perfect guy for you is not necessarily going to be the next one that you meet. Most likely, you will end up going on many dates before you connect with a guy that is compatible with you. Do not let this simple fact discourage you. Dating does not have to be a quest for a husband. It can be a fun hobby. After all, what's wrong with going to dinner and expanding your conversational skills with enjoyable (or maybe not so enjoyable) company for a couple of hours on a Saturday night. You can always meet up with your friends later if the guy turns out to be a slob. And if he turns out to be Mister Right, you'll be glad that you accepted the date. If the guy seems like an acceptable date, go out with him. Do not inspect each prospective date under a magnifying glass as though you expect him to be your future husband and partner for life. Lighten up! Go out with guys who might not be acceptable to you as a life partner, but are decent, genuine human beings. You might surprise yourself by having a good time! Along the way, you will most likely make friends with many of the guys who are not compatible as your husband, and there is nothing wrong with having another friend.

Girls, dating can be very trying if you approach it with the wrong attitude. Remember, dating can be fun and enjoyable. You might even come up with a few friends along the way. As long as you follow these expert guidelines and criteria for dating, you can have a good time as well. There is no such thing as the perfect male, looks aren't everything, make sure that the guy pursues you, and accept dates with men who may not fit your ideal just for fun, and your dating experiences can be devoid of the useless and awkward evenings that I have suffered through in order to come to these conclusions. Good luck and happy dating!

QUESTIONS

1. What about the title? Is it good, provocative, evocative? Or is it just a name? Now that you've read the paper, think up a new title that correctly identifies the point of the essay but that also gets us excited about reading it.

2. One of the first things you'll notice is the "tone" of the essay, or the kind of language the writer uses. Does it work for you? Do you like the casual, breezy feel or not? If you like it, point out two examples that you think are good examples of friendly, creative, and inviting writing. If it doesn't work for you, find two examples where the casual and informal writing turns you off.

3. Like we did with Sarah's essay about the talk shows, find the criteria the writer is using here. Write them down and look them over. Do her criteria match the overall evaluation she is trying to make? If so, how? If not, what's wrong?

4. Keeping in mind how we worked on the talk show paper, rewrite the opening and closing paragraphs of this essay. I think there are flaws in each.

WHILE YOU'RE WRITING

While the essay is in progress seek help from other writers, your instructor, and other readers whose opinion you trust. These are some of the points that you should address.

▪ Start early. We often are experts in things we often don't think of. Are you good with VCRs and stereos? Did you recently buy something? Have you ever been asked to evaluate your boss or a co-worker, or maybe even your teacher? Do you own something you like, like a really good razor or a really good mascara brush? You're an expert on something, I swear.

▪ Work on your expert status. If you think you know a topic, test it out. Spend some extra time studying your topic. If you think you're an expert on cars, go to a parking lot and look at a hundred of them: "That red one is a good car, but why? I don't like that blue one, but why? What makes one better than the other?" Pressure yourself to find an intelligent and clear way of talking about your topic. Don't allow yourself to rely on the very weak support of "I like it . . . uh . . . because I like it!"

▪ Put yourself on the spot when evaluating things. Ask around to find topics where you might differ from your friends' evaluations. If your roommate loves the cafeteria food and you hate it, spend ten minutes talking about each of your reasons. Practice the job of evaluating and trying to persuade at the same time: "Matt, you've got to quit eating that stinking food. Come with me to Denny's!" Remind yourself about your purpose. You've got to get Matt out the door to join you.

WORKSHOP QUESTIONS

▪ Has the writer identified the subject to be evaluated?

▪ Has the writer proven to you that he or she has "expert" status? (Remember, they can do this through examples and stories of their involvement with the subject; they don't necessarily have to work in the field.)

▪ Has the writer specified some criteria that will allow him or her to evaluate the overall topic in smaller ways?

▪ Do you think these criteria "match" in some way what a typical reader would require? (Remember, while the writer gets to be in charge of the criteria, he or she still has the responsibility to address the most common and expected needs of the reader.)

- Is there a clear overall judgment of the topic at hand? That is, has the writer clearly stated the evaluation?

- Are examples given in each "criteria" paragraph? In order to prove that he or she is right about the evaluation, it's expected that the writer will point to specific items.

- Do you feel that you've been "taught" by the writer? A good evaluation paper will leave you with the sense that you now know a good deal more about what makes a good TV show, or toothpaste, or anything else!

The Problem–Solution Essay: The Call to Action

Something to think about

There are times when things must get done. Sure, we live in a society that treasures leisure and relaxation, but we have all faced moments when action was needed, either by us or others.

Lots of little things annoy us but we just don't do anything. I get my change at the fast-food place and I'm halfway down the street before I realize I got short-changed a quarter. I'd like that quarter as much as the next guy, but I keep going this time. Or I hit that huge pothole on my street and my coffee spills all over the front seat of my car. I could do something. I could complain. But I usually don't.

Sometimes we see something happen in our world and it angers us. "Why does that happen?" "Why can't people be better, smarter, act kinder?" We bump through the world and often it can seem there are problems all around us. When we see problems we have options: Do nothing, or do something. Eventually, some bigger problem makes itself known to us and we decide to do something, to act.

That pothole? It could be fixed. It should be fixed. But what do I do? Get some concrete and fill it myself? Ask my neighbor to help me? Call the neighborhood committee? Write the mayor? Tell the local newspaper about it?

Maybe all of those are good ideas; maybe none of them are. The fact is, though, there are always options. If a problem exists in your world, there's a response to that problem. You don't have to keep banging your car into that silly hole. There are people out there who will listen to us. We simply have to find them, approach them properly, speak to their hearts and heads and souls, and tell them what we need or want or demand.

Getting started

The call to action essay takes some different shapes. Every semester, I encourage my writers to write at least one of their essays directly to a single person as a letter. I find that this essay or the Rogerian generally works best in that kind of format. (The Rogerian is discussed in Chapter 10).

Why a letter? Well, first of all, in a very practical sense, a letter is a type of communication you're likely to actually use in your life; it's a good idea to know something about it. Second, there is a kind of immediacy and intimacy that comes when you address a specific person rather than a large group. One of my pet peeves as a teacher, actually, is the practice that many developing writers have of writing to a "general audience." I don't know what that means. Does that mean "everybody"? You can't possibly really think your essay is just right for everyone on the planet! I think it's just a lazy way of saying "I have no idea who my audience is." And if that's the case, then there's no way I'm allowing you to use "general audience" as a way out of actually knowing who is best reached by your work. Writing a letter allows you to focus the topic and direct your energies to a real audience who can help. Why waste your time with folks not interested in the issue?

ELEMENTS OF THE CALL TO ACTION

I'm going to offer you five important elements of a call to action paper, but I want to stress that these elements can be moved around to suit your needs. They don't all *have* to be used, but in many cases they all *can* be used. It's up to you and your instructor. As always, check with your instructor to see how you're doing.

IDENTIFICATION OF SELF

Who are you? This is often the first question a reader asks when reading a letter. (The other main question is, as you already know, "So what?")

You'd better let the reader know fairly early on that you're somebody worth hearing from; you're asking him or her to take some time out of the day to read your thoughts, after all.

In a corporate or business letter (which many of these call to action papers become), at the very least you'd better let your reader know how you're attached or connected to their business. "Hi, I eat at your Taco Bell restaurant twice a week." "I bought my last set of tires from your location." "I'm a student at this university, taking 12 hours a semester." "I'm your son; I live in the basement apartment."

This announcement is designed to convince the reader to listen to you. You are someone they need to pay attention to.

IDENTIFICATION OF PROBLEM

At its heart, the call to action paper is a problem–solution essay. Of course we're going to do more than that, but if this paper resembles any traditional essay type, it's the problem–solution model.

Many developing writers only make a vague reference to the problem. The problem is so clear in their heads, they don't think to emphasize or describe it fully. But you don't know if the reader will see it as you do. In fact, that's often why problems go unchecked; the reader has missed the problem. You have to be specific and pointed in bringing the problem to the eyes of the reader. You must identify it clearly: "I've discovered that there is a one foot by two foot oval pothole at the corner of my block, Edgefield Avenue and Colorado Boulevard." "Twice this past week when I ordered the bacon cheeseburger at your restaurant, I received a plain cheeseburger instead." "When parking overnight at the airport's West Reduced parking area, it's impossible to retrieve the car until six the next morning."

Be plain and clear with your description. Keep in mind that many folks read letters fairly rapidly. We're a short-attention-span society, and being vague or general with the problem may result in your audience missing the whole point.

PROOF OF PROBLEM THROUGH EXAMPLES

Once the problem has been identified clearly, you will have to support its existence in some way. This might seem redundant. For example, let's take a sentence from the paragraph above: "There is a one foot by two foot oval pothole at the corner . . . " Because the writer knows the problem personally and has seen that silly pothole a hundred times, that seems like enough proof. But keep in mind that readers of problem–solution essays are usually hearing about the problem for the first time. They're going to read a sentence like this one and think, "Really?" So, always further support the notion of the problem with more examples.

> ▶ I've discovered that there is a one foot by two foot oval pothole at the corner of my block, Edgefield Avenue and Colorado Boulevard. I see it or hit it almost every day. I would swerve out of the way of it every morning, but if there is oncoming traffic in the other direction, I have no choice but to hit it.
>
> One morning, after hitting the hole and spilling coffee all over my shirt, I had to go back and change my shirt for work. While at home I got my tape measure and when I passed the hole the next time I measured its depth. Eight inches! Look at your own ruler or tape measure. Do you see how deep an eight-inch hole is? My entire tire dips down into it; my car shakes; a loud thud is heard, and now I fear that my shocks are going bad. I have no other route to take to work. Neither do my neighbors. My neighbor John hits it every morning too. We just call it "the black hole of Edgefield Avenue." ◀

By this point I bet the reader understands the problem. By re-creating the scene of the pothole in some imaginative and detailed ways, our writer ensures that he will get a chance to be heard. Only the worst reader will deny that a problem exists after those examples above. Don't settle for merely stating the problem; support it with examples.

SOLUTION AND SUPPORT

If things have gone well for you in the essay or letter so far, you'll have earned the right to really talk to your reader. If you don't properly show the problem and prove it exists, it doesn't matter how brilliant your solution is. So, getting to this point is essential.

However, what good is getting the reader this far if you don't really have a payoff? Your solution has to make sense. I can stress nothing more than that. Once confronted with the problem, the reader is a little off-balance. The world as the reader has seen it is slightly different. If you send your pothole letter to the mayor, she's liable to say "Holy moley! Potholes as big as a toaster oven?! My city is in shambles!" You've got to make use of this opportunity. If a reader has come this far, he or she is waiting for you to deliver the goods. Your solution has to be great, reasonable, sensible, and do-able. It does no good to suggest a silly or unworkable solution.

> ▶ I've been bugged by this pothole, and it's caused me severe distress. I'd like the city to give me a check for pain and suffering in the amount of

◄ $53,210 and fix the pothole, and give me the key to the city, and give me a job as mayor's assistant. ◄

That's silly, but lots of developing writers go nuts when they get to the solution section. We're asking for something; we need to be reasonable. Acting unreasonably or asking for more than we deserve will cause the reader to be defensive. We must be thinking about the needs of our audience as we write. The mayor is not going to give you money for pain and suffering. But the mayor will get someone to fix the hole if you ask the right way and explain why fixing the hole has some value for her, too.

CALL TO ACTION

Many writers confuse the call to action with the solution. That's understandable. However, the solution you suggest in the section above is only the beginning of the process. Oftentimes, the reader of your letter can't personally fix your problem. The mayor is not likely to bring a bucket of tar and gravel to your street and fix that hole. Instead, you want to make sure in the closing of your letter or essay that the reader will do "something" to start the solution process.

The letter or essay fails if you don't get the reader involved. Getting the reader involved means making him or her act. Think of the call to action as an intermediate step between "nothing" and the solution.

In our pothole example, it would be this.

▶ Now, obviously Mrs. Mayor, I don't expect you to fix that pothole yourself. But I know you've got the resources and the power to make sure it gets done for the betterment of all of this neighborhood's drivers. I'm asking you to call the city department of roads and alert them to this problem. And, would you please have someone in your office call me at (214) 555-5555 to let me know that this process has started? That way I won't call or write to you again; I know you're very busy.

Thanks so much. ◄

A couple of nice things are done in this closing call to action. The first step to the process is clearly laid out with "call the city department of roads." Not only that, but a secondary call to action is suggested by "please have someone in your office call me." That's a terrific suggestion. That allows the mayor the chance to act, which is, after all, the point of the paper.

Warmups

GENERATE PROBLEMS

Begin some free-writings based on the list below about "Problems." Do them one at a time and keep the writings separate from each other. Deal with them as individual assignments. If a couple don't strike you as being useful or interesting, skip them. But do most of them. Spend five to eight minutes on each.

- Problems at home
- Problems at work
- Problems with friends
- Problems with family
- Problems with my school
- Problems with my town or city
- Problems with my state
- Problems with my country

The idea is not to depress you, but to help you generate as many long lists as you can. Things that you think of as problems sometimes aren't as bad as they seem. By getting these lists together we empty the "problem" file in our brain! That's always good. It helps us see what really bothers us and raises a number of possible topics for our essay.

You should now have a few free-writings full of problems. Take them one at a time and study them. Recopy them if they are too messy, and make sure the only thing you have on your new copy is a list of problems.

Once you've got a nice clean list of problems, go down the list and next to each mark an "S" if the problem is solvable or an "N" if the problem is not solvable. (Be realistic as you do this. The problem of global warming might be a little too big for you to handle this week. The problem of your boss keeping you after hours without paying overtime might be a little easier to deal with. Your roommate leaving the top off the toothpaste might be easier yet.)

What you'll be left with after you do a number of these (ask your teacher how many you should do) will be a list of solvable problems (those marked with an "S"). All of these probably qualify quite nicely as possible topics for this paper, and all of them will likely be within your interest area. That's not a bad place to begin looking for a topic.

From one of your lists, pick a problem that relates specifically to one single person who is in your life right now, someone who you can actually talk to today or this week. Sit down in person or on the phone and tell them how you see the problem. Let them tell you their version of the problem (if they even see it as a problem at all—it may just be your problem), then discuss ways the two of you could solve the problem. Take notes to keep track of what you come up with. When you're done, spend a few minutes on your own trying to write down a step-by-step solution. Here's a brief example.

Problem

▷ Mother is calling too much to check up on me. ◁

Discussion with Mother About Problem

▷ Mom says it's not real. She just loves me and wants to know how I am and what's up. I tell her that it bugs me and that I feel I don't have independence. Mom tells me that she doesn't want to bug me, but that she worries about me. She wants to know if we can meet halfway. I write up the plan as a solution: ◁

Solution

▷ In order to meet the needs of both my mother and myself, we are going to set up a new method of "checking in." My mother will only call me during the week, one night usually, twice in one week if something "special" or "urgent" occurs. She will NEVER call on the weekend! However, I will make one call on the weekend, between Saturday morning and sometime after I'm "in for the night" Sunday. Any breaking of this agreement will result in the offender having to do the other person's laundry for one whole month. ◁

PRACTICE LETTERS

Write five different notes for people in your life: roommate, friend, sibling, mother, father, teacher, boss, co-worker, and so on. Feel free to draw on any of the free-writings you generated earlier when you were writing about "problems." Each note must have a purpose (like any good piece of writing), but each note must also have a "call to action," a section of the note that requires the reader to do something specific. This may take some creativity. It's not as easy as simply finding something for your reader to do; you must also write persuasively enough to convince the reader that your request is worthwhile. You can make these short. We're not even up to the essay yet, but we must get some practice on moving our reader. Here's a note one of my students tried a few years ago.

> Dear Dr. Pfefferle:
>
> I'm going to be out of town with the volleyball team this coming Friday, so I'll be missing our class. I'm really sorry; you know how I miss those funny stories you always tell! (No, seriously.) Anyway, since I don't want to miss anything while I'm gone, would it be all right if you gave any handouts or assignments to Mark Curry in our class? (He sits right behind me.) He's a good friend and I'll see him over the weekend. I could get the notes from him so as to be ready for Monday.
>
> If that's okay, just give the material to Mark on Friday.
>
> If this is not okay, then we'll have to make separate arrangements for me to get the missed work. Please call me at my dorm before Thursday evening at (817) 555-5555.
>
> Thanks very much.
>
> Katie.

Now, do you think I did what Katie wanted me to do? Absolutely. Do you know why? Go through the letter and find as many of those five call to action elements as possible. See if you can find all five. If all five aren't there, do you know which ones she skipped and why?

Letter format

Let's look at a typical letter format. Here's that pothole letter we were writing earlier. I've put it into a perfectly acceptable and standard business letter format. (It's just a suggestion, however; your instructor may offer you something different, or you may already have a letter format you like to use.)

```
9999 Edgefield Avenue
Apt. 23
Dallas, TX 77777


January 1, 1999
```

continued▶

Mayor Thea Bosley
City of Dallas
201 Young Street
Dallas, TX 77777

Dear Mayor Bosley,

I'm a longtime resident of Dallas, and have lived along
Edgefield Avenue in historic Oak Cliff for almost ten
years. I'm proud of my neighborhood, just like I know
you're proud of the whole city.

That's why I regret that I have to write this letter to
you. I've discovered that there is a one foot by two foot
oval pothole at the corner of my block, Edgefield Avenue
and Colorado Boulevard. I see it or hit it almost every
day. I would swerve out of the way of it every morning,
but if there is oncoming traffic in the other direction,
I have no choice but to hit it.

One morning, after hitting the hole and spilling coffee
all over my shirt, I had to go back and change my shirt
for work. While at home I got my tape measure, and when I
passed the hole the next time I measured its depth. Eight
inches! Look at your own ruler or tape measure. Do you
see how deep an eight-inch hole is? My entire tire dips
down into it whenever I hit it. My car shakes; a loud
thud is heard, and now I fear that my shocks are going
bad. I have no other route to take to work. Neither do my
neighbors. My neighbor John hits it every morning too. We
just call it "the black hole of Edgefield Avenue."

Now, obviously Mrs. Mayor, I don't expect you to fix that
pothole yourself. But I know you've got the resources and
the power to make sure it gets done for the betterment of
all of this neighborhood's drivers. I'm asking you to
call the city department of roads and alert them to this
problem. And, would you please have someone in your office
call me at (214) 555-5555 to let me know that this
process has started? That way I won't call or write to
you again; I know you're very busy.

```
With thanks,


Randy Severance
```

We can send this to the mayor now and be confident that we've addressed all the necessary elements of the call to action.

It is also certainly possible to do this kind of essay in a regular shape and not in a letter format; your instructor and you will have to decide how your essay would work best.

The essay assignment

Write a letter about a problem that exists in your world. Make sure the problem is solvable and that you target the best, most effective audience. Try to deal with a manageable problem for which you can offer a reasonable solution and a clear call to action. In the space of a good letter (250–500 words, perhaps?), you can take on large problems; just make sure that your solution is one that is manageable by your audience.

Keep in mind that your paper will fail if you are not able to move the reader to a specific action. It is not enough merely to make the reader aware of the problem in question. You must get beyond that.

Sample essays

Our first letter is by a student named Lisa. As you read the letter, keep in mind the five essential elements that any good call to action must have. Keep track as you read.

- Identification of self
- Identification of problem
- Proof of problem through examples
- Solution and support
- Call to action

LETTER TO A RESTAURANT

9999 Northridge Place
Dallas, Texas 77777
11 November 1996

Joe Harkey
Friday's
4444 North Central Expressway
Dallas, Texas 77777

Dear Mr. Harkey,

I am a longtime customer of Friday's and have visited
your establishment frequently. I manage a nearby business
that also caters to the public and I eat at your restaurant about once a week. I have always enjoyed the food
and the casual atmosphere—(I have a particular fondness
for your Pacific Coast Chicken and Tuna). On my last few
visits, however, my experiences were not on a par with
what I have come to expect from Friday's.

On Thursday, October 24, at 4:30, my son, his friend, and
I came in for dinner on my way to work. I did not have to
be at work until 6:00, so we felt that we had more than
enough time. When we arrived, the restaurant was fairly
empty, but did get busier during the time we were there.
We were seated promptly, but I could not catch the attention of any waitstaff to place an order. After fifteen
minutes, our drink orders were taken. Ten minutes after
that, we received our drinks and our meal order was
taken. Another 25 minutes passed before we were served
our meals. (By now, we had been seated for an hour). My
order had not been cooked as ordered, but I did not have
the time to have it done again. There seemed to be ade-
quate waitstaff on duty to handle the number of patrons,
I just had trouble finding someone and getting their
attention.

On another visit a week later, the experience was much
the same. We came to Friday's on Saturday, in the middle

of the afternoon, and even though there was less business, it still took 65 minutes from the time we were
seated until our meals arrived, even though I had
informed our waiter that we were under a time constraint.
(In his defense, I don't believe that our waiter knew
that we had been seated until we asked a busboy to have
him come to the table.)

Up until this point, I have always been more than satisfied with the service at Friday's. Its convenient location
and the menu variety is always a factor when choosing
between the numerous restaurants in our area. I hope that
these last experiences are not indicative of a new trend
in customer service at Friday's, as I would like to be
able to continue patronizing your establishment. Perhaps
a review of communications or serving procedures would
help. If you have any comments on this matter, or feel
that my inconvenience is worthy of a free meal coupon or
two, please feel free to contact me at the above address,
by telephone at (972) 555-5555, or by facsimile at (972)
555-5005.

Thank you for your attention in this matter.

Sincerely yours,

Lisa Petty

Great letter! Now, let's pull out some sample sections and look at what Lisa has done to make the letter so ambitious and so effective.

IDENTIFICATION

> ▶ I am a longtime customer of Friday's and have visited your establishment frequently. I manage a nearby business that also caters to the public and I eat at your restaurant about once a week. ◀

In the opening two sentences, Lisa establishes two critical and essential facts that will help her letter get the best reading. In one sentence she shows herself to be someone this restaurant must recognize. She's a customer; she's been there "frequently." Not only does it place her in the building, it also sets the tone that she's a good customer, one that comes back a lot.

The second point she makes—this one is in the second sentence above—is one that not all of us can make, perhaps. Not only is Lisa a good customer, she's a customer who has special or advanced knowledge of the topic. If this had been a letter about a pothole, and she had worked on a tar crew on the highway department, it would have had the same impact. Or if she was concerned about the sackers at a grocery store and she once did the same job, it also would show her to have special knowledge.

Now, the reason this bit of info is so important (and why it's something you should use to your advantage if you happen to have it), is that it makes it more likely that the reader will have some faith in or a reason to believe Lisa's comments in this case; after all, she knows what she's talking about. It's a very persuasive moment in this letter.

PROBLEM

Let's go on to some other good things Lisa does.

> ▶ On my last few visits, however, my experiences were not on a par with what I have come to expect from Friday's. ◀

This is an easy one, right? This moment is the transition from the first to the second paragraph, and it also happens to be a move from a positive comment to a problematic one. In our assignment section of this chapter you are urged to try and be reasonable in your letter or article. This writer has had good service and good times at Friday's, but this letter is not going to be about those! So, you open positive, and then prepare your readers for the next stuff with a smooth transition. Lisa acted reasonably by pointing out that she's had good experiences, and in doing that, she's earned some goodwill from the reader. Nice work.

> ▶ On Thursday, October 24, at 4:30, my son, his friend, and I came in for dinner on my way to work . . . ◀

In any kind of problem section, the re-telling or re-creation of the scene is crucial. (In fact, it's one of the reasons we took care with the personal narrative and the observation essays earlier; those skills are useful in lots of ways.)

Throughout the paragraph Lisa is careful to give exact details. A line that reads "I was at your restaurant last week and had a bad time," is almost useless. It doesn't help the reader know much. Was it at the dinner rush hour? In the morning? Who was the waiter? What does "a bad time" mean? Bad server? Bad waitress? Bad food? Music too loud? Not loud enough? Not enough light?

Do you see the problem?

Lisa avoids that problem by knowing that to be convincing she has to be factual and help her reader see the situation clearly. If Lisa had a bad experience, re-creating it just as it happened will give her reader the same experience. That's exactly what she wants!

PROOF

Look back at Lisa's second paragraph again. Look at the details: date, time, minute-by-minute account of her attempts to get service. It's very thorough and detailed and it sounds believable. She helps her cause by being specific as to the amount of time she has been made to wait and about the fact that her food was not cooked as ordered.

CONCLUSION
(SOLUTION AND CALL TO ACTION)

Two things should happen here at the conclusion. Some kind of solution to the problem should be suggested, and a call to action should be made.

As we've said before, the heart of this essay is the "call to action." As we've defined it, it's the moment in the essay or letter at which the reader is compelled to act, to do, to respond, or to move. Without action this essay is a failure. Indeed, all that you do in the early part of the essay is in some way a lead-up to your call to action. If by the end you've earned the trust and the belief and the goodwill of your reader, he or she is liable to act for you!

What does Lisa do with her chance? Let's check out the closing.

> ▶ Perhaps a review of communications or serving procedures would help. If you have any comments on this matter, or feel that my inconvenience is worthy of a free meal coupon or two, please feel free to contact me at the above address, by telephone at (972) 555-5555 . . . ◀

I'd suggest that the first sentence in the above section serves as her "solution." She has an idea for how the restaurant can address their problem. (Of course, there are other possible solutions, too. Perhaps the problems stem from hiring bad employees.)

Look at the subtle way Lisa fits in the call to action. (It's the free meal coupon line. Very sneaky!) Giving her telephone number is also crucial, as it suggests that this dialogue is not finished yet. It suggests to the reader that he should probably call her on the phone—another call to action.

This is a persuasive and good ending.

Another sample

I want to show you one more essay, this one by a student named Corey. As you read, ask yourself how you would react if you were the intended reader. Watch to see if all the call to action elements are present.

LETTER TO A TATTOO PARLOR

```
November 13, 1996
Skin and Bones
2222 Second St.
Dallas, TX 77777

To Joanne Buhner,

I had toyed with the idea of getting my navel pierced for
quite some time. When I finally decided to go through with
it I wanted a place where the instruments and environment
would be sterile and the staff would be knowledgeable and
helpful. After checking around with some friends, I
decided to try your salon, Skin and Bones.

I went to your salon in Deep Ellum. I was very nervous
about the whole procedure but from the moment I walked in
I felt completely at ease, just the way I hoped it would
be. The woman behind the counter was extremely support-
ive, cooperative, and skilled in what she was doing. This
woman's name was Alicia Patterson. Alicia helped me pick
out the jewelry that would be the most comfortable and
appropriate for me. She made me feel completely at ease.
She walked me back to the piercing room and explained
each step thoroughly, showing me what she was going to do
before actually doing it. When I asked her to stop a
minute while I got comfortable, she did and helped me
understand the small amount of discomfort I was feeling.

I was very proud of my new ring, but disappointed over
the next several days when I developed a bad rash and
```

infection from the piercing. I wasn't given explicit instructions by anyone at your location before I left and when the rash appeared, I didn't know what to do. I panicked, took the ring out, and began cleansing the area with alcohol and ointments. When I tried to get help over the phone from someone at your store, I was simply told "Keep it clean."

Now, two months later, everything is fine. My ring looks great; the infection and rash went away in a few days, and I've since learned that I could have avoided all the problems with some preventative instructions on the day of my piercing.

The purpose of this letter is to let Alicia know how much I valued her help and to urge you to spend more time on the "after-care" of future "piercees." My experience could have been perfect had someone helped me understand what I had to do to take care of my new piercing.

Thank you.

Sincerely,

Corey Melman

QUESTIONS

1. Go through Corey's letter carefully and determine if all five elements are in there. Find as many as you can and mark the important parts. If you were asked to defend this letter as a good example of a call to action writing, could you?

2. Which of the five elements does Corey do the best job with? Why? Which element needs the most assistance in a rewrite? Rewrite that one element on a separate sheet of paper.

3. Are there essential details or ideas missing from the paper? What are they?

Professional sample

Our last essay is written by *Flying* magazine's editor, J. Mac McClellan. It's not in the "letter" format of our other samples. It's merely an editorial-type essay that McClellan wrote recently about the problems of air safety.

In fact, it's a lot more like a traditional problem essay, and that's one of the reasons why I've included it here. McClellan recognizes that a problem of perception exists in the flying industry. He's trying to solve this problem by providing a more correct way of viewing the hazards of air travel. That's the solution.

I'm not going to offer you any comments or evaluate it. Read it on your own, or with your classmates, and discuss it as a model or an example.

HOW SAFELY CAN WE FLY?

When was flying transformed from an activity with obvious risks into a mode of transportation that never fails? Who did it? Was it the airlines, the government, pilots or the news media that convinced the public that flying is as safe as hiding under the covers? I don't know who to blame, but the public's attitude toward aviation safety is now out of whack.

Airline safety has been unchanged for at least 20 years, but the public's current perception is that airplanes are plunging out of the sky. Commentators always note that flying is the safest mode of transportation, and then launch into the latest scare story about rudders on Boeing 737s, old computers in air traffic control centers, military airplanes flying too close to airliners, or whatever the panic du jour may be. Instead of taking the excellent safety of our aviation system for granted and feeling as safe as the statistics show airline flying to be, the public frets that flying safety is eroding.

Last year there were three fatal crashes involving U.S. jet airlines, and only one involving a commuter. The record for the jet airlines was average for the past 20 years, and the commuters had a much safer year than average. But based on media coverage—and comments by the National Transportation Safety Board—you would believe that pilots forgot how to fly.

For the past 20 years the U.S. jet airlines have averaged just over three fatal crashes per year, so 1996 was statistically an average year. But the number of people killed was significantly above average, and that fact fuels the worry. The number of people killed in aviation accidents is just that, an accident. Whether the airplanes involved in the crashes were full or empty, jumbos or narrowbodies, is random. It's crashes that count, and and crashes that must be prevented, and in doing that we prevent fatalities.

The three jet airline crashes were also unusual because in two of them the pundits and experts instantly identified a cause, which turned out to be wrong. When ValuJet's DC-9 plunged into the Everglades the "experts" quickly determined that the accident was caused by low fares: Because the start-up airline charged less it must have been scrimping on maintenance, pilot training, and who knows what else. Maybe ValuJet did all of those things, but it seems certain that the accident was caused by a fire in the cargo hold. Maybe the fire was caused by oxygen generators that were improperly packaged for shipping, but hazardous materials could find their way onto any airliner. In any case, the crash wasn't caused by low fares.

When the TWA Boeing 747 blew up just south of Long Island the cause was "obvious" to all experts, including those in and out of government: It was a bomb or missile. New security measures were implemented at airports, passengers said they would agree to a strip search to prevent another such accident, and the government laid out millions for new bomb-sniffing luggage screening devices. Despite the most exhaustive and expensive aviation accident investigation in history, the cause of the TWA 800 crash remains a mystery. No airliner flying from a U.S. airport has ever been bombed. Perhaps some yet to be found clue will prove that TWA 800 was the first, but the lack of evidence so far has not calmed the panic caused by continuous speculation. The public sees terrorism as the major threat to airline safety after the TWA 800 crash even though no evidence of any sabotage can be found.

The third fatal airline accident had an obvious cause but generated no cries of alarm. In that accident, an engine on a Delta MD-88 suffered an uncontained failure on takeoff and the flying shrapnel penetrated the cabin, killing two passengers. Flying parts from an uncontained engine failure could disable an airplane in flight, so this is no minor matter. But since only two people were killed and no sinister terrorists were suspected, the Delta accident faded from the news almost instantly. The fact that more recently certified airplanes and engines have much more stringent safeguards to deal with engine failure was never mentioned. Uncontained engine failure is a very real threat, the certification rules have been adjusted several times to address the problem, but the media, and thus passengers, don't seem to notice.

Compare the reaction to the Delta engine failure with the Boeing 737 rudder controversy. Two 737s in the life of the world's most common jet airliner have gone out of control and crashed for no apparent reason. The first was at Colorado Springs and the second near Pittsburgh. No probable cause

continued ▶

has been determined in either accident, but the NTSB continues to speculate that the rudder was somehow involved. There is no evidence pointing toward any particular cause in the two 737 crashes, but the Board and the public are demanding that completely new rudder power control units be installed in all 737s. The 737 fleet has a better than average safety record, there have been only two unexplained accidents in the millions of hours of fleet history, yet the government, at the urging of the public, seems ready to make radical changes in a proven airplane. What if a new rudder control system is less reliable than the one we have now? We won't know the answer to that for many years.

Which brings me back to where I started. Ask anybody if there is risk involved in traveling hundreds of miles per hour thousands of feet above the ground and they will get the answer right. But when things do occasionally go wrong and an airplane crashes, there is disbelief. Flying is no less safe than it was five, 10 or even 20 years ago. But neither is it significantly more safe because we have eliminated the predictable causes of accidents in jet airline flying. Future improvements in safety will come slowly and won't be noticed by the public. If three fatal accidents can cause the long-lasting impact we saw growing out of 1996, then even one accident can have the same effect. And unlike our departed Secretary of Transportation, I know too much about airplanes and flying to believe zero accidents is a possibility.

QUESTIONS

1. Which paragraphs are used primarily to explain the problem? Which ones for the solution?

2. Do you think the ratio of problem to solution in this essay is appropriate?

3. By paper's end do you feel differently about flying? How do you feel? Based on your new feelings, did the writer succeed in his stated goal?

WHILE YOU'RE WRITING

While the essay is in progress seek help from other writers, your instructor, and other readers whose opinion you trust. These are some of the items that you should consider.

- Start early. We all see problems in our world around us. Don't settle for the first problem you can think of. Look at all phases of your life: school, home, family, friends, work, and so forth.

- Try making lists of problems. Choose from those lists the problems that seem most in need of solving and most solvable. Ask yourself: What do I know about this? Why do I care about this? What do I have to say? Free-write. Loop.

- Remember your purpose? You've got to prove the problem exists and that it's in need of solving. You've got to prove that you've got a decent, workable, and reasonable solution. You've got to move your reader to some kind of action at the essay's end.

- Have I come prepared to the workshop with a rough draft of my essay? Am I willing to let my colleagues help me better my essay? Am I willing to help others see their good and bad points?

WORKSHOP QUESTIONS

- Has the writer targeted exactly the right audience? Help the writer imagine some other audiences who might be better.

- Does the writer seem to have "credibility"? That is, has the writer identified him or herself as someone who our reader should listen to?

- Are you confused by anything? Is there enough background in the telling of the problem? Will the reader of the letter "get it"?

- Has the writer provided a solution, and does that solution seem reasonably accomplished by the means suggested?

- What's your opinion of the call to action? Is it clear enough? Is it a good, first step in the solution? Will the reader feel compelled to act upon it? Can you think of a better call to action for the writer to push instead?

The Research Essay

Something to think about

Try not to panic.

Above all other essays, this is the one that terrifies writers most. It's an unfortunate thing that the word "research" scares so many people. Just hearing the word tends to make many people think of libraries and lots of books and weird, arcane footnotes and bibliographies.

I can remember writing research papers in middle and high school; they were terrible beasts. I can clearly remember one teacher telling me to write a research paper about the Civil War. That was it. No other direction. I wasn't given the option to pick my own topic, and I wasn't told what part of the Civil War I should write about.

What I did was go to the library, check out the first five books I found that talked about the Civil War, and then copy a bunch of those ideas into my finished paper. The paper was horrible, dull, vague, uninspiring, and I hated every moment of the process.

What good was that? None.

I'm not going to let you have a bad experience with the research paper, because the truth is a research paper can be a very cool experience. A research paper is any paper you choose to write that relies on outside documentation for a primary part of its message. In fact, many of the essays that we discuss in this book are suitable for a research paper: argument, evaluation, call to action, creed, and so on. All can work extremely well when you bring the work of other writers in to help make your point.

Research paper FAQs (frequently asked questions)

Over the years I've been doing my best to change the way writers look at research. I've designed a series of steps for the research paper process that I believe will help you along the way to the best paper you can write. I've been keeping track of the most commonly asked questions about this kind of essay, and I've been trying to answer those questions as cleanly and clearly and briefly as possible. Read through the entire FAQs and I believe most of your early concerns will be addressed. Then we'll get on with the paper.

WHAT IS A RESEARCH PAPER?

It's synthesis! A research paper is primarily the synthesis of a number of other writers' ideas. Picture a wall of books about gun control. Your job would NOT be to summarize one or two of those books in great detail. Your job is to bring together all the ideas from that entire wall of books and extract a manageable and common thesis. I can't warn you enough about the number of sources you use. Too many writers may cite ten or more books in their research, but cite one or two books countless times. That sort of paper doesn't work, because if you spend ten pages re-telling what's in one book, why isn't it easier for me to go read that book? You've got to bring me the whole wall!

A lot of developing writers have trouble with this notion simply because it's a daunting task to do so much varied reading and writing at one time. Usually, the research paper comes late in the semester and writers have gotten in the habit of writing their essays on their own, with limited outside research—or none at all. Adding the responsibility of bringing other texts together makes this essay far different.

It's easy, too, to get caught up in one or two texts. Invariably in research, you find one text that really says what you've been looking for. For various reasons it becomes the book you read the most, know the best, and trust. It only stands to reason that you are more likely to quote from it than all the others. However, you must keep in mind that your responsibility is to bring the whole field to us, not just one perspective on the field. Resist the temptation to write a book report!

Instead, let your thesis or your point develop after you've read and considered books from the field. Your thesis likely will grow and change every time you pick up a new book.

Let's say you're doing a paper on dreams. The first book talks a great deal about how easy dream interpretation is. Your thesis begins forming: "Dream interpretation is quite easy to do." You read a second book, though, and learn that dream analysis offers many difficulties, because the same dream might mean several different things. Your new thesis becomes "Dream interpretation seems quite easy; however, a single dream may have many different meanings."

You read a third book and discover that dreams hold the key to our future, and a fourth book that says dreams are all about our past. Keeping in mind that your thesis and your paper are supposed to synthesize the entire field, you write

> ▶ The field of dream analysis is full of contradicting theories supporting the importance of our dreams. Perhaps dreams hold our future, perhaps our past. Regardless, dream analysis is an active and fascinating field. ◀

That thesis, still in progress perhaps, captures the variety of ideas you find in all the research you do. That's always your main responsibility.

WHAT VALUE IS THERE IN USING OUTSIDE SOURCES?

Bringing in these outside sources greatly enhances the paper writer's credibility with his or her readers. If no sources are documented, the reader can dismiss the entire paper by saying "What does this guy know about dreams?" If the writer cites sources to back up or support the major thrust of the essay, the message is much more credible. If a reader wants to discount the essay now, he or she has to discount not only the essay writer but all of the experts cited throughout the essay, clearly a daunting task.

WHAT ARE MY RESPONSIBILITIES AS A WRITER OF A RESEARCH PAPER?

Well, in addition to writing a good essay that brings together an entire field, you have to make sure you give credit to the original writers when you use their ideas! The whole point of documentation—which we will do through the Modern Language Association (MLA) style—is to make sure writers get their just due. Plagiarism is one of the most nefarious forms of stealing, because it deals with the special quality of the mind. Taking my thoughts and using them uncredited is like stealing something of my ideas, my beliefs, even my humanity.

Your chief responsibility as a research paper writer is to document those sources from which your work comes. The MLA style is discussed in its own little section. It's advisable to pick up a recent copy of the MLA guidelines, however, because electronic research is quickly changing the face of how we document material found on the Internet and the World Wide Web. Your instructor will likely suggest you spend some time with a good MLA guide, like the MLA's own publication, the *MLA Handbook for Writers of Research Papers*. Still, MLA style is found in nearly every decent college grammar handbook. You may already have one of these in your possession.

WON'T I HAVE TO DOCUMENT EVERY SENTENCE?

No. In fact there is a rule already in place dealing with the problem. It's called the "common knowledge" rule. If you're writing a paper on George Washington, you do not have to document where you found the information that he was the first president of the United States. Why? Because it's common knowledge. You would find that fact in hundreds of books. The common knowledge rule is partially interpreted by you as the writer. You have to decide if a piece of information is easily enough found and attributable to several sources in the field to declare it common knowledge and be able to avoid citing it.

One great teacher I know always reminds his students "If you didn't know it before you began your research *or* if you don't think your reader will know it, then you should cite its source."

Be careful, however. Don't overuse the rule. One of the other ideas in a research paper is to bring to a reader a source of further information. If you use the common knowledge rule on everything, the reader will never be given a hint about where else to go for more information in the field. Think of it from the reader's point of view for a moment. If a reader is taking the time to read your essay on dream analysis, wouldn't that reader be a prime candidate to read some of the books and articles you used?

HOW DO I AVOID PLAGIARISM?

Plagiarism is using anyone else's ideas or words as your own without credit. (In a research paper, you give credit through proper MLA style— parenthetical cites within the paper and a Works Cited page at the end.)

Plagiarism has three possible punishments in different colleges and universities around the country: 1) failure of the paper, 2) failure of the class, 3) expulsion from the college. I've seen all three of these punishments used, and it's not pretty. The harshest penalty is rarely applied to first-year students. Usually, expulsion is reserved for a grad student or even a professor who knowingly and broadly uses someone else's work, failing to give credit. An advanced writer, of course, is much more guilty because he or she is more aware of the rule. There's a big difference between plagiarizing because you didn't know the rules and plagiarizing even though you knew the rules.

Developing writers may sometimes make a mistake in not documenting something. That qualifies as plagiarism in the strictest sense of the word. But the nice thing about our writing process is that through workshops and conferencing, your peers, your instructor, and you will have multiple chances to review your work. I've always found it pretty easy to find examples of plagiarism in texts. Here's a fairly common mistake.

> ▶ Most of the cheese manufactured in Wisconsin is of the cheddar variety. In fact, 55% is "American" cheddar, a variety made exclusively with whole rather than lower fat milk. ◀

Why is that plagiarism? Because that "55%" figure came from somewhere, right? You and I and your instructor know that you didn't go to the cheese and dairy farms of Wisconsin and count how much cheese was made over the past few years. That info came to you from a book or magazine somewhere.

The tough part for some writers is to realize it's okay to get information from other sources and use it! In fact, it's one of the points of this whole essay.

Still, writers get it in their heads that it's an almost shameful thing to use other people's work at all. Writers have told me "But if I cite something, that shows I'm not writing enough." That's crazy! Part of the research paper is to prove you can pull together other writers' ideas to help make a point. And in any essay that uses outside sources, it's always a good idea to reinforce your own ideas with the words and ideas and facts from experts. That's the power of a well-chosen and well-used cite.

WHAT DO PARENTHETICAL "CITES" LOOK LIKE?

Okay, I keep using these terms "cite," "parenthetical cite," and so on. Let's see one. We'll carry on with the cheese example:

> ▶ Most of the cheese manufactured in Wisconsin is of the cheddar variety. In fact, 55% is "American" cheddar, a variety made exclusively with whole rather than lower fat milk (Seaver 41). ◀

There. That's a cite. We call it, in fact, a parenthetical cite. With no explanation at all I am sure you can guess how a cite works. First, you see that it is separated from the regular text by parentheses, thus its name. Second, you see it's rather short, containing only two pieces of information: the last name of the author being cited (Seaver), and the page number (41). In most cases, that's all that appears in a parenthetical cite. The writer of this paragraph knew that the 55 percent stat he had gotten had actually come from someplace. He checked his notes, found the article or magazine that it came from, and gave proper recognition to the originator of the information.

WHAT DOES A "WORKS CITED" ENTRY LOOK LIKE?

This is the second place in your essay where you give credit; the first was the parenthetical cite. The second occurs on the last page of your essay. That page is reserved for a listing of all the books, articles, magazines, and so on that you've cited during your paper. It's called, not surprisingly, the "Works Cited" page. (Remember, there's more about this in the MLA documentation section later in this chapter.)

On that "Works Cited" page is where (Seaver 41) is explained in more detail. In fact, a parenthetical cite is specifically there to let us know that should we need more information about that particular text, we can get it from the "Works Cited" page.

(Seaver 41) becomes:

```
Seaver, George. Cheeses of the World. Fresno: USC
     Press, 1997.
```

Does that look a little confusing? Well, don't worry too much; it's pretty easy to figure out. This tiny example, in fact, tells you much of what you need to know about a typical Works Cited entry.

It starts with the name of the author, last name first. This author's name is George Seaver. Then there's a period. Next comes the title of the book. You know it's a book and not a magazine article because books are underlined (or sometimes italicized), and articles simply have quotation marks around them. Another period. Then the name of the city in which the book was published. How do you find that info? Usually it's in the "frontmatter," the first few pages of the book. It's sometimes small and at the bottom. Just keep looking. You'll get good at finding these bits of info.

Fresno is the city where the publisher is located. After the location comes a colon and then the name of the publisher or press that made the book, followed by a comma and the year the book was published. Think of it this way.

```
Last, First. Title. City: Publisher, Year.
```

Or,

```
Seaver, George. Cheeses of the World. Fresno: USC
   Press, 1997.
```

Keep in mind that a single-author book (like the Seaver example) is the easiest form of MLA citation. But the theory and the system is based on that basic format. We'll get into more complicated and exotic uses of the MLA style later on.

WHAT ARE PARAPHRASING AND SUMMARIZING?

Paraphrasing is a vastly misunderstood and misused piece of writing. There are some writers—and even some teachers of writing—who believe that by changing around some words you have made an idea your own. This is insanity. Changing words around does not take away the spirit or the idea of the original. A *paraphrase* can be used in a research paper to avoid quoting long sections verbatim—maybe the same length as the original, with simplified word choices, or oftentimes it's shorter than the original—but the paraphrased section still needs to be cited.

I find that the most useful form of paraphrasing comes from substituting simpler, easier to understand text in place of highly technical (or unnecessarily complex) jargon or information. Sometimes it is just not necessary for us to be bowled over by fancy language. As the researcher, one of your jobs is to bring information to your reader as clearly as possible. Obviously, some paraphrasing is necessary, as in the example below.

▶ The action of the new Telecaster is substantially higher than the Bullets or the Squiers in the same price range. Still, with a setup you can expect less buzz and scrape than you would on the less adjustable Pauls (Thompson 19). ◄

You can paraphrase to take care of specialized knowledge or jargon, making the text more easily read by a typical reader. A paraphrase is sometimes longer than the original, because some technical language has to be explained. Here's a paraphrase of the above.

▶ The strings of the new Fender Telecasters are quite a bit higher off the fretboard than in comparably priced guitars also made by Fender (like the Squier or Bullet brand.) However, getting your guitar "set up" by a knowledgeable guitar repair person will help you avoid the common "buzzing" and "scraping" of strings that occur fairly often on the Gibson Les Paul model, a model not nearly as adjustable as the Fender products (Thompson 19). ◄

On the other hand, a *summary* is always an abridgment, a "making smaller" or shorter. It has elements of paraphrasing as well, but it always involves making a section of text you've read smaller. It's very useful when you're trying to maintain just the overall "gist" or meaning of a section, without its entire bulk. Here's an example.

▶ The biting incident involving Mike Tyson and Evander Holyfield has tainted the professional boxing game. A sport already partly in ruins has seen its immediate future put in jeopardy by immature and animalistic actions by one of its leading figureheads. The sport has been shaken to its core, and despite the findings of the Nevada Athletic Commission, boxing—which has been feeling poorly—is going to feel a lot worse.

— Johnny Sanders ◄

Which summarizes nicely to

▶ Sanders believes that boxing is in trouble (Sanders 142). ◄

You may think that's an extreme example, but it really isn't. One of your jobs in the research paper process is to bring together a world of information about your field of research. That often means you have to condense long sections, even entire books and articles, into brief, conclusive statements.

The main and unstated rule about summarizing and paraphrasing is that while you may be substantially changing the actual text, even so much as to be changing words completely around, replacing jargon, and so forth, you are still held to the rules of documentation. That is, if the idea belongs to the original author, you must give credit for it. More about documentation style, which we do according to MLA rules, later in this chapter.

HOW DO I CHOOSE A TOPIC?

Writers really get stressed out about topic, mostly because of how we've been assigned research papers in the past. I can remember being in school watching Mr. Partridge bring around a big stovepipe hat (left over from our Abraham Lincoln play) filled with slips of paper. We all reached in and pulled out a folded piece of paper.

"Don't open it," Mr. Partridge said. We had no idea what this slip of paper was all about. He hadn't told us anything. Like the bad student I was, I peeked at my slip and saw the word "Cheese." I was excited. I imagined that the slip of paper was a gift or prize I was going to win. I'd love to have a big block of cheese, I thought to myself. Nothing goes down smooth like cheese.

Mr. Partridge got to the front of the class and said "Open your slip of paper; that will be your research paper topic for this quarter."

We all were horrified. Cheese? At least I wasn't like my friend Cindy Monahan. She got stuck with Ballroom Dancing.

The point is, research papers have a bad reputation. Usually we think of large, unwieldy, and oftentimes dense topics like The Civil War, The History of Gasoline, The Industrial Revolution, The Musicals of Gilbert and Sullivan, or Diamond Mining. For the right writer, each of those topics can be terrific. But too often developing writers pick or get stuck with topics that simply don't excite them.

Try to keep in mind that we do this research paper because the skills of researching and reading and understanding are important. Those skills can be explored and developed regardless of the topic. I don't know about you, but I'd like to spend my research and writing time on a cool topic, a topic I like. So, here are the rules for deciding on a topic if the choice is yours.

PICK A TOPIC IN WHICH YOU ALREADY HAVE AN INTEREST AND SOME KNOWLEDGE OF

I make this rule because usually you'll only have a few weeks to do this essay. That really doesn't give you enough time to start completely from scratch. It's best to work on a topic that you already have some experience with. You may already have some books and magazines around that will help you start your research. For example, if you're a big guitar fan and think you might want to write about a guitar-oriented topic, you've probably got some guitar or music magazines. It's nice to start your research that way, with some familiar and comfortable resources already stored up.

PICK A TOPIC THAT YOU KNOW HAS BOOKS AND MAGAZINE ARTICLES THAT CONCERN IT

If you can't instantly think of a book, journal, magazine, or newspaper that publishes or has published articles and ideas about your topic, you may want to rethink things. Simply put, you have to do research for this essay; you'd be better off with a topic that's huge than one that is too small. You need the raw material of books and magazines before you can even start. Your instructor will help you with this, of course; he or she has seen lots of research papers and topics come down the pike and will be able to help you gauge if your topic is a good one.

PICK A TOPIC YOU ARE WILLING TO LEARN MORE ABOUT

Here's one that stumps some people. The truth is that the research process is an enlightening one that often opens the researcher's eyes a great deal. Oftentimes, we may have a very specific interest in a field. For example, I'm a huge guitar fan, but really only know a great deal about Fender products. If I began to work on a research paper about electric guitars, I would learn tons of new stuff about the Gibson line, the Vox products, Kramer, Charvel, Ovation, and the others. If I go into a research process thinking I know it all, I won't have my eyes opened wide enough to get all the material that's there. I'll only be thinking Fender, when in fact I should be thinking Guitars!

Be ready to learn.

WHERE DO I GO TO LOOK FOR INFORMATION?

Typically, books, magazines, newspapers, journals, and encyclopedias are first sources. They exist in almost every field in varying amounts. Here's a little checklist.

ENCYCLOPEDIAS

Most of my writers find very little real help in so-called general encyclopedias such as *Encyclopaedia Britannica*. Fine books in their own way, they are necessarily abridged and too brief to be classified as an essential source. They make excellent starting points for sifting through a large number of topics, however. Grabbing one volume and flipping pages brings me these topics within ten seconds: Aardvarks, Airplanes, Alabama, Amateur Athletics, Astronomy. But I discourage writers from relying too heavily on them.

On the other hand, subject encyclopedias (*Encyclopedia of Religion, Encyclopedia of Philosophy, Encyclopedia of Sports Medicine,* and so on) are rather useful. Very often, reading a short note about a topic in a subject encyclopedia can lead you to a large number of excellent book and/or periodical resources that the encyclopedia includes in its own bibliography. You can then go directly to more essential sources.

BOOKS

Good, old-fashioned books with pages and binding, stacked up in libraries, are still the number one source. Of course, other sources are important, and electronic or online sources are the most cool of all, but for sheer volume, for raw data easily accessed by anybody, books are the king. The key to searching books well is to understand the library's computer catalog system. They all vary slightly from one another, but most offer you the option of searching the library's catalog of books in various ways. The first choice might be:

■ subject

This search is the best search of all for a research paper. Once you have a general area of interest—volcanoes, hang gliding, DNA, soda—enter your topic here and collect a wide variety of books that address that subject. Read the description of the book right on the screen, but don't put all your faith in that. Oftentimes the descriptions are necessarily brief, and therefore may skip crucial information you may be looking for.

Many computer catalogs offer you the chance to print out this information, and by all means do so. But even if you have to write out your choices, do so, then take the sheet to where those particular books are kept in your library. Most books of similar interest are grouped together, so even starting with one good call number (the number on the spine of the book) will get you to a small collection of appropriate texts.

You can also search on:

■ keyword

This search seeks out a word you type in anywhere in the catalog. It searches the description of the book, the author, the title, and so on. It's all-encompassing, and a good choice if you are working in a small library. On the other hand, typing "crime" as a keyword in a large library will bring back so many sources that you'll have a difficult time narrowing them down to a usable number.

One note for you if your computer catalog is a little more advanced: You may be able to use what are called Boolean terms or operators. The most common use of Boolean terms is in the addition of the words "and" and "or." For example, if you know you want to focus on juvenile crime, enter as your keyword "juvenile AND crime." If you're more flexible, use "or," as in "crime AND juvenile OR child."

If you know the name of a source, you can search on:

■ **title**

This will be the fastest way. In addition, it's a good cross-reference for you. It works similarly to the "keyword" option above, but only searches for your word in the book titles. Entering "crime" here will bring back a more manageable number than you found by doing it in the keyword search.

Finally, you can search on:

■ **author**

You'll usually begin seeing names multiple times as you search your subject. That's because authors who work in a field tend to do so for many years and in many books. If you find a great book about urban crime by Chris Peacock, then enter that name in the author search for a quick check of all other books she's written.

PERIODICALS

It's not universal, but most instructors mean "magazines, newspapers, and journals" when they say periodicals. That's how I use the word.

I stress that the combined use of books and periodicals makes the most sense in your research. Books, by their nature, are going to contain slightly older information. Magazines, by their nature, will include the most recent developments or ideas in the field. It's not a good idea to only use one or the other because you'll be missing an essential part of your research. Using only books will skew your paper toward older material. Using only periodicals will skew it toward only the most recent. A balance is key.

The best method of finding articles for your research involves a computer database of magazine and journal articles such as InfoTrac, a system available at most colleges in the country. Lacking that, the standard book series called the *Readers' Guide to Periodical Literature* will do the job, too, although you will need more time. The *Readers' Guide* comes out several times a year and is commonly bound in year-length volumes. You can search your topic or subject in the index and that will lead you to a number of magazine and/or journal articles. Cross-referencing your library's holdings (a list of magazines your library has on hand) will allow you to track down articles.

The InfoTrac system is much easier, as the searches are rather faster. Instead of looking up your topic, you can just type the topic into an InfoTrac field and the machine does the rest, often highlighting articles and magazines known to be at your library.

Additionally, many InfoTrac entries show you a portion or the complete text of the article. With a printer hookup, you can print these articles out for your research. It's a convenient system to be sure, and one that makes your research easier.

You still have to do the reading, though. Technology doesn't make *that* any easier.

ONLINE SOURCES

The amazing online world has revolutionized how research papers get written. I now have many writers writing research essays while never actually setting foot in a real library. That's how complete and available sources are online. And the field keeps exploding. By the time this book reaches you, the technology and availability of online research will be even greater than it is as I am writing this.

In Chapters 17 and 18, I discuss a number of concerns regarding online sources, and therefore I direct you to those chapters for more specific information. For now, though, many writers don't have the equipment to access online resources.

Additionally, unlike venerable documents such as books and journals, information found on the Web (for example) is somewhat suspect. Anyone with a computer and a modem and some time can construct a viable, professional-looking site that says the world is flat. (I found ten Web sites that support this laughable theory, just during the writing of this paragraph. Each one is fairly reasonable and well written. Some of them are written by various folks identified as Ph.Ds.)

Still, it's very likely that you will use the Internet in some way during research, so try to stick to legitimate and recognizable sources. In Chapter 18 I've identified 50 terrific links to get you started on almost any kind of research. Start there.

One more caution about online research: Just as it's changing the face of research, it changes itself from day to day. Sites that seem fruitful can disappear without warning. Web masters (people who keep sites running) change addresses, lose their service, or just change their minds. Making and keeping records of everything you find is even more important online than it is for traditional research sources.

Some encouraging words

There is no way that I can stress how difficult and important the research will be on this paper. It is a task quite different from the other tasks we've done this semester. Usually, we start writing right away; however, due to the size and the complexity of most research papers, we must change from a writing intensive to a reading intensive focus.

It's true that even during the early reading of your source material, you'll be making notes, free-writing, looping, and so forth. But the majority of your time must be spent immersing yourself in the books and articles and sources that make up your field of study.

Here are three keys to keep in mind.

GET STARTED RESEARCHING AND READING RIGHT AWAY

In one of the steps below I suggest that you do a quick sources check for as many as ten different topics. A source check is fairly simple and fast. Go to the catalog system at your school's library and see how many sources appear in the general area of your topic. Do the same for the periodicals available in your library. If you only find a handful in each, you can be sure that you'll have a difficult time gathering enough material for an entire research paper. On the other hand, finding ten or twenty in each category (books and periodicals) will assure you that your topic is researchable.

But getting started right away also refers to reading. You'll quickly discover why I urge you to write about a topic you have interest and knowledge in already. There simply isn't time to do all the reading that is necessary to cover a whole field. And you need a sense of the overall field of study if you're going to fulfill the goal of the research paper. So, start reading right away. Read a lot. Read often. And during all of it, TAKE NOTES. If someone was throwing free money at you, wouldn't you grab it and stick it safely in your pockets. Would you allow the bills and coins to collect around your feet or fly past you? No. You'd scoop the stuff up, stick it in pockets and in your hat and your bookbag.

Do the same thing with the information you get!

Also, you should make photocopies of as much of your research as possible. At the very least, write down all the information you will need for documenting the text later: author, name of book or article, name of magazine or journal (if applicable), date, city of publisher, publishing house, volume number, pages, and so on, on the back of your copies. If you need that source again, and/or when you need to give credit for it, you'll have the information at your disposal. Believe me, this is much easier than having to track down a book that you've already returned to the library or find an old magazine that your roommate or sister has thrown in the trash.

You're better off dropping some dimes into the copy machine now rather than scrambling to refind that "perfect" article or quote or crucial Works Cited information on the last day of the project. It's easy to become overwhelmed as you research. Sometimes it seems like you're a paper magnet. Paper is everywhere. Pages of books and magazines and your notes cling to you.

You need to keep track. Keeping ten or twenty books checked out of the library for the entire duration of your research paper is not usually a possibility. So when you get books, read through them right away, looking for sections that are especially helpful to your ideas or the points you're trying to make. When you find specific information that you think fits your paper, make photocopies of these sections.

Many instructors will also tell you to keep this info on notecards (small 3 x 5 or 4 x 6 cards, lined or unlined). I say "The more, the merrier." Keeping track of where your info came from is no small matter. Use the photocopy method first, and anything else along the way to help.

LOCK IN A THESIS TO GET STARTED

A thesis and a topic are two very different things. The thesis is the central, controlling idea of your essay. It is not the topic! A topic is something like Recycling. The thesis would be "Only through aggressive recycling mandates can large cities begin reclaiming their environments."

Lots of developing writers have trouble with this distinction, but think of it this way: A topic can be one word; a thesis must be a complete sentence. A topic can be static or motionless; a thesis must move. A topic is a thing; a thesis is what you're saying and doing about that thing.

I like to promote a good thesis at the beginning of the research process simply because it helps you focus your attention. There are lots of ways to get off track when the researching begins. You simply find so many little side roads and side topics that it's easy to lose your way off the main highway of your essay. So, by committing to a thesis early on, your paper gets some direction.

CONSIDER YOUR THESIS A WORK IN PROGRESS

Now get ready; don't be mad at me. This step and the previous step really can both survive together. I want you to lock in on a thesis early; that is definitely true. You need focus.

However, I often find that too many of my writers fail to let their thesis develop. The truth is as you work, you'll find new information in your research that will likely influence and shift your thesis into a slightly (or drastically!) new creation. Don't deny it. Don't ignore it. The research should inform the thesis, just as it did earlier in the example about a dream analysis paper. One book gives you one thesis; the second one modifies that original thesis; books three and four offer more ideas; finally, when the research is done, your thesis is a natural combination of ideas based on your wide and varied reading.

Have you ever seen ants walking in a long line? If you drop a rock or a pebble in front of them, they simply go around it. They don't stop working. They don't go home and tell their ant-parents that life is rough. They just swing around the pebble and keep moving.

That's how you have to be about the thesis. If new information comes along that modifies your paper, just swing along with it.

When a rock falls in front of you during the research paper, as it most surely will, just find your way around it and keep going. Don't think a changing thesis is a sign of weakness; it's a sign of strength. You've discovered new and vital information, perhaps, and it's reasonable and responsible to let your paper grow and change as your knowledge does. The only thing that can stop you is time. When the paper is due, it must be done. So to arm ourselves for that, let's begin talking about some actual steps we can take as we work on this essay.

Research paper steps

Because this is usually the longest writing assignment of the semester, I try to encourage you to think of it in pieces. It's all one essay, but by breaking up the long event into a series of tasks, I find my own writers are able to stay focused for the long haul. (Of course, it's important to get your schedule figured out with your instructor. He or she may have some special schedule in mind.)

When I was a kid I always wanted to do grown-up things. My family used to have a big breakfast on the weekend: eggs and ham and pancakes and toast and greasy potatoes and corned beef hash and every-thing else. So I began begging my mom to let me make a big breakfast. Finally, after months of begging, she said "Go ahead."

Well, making a whole breakfast was a little beyond me, but I was game to try. When she left the room to answer the phone, I started in. When she finally came back (way too late, of course), there were broken egg shells on the floor, eggs uncooked in a cold frying pan, a burner on the stove doing nothing but burning bright red, a big piece of ham in the oven at about 800°, black to a crisp. Oh yeah, and about seventeen pieces of toast in a big pile on the table, some white, some black like a piece of coal.

Now, whose mistake was that? Sure, it was my mom's. Of course, it was my fault for taking on a difficult and complex task all at once. But had my mom given me one small step to complete, I could have made that big breakfast one step at a time. She could have shown me how to break eggs into a bowl first. Just one task. I could have concentrated on it and learned that skill. Then, when I had that mastered and done, she would show me how to put oil in a pan, start the range up, and cook a nice piece of ham.

I could have been taught step by step. At the end of the training I would have been able to present a cool plate full of great breakfast stuff. She could have checked my progress and steered me right when things went wrong. "Oh, honey, that ham has caught fire now; call your dad and bring the hose." That could have saved me a lot of trouble.

So, as you move through this process, I want you to stick to these lit-tle tasks as you go. Each of the headings below represents a small, inter-mediate step. Each step tells you what to accomplish and how to pre-pare the work. Your instructor may ask you to turn these in as you go, or to collect them all in a folder until the end. Check to see what you should be doing.

TEN POSSIBLE TOPICS

Don't be satisfied with your first choice. Too many times I see good writ-ers get hampered by a quick topic choice. This is usually a long project, so there is more time for you to get tired or bored with your topic. I'd prefer you took a little extra time at the beginning, thinking through a number of different topics rather than ending up halfway done with an essay whose topic you hate.

A broad consideration of topics will better prepare you for the suc-cessful completion of one. If you won some award and were going to have your picture in the paper, would you want the photographer to come, shoot one picture, and publish it, or would you want the photographer to shoot a few, to make sure your eyes weren't closed, or your hair wasn't standing up weird, or just to make sure you were in focus? It's the same principle here.

I sometimes ask students to come up with 40 possible topics. It's surprisingly easy once you get started. And just like any topic search process, there are many good ideas our minds sometimes have hidden that might be unearthed with a little searching. Go through some newspapers and magazines, cutting out or marking articles that catch your interest. Anything might spark you toward a good topic.

Sit down or walk around, but start thinking of topics. Use some of our inventing strategies from earlier in the book (Chapter 3). Do some brainstorming with your friends. Do a free-writing. Write in your journal.

Whatever you do, think of as many topics as you can and then write the ten best on a piece of paper. This will be a neat list to have when you talk to your instructor about topics. Try to blow your instructor away, and then get his or her guidance on what some of the best ones are.

PAPER TOPIC

As we've often seen in our other essays, an essay must have a topic, an audience, a purpose, and some significance. Early on in the procedure of any essay it's good to make sure that you can envision the perfect audience and that you understand your actual purpose.

Without those things in place, it's too easy to get sloppy or casual in your research. Remember, good writing "does" something.

AUDIENCE

If you've chosen the topic "Dreams" for your essay, begin imagining an appropriate audience. Who cares about dreams? People who have dreams. People who have nightmares. People who believe that dreams tell us something about our lives. People who think dreams might tell the future. There are some interesting audiences already.

What if I suggested you also might reach people who think dream analysis (the study of dreams and their meaning) was all bunk, nonsense? Wouldn't that audience segment change your essay? Writing a research paper to people who are cynical about the meaning of dreams would mean you'd have to treat part of your paper as an issue paper, spending some time convincing your "cynical" readers that dream analysis has merit. If you simply wrote to people who dig the idea of dreams and who believe dreams mean something, you could spend more time simply covering the field.

That's how important audience is. The topic is the same, but if we modify the audience, suddenly we're talking about two different essays. That's why it's important early on to invest some time in finding out who you want to reach and why.

PURPOSE

Of course, purpose in this essay is already spelled out a bit for you. Earlier I told you about "synthesis." Your purpose in the essay is pretty much to synthesize the information available about your field. But purpose in the essay can also go beyond that. Your dream paper may turn into a document in which you actually urge readers to trust their dreams, analyze them themselves, and modify the way they live based on these analyses. You might write a dream paper that urges readers to enjoy the possibility that dreams mean something, but you may treat the topic lightly and suggest that dream analysis is just "fun." On the other hand, you could write a paper where you expose dream analysis as pure fraud.

Those are wildly different essays, and you should begin wondering what direction your paper is headed as soon as you can.

This step requires you to write down your topic and give an explanation of audience and purpose. It might be something like this.

Topic: Dream Analysis
Audience: People who believe that dreams somehow foretell our future
or offer us warnings.
Purpose: To synthesize the material in the field but also to provide
enough examples and interpretations so even a lay person
will be able to get started analyzing his or her own dreams.

START READING

This seems funny, but this may be the most important step of all. Find some books and articles that concern your topic and start reading. Now. Read. Think. Write. Repeat.

THESIS STATEMENT

There is no section of your paper more important than the thesis statement. Contrary to common belief, the thesis can be more than one sentence. Earlier I talked a little about the differences between a thesis statement and a topic. The thesis really can only come after the topic. The topic is what you're researching; the thesis is what you're saying about the topic. Here are some more examples.

Topic: Bicycling
Thesis: The sport of bicycling, often thought of merely as a child's pastime or an Olympic event, actually is most significant for its health and well-being benefits.

Topic: The Bill of Rights
Thesis: The Bill of Rights is not a static document anchored in the past but a living, breathing text that we as citizens have the right to revise and strengthen when the need arises.

Your instructor will really be interested in either of these theses. It's been my experience that in the same way the thesis sells a paper to a reader, it also sells your idea to your instructor. In offering your thesis to your teacher, you're in a sense asking your dad for permission to take the car out on a long drive. "Look, here's my driver's license. I have a map. I have money for gas. I know how to get there and how to get back." The thesis is authorization to go on.

Your thesis should say "Look, this topic is important; I know how to research it and, more important, what to say about it. I know my audience, and I'm going to give them information they'll be hungry for."

I know it sounds like a lot, but it's important. Get the thesis right and the rest of your job will be easier.

ABSTRACT

At this point you've got a topic and a thesis and I hope you're well into your reading. Next, because the essay is usually fairly long and complex, it's a good idea to work out some structure for it to follow.

An abstract is a small version of your paper. Consider it a one- or two-paragraph outline of your research essay. I think you will find it difficult—but also very useful—to compose such a thing this early. It, of course, will likely change as you move through the process. But you have done considerable research by this point, and it's not a bad idea to commit to some direction.

Your abstract should condense the entire planned paper. I recommend about 150 words as a good length for an abstract. The finished abstract will have a much more finished and formal look than a simple sentence or topic outline, and I find that my writers are better able to follow it as a guide.

Here's a sample abstract. As you read it, you should be getting the overall picture of an entire essay-to-be.

KILLING THE PLANET

Through long-term neglect, the Earth has been severely depleted of many crucial resources. At this moment South American foresters are burning hundreds of acres of rain forests, eliminating the planet's greatest single oxygen reservoir. American politicians leisurely debate bills that would dictate safer measures of waste disposal, enact efficient control of fluorocarbons (those chemicals that deplete the ozone layer and contribute to increased incidences of skin cancer), and educate the youth of America about available means of recycling.

There are things that can be done to impede the seemingly inevitable destruction of the planet. Major corporations like First Brand—the producer of Prestone—and DuPont Chemicals are trying to educate the public through advertising their products' biodegradable qualities. The private sector is raising awareness with events like Earth Day. Ultimately, however, the fate of the planet rests with individuals. The planet's verdict is something each one of us must decide now.

ONE PEER EVALUATION OF YOUR ABSTRACT

Simply put, have one of your fellow writers look at the abstract described above. It's a good idea to exchange abstracts with another peer in class so you can respond in the same kind of way. Critical issues to be decided at this point in the research paper process are

- Is the topic interesting, or has it been made interesting?
- Does the writer sound knowledgeable about the topic?
- Will the topic be covered in a number of different ways? (That is, does the writer seem to be covering different aspects of the topic?)
- As a reader, are you completely clear with the direction and purpose of this essay plan?

Your responses to your fellow writer should be honest and helpful, just like one of our workshop meetings. A single peer evaluation, of course, is even more intensive than our normal big or small group meetings, though, so be prepared to be more helpful than usual. The key is to help the writer establish direction.

MINDSET PARAGRAPH

I think we've done a good job so far discussing opening or "mindset" paragraphs. A research paper requires the same kind of setup, perhaps even more so, as our other papers. You are asking the reader to embark on a fairly lengthy journey; therefore, it seems fitting that your mindset paragraph may be more lengthy and more involved than in other essays.

Some writers, however, still get opening paragraphs and thesis statements confused. Let me explain it one more time within the context of this research paper.

The job of an opening paragraph is to entice readers to read your essay, to hook them, to grab them, to introduce the overriding idea of your essay, to set the reader's mind. It's like synchronizing your watch with the readers. You've been thinking about your topic; you want your reader to think about it, too.

The job of a thesis statement, however, is to state the central, controlling idea of your paper. The thesis often takes place in the opening or mindset paragraph (toward the end, perhaps), but can occur even later.

DISCOVERY DRAFT

As you know, this is your first draft. Once you've got some reading and research done, decided on a purpose or point or thesis, and come up with an interesting, evocative, and inviting opening paragraph, it's time to move ahead into the rest of the draft. Keep your abstract handy, and also keep your mind on the thesis statement. These two early steps should help you maintain focus as you write.

As I've suggested elsewhere in this chapter, think of your essay as being made up of parts or "little chapters." Don't sit down with the express notion of writing the whole draft at once. Do it in chunks. Say to yourself, "For the next thirty minutes, I'm going to discuss the dream analysis ideas that I learned and understand from the book by Sanders." Then you present your understanding; you throw in a couple of parenthetical cites or direct quotes from the Sanders source, and suddenly some paragraphs are born.

You write some kind of transition to the next idea or next author, or the next concept, and you write another paragraph or two, using the strategies of promise and delivery, paraphrasing, summarizing, and so on.

Keep in mind, you're presenting us the entire field. You're a tour guide to the material within your topic. Show us around. Have fun.

ONE PEER EVALUATION OF YOUR DISCOVERY DRAFT

The procedure is exactly the same as the earlier peer evaluation: Find a reader and switch papers. Your role as a peer evaluator in this step is to answer the questions that follow. Give your best effort and answer as honestly and completely as you can. I'd encourage you to answer on paper in addition to chatting with the writer. This will provide the writer a written set of ideas and comments to refer to later.

- Is it long enough? Does it meet the instructor's requirements?
- Are there enough outside sources? Do they meet the instructor's requirements?
- Is it clear what ideas come from the writer and what ideas come from research?
- Is this draft representative of what the writer has earlier promised in the abstract?
- Does the paper seem to make sense?
- Is it complete?
- Do you understand what the writer is telling you?

PRELIMINARY WORKS CITED PAGE

This step is here so that you can avoid any possible citation problems later. It's good to keep checking your MLA style as you go. Having your instructor look at your Works Cited while you're still compiling sources is also a good idea. Perhaps you're making a small error in citing certain things, and another reader can help you avoid that problem later. (A complete guide to MLA style is coming up in the chapter shortly.)

KEEP DRAFTING

There's no telling how long this step will take, but it's imperative you take your first discovery draft through a good, solid revision. You obviously have more knowledge of your topic now than when you first started that early draft. Now you have a clear idea of all the parts of your essay, plus you've had the benefit of getting at least some feedback from a peer.

Any revision of any paper begins with a check of promise and delivery. Your thesis should match your support or your proof. Have you done what you set out to do? Have you addressed all the parts of your thesis?

Additionally, during this time you should take your essay through the workshop and conference exercises. Because this essay involves more complex planning and execution, these "support group" activities will be even more important than usual. A complete list of workshop questions to guide you appears at the end of this chapter.

A COMMON DRAFTING PROBLEM: NOT ENOUGH TO SAY

Despite all my warnings about doing a great amount of research, some writers end up a week away from the due date with a tiny paper. (Most of my writers write in excess of ten pages; anything six pages or less is pretty tiny.) In many of these cases, the pages they have are terrific. What's missing is depth or complexity of thought in the field.

It's always better to do too much research than not enough. If you read widely and research a variety of aspects of your overall topic, you'll usually have enough to work with. However, if you find yourself stuck, the best last-minute fix is to redesign your overall topic. Let's revisit the topic on bicycling. Here's the topic and thesis our writer began his work with.

Topic: Bicycling
Thesis: The sport of bicycling, often thought of merely as a child's pastime or an Olympic event, actually is most significant for its health and well-being benefits.

Let's say he's worked on that paper for a while, has supported his thesis well, but is still short of the required pages. I'd advise him to go back into his thesis and expand it, adding another area of research, another "mini-chapter." How about this?

Topic: Bicycling
Thesis: The sport of bicycling, often thought of merely as a child's pastime or an Olympic event, actually is most significant for its health and well-being benefits. **People eager to profit from**

**these benefits can explore two subgroups of cyclists:
mountain, all-terrain cyclists and health club "spinners."**

I've boldfaced the additional information. Now, in addition to what the writer had intended, he or she will be writing some practical ways in which readers can benefit from cycling: mountain biking and "spinning," an organized sort of stationary biking under a fitness expert's instruction.

This addition to the thesis allows the writer to stay completely within his or her field. If you get into a "not enough pages" jam, resist the temptation to start over on a new topic. A reconfiguration of the thesis can often save you. Obviously, consult with your instructor as soon as you can if you feel you're coming up short.

FINAL CITATION CHECK

This step is different from the previous in that it should be done near the very end of your process. Show your instructor your final Works Cited page, plus some sample parenthetical cites within your essay. It's your last chance to get your MLA style checked for correctness and completeness. Feel free to show this material to some peers, too. This step also allows your instructor to make sure you've met requirements for the number of outside sources.

TURN IN FINAL COPY

This is the last step, where you turn in your finished essay. At the very least, your instructor will want the essay, complete with Works Cited page. He or she may also want you to turn in all your other materials (ten topics, paper topic, thesis statement, etc.).

Documentation of outside sources

Whenever a writer uses material from another source, he or she is expected to give credit for the material. In short, you must let your reader know that the material you're using from another source belongs to someone else; you must tell your reader where you got it, where it was published and when, and show them how to find that article or book if they should ever want to read it.

There are a variety of documentation styles, but courses in the humanities, like this one, favor MLA (Modern Language Association) style.

Now that you're surrounded by books and magazine and journals, I want you to know how to give credit correctly to those writers who are helping you with your research essay. Below, I'll show you examples of MLA style for traditional and electronic sources.

MLA STYLE—TRADITIONAL SOURCES

Here's a brief and concise guide to using MLA style in your essays. For the complete version of MLA documentation, with all its intricacies, direct your research to the most current version of the *MLA Handbook for Writers of Research Papers,* published every three to five years or so.

What I offer below is a collection of parenthetical cites and Works Cited entries of the most commonly needed types for sources used. Keep in mind that whenever you use material, quotes, ideas, stats, and the like from another writer or source, your responsibility as the writer of a research paper is to give credit to that original source.

You give that credit in two spots: inside the essay and at the end of the essay. My examples that follow will show you how to cite in both places. The first entry will always be the parenthetical cite (PC). That's an example of how you actually give credit to the outside source in the text of your written essay. The second entry will be for the Works Cited (WC) page. That's the last page of your essay. Here we go.

ONE-AUTHOR BOOK

Parenthetical Cite (PC)

```
Jones also finds the extinction of dinosaurs to be "an
amazingly complicated puzzle" (Jones 41).
```

This is a simple example. We just have the last name of our author and the page number. Note that the quotation marks close before the parentheses, but that the final punctuation comes after the parentheses.

Works Cited (WC)

```
Jones, Monte. The Test of Time. New York: Harper, 1996.
```

Just to remind you: Last name of author, First name. Title of Book. City: Publishing Company, Year.

Remember, most Works Cited entries will look a lot like this one.

MULTIPLE-AUTHOR BOOK

PC

> "When the truth was discovered, many people didn't want to know" (Torrance and Smalls 119).

Use this for two or three authors.

> But other studies proved too "unruly" for a clear understanding (Torrance et al. 134).

Use this for four or more authors.

WC

Torrance, Michelle, and Rachel E. Smalls. <u>Mysteries of the Half Light</u>. Austin, TX: Rochelle, 1994.

Use this for two or three authors. Note that after the first name given, all other author names go in forward order.

Torrance, Michelle, et al. <u>Mysteries of the Half Light</u>. Austin, TX: Rochelle, 1994.

Use this for four or more authors. With four or more authors it's not necessary to list all of them, but it's also not wrong to do so if you want to make sure everyone gets credit.

MULTIPLE BOOKS BY SAME AUTHOR

PC

> What still confuses us today is "the inevitable decline of test scores into near-record low levels" (Thompson, <u>Anxious</u> 181).

Because Thompson has more than one book in your essay, you have to use a portion of the relevant book's title in your parenthetical cite. In this case, just the first word of the title is enough to differentiate it from the other Thompson books.

WC

Thompson, Jennifer. <u>Anxious Testing = Anxious Results</u>. Chicago: U of Illinois P, 1993.

This is the Thompson book you cited above in the PC section.

---. <u>Too Much Time; Not Enough Pencils!</u> Chicago: U of Illinois P, 1993.

This is how you cite other books by Thompson used in the same essay. Note how the author's name in the second entry is simply replaced by three hyphens.

REFERENCE BOOK WITH AUTHOR

PC

> The Emperor penguin is as tall as it is because of the cantilevered shaping of its upper vertebrae (Mitchell).

Note that there are no quotation marks in this section. The writer is not using a direct quote, but the information still comes from the research, hence the cite. Also, no page number is necessary in reference books that present their information in alphabetical format, like an encyclopedia.

WC

Mitchell, Donald. "Emperor Penguin." <u>Encyclopaedia Britannica</u>. 1997 ed.

REFERENCE BOOK WITHOUT AUTHOR

PC

> But the other penguins wouldn't let Rudolph join in their penguin games, thus forcing the penguins' owner to "give Rudolph a new position in front of the sled" ("Penguin").

Reference books, because of their almost universal alphabetic organization, don't need page numbers cited. The title of the section cited (Penguin, in this case) is all you need. It's in quotes because it's an article title.

WC

"Penguin." <u>Encyclopaedia Americana</u>. 1987 ed.

ONE-AUTHOR MAGAZINE ARTICLE—WEEKLY

PC

> Johnson describes how he knew freedom was his when "the guard put his head down and left the usually locked door wide open" (34).

Only the page number is necessary here because the author's name is included in setting up the cite. You don't always have to leave the author's name out of the cite, however; it's an option.

WC

```
Johnson, Wilmer. "Getting Out: The Hard Way." Time 17
    Jan. 1997: 34-40.
```

Notice here how we have both an article name (in quotation marks) and a magazine title, (underlined). The order of the date is important, too. Day first, then the month, then the year. Months longer than four letters are to be abbreviated. Finally, you'll see that actual page numbers appear in this cite, as they should for all magazines, newspapers, and journals.

ONE-AUTHOR JOURNAL ARTICLE—MONTHLY

PC

```
Nobody has found the link necessary, but many scien-
tists believe that "the dynamics of hair growth may
hold the key" (Stubing and Tenille 111).
```

WC

```
Stubing, Thomas, and Anthony Tenille. "Hair Apparent."
    Journal of Follicular Biology Dec. 1995: 109-124.
```

MLA STYLE—ELECTRONIC SOURCES

At the time I'm writing this book, the Modern Language Association is still standardizing MLA documentation style for the new and ever-changing online world. Even though their most recent text edition includes some passing remarks about documenting online sources, they have posted to their Web site (available http://www.mla.org) the first official MLA-sanctioned guidelines for citing electronic sources.

The examples below are limited to some major categories of sources you are most likely to come across during your online research. My warning is, however, that the documentation style for electronic sources will be in flux for quite a while yet, as we explore the current online world and try to assimilate coming trends and modes of information that will become part of the Internet. Your best source for MLA style will be the organization's Web site (mentioned above) and their newest traditional paper edition.

Here's a general form that I've adapted from the MLA's own Web site for you to follow as you get comfortable with this style.

```
Name of the author of the source, reversed for
alphabetizing and followed by an abbreviation, such
as ed., if appropriate. Title of a poem, short story,
article within a Web site, database, or periodical
(in quotation marks). Title of a book (underlined).
Name of the editor or compiler of the text (if not
cited earlier), preceded by the appropriate abbrevi-
ation, such as Ed. Publication information for any
print version of the source. Title of the Web site,
database or periodical (underlined); or, for a site
with no title, a description like Home page. Name of
the editor of the scholarly project or database (if
available). Version number of the source (if not
part of the title) or, for a journal, the volume
number, issue number, or other identifying number.
Date of electronic publication, of the latest post-
ing. The number range or total number of pages,
paragraphs, or other sections, if they are numbered
(this is slowly becoming an ingredient on many
pages, but you will find many sites with no marked
pagination at all). Name of any institution or orga-
nization sponsoring or associated with the Web site.
Date when you accessed the page. The URL (Universal
Resource Locator) in angle brackets (that means
<http://something.com/something-else.html>).
```

That's a mouthful, right, or at least a brainful. Here are some specific examples from Web sites, e-mail correspondence, and Usenet news-groups, for you to look at. Just as in the traditional documentation section, use the rules of MLA documentation to give credit in the best way you can for the work you've researched.

WORLD WIDE WEB PAGE: A BOOK

PC

```
What Shelley sees in the monster, however, is some-
thing "sweet and sublime" rather than monstrous
(Jelotto).
```

Many online sites don't have a well-developed pagination system, so knowing what page anything is on might be quite difficult. Some large

Web sites are really just one big page, in fact. So, you'll notice in this example that we just use the last name of the author in our parenthetical cite. If Jelotto is a source for two different Works Cited entries, then you'd use this format in a PC.

```
What Shelley sees in the monster, however, is some-
thing "sweet and sublime" rather than monstrous
(Jelotto The Monster . . .).
```

WC

```
Jelotto, Darryl S. The Monster Within, the Monster
    Without. Boston: Houghton Mifflin, 1978. Women &
    Writing Project. Ed. Matthew Kudzu Smollet. Jan.
    1998. Ohio U. 29 Mar. 1998 <http://www.ohio-u.
    edu/txt/vwwp/jelotto.html>.
```

In this first example, you'll see some familiar forms. Author comes first, then the name of the book and its traditional publication information. (The Web site you've used for this source may or may not have full information. The rule is to use what you've got. You aren't expected to find the hard copy of the book in addition to its electronic version. In this case you can see that the full publication information was available, and thus was used in the cite.)

Next comes the name of any scholarly project, database, periodical, or professional or personal home page that houses the book in question, and then the editor of that project, if available.

Next is the identifying volume number, issue number, or date of the document, followed by the name of any institution or organization sponsoring or associated with the Web site, date of access, and then the address.

WORLD WIDE WEB PAGE: A POEM

PC

```
What the poet intends to imply with his image of
"sunlight on a broken column" is anyone's guess
(Eliot).
```

WC

```
Eliot, T. S. "Hollow Men." Art of Europe. 16 Mar. 1998
    <http://www.penwith.co.uk/artofeurope/poetry.
    htm#eliot>.
```

This example is substantially more simple than our previous one, but that's just because the Web site in question simply doesn't give us as much information. As before, give what you can. Here, we simply have the author, the name of poem, the name of the Web page, the date of access, and the address.

WORLD WIDE WEB PAGE: ARTICLE IN A REFERENCE DATABASE

PC

Most contemporary poets haven't felt constrained by the traditional rules of versification, rhyme, or meter. In fact, "free verse" has reigned as the primary language of the "people's poets" ("Free Verse").

WC

"Free Verse." <u>Brittannica Online</u>. Vers. 98.2.2. Mar. 1998. <u>Encyclopaedia Britannica</u>. 18 Aug. 1998 <http://www.eb.com:140>.

WORLD WIDE WEB PAGE: ARTICLE IN A JOURNAL

PC

Until Milton's own pages were found, many critics "simply had to play hopscotch with small sections of the poem" (Flannagan).

WC

Flannagan, Roy. "Reflections on Milton and Ariosto." <u>Early Modern Literary Studies</u> 2.3 (1996): 16 pars. 22 Feb. 1997 <http://unixg.ubc.ca:7001/0/e-sources/emls/02-3/flanmilt.html>.

WORLD WIDE WEB PAGE: ARTICLE IN A MAGAZINE

WC

Landsburg, Steven E. "Who Shall Inherit the Earth?" <u>Slate</u> 1 May 1997. 2 May 1997 <http://www.slate.com/Economics/97-05-01/Economics.asp>.

WORLD WIDE WEB PAGE: GENERIC

PC

> Some independent music distributors are selling their product right online, using sophisticated and secure forms for credit card purchase. Dragtown Records, a small label in Milwaukee, Wisconsin currently offers 30 of their recent releases in this way (<u>Dragtown</u>).

WC

<u>Dragtown Records</u>. Home page. 13 Feb. 1998 <http://www.dragtown.com/index.html>.

In this example, we have no author—such is the case with many Web sites you'll find. We treat it like we do any unknown author, however, by alphabetizing it by the name of the document (just like a newspaper editorial, for example). The modern angled parentheses enclose the full Universal Resource Locator (URL) for the Web site. Take great care when transcribing URLs, as they sometimes are upwards of thirty or forty characters long.

E-MAIL

Now we move away from the World Wide Web to discuss personal e-mail correspondence. This is a very useful method of research, and after a while online you'll develop the courage and the inquisitiveness necessary to send e-mail questions and comments to researchers and writers in your field. One of the most compelling reasons to gather research info this way is touched on in the section about personal interviews. Namely, being able to ask exactly the question you want during research often will help unearth exactly the information you need rather than having to get along with only what you find.

PC

> Many theorists like Josephine McMillan believe "radar images from space are confusing the issue more than CNN or NBC would like to believe" (McMillan).

Most experts will tell you that putting the author's name in the parenthetical cite above might not be necessary; after all, you've mentioned her name in the sentence. However, it's not wrong to list her both places, and since this a new kind of MLA formatting, it might ease confusion for your reader to do it this way.

WC

```
McMillan, Josephine. "Re: Radar Image Request" E-mail
    to the author. 16 July 1998.
```

The author's name remains first, in the standard MLA way. If the correspondence had a title or subject line, that appears next. The date that ends the cite is the date the message was sent, not the date you received or opened the message.

USENET NEWSGROUP POSTING

Newsgroups, those great "bulletin-board" type gathering spots in the online world, vary from the ridiculous to the sublime. For every really great newsgroup about news, sports, medicine, culture, and so on, there seems to be about a dozen about professional wrestling, frozen waffles, and Leonardo DiCaprio. (Although I'm sure there's some good information in those newsgroups, too.)

While the online world continues to expand, recognize that readers still trust traditional sources more than they do electronic ones. Just like we will trust a source that comes from a big publisher like Prentice Hall over a publisher called Eddy's Big Toe, readers also will look askance if your newsgroup research includes too many like the very care-free and often silly <alt.food.blueberrywaffles>, and not enough of something established like <rec.food.nutrition>.

Still, there is great information shared around the world in Usenet newsgroups every day. Don't close yourself off.

PC

```
Some experts want to replace UNIX systems world-wide,
simply because they believe we've reached "platform
saturation that will water down the good computing
can do" (Slopper).
```

WC

```
Slopper, Theodore. "UNIX Must Die!" 11 Jun. 1997.
    Online posting. Newsgroup rec.computing.unix.
    Usenet. 21 Oct. 1998.
```

Unlike the e-mail example above, we do not include the e-mail address of the original poster, but notice that after the creation date we also have a listing of the particular Usenet newsgroup where the message was found. This entry closes with the date you read or found the document, what we often call the access date.

The essay assignment

Write a research paper about a topic of interest to you. You should recognize that in this kind of essay, your personal point of view is not nearly as important as your ability to synthesize the work and ideas of other writers.

Primarily, you are bringing together a body of knowledge. Your topic, be it small or large, has around it a common or shared knowledge. Your research should lead you to the heart of that knowledge. You are expected to report all sides and all positions of a topic without bias. You certainly can have an opinion in the latter stages of the paper, but not until you have presented the field fairly. A reader of a research paper expects a more objective sort of treatment by the author than in most papers. You are acting as an authority in the field, and therefore you are held to a higher standard of impartiality.

Your essay should consist of a number of different ideas, as many major ideas or sections as you think are needed to present the field properly. If your topic is "Bicycling," it would not be sufficient to merely discuss recreational riding. Recreational riding does not explain or cover or encompass all of bicycling. You'd have to do something more in line with this:

Topic: Bicycling
Areas within field: Competitive
                  Recreational
                  For Health

Many of my most successful writers think of their research paper as a mini-book, made up of one overall, overriding idea, but explained through a series of linked chapters.

If during your research you discover that you'd rather just work on the health benefits of bicycling, you can do it; you just have to redesign your topic and areas.

Topic: Health Benefits of Bicycling
Areas: Muscle
        Cardiovascular
        Anti-Aging

You can modify your topic as you go, but always make sure that your paper covers the overall topic, plus a number of areas within it.

Sample essay

Research papers are a varied lot. Unlike other chapters in this book, I don't think I can give you a representative example of a research paper to guide you. In some of the other chapters in this book, the samples could be modeled exactly using your own ideas and writing. However, research papers take so many different forms and shapes and structures that I am not suggesting you model or imitate the following essay by a student of mine named Linda. I will go through it with you, stepping in every once in a while to point out something that she has done well.

DESTINY IN OUR HANDS

The prospect is exciting. "By mapping and manipulating tiny genes, man could conceivably conquer diseases, improve upon his natural abilities and perhaps even control his own destiny" (Elmer-Dewitt 70). The new technology of gene therapy promises to revolutionize medicine in the next century. However, just because miracles might someday be possible does not necessarily mean they should all be performed (Elmer-Dewitt 70). Gene therapy has an enormous potential for both good and evil.

Including a quote or a citation early on in the paper has a couple of effects. First, it lets your reader know that you are comfortable with the use of outside sources. Second, it helps you define your thesis. Look how Linda allows two separate small quotes from an outside source help her. The last sentence in this paragraph is her thesis.

Also note that the first cite is an actual quoted section of text, therefore the quotation marks. Further, the next section has no quotes, yet Linda still gives credit for the idea. Although she hasn't used the Elmer-Dewitt source word for word, she does feel she is using the writer's idea. That, of course, must be cited, as she's done it here.

One thing Linda doesn't do very well, however, is provide a necessary mindset paragraph. I'd suggest that she try again in her next revision by moving her first sentence, "The prospect is exciting," to its own space, and then raise the very complex issues of gene therapy and gene experimentation. Surely she's found several interesting stories or case studies that would whet our appetite for the paper to follow.

"Gene therapy is an experimental technique for treating or preventing diseases by inserting a gene into a patient's cells" (Blaese 81). Each person has an estimated 100,000 separate genes, strung side by side, along twenty-three pairs of chromosomes. "An identical set of these 100,000 genes—the full set is known collectively as the genome—is tucked into the nucleus of all but a small fraction of the 100 trillion cells that make up the human body" (Lyon and Gorner 32). Genes are the basic unit of heredity. They carry the chemical instructions that determine the form and function of every cell. Genetic diseases result when a gene is defective or missing, causing affected cells to malfunction. Gene therapy is in the early stages of development but offers hope of treating or preventing genetic diseases that today are incurable (Blaese 81).

Okay, can you spot where Linda must have used the common knowledge rule to avoid having to cite something? Remember what we said earlier: The common knowledge rule says that we don't have to offer a cite if the piece of information we use is readily available in many sources in the field. Found it yet? Look up at the paragraph again. It's the sentence that reads "Each person has an estimated 100,000 separate genes, strung side by side, along twenty-three pairs of chromosomes." That's clearly a fact, correct? It's something Linda wouldn't just know on her own, yet no cite was given. In this case the number of chromosomes in the human body is a well-known fact within the field of science and genetics. There's no need to cite it.

However, in the very next line Linda does cite something. Why? I'd suggest it was because it was a specific bit of information she only saw in one place, or perhaps she really liked the way the authors of that source stated the idea. Remember, it's never wrong to cite a source. It's often wrong to *not* cite a source.

"Nearly 4,000 known medical conditions can be blamed directly on the influence of defective genes" (Lyon and Gorner 26). These include diseases such as cystic fibrosis, muscular dystrophy, sickle-cell anemia, and hemophilia. Each is caused by a single deficient gene. Genetic conditions may also be polygenic, which means they may be caused by the interaction of two or more improperly functioning genes. These conditions may even involve whole groups of genes, as in Down's syndrome (Lyon and Gorner 27). There are also ailments caused by genes acting together with certain environmental agents such as viruses, foods, or toxic chemicals. Examples of these disorders are diabetes, high blood pressure, multiple sclerosis, asthma, and spina bifida (Lyon and Gorner 27). Recent research has also hinted that schizophrenia, manic depression, alcoholism, Alzheimer's disease, arthritis, and Parkinson's disease all have a genetic component (J. Miller 201).

> Of even broader significance to the general population, science is demonstrating a correlation between genes and the primary human killers—heart disease, cancer, high blood pressure, and stroke. (Lyon and Gorner 28)

> Having the wrong genes can trigger clogging of the arteries. Similarly, our prospect of acquiring cancer appears to hinge on environmental effects on certain growth-regulating genes we all harbor within our cells. Researchers have concluded that almost all human illness has some relationship to genetic endowment (Anderson 124).

Beginning a paragraph with a quote often helps writers find focus. In a sense it's like starting a paragraph with a topic sentence. You then know that in the rest of the paragraph you should concentrate on addressing and responding in some way to that opening quote.

Additionally, note the indented quote above attributed to Lyon and Gorner. Typically, if you're going to quote a section four lines or longer, it's helpful to indent that text ten spaces from the left-hand margin. Note how the punctuation differs with the longer quote. The period follows the quote, and there is no punctuation after the parenthetical cite.

> Therefore, the number of potential beneficiaries of gene therapy is awesome. While only 15% of the public suffers from the rarer forms of genetic disorders, the percentage of those affected swells if we consider cancer, cardiovascular disorders, Alzheimer's disease, and others. Together these ailments are responsible for 75% of all deaths (Lyon and Gorner 29). Genetic illness will become a concern of everyone, and we may all profit from ongoing research into gene therapy.

> Doctors first used gene therapy as a treatment in 1990. The case involved a girl whose immune system became defective because of the lack of the enzyme ADA. Scientists at the National Institutes of Health in Bethesda, Maryland, inserted a normal human ADA gene into immune cells taken from her body. Then they returned the treated cells to her body through a transfusion. The inserted gene instructed the cells to produce the missing enzyme, and her immune system began to recover (Anderson 124).

continued ▶

Gene therapy also has the potential to treat some non-genetic conditions. By introducing new or modified genes, the cells can be told to perform new functions. For example, researchers have placed genes into cancerous cells to make cancer therapy more effective (Blaese 81). Scientists are also attempting to genetically modify cells of the immune system to make them resistant to HIV (Blaese 81).

The type of gene therapy presently used is called somatic cell gene therapy. Somatic cells consist of all cell types except reproductive cells (Anderson 126). Genetic alteration of somatic cells affects only the patient undergoing the treatment. "In theory, gene therapy could also be applied to the reproductive, or germ cells" (Anderson 126). This is called germline gene therapy. Modifying these cells would mean that patients would pass along the inserted genes to their offspring.

Gene therapy may involve one or more of the following:

1. Gene replacement therapy, in which the normal form of a gene replaces a mutant gene. This type of gene therapy becomes important if the gene's location at a specific point on a particular chromosome is essential for it to function properly (Levine 86).

2. Gene augmentation therapy, which inserts the normal form of a gene into one of the cell's chromosomes without removal of the abnormal gene. This would be effective if the genetic disease is caused by a deleted gene or one which has little or no activity (Levine 86).

3. Gene inactivation therapy, where the transferred gene produces a protein that neutralizes either a defective protein formed by a mutated gene or the excess number of proteins by a gene that is duplicated wrong to give many extra copies of itself (Levine 86). Therapeutic genes can be introduced directly into a cell by using chemical or physical processes that make the cell membrane temporarily permeable to foreign DNA. This method of gene transfer is called transfection (Levine 86). Transduction is another method which incorporates a beneficial gene into the genetic material of the virus and then infects the target cell (Lyon and Gorner 62). "The most efficient method of transferring genes is transduction using a type of RNA virus called a retrovirus. After infecting a host cell the retrovirus makes a DNA copy of itself, which is then inserted into the genetic material of the host cell" (Levine 86).

Setting up some kind of numbered list is usually quite valuable, especially when presenting such a lot of material as the typical research paper. Here Linda realized she had three rather large ideas to discuss at the same time. She decided to let the visual makeup of a numbered list help the reader along. A reader sees those numbers and can much better bite off the chunks one at a time. This style is even better than simply having three separate paragraphs, because the numbered list suggests that while we look at each number separately, the combination of all three sections actually adds up to a single, large, and complex idea.

> While gene manipulation holds promise, it also presents a wide spectrum of ethical issues and possible social perils. "Lurking behind every genetic dream come true is a possible Brave New World nightmare" (Elmer-Dewitt 70). The opportunities and dilemmas created by the new genetic knowledge begins even before birth. The question of what to do with genetic informa- tion gained through prenatal tests runs squarely into the highly charged issue of abortion. Many could sympathize with a woman who chooses to termi- nate a pregnancy rather than have a baby doomed to a painful struggle with a terrible genetic disease. But what about the prospective parents who abort fetus after fetus until they get the "perfect" baby (Elmer-Dewitt 70). Some fear that mapping the human genome may lead to a very narrow idea of what a physically normal person is. This could promote an increase in the number of abortions, or even create a market in pre-screened high-grade embryos guaranteed to look like Robert Redford or to make the Olympic team (Leo 59). If a child risks an array of biases because of a minor physical weakness, the pressure will be on to produce the ideal child.
>
> "The debate between insurance companies and AIDS patients fore- shadows the demands such companies will make when screening exists" (Leo 59). Imagine a world in which millions are denied insurance because of their genetic profiles. There could also be major insurance fraud as adults are screened and then load up on insurance without telling the company about problems. Insurers have already used a similar policy to avoid covering individuals at high risk for AIDS (Elmer-Dewitt 70).
>
> Some industrial physicians already reject certain job applicants because of mild diseases that have no effect on work performance (Leo 59). If employers could genetically screen applicants this could result in genetic bias. All but the best physical specimens could be subject to subtle preju- dices. The disabled movement has already recognized the potential for greater prejudice once genetic alteration is possible. Deborah Kaplan of the World Institute on Disability predicts "an immense pressure on myself and my peers to undergo different forms of treatment" (Leo 59). The handicapped may no longer be seen as unfortunates worthy of special treatment but as genetic errors committed by parents who failed to take proper action against a defective gene (Elmer-Dewitt 71).

continued ▶

Issues of privacy are also involved in genetic screening. Once someone's genes have been screened, the results could find their way into computer banks. Without legal restrictions this personal information might be shared with companies and government agencies. A DNA analysis could become part of a person's electronic dossier, just like a credit rating or an arrest record. Individual privacy would then disappear (Elmer-Dewitt 70).

Even if genetic information is kept private, the knowledge gained could be difficult for individuals to deal with. What if an individual discovers he has inherited a disease which has no treatment or cure? Some people might prefer not to know.

Another issue regarding gene therapy would be equality of access. Would those with the greatest need be treated first or would those best able to benefit society be chosen first? Perhaps ability to pay eventually would decide who would be treated (H. Miller 316).

Even to label genes as defective can be dangerous. In the nineteenth century new discoveries about heredity and evolution started a eugenics movement whose followers thought undesirable traits should be purged from the gene pool (Elmer-Dewitt 71). The German geneticists gave scientific advice to the leaders of the Third Reich, telling them how to purify the species by selective breeding and by exterminating whole races at a time. Of course, no geneticist today would even talk about creating a master race. Scientists are careful to point out that experimenting in gene therapy will be aimed at curing hereditary disease and relieving suffering, not at producing some sort of superman (Elmer-Dewitt 71).

This is the part of gene therapy that sounds so frightening. If biologists can change heredity, they can try to play God and influence destiny. No geneticist is currently planning to transfer genes to human germ cells. However, medical scientists have an obligation to protect humanity against disease. "Once it is possible to eradicate a gene that causes a fatal disorder, and thus keep it from passing to future generations, it would be criminal not to do so" (Elmer-Dewitt 71).

The future of gene therapy may hinge on a fifteen-year $3,000,000,000 project called the Human Genome Project. This project began in 1990, and its purpose is to map, sequence and decipher all of the approximately 100,000 genes possessed by human beings (Ward 63). This information should provide a giant leap forward in our understanding and ability to successfully deal with human diseases.

Fortunately, the biggest supporters of genetic research are the first to admit the potential for abuse and see the need for guidelines. Many scientists agree on certain principles. Individuals should not be tested against their will, and testing should be confidential. Information gained should be used to inform but not to harm. And genetic engineering in humans should be used to treat diseases, not to create genetic uniformity (Elmer-Dewitt 71). The potential for good is enormous, but as with every fairy tale come to life there is the dark side to be guarded against. "One thing is certain: The genie cannot be put back in the bottle. The task ahead is to channel that force into directions that save lives but preserve humanity's rich genetic heritage" (Elmer-Dewitt 71).

Currently, to provide a forum for concerns about gene therapy and to help monitor its use, all proposals for gene therapy in the United States must be approved by government regulatory groups. These include the Food and Drug Administration and a special panel called the Recombinant DNA Advisory Committee (Blaese 81).

Because of the dangers, some critics demand that gene therapy research be stopped. However, I believe that attitude is mistaken. "One of the best aspects of human nature is the drive to explore new areas, to find new truths, and to solve problems by constructing new technologies" (Ward 66). We should definitely go cautiously, but the promise of gene therapy in easing human suffering is worth the risk.

Let's compare her closing thesis with the one that opened her paper. Her early thesis says "Gene therapy has an enormous potential for both good and evil." That suggests that she will show both sides during the paper, which she does. By the end, though, the evidence has over-whelmed her, and her thesis modifies in such a way that she is clearly on one side of the issue.

As I've said often in this book, you should recognize that as you write you will learn. Linda has experienced that firsthand during this essay. After Linda has developed and shown the field of gene therapy, she con-cludes with her opinion. What she hopes is that you will feel like she does at the end. After all, her opinion was formed from reading and considering the same research she has brought forward to you.

In a research paper you must persevere, present the information, and at the end if you think a single point or thesis can be made based on the evidence, then make it.

WORKS CITED PAGE

The Works Cited list belongs on its own page and is an essential part of research essays. Developing writers tend to miss the importance of the page, and often do a bad job of preparing it. However, a good reader will certainly look at your Works Cited when he or she wants to find more information on your field. So it needs to be in good shape, with the facts given properly and in the correct, accepted order.

Using the MLA style correctly is like speaking a foreign language properly. If you misuse the MLA, it's the same kind of error as asking a shoe salesman in South America for a nice pair of leather lace-up cats.

Here's Linda's Works Cited page, which is done expertly.

WORKS CITED

Anderson, W. French. "Gene Therapy." <u>Scientific American</u> Sept. 1995: 124-127.

Blaese, R. Michael. "Gene Therapy." <u>World Book Encyclopedia</u>. 1996 ed.

Elmer-Dewitt, Philip. "The Perils of Treading on Hered-ity." <u>Time</u> 20 Mar. 1989: 70-71.

Leo, John. "Genetic Advances, Ethical Risks." <u>US News and World Report</u> 25 Sept. 1989: 59.

Levine, Louis, "Genetic Diseases." <u>Academic American Encyclopedia</u>. 1993 ed.

Lyon, Jeff, and Peter Gorner. <u>Altered Fates: Gene Therapy and the Retooling of Human Life</u>. New York: Norton, 1995.

Miller, Henry I. "Gene Therapy for Enhancement." <u>Lancet</u> 30 July 1994: 316-317.

Miller, Jeff. "Gene Therapy: What It Is and How It Saves Lives." <u>Good Housekeeping</u> June 1993: 201-202.

Ward, Darrell E. "Gene Therapy: The Splice of Life." <u>USA Today</u> Jan. 1993: 63-66.

If you need a refresher about the style of any of those entries above, turn back a few pages to the MLA examples.

WHILE YOU'RE WRITING

■ This is an easy one. Keep track of everything. You will process more outside information on this essay than you will on any other essay all semester. It will be crucial that you have a system of keeping all your facts straight. I always suggest using a single, closable folder so that all of your material can always be in the same place. Having some notes in a notebook, some in your backpack, some written on cards, and some somewhere else, often makes it difficult to put your hands or your brain on info when it's needed.

- Get in the habit of storing all your research material—including guidelines from your instructor and this textbook, too—together at all times.

- Keep reading what you've written. A big essay is a different kind of problem from a small one. I often have research writers tell me they're surprised when they go back and look at the opening page of a long essay. That's bad. You should keep the entire process, the entire message of your essay, in mind all the time. This is a much longer piece than perhaps you've been used to, so it's a good idea to take five or ten minutes every day or so and reread what's there.

- Try to balance the duplicate jobs of writing and researching. It's not as simple as "Find books. Write paper." You'll likely find that you're doing a little of each all the way up to the last days. Many of my writers go scrambling from library to library at the end of the process looking to fill in that one critical, missing piece of information. Being well organized and beginning the process early will help alleviate such problems, but you should be prepared for the same kind of challenge.

- In fact, I think it's a good idea to research up to the end, for exactly the reason I mention above. You are learning the entire time you're writing this paper. You may not know all you want to say or cover until you're done. It also happens many times that the writer gets to the end and needs just one more fact or one more perfect quote to bring it all together. Don't sell your paper short by being satisfied with it too soon.

WORKSHOP QUESTIONS

Two workshops are mandatory for a research paper. That way, the first one can be utilized just to discuss content and the second one to discuss presentation. Here's how I break it up, with appropriate questions for each.

CONTENT WORKSHOP

- Does the writer seem fluent with the details and language of the topic? If so, give an example where he or she impressed you with strong understanding of the field. If not, give an example of where you were confused and where the writer didn't seem to know how to teach you.

■ As best as you can, reflect back to the writer what elements of the total field of his or her study seem to be the most interesting to a general reader or layperson. Your writer friend has got lots of material to work through; help him or her narrow it down.

■ If you've visually seen the essay being discussed, do you think that there are an appropriate amount of parenthetical cites? While we haven't talked too specifically about number of cites, I'd bet your instructor will give you guidelines. I usually suggest a minimum of one or two cites per page of text, although it's not unusual that a paper may have more than six on a page.

PRESENTATION WORKSHOP

■ Is there a balance of outside information and the writer's own attempts at making sense of the outside information?

■ Has the writer incorporated the quotes seamlessly into his or her own text? If so, find some especially smooth transitions. If not, find some areas where quoted sections are awkwardly introduced.

■ Is the MLA style correct? Are the parenthetical citations done correctly? Is the Works Cited page correct? Suggest needed modifications to the writer.

The Argument Essay: The Rogerian

If you've somehow arrived here without going through the extensive research paper chapter, you might want to go back and do some reading there, especially the sections that discuss documenting outside sources in MLA style. That will be imperative in this essay, and I'll assume throughout this chapter that you're familiar with those skills.

Something to think about

One of the reasons I teach writing is my experience with arguments. I've been a part of thousands of arguments in my life. Some were serious enough that there was an ambulance at the end of the night; some were so minor that no one remembered them five minutes later.

But each argument has at its base a simple fact: We don't understand each other. That's it. We don't know what the other person is thinking. We even shout out sometimes when we're arguing, "What were you thinking?" "Are you nuts?" "How could you do that? " "What was in your head?" It perplexes us when people do or say things that we don't understand.

Of course, shouting those things has never solved any of my arguments. The problem with shouting is it sends two messages: 1) We're no longer willing to listen to you; and 2) We're going to express ourselves, regardless. If that's how most arguments end, then clearly one of the main problems we face as human beings is finding a better way to react within an argument.

When I'm in an argument I'm looking for a way out, for a way to solve the problem, for a way to answer my concerns and the concerns of the person on the other side of the argument. And it doesn't take brain surgery. It just takes listening and thinking. Instead of being mad, I clear my head and start listening.

I still say, "What were you thinking?" but I say it in a nice way. What I mean is "How come you and I see this so differently? Explain your side, and then I'll explain mine."

Getting started

In any writing or communicating situation, you have a wide variety of options about audience. But in an issue or argument essay, three specific groups appear more prominently than the rest. Each of them requires a different kind of approach.

THE HIP-HIP-HOORAY ESSAY

This essay is written to someone who knows what you know and who agrees with you. This sounds like a nice group of folks, right? But as it relates to the usefulness or utility of an essay, they're a group we can't do much with.

It's fairly easy talking to someone who thinks the same as you do about the designated hitter rule, about no-smoking laws, about the President, etc. You say, "Yeah, get rid of it," and your buddy says, "Yeah, you're right!" Or, "Let's send all the smokers to an island somewhere," and your buddy says, "Yeah, forget the island, let's just dump them in the ocean!"

There isn't much to accomplish in a "hip-hip-hooray" essay. You believe something; your audience believes the same, and you mostly stand around patting each other on the back, saying "Hooray for us," or "Hip-Hip-Hooray." (I know you were waiting to find out how this essay got its name.)

So, when I think about writing an issue paper—because that's what this chapter is all about—I stay away from this audience.

THE FILL-IN-THE-BLANKS ESSAY

This is the kind of essay you must write when your audience is uninformed about the issue and therefore has no opinion.

This is a group of folks who aren't up to speed on the topic you're interested in. You walk up to them and say "We gotta get rid of the designated hitter rule," and they say, "What's that?"

It's hard to debate or discuss the issue with this group because they don't have the necessary background to be fully involved in the topic. It is certainly possible to write an essay for these folks, but it would be primarily an informational essay. By the time you explained the issue appropriately, you would have used up too much time to move on to debating the issue. In addition, it's not fair to debate an issue with someone who has just learned about the issue. There has to be some time for a newly indoctrinated reader to sort out the information and make up his or her own mind.

So for this essay, we skip this possible audience, too.

THE LET'S-MEET-THE-ENEMY ESSAY

This is the kind of essay we're going to write in this chapter. More formally we call this the Rogerian essay. The Rogerian argument style comes from the psychologist Carl Rogers. He believed, among many other things, that the essential part of speaking to someone who is opposed to you or your beliefs is to eliminate any fear or discomfort that your audience may feel. Think about that for a moment. If I'm at a cocktail party and someone says to me "Hey, that guy over there thinks you're a nut; come over and meet him," I immediately put my guard up. I'm preparing for the worst. If you think your instructor is a wonderful person, then meeting someone who proclaims right away that "Our teacher is an idiot" will put you on the defensive.

Rogers believed that the only way to communicate effectively with someone who is opposed to you and your ideas is to be reasonable and responsible, eliminating confrontation and instead stressing an open and honest communication between sides with no goal beyond allowing the opposition to understand your point of view.

Our audience in this essay is that group of people who knows the issue well but who holds a viewpoint directly opposed to ours.

I'm not eager to simply stand around with people who agree with me, nor am I eager to explain the issue to a group unfamiliar with it. When a burning issue is on my mind, I want to talk to someone who knows the issue and who can argue with me.

This is a principle we have to understand. Argument is not bad. Well, it can be if you're arguing with some bonehead who dinged your car in the parking lot. But you know I'm not using argument in that way. I'm using *argue* in the sense that means "to debate, persuade or prove." It's a means to making ideas clear. It's a way to make sense of the things you think.

Carl Rogers's ideas have been adopted by the composition field in the following ways.

Rogerian essay goals

TO AVOID CONFRONTATION

This is our first goal because it is often the key to the success or failure of your essay. What I tell my writers every semester about this essay is this: "If you can get the opposing reader all the way through the essay, then you've won. If you can't get the reader all the way through, you fail." I see it as simply as that. After all, the Rogerian philosophy stresses that our goal is to get the reader to understand us and our point of view. If the reader doesn't read our essay, or get through our ideas, how will he or she ever understand us?

So, avoiding confrontation is a key.

It's easy to think of moments in arguments or disputes when you turn your reader away. If you're talking to someone who expresses their belief to you and you respond by saying, "Oh, you're one of the pathetic, bleeding-heart liberals," how do you think that will affect the conversation? Won't your companion immediately be on guard? It's like writing an abortion essay and calling it "Baby Killers." Regardless of what you think, or what your opinion is, you must recognize that inflammatory language like that will have an explosive effect on your reader.

Once we get to that confrontational level, we stop listening to one another and instead begin hurling insults. It leads nowhere. When tension becomes too high either we separate and communication breaks down, or we escalate to some kind of physical violence.

And I'm not joking. A simple argument can lead to pushing and shoving and actual violence. That seems weird, I know. After all, it's just issues and ideas, right? And words? Well, nations have gone to war over words, and people have lost their lives.

I look at it as a serious matter. Avoiding confrontation means getting your reader through the text. Confronting or bullying your reader might work in a situation where your reader was uninformed. But our essay is going to follow the Rogerian style. The Rogerian essay is directed to an audience as knowledgeable as you. They can't be bullied.

One of the most effective and often overlooked ways to avoid confrontation is to maintain a reasonable tone in your essay. Reason is a cool word that has as a synonym: sanity. We all strive for sanity in some kind of way, so being reasonable is what we want.

Imagine you're asking your dad for a huge favor; you need to borrow his car because you want to take five friends to the mall. He says he isn't sure and then you say:

> ▶ What? Dad, you don't understand. You don't know what it's like to be a kid. If I don't take my pals to the mall, I'm going to be left out of all of their cool parties forever! No one will hang out with me. I'll be so upset that I'll start flunking classes; I'll have to live at home the rest of my life and be a failure. ◀

Sounds funny, huh? Well, my dad didn't like it much either. It's over the top. It's unreasonable. The tone is wrong. Here's another example of "reasonable tone" getting away from a person.

> ▶ You're the worst dad imaginable. A good dad would just give me the car to use on weekends. A good dad would realize how important my friends are to me. You're a communist. You're an evil autocratic dictator! Down with the dictator; power to the teenagers! ◀

Name-calling. It's surprising how often we reduce ourselves in an argument or a discussion to simple name-calling and labeling. It's not reasonable. People are people, unique, individual, and complex. We often try to label folks with terms because it makes it easier for us to understand them.

The dad in these examples is probably a pretty complex guy, a little conservative about some things and a little liberal about others. He's probably not a dictator or a communist. But the kid who's screaming because he wants the car has lost touch with reason and sanity. He's out of control, and the worst part of going out of control in an argument is what happens to the reader (or the opposition, in this essay's case). They begin reacting to the name-calling and labeling and are more than likely no longer listening to the part of our tirade that's an actual argument.

The whole point of this essay is getting the reader all the way through. In our scene above, Dad is getting out of his chair and heading down to his work room, or flipping channels on the remote, and has effectively said "I'm not listening any more; you ain't getting the car."

So, we must remain sane, keep a reasonable tone, and do our best to avoid a confrontation. How's this?

> Dad, remember my friends from the volleyball team? The five of us were so happy that we did so well at the tournament last week that we wanted to go and have fun this afternoon at the mall. We thought we'd grab some lunch at the food court, and maybe go skating. Mike's dad used to drive us last summer before any of us had our permits, but I was thinking that since I've got my license now that maybe you and I could work out a deal where I could borrow your or Mom's car once a week, maybe in return for me doing an extra chore around the house or maybe helping you when you go in to work at nights.

That's much better, and it shows a mature and reasonable attempt on the writer's part to talk to the opposition.

TO EMPATHIZE WITH THE OPPOSING VIEWPOINT

This is a hard one for some folks. I understand completely. We believe what we believe, sometimes very strongly. And we've often thought long and hard about beliefs, including those of the other side. In fact, we've already considered and rejected the other side!

But to "empathize" with your audience simply means that you are able to see their side and understand where their position comes from. You don't have to agree with them. Oftentimes, empathizing can be done simply.

▶ While I'm against smoking, I can certainly understand how smokers believe they have certain rights to their habit. ◀

Or,

▶ I would never wear fur, but I see why people from another generation may see fur not as the coat of an animal, but instead as a reward for hard work and a symbol of the good life. ◀

Neither of those two statements jeopardizes the strength of the writer's own position. In fact, his or her own belief is a central part of each of those statements. You must maintain your own position; but you must also show understanding of the opposition.

TO ESTABLISH COMMON GROUND

Establishing common ground is a critical step in the essay. Once we make it clear to our audience that we aren't going to fight, and that we understand that they hold an opposing viewpoint, we must go somewhere from there.

You must figure out what you and the audience have in common. It's a very healthy step and it allows you and your reader to talk and communicate along lines that are similar.

For example, imagine a paper about teenagers and their right to an abortion. This issue is heatedly discussed and argued all the time. One side believes that a teenage girl or a teenage couple have the right to decide if she or they want either to carry the pregnancy to term or to end the pregnancy before the birth. The other side thinks of abortion as murder, and also thinks that both a teenage girl and a teenage couple are far too young to make such an adult and important decision.

In a paper about this topic, you must ask yourself, "What do we have in common?" As the writer, the impetus is on you. The reader is out there in society waiting for you. If you're writing the essay, then you're the one making the move toward understanding; it will be up to you to come up with a reason for your reader to listen to you.

In this teenage abortion issue, what do both sides have in common? How about the fact that both sides surely care about the teens? Finding that "common ground" allows you and the reader to momentarily agree on something. That step toward understanding indicates respect and even compromise may lie ahead.

> ▶ While these two sides may seem to be miles apart, it is clear that we both value the lives and futures of the teens. They are our sons and daughters. We've raised them and loved them and cared for them. We've dreamt big dreams of college and family and kids and careers and happiness and love. None of us wants bad things to happen to our kids, and regardless of where we line up on this issue, we are rallying now, trying to do what's right for them. ◀

That's a pretty terrific paragraph, and it actually was pretty easy. Look at a simple thing like the use of the word "we." Without even mentioning what the common ground is, during the first sentence the writer has made a step toward joining forces with the opposition.

Rogerian essay parts

Now that we've established some of the goals of this very important essay type, let's look at some actual parts or sections of the Rogerian essay.

These parts do not necessarily have to appear in your essay in this order. Don't follow this strictly as an outline. These are essential items that should exist somewhere inside your Rogerian paper. The sequence as I give it here happens to be one of several successful ways of arranging the material. You will need to decide in what order you present your information.

MINDSET PARAGRAPH

As with any good essay, you must set the piece up. In this case, you try to create an introduction for the paper that will make clear the issue to be discussed. You should not start with your position, however, since opposition readers may simply ignore the issue and stop reading once they find you disagree with them. You won't even get the chance to talk to them before they tune out. You don't want to take that chance. It is sufficient and reasonable to write this paragraph creating the mindset of the issue at hand.

> ▶ The battle over gun laws in this country has raged for years, especially feverishly in the past two decades, as pro-gun and anti-gun political lobbies have poured millions of dollars into advertising campaigns and political elections, looking for an edge. ◀

The paragraph accurately identifies the issue to be discussed, but the writer is also careful simply to raise the issue and not attempt to take a stand on it. It's too early for that. It's an excellent opening.

POSITION

Any good position paper, however, needs a position, and despite the fact that we want to remain reasonable and keep our readers involved, I would not ask you to weaken or dilute or hide your opinion. You do, however, have to express it reasonably. I call this part of the essay your chance to "come clean." If someone asks me about gun laws, I know at some point that after I give my opinion, that person is going to give theirs, too. We all have to come clean at some point and reveal what we think. In this paper I would like you to make your position clear fairly soon. Not in the first paragraph but perhaps by the end of the second, as in our continuing example.

> ▶ As the battle over gun law rages, I find myself wondering about guns. Do I want one in my house? Do I want my neighbor to have one? Would I feel safer if I had one? Do I feel safer to know that my neighbor has his in a shoebox beneath his bed? Do I feel safer knowing that I could buy one if I wanted to? Do I feel safer knowing that anyone with a driver's license can walk into any pawn shop or gun shop in this city and buy a gun and bullets? I decide that I don't feel comfortable. I don't want my neighbor to be armed, or myself, or any kid who wants to have a weapon of his own. I think our nation's gun laws need to be strengthened, and that we must begin doing something about getting guns off the streets. ◀

That's a pretty powerfully stated position, but done in a reasonable, nonconfrontational way. Now, of course you recognize that some readers may check out of the paper right there. You know that some folks are unreasonable and no amount of preparation or size of mindset paragraph will keep these readers listening once the writer has come clean. But, we try to write and compose using what I call the "reasonable reader" rule.

There's not much I can do when my Boston Terrier named Tucker decides he wants to play with his ball in the backyard. I can tell him it's 4 AM. I can show him how dark it is and I can explain how tired I am. But what I always remember is that when it comes to his ball, Tucker is NOT reasonable. So, he gets to play.

And what about the unreasonable reader? Well, he or she gets to leave the essay at any time. We try to reach that reader with a good opening paragraph. If we lose them, we lose them.

OPPOSING ARGUMENT

When someone starts telling me their opinion about something, I'm usually gearing up for my turn. It's fairly easy in a conversation to do this because there's a natural give and take to a conversation. When someone takes a breath, we can always jump in and say "Yes, but, don't you see . . ." In an essay, the reader doesn't have that same chance. The essay is an unstoppable one-way bit of communication. The writer writes and continues to write and writes some more. The reader may object and/or want to interject an idea, but he or she can only keep reading or quit reading. If the reader decides to quit, we lose, remember?

So, what do we do in this case? Well, we give the reader his or her chance to talk by giving some portion of the paper to the opposing point of view. You can see how imperative it is that you "know" your reader fairly well. Look and see how it works in the following paragraph.

> ▶ But of course there are many reasonable folks who disagree with me. I know this because I know some. My own brother lives peacefully and happily two miles away from me. You would not know it from a visit to his house, but he has a loaded .357 pistol that he keeps on a high shelf in his bedroom. He's a wonderful man, a great husband, a great father to his two little girls. But he wants protection. He doesn't wave his gun around at parties; he's no threat to the neighbors or others, but he believes in protecting his house and his family with whatever means the law allows him. I love my brother. He would use that gun to save his life, his wife's, his kids', and even mine. ◀

That's a pretty good way to deal with the opposition. In our sample essay, the writer is able to prove fairly easily that he understands the opposing point of view. That is key in the Rogerian essay. We must earn the trust and the goodwill of the opposition in this way because, after all, our goal for the paper is for them to listen to us and understand our position. How better to attain that than by showing them the same respect?

You don't have to have a family member who believes the opposite of you—that was just a happy coincidence for the writer above—but it does help to be able to identify with someone who is opposed to you. It shows you being reasonable.

REFUTATION

The refutation is a unique part of the Rogerian essay. There are elements like it in other kinds of writing, but it is special to the issue paper. To refute means to rebut or disprove, to contradict. Offering a refutation of the opposite case or argument is an essential part of your ability to succeed in this essay.

After offering the opposing point of view, your audience should be thinking "Yes, this writer understands why I believe it's appropriate for me to own a gun and possess it legally for protection." You've shown your ability to be reasonable, and the goodwill you've earned for that will allow you the opportunity to begin making your own case, making your own point.

Think of a refutation paragraph as a delivery on an earlier promise. Earlier you indicated that you were against gun ownership (this happens in our example in the second paragraph). Shortly after that announcement—after you came clean—you began to show the opposition's point of view. Now it is time to assert yourself. Here's how refutation works.

> ▷ . . . I love my brother. He would use that gun to save his life, his wife's, his kids', and even mine.
> But, my brother thinks his gun is safe. He's careful, of course. But so are other people. So was Dominique Marcelle, of Detroit, Michigan. Her gun was kept out of reach of her two little boys, Joshua and Kevin. Out of reach until Joshua and Kevin stacked phone books on a chair and pulled the gun down one afternoon last year (Dalrymple 12A). When Mrs. Marcelle got home, her son Joshua was already dead, killed accidentally by his own 5-year-old brother. ◁

The refutation starts with the word "But." The writer is now returning to his position and its support.

> ▷ "I loved my boys," she said. "I never wanted them to get hurt" (Dalrymple 12A).
> Gun owners know the dangers, yet keep the dangerous weapons in their own homes, sometimes hidden, sometimes under lock and key. But what do we do about Mrs. Marcelle. Or Earl Thompson of Binghampton, New York, who was killed by his own gun one afternoon after his 9-year-old son unlocked a locked cabinet that held the gun, brought it to his dad, muzzle first, then pulled the trigger, playing ("Safe in Our Homes?" 9). ◁

In both of these paragraphs we see outside sources added to help make the writer's point. Supporting your ideas with the ideas of other writers is always good; it's like bringing along a couple of extra friends to a bar fight.

COMPROMISE

This is an optional part of the Rogerian essay. Some writers become eager to offer compromise, so great is their desire to help end the confusion and bitterness that often divides people on an issue. Others reject the notion, preferring to stand firm in their convictions.

I don't think either one is necessarily right or wrong, although I do tend to urge writers to go for compromise. In one way, I believe it's the most you can ask for in a hotly debated issue. Remember who you're writing to. This is a group of people who are knowledgeable about the issue at hand. These aren't people who will be swayed into changing their entire belief system by a handful of pages you're writing.

Compromise is a reasonable and mature solution in an unwinnable situation. Let's look at an example.

> The two sides of the gun law issue are not likely to resolve their differences easily. Our positions are strong and well supported. However, the needless accidental deaths that occur every year, oftentimes the deaths of our own children and loved ones, must be taken into consideration. Safe placement of a gun in the home is not so easy to achieve when children are as inquisitive as they are. One gun magazine suggests storing the gun and its bullets in two separate and locked places in the home (Tolson 121). A gun advocate suggests mandatory "child-proof" safeties on all guns kept in homes with children. While not an answer to all the problems, these compromises would show an understanding between the two sides.
>
> My two beautiful nieces sleep every night in a home with a gun. Every Christmas they turn that house upside down looking for gifts and red ribbon and boxes and bows. I pray they never find a box not meant for them. I pray they never find my brother's gun. ◄

There are two very good items in place in this closing. First, as we've just discussed, we have compromises raised. In this case they are: 1) keep guns and ammunition in separate places, and 2) add suggested "child-proof" safeties on guns kept in the home. When offering compromises you have to decide how many you think the reader will be willing to listen to. Some readers may not listen to any, of course, but in this case the writer feels comfortable.

And because the topic is a very personal and powerful one for the writer, he is prepared to make an "emotional appeal" to the reader. He reveals his concern for the children in a house with guns, and obviously that's a "common ground" he and the reader share.

Whenever you can express "common ground," do it. In this closing paragraph, it strengthens the argument.

Warmups

■ For your first warmup I want you to become more aware of how you talk to people and solve little disputes. Even if it's just explaining to the guy at Arby's that you actually ordered curly fries instead of potato wedges, pay attention. Observing and listening to how you deal with disputes and arguments will give you an idea of why you are or aren't successful in those kinds of situations. Chances are if you often get your way you have some of those Rogerian elements going for you.

Once you find yourself in an argument or a conversation with another person, where you're on one side and he or she is on the other, pay attention and later write it down. Write a couple of paragraphs and try to make sense of how you argued and if you did it well. Some likely sources of an argument are

- a roommate
- a teacher
- a friend
- a parent

For each of the positions below, write two paragraphs. The first paragraph should be a mindset paragraph, that all-important paragraph that raises the issue. You already know that in this essay the mindset paragraph must be free of your position. The second paragraph you write should be the paragraph that contains the thesis. Remember to state it reasonably so that it will be considered carefully by the reader. If your reader rejects you at this point, you will never have the chance to move further into an essay.

- Convicted murderers on death row should not—under any condition—be given the death penalty.
- Young women between the ages of 13 and 18 should be able to obtain a legal and safe abortion without needing parental consent.
- The private and recreational use of marijuana, cocaine, and amphetamines should be legalized.
- Private individuals should have no rights to own and keep guns in their home.

One of the reasons I like this list of topics is that they all make good subjects for the Rogerian essay. Because these are highly contentious issues, they might be much more difficult to stay reasonable with than other issues of students' choosing. So, be forewarned. If you're feeling exceedingly brave, and if these topics are of interest, then try one of them out.

The essay assignment

Write about an issue that is important to you. Direct the essay at an audience who holds the directly opposing view—called the Rogerian audience. You should assume that your audience is as knowledgeable as you about the subject, but of course you can also assume that your audience is less knowledgeable about your side of the issue. Use the guidelines of the Rogerian argument to guide you as you go, keeping in mind that the goal of this paper is to keep your reader interested and reading until the end. Your purpose is not to sway the opinion of your reader; that task is likely outside our time and length constraints. Keep in mind the goals and the parts of the Rogerian essay.

Sample essays

Here are some sample Rogerian essays. As always, read with the idea that you are attempting to learn how these essays work, but also that you are looking for ways to do your own work, and ways in which you would help this writer fix his or her essay. In our first one I'll jump in from time to time to show you some essential Rogerian essay features.

PORNOGRAPHY—PLEASURE OR PERVERSION?

The question of the relationship of pornography to violent crime has been debated for many years. Sensational news stories such as the Ted Bundy and Jeffrey Dahmer cases have kept the issue in the public eye. These cases have more than likely led some people to believe that adult material poses a very real threat to society, and many contend that making it illegal would prevent future occurrences. These people view pornography as an invasion of society, and believe that it leads to violent crime, especially against women (Gorman 26). Currently, citizens have the right to purchase, read, or view adult material; they also retain the right to boycott or object to it.

Is this an appropriate first paragraph? What I mean is, do you think it's a sufficient mindset paragraph? Is it too abrupt? Based on ideas already in the paragraph, what kind of story or case history could the writer retell to get us thinking about the issue?

The topic of pornography is a sensitive and emotional one. When polled, many people would claim to harbor negative feelings on the subject for fear of appearing socially incorrect. Some people find it distasteful and, because they do not understand how anyone can find it helpful or intriguing, they condemn it. Many people believe that if you are not against it, you must be for it (Eve 1). In the past few years, social science research and opinions rendered in courts of law suggest that although adult material may have some negative effects, they are not as common or heinous as commonly believed. For lack of a better reason or defense, it is often used as justification for violent crimes. While it would be ludicrous to suggest that adult material has never played a part in violent crime, harm has also resulted from alcohol, religion, patriotism and even brand name sneakers and clothing; yet, as research author G. L. Simons points out, these causes have not compelled people to demand abolition (197). These cases have been dealt with by creating a set of legal guidelines tailored specifically for each.

Remember that this essay is written to the opposition. Are you at this point clear about the writer's point of view? If so, when does the writer's position become clear? If not, where should she make a more clear claim?

Most modern scientific research suggests that adult material actually plays little direct role in sex crimes. Many rapists or perpetrators of violent crimes come from sexually repressed backgrounds in which there was little or no discussion of sex, and sex was generally believed to be sinful (Eve 2). Scientists have created the phrase "spurious correlations" to describe cases in which two phenomena are statistically associated but are not causally connected. For example, "It may be true that more storks appear in Sweden in the spring, and it may also be true that the birthrate goes up in the spring, but it does not causally follow that storks bring babies" (Eve 1).

So far, we've seen the writer use a number of interesting quotes from Eve. What do you think of our writer's use of sources? Have they been effective? Have they been used to support an idea the writer has forwarded? Do you have any concerns that Eve is the only source shown so far?

Some would make the claim that pornography is a threat to society because of the actions it may provoke. When judged by certain moral guidelines, the claim that porn is wrong actually can be substantiated by the belief that, since pornography is representative of sex, and since sex for any reason other than procreation is immoral, so then is pornography immoral. This commonly stated claim supports the causal effects of pornography. According to an interpretation of social scientific data, if the use of adult material causes people to commit crimes or to exhibit other socially unacceptable behaviors, then this material is considered a threat to society

continued ▶

because of its causal effects. In order to identify pornography as the cause of a violent crime, though, all other possibilities must first be ruled out.

I'd suggest that this paragraph contains the writer's attempt at discussing the opposition's viewpoint. Can you in one sentence state what our writer thinks the opposition believes? Has the writer been fair in her attempt? Do you think the opposition in this paper (the reader) would continue past this paragraph? Why or why not?

There are several characteristics of pornography that can generally be accepted as a given. First, adult material is sexually explicit. Second, it is intended to arouse. Third, it is available for sale to the general public. Several arguments can be made to support the continuation of legalized pornography. One—people enjoy it and derive pleasure from it. Two—the availability of adult materials may actually aid in normal sexual development when the usual social or educational situations are absent. And three—it has the ability to serve as a substitute for actual sexual activity; whether as an outlet for lonely or deprived people or for the enhancement of a couple's sexual relationship. Sex therapists commonly use adult materials as a tool for overcoming negative attitudes toward sexual desire and pleasure. A major function of such therapy is not to teach erotic skills, but to give patients "permission" to enjoy sex; even married people have been unable to overcome their learned attitude that sexual desire and pleasure are morally bad (Christensen 107). Many married couples will find that their sex lives become routine or boring after a period of time. After incorporating films, books, magazines, etc. into their private lives, often they find their sex lives enhanced appreciably. "Before turning to erotica, these couples made love infrequently, found it either boring or unexciting and realized that much of their sexual desire was directed at people other than their partners. But, they did not want to have affairs. Rather, they preferred to rekindle passion for their own spouse" (Zilbergeld 87). Circumstances brought on by varying reasons (travel, illness, death of a partner) may lead a person to accept adult material as an interim substitute. It can allow a person to express repressed or unsatisfied sexual desires without endangering one's health or welfare (Simons 199).

Here's where our writer is attempting to provide a number of different supports for the continued availability of pornography. I think the paragraph might be a little dense and too complex. Could you make an outline of this paragraph, drawing out what you think the main ideas are? You should be able to come up with multiple statements that the writer makes and supports. What I'm hoping you'll come up with will be a list.

A study of the number of adult bookstores across the country showed no correlation with the reported rates of violent sex crimes. Those areas with a higher concentration of adult bookstores, video stores or theaters did not show higher incidents of violent sex crimes (Scott 132).

Where does this paragraph belong? Hint: It doesn't belong here. Tell me where it should be, or if it should be in the essay at all.

Much more could be and should be said in the defense of adult material. The issue of pornography raises questions about human sexuality, morality, and our legal rights as a free society. It is important that people gather information from both sides of the issue and consider all aspects of the issue, whether they are moral, legal, or religious aspects. Perhaps then we can agree on how the issue of pornography should be resolved, and turn our collective attention to other, more serious social issues.

One of the steps in the Rogerian essay is to come to some sort of compromise between the sides. Do you think this paragraph does that? If so, what is the compromise? If there is no compromise here yet, do you think the paper needs one? I'll suggest that I think the paper ends rather quickly, without a full conclusion. I'd like you to rewrite this entire paragraph, using most of what's already there, but including some other things you think might be relevant or useful.

WORKS CITED

Carter, D. L., et al. "Use of Pornography in the Criminal and Developmental Histories of Sexual Offenders" Report to the National Institutes of Mental Health, 1985.

Christensen, F. M. Pornography--The Other Side. New York: Praeger, 1990.

Eve, Ray. Personal Communication. 1 Mar. 1981.

Gorman, Carol. Pornography. New York: Franklin Watts, 1988.

Gosselin, Chris, and Glenn Wilson. Sexual Variations. New York: Simon and Schuster, 1980.

Hawkins, Gordon, and Franklin Zimring. Pornography in a Free Society. New York: U. of Cambridge P, 1988.

continued ▶

Simons, G. L. <u>Pornography Without Prejudice</u>. New York: Abelard-Schuman, 1972.

Scott, Joseph E. Report on "Violence and Erotic Material--The Relationship between Adult Entertainment and Rape." Los Angeles: American Association for the Advancement of Science, 1985.

Zilbergeld, Dr. Bernie. <u>Taking Sides: Clashing Views on Controversial Issues in Human Sexuality</u>. Hartford, CT: Dushkin, 1991.

Another sample essay

I'll leave you alone on this one. Read it carefully and get prepared to answer questions at the end that will ask you about its appropriateness as a Rogerian essay.

HUNTERS VS. NON-HUNTERS

It is safe to say that thousands of people go camping as a retreat or vacation at some point in their lives. It is also safe to say that these people go out into the wilderness to get away from the drudgery of the city. They go to commune with nature, enjoy the beauty and tranquillity of lakes and views offered by the outdoors. They relax with their families and loved ones while appreciating the solitude around them. While these people are taking in the sunshine and beauty around them they do not have to worry about getting shot or being hunted . . . animals do.

Until the beginning of the twentieth century, the United States was predominantly a rural society. Hunting was a deeply ingrained tradition in the towns and farms where most people lived, places where hunters hunted to put meat on the family table. Today, in contrast, the United States is overwhelmingly urban, and relatively few Americans know much about hunting.

Some people oppose hunting because it endangers hunters and non-hunters alike. According to the National Safety Council, 138 people died in firearm-related hunting accidents in 1989, the last year for which complete data is available (Petzal and Tanenbaum 14). In a widely publicized incident in Maine on Nov. 15, 1988, Karen Wood, the mother of twin girls, was fatally shot in her chest by a deer hunter. The tragedy initially attracted attention because it had occurred while Wood was standing in her own back yard in a suburb of Bangor. Interest was rekindled when a grand jury declined to indict the hunter for manslaughter. However, a second panel indicted him, and he went to trial in October 1990. He was found not guilty. The verdict seemed to show that hunters receive the benefit of the doubt in areas where the hunting ethic is well established (Reiger 8).

Animal-rights groups oppose hunting from what they describe as the philosophical/ethical position that animals have inherent legal and individual rights, just as humans do. According to this viewpoint, humans do not have the right to use any animals for any reason, including research, recreation and food—or sport hunting. This belief is not embraced by all anti-hunting activists, however. Luke A. Dommer, chairman of the Committee to Abolish Hunting (CASH), describes his organization as "a nature-preservation group dedicated to the preservation of biological diversity. We feel that hunting as it stands now and the management of wildlife for that purpose contribute to the loss of biological diversity. And on top of that, we don't believe in recreational killing" (Atwill 46). Echoing an argument often made by supporters of hunting, Dommer says animal-rights activists often display a lack of knowledge about how nature works. "We have to come to grips with the reality that all life on Earth subsists on other life, from the highest to the lowest forms," he says. "That's the way it has always been. But we as human beings have the capacity to eliminate as much unnecessary suffering and unnecessary killing [of animals] as we possibly can" (Atwill 46).

In defense of hunters, *Field & Stream* Executive Editor David E. Petzal wrote last spring that ethical sport hunters should confront the "slob hunter" problem head-on. "As we come under increasing attack," Petzal wrote, "we can deny until we are blue in the face that . . . yahoos who chase game in pickups" and shoot in the direction of sounds they hear in the woods are not truly hunters. "But in the court of public opinion where our case is being tried, they are and we stand accountable for them." Petzal goes on to say hunters have an obligation, to see to it that everyone that kills animals for sport possesses a basic set of skills, including the ability to track wounded game. Failure to adopt a skills testing program, which would be funded by the hunters themselves, could lead to the demise of sport hunting (Reiger 16).

Hunters are trying to enhance their image among non-hunters by helping to shape legislation to promote hunter ethics and competency. This

continued ▶

approach bore fruit last year with the passage of New Jersey's Sportsman's Responsibility Bill. The measure requires game-law violators to pay the state for the loss of wildlife ($200 per deer, for instance, plus possible criminal penalties). The law also makes hunters responsible for the careless handling of a weapon, regardless of whether it caused any damage, mandates the loss of a hunting license for two years for repeat violations; and requires game-law violators to take a remedial hunter-education course (Reynolds 56).

A more difficult task, hunters have found, is showing non-hunters the positive aspects of stalking game for sport. Hunters and many wildlife biologists say, for example, that hunting prevents the abundant whitetail deer from multiplying beyond the capacity of its habitat to sustain the species. Some experts think that without hunting the whitetail population might even "crash," transforming a robust wildlife species into a threatened or endangered one. In the like manner, hunters argue that hunting and trapping of predators is sometimes justified to protect other wild creatures. In addition, in some parts of the country where there has been a deer explosion, deer have caused a serious safety hazard. The National Safety Council estimates that motor vehicles nationwide kill more than 350,000 deer—and about 100 drivers and passengers—each year (Pattison 8).

There is one form of hunting, however, that supporters and opponents of the sport condemn with almost equal fervor: "canned" hunts of animals that are released into small enclosures to be gunned down by trophy hunters. Prices are pegged to the rarity of species, many of them are not native to North America, among them are exotic "big cats" obtained from breeders, dealers, and zoos.

The argument between hunters and non-hunters has been going on for decades. I feel the only way to ease the tensions between the two would be for them to join forces and work towards a common goal of compromise and understanding. If two such influential powers were to merge, and a common goal was in sight, half the battle would be won.

WORKS CITED

Atwill, L. "Anti-Hunting 101." Field & Stream 17 August 1991: 46.

Pattison, S. "When Animal-Rightists Have Their Way." Consumer Alert March/April 1995: 10-11.

Petzal, D. E., and Tanenbaum, R. "One of Us." Field & Stream 30 May 1991: 14.

Reiger, G. "The Untold Story." Field & Stream 25 June
    1994: 16.

---. "Our Achilles' Heel," Field & Stream 24 January
    1992: 8.

Reynolds, J. "Sportsman's Responsibility Bill." Field &
    Stream 14 February 1991: 56.

QUESTIONS

1. Has the writer met the main goals of the Rogerian essay: avoiding confrontation, empathizing with the opposing viewpoint, and establishing common ground? Find elements in the paper that prove or disprove each of these elements. If the writer has done a good job of empathizing, show me where that happens exactly. If you think the writer has offended the reader through name-calling or labeling, show me where she goes wrong *and* what could be done differently.

2. I think there's a problem with how quickly the essay starts. I believe that the shocking and abrupt closing line of paragraph 1 might turn her readers (the opposition) off. I'd like you to rework the first paragraph so that the closing line (which is good) comes after a bit more of a setup. (You won't have to write anything new; use some text from elsewhere in the essay.)

A "working" sample essay

Let's use our last sample as a bit of a teaching model or quiz. I've boldfaced a number of different sentences and put a number next to them. Your job is to go through the essay and match the numbered sentence with one of the Rogerian essay elements I've listed below.

- Refutation
- The opposition's position
- Thesis or position
- Mindset
- Compromise

Tell me what each numbered sentence or section is doing. If I bold-face something that is the thesis, then that's your answer. If I boldface the compromise, tell me that. There's a word or sentence match for each of the five items listed above.

GETTING STRICT ON THE UNINSURED DRIVER

Imagine that you are driving your car to pick up a friend.[1] You have your night all planned out and it's going to be the best night ever. You're in a great mood because you just figured that next week's paycheck will buy a new computer. You pull up to a stoplight and turn the radio up as your favorite song comes on. The light turns green, and you pull into the intersection.

The next thing you know, a car appears and slams into you; you're facing the way you just came, your head and neck hurt badly, and you can see that the whole front side of the car is totaled. The next day you get back from the doctor's office diagnosed with a concussion and whiplash, and you know you'll never see your car again. The only comforting thought is that the other guy's insurance will take care of it all.

Only hours later do you find out that the man that ran the red light and smashed into you has no insurance as well as a fake driver's license. Because this guy decided that the law does not apply to him, you are now in serious pain, thousands of dollars out, and you can't work for the next week. There goes that computer. This is what happened to my brother and is happening to many people all over the country. Uninsured drivers are costing honest Americans billions of dollars and, in many cases, hundreds of human lives.

An epidemic of uninsured drivers is sweeping across the nation leaving insured drivers with higher premiums. Jerry Sinclair of Nationwide Insurance says their records show that in 1990 an average of two out of ten drivers that were involved in accidents with their clients were not insured. Five years later the number has risen to almost five out of every ten drivers (Sinclair). "It's terrible," Sinclair says. "People get hit right and left and now you can't even be sure if the responsible party can finance the pain and suffering they've caused." This has become especially bad in major cities such as Dallas, New York, Los Angeles as well as many others. Already it is illegal to drive without car insurance, but judging by the increasing number of uninsured drivers, obviously the methods of prevention and correction aren't effective enough (Harper). Should the penalty be raised to stricter measures to keep uninsured motorists from driving? **I believe that laws should be enacted to withhold the privilege of a driver's license, as well as owning a car, from anyone that does not have car insurance.**[2]

Many people argue that the laws should not be too strict because insurance payments are too high for some drivers to afford.[3] For example, a seventeen-year-old boy with insurance covering only the bare minimum required by law and only drives occasionally, must pay at least $1,400 a year (Sinclair). Also, those with bad driving records can even be denied coverage by most reputable insurance companies. **However,**[4] the high prices of insurance premiums usually arise because of all the uninsured drivers. Insurance companies must make up for the money lost in cases when an uninsured driver cannot pay any damages that they had incurred. The same goes with bad drivers. As the old saying goes, "We are only as strong as our weakest link." Many good drivers are paying for the country's "weak links," which in turn raises the insurance premiums for everyone, making us all weak links.

Everyone agrees that a person's driver's license should be suspended and even taken away after so many instances. Many states work on the "three strikes and you're out" plan. Still, many people foolishly continue to drive without a license or insurance and end up putting others at risk, such as my brother. The victims are always the insured drivers. The uninsured usually get off with a ticket while the insured become thousands of dollars in debt. Mandatory imprisonment should be applied to drivers caught without insurance, even if it is the first offense. In the more severe cases, such as the uninsured causing a major accident, the state and local government should consider repossessing the uninsured's car. The state of Texas defines a license to drive as ". . . a privilege and not a right" in the state's driver's manual. Therefore, owning a car for the sole purpose of driving is also a privilege and not a right. These privileges are freedoms, and with every freedom comes responsibility. If a person cannot responsibly hold this privilege, such as obtaining insurance and maintaining a good driving record, they must pay the strictest price possible. Anyone who owns a pet knows they must feed, bathe, and clean up after them. If they don't, the pet will die or possibly be taken away. If someone cannot maintain the responsibility of obtaining insurance, they must have their privilege to drive taken away. **The government should be able to repossess the uninsured's car and auction it off to compensate the insured driver's finances caused by the uninsured driver.**[5] My brother's suffering would have been greatly lessened had this plan been enacted to protect law-abiding insured drivers.

WORKS CITED

Harper, William. "Citizens Against Outrageous Car Insurance Practices." 1 Sept. 1996. Online posting. Newsgroup alt.insurance. Usenet. 30 Oct. 1996.

Sinclair, Jerry. Telephone interview. 1 Nov. 1996.

State of Texas. Department of Motor Vehicles. <u>Texas Driver's Manual</u>. Austin: GPO, 1992.

WHILE YOU'RE WRITING

While the essay is in progress, seek help from other writers, your instructor, and other readers whose opinion you trust. These are some of the ideas you should be considering.

- Start early finding your point of view on issues that matter. Reject the notion that many developing writers have of picking an "established" or "big" issue such as abortion or drunk driving or gun control. It's perfectly fine if those issues interest you, if they are topics you have real insight into. But if you're just picking them because you think that's what a reader wants, then forget it. The neat thing about this essay—like some of the others—is that as long as you can imagine one reader out there, then you've got yourself an audience. The things that you feel passionate about are likely to inspire strong feelings in others as well.

- Issues can be as big as the planet, or as small as your house. Too many writers focus on global issues when in fact issues that are the most pressing on us are usually from our personal life: family, job, school, and so on. Often, writing about issues and ideas close to our lives results in our being as writers more dedicated to the project. (After all, we like talking and thinking about ourselves, right?)

- Once you get a topic and begin work, do your best to seek out folks who disagree with your position. You need to be familiar with their thoughts and ideas and beliefs. Writing the paper without knowing your opposition will likely work against you; you won't be able to show the reader any real empathy for their viewpoint if you don't know what it is.

- Make sure you go in search of outside sources to help your paper. But don't simply rely on sources to support your view. Sometimes it's easier to find sources that support the opposition. That way the opposition has an actual "expert" supporting their point of view.

In fact, your reader may feel more comfortable with that arrangement than with you trying to pronounce their views for them.

- Think long and hard about including a compromise. While it's not a mandatory part of this essay, I believe it can be a rather mature choice. If you find one that you really can live with, it's an excellent idea to offer it.

WORKSHOP QUESTIONS

- Your biggest responsibility in reading this essay is, of course, to represent the opposition as it's described in the paper. You must do your best to put yourself in the shoes of the opposing side of this argument so you can give feedback as accurately as possible. What your writer needs most is the assurance that he or she can get you to read all the ways through the paper. So as you study the essay, listening to it or reading it, you must always be aware of what an opposition reader might do. If you become offended at anything, a word choice, a generalization, a falsely attributed belief, you must let the writer know.
- Do you think the writer is genuine or sincere in how he or she presents the issue in the mindset paragraph?
- Are you turned off by any language, labeling, or name-calling?
- Has the writer correctly and honestly offered up the opposition argument so you feel comfortable?
- Has the writer in some way established common ground with you? That is, do you feel like the two sides of the issue share some common beliefs and concerns?
- Are you willing to read the whole paper?
- By paper's end do you have a clear understanding of why the writer feels the way he or she does?
- By the end of the paper, are you inclined to agree to or take part in some compromise position with the writer? Why or why not?

A brief argument reader

Argument papers need an issue to spring from. You need to argue with someone about something. Many developing writers, in fact, tell me as they start this chapter, "Oh, I don't know any issues. I've got nothing to write about." But, if I ask them about smoking in public places, or ask them how they feel about 5 percent of their tuition going to pay for the new faculty parking lot, suddenly they're interested. Now they've got something to argue about.

So this very brief section of essays is designed to offer you a few ideas or issues to bounce up against. Maybe you'll agree with these writers, or disagree, but chances are one or all of them will make you want to say something.

MAKING THE CASE FOR SMOKERS' RIGHTS

BY ROBERT SAMUELSON

The media are deeply sensitive to the rights of "minorities": the poor, the disabled, blacks, gays, and immigrants, among others. But there is one minority much larger than any of these (at least 25 percent of the population) whose rights we deny or ignore: smokers. The debate over cigarettes has been framed as if smokers are the unwitting victims of the tobacco industry. They lack free will and, therefore, their apparent desires and interests don't count. They are to be pitied and saved, not respected.

This is pack journalism run amok. We media types fancy ourselves independent thinkers. Just the opposite is often true: We're patsies for the latest crusade or fad. In this case, the major media have adopted the view of the public health community, which sees smoking as a scourge to be eradicated. The "story" is the crusade; the villain is the tobacco industry. Lost are issues that ought to inform this debate.

The simplest is whether, in trying to make Americans better off, the anti-smoking crusade would make many Americans worse off. Smokers would clearly suffer from huge price and tax increases. The cost of the $368 billion agreement between the tobacco industry and the state attorneys general is estimated at 62 cents a pack. President Clinton suggests raising that to $1.50 a pack—about six times today's federal tax (24 cents). The cost would hit the poor hardest. They smoke more than the rich.

Consider. About half (53 percent) of today's cigarette tax is paid by taxpayers with incomes of less than $30,000, estimates the congressional Joint Committee on Taxation. Higher prices will deter some people from smoking. But for the rest, would siphoning billions away from poorer people be good policy? Or fair?

The anti-smoking crusaders try to seem fair by arguing three things: 1) There's growing smoking among teenagers who, once they try cigarettes, may become addicted for life; 2) tobacco ads cause much teen smoking—

teens are, therefore, victims; and 3) passive smoking (the inhaling of smoke smoke by non-smokers) in public places is a serious health threat, justifying action against smokers. These assumptions also permeate media coverage, but the first two are open to question and the third is untrue.

Start with teen smoking. One survey from the University of Michigan does show a rise. In 1996, 34 percent of 12th-graders reported smoking in the past month—the highest since 1979 (34.4 percent). But the government's survey on drug abuse reports the opposite: In 1996, only 18.3 percent of teens between 12 and 17 had smoked in the past month, the lowest since 1985 (29 percent). It's hard to know which survey to believe, but neither depicts runaway teen smoking.

As for ads, teens do a lot of dangerous things (drugs, early sex) that aren't advertised and are often illegal. The tobacco industry no doubt targets teens; but the ads may affect brand choices more than the decision to smoke. A new, comprehensive study—financed by the National Institutes of Health—suggests that teens' home environment is more important in determining who smokes.

"Children who report feeling connected to a parent are protected against many different kinds of health risks including . . . cigarette, alcohol and marijuana use," it says.

And even teens who smoke do not necessarily become lifetime smokers. Among 12th-graders, about twice as many (63 percent) once smoked as currently smoke. The "addiction" isn't so great that millions haven't broken it.

Finally, passive smoking isn't a big public health risk, as many stories imply. The latest example of misreporting involved a study from the Harvard Medical School. It purported to show that passive smoking doubled the risk of heart attacks, indicating a huge public health problem. That's how both the *New York Times* and *Washington Post* reported it. In fact, the study—at most—showed that passive smoking doubles a very tiny risk.

Here's why. The study followed 32,046 non-smoking nurses between 1982 and 1992. Of these, four-fifths said they were exposed to passive smoking. But there were only 152 heart attacks (127 non-fatal) among all the nurses: a small number. Many heart attacks would have occurred even if no one were exposed to smoke. And most exposure to passive smoke is now private or voluntary, because public smoking has been barred in so many places. Will we outlaw husbands smoking in front of their wives—or vice versa?

You don't hear much of this, because the press has an anti-smoking bias. The crusaders do have a case. Smoking is highly risky for smokers. But lots of things are risky, and do smokers have a right to engage in behavior whose pleasures and pains are mainly theirs without being punished by the rest of society?

continued ▶

There is almost no one to make smokers' case. They have been abandoned by the tobacco industry, politicians and the press. Do smokers have rights? Apparently not.

QUESTIONS

1. In your class, or with a group of friends, divide up into smokers and nonsmokers. Raise the idea that Samuelson has that there is an anti-smoking bias in the press. Is that true? Are there anti-smoking biases elsewhere?

2. Samuelson's article has a certain tone. It's a little informal, and certainly a bit "cocky." Is it possible that readers could be put off by this? Where would an opposing reader be most likely to feel angered or upset?

SAFE SEX AND THE SINGLES CLUB

BY ELLEN GOODMAN

There is a new club in West Bloomfield, Michigan. You might call it a health club although it doesn't offer barbells, treadmills or aerobics classes. All it promises is a membership that is AIDS-free. They call the club Peace of Mind.

There is a new dating service in Manhattan. They don't check your pedigree or your credit rating. What they insist on is an AIDS test. It is named the Ampersand Singles Club.

There is another dating service in Vermont that demands tests, and a fourth in Massachusetts, and I'm sure a fifth, sixth, sixteenth. What they give members in return for a hefty fee is admission to a population of the certifiably clean, people who carry a card symbolic of their status in the dating world: AIDS-free status.

This is what's happening in the second phase of the AIDS epidemic. The hottest item in the marketplace of supply and demand these days is safe sex. So, a new breed of anxiety entrepreneurs have come out hustling and a new breed of the anxious are buying.

Just a few years ago, the people looking for love developed their own code in the personal ads. SWM for single white male, DF for divorced female. Now, the most desirable credentials are AF, AIDS-free. They are in pursuit of guaranteed certified safety.

It's part of the same anxious pattern that has escalated along with the numbers of people infected with the virus. Early in the AIDS epidemic, there was serious debate about quarantining carriers. Today the healthy want to quarantine themselves. And among them are those who want, as one entrepreneur put it, "romance without risk." The want, in effect, to save the sexual revolution in its 1970s form.

But sex just doesn't come carefree anymore. A few weeks ago, in a conversation in San Francisco, Dr. Mervyn Silverman, president of the American Foundation for AIDS Research, put it succinctly: "This is a disease of consenting adults. You have to 'place' yourself at risk. If everyone was educated, if everyone listened, you could stop the spread of the virus tomorrow. I can't do that with the flu."

For all that's been said in the past years about "safe sex," there is only one kind that is foolproof: sex with someone who is uninfected. What "peace of mind" does the Michigan club offer for its deluxe-plan price of $649? Only what potential lovers can get on their own for the price of a test.

What they are really proffering is the notion that people don't have to change their behavior at all: the illusion that an entire world of singles bar and single nights can be quarantined off, protected from threat.

At Peace of Mind, those who pass the entry exam not only get a list of local bars where members hang out, but a stickpin with the club's insignia and an ID card. These badges become a magic talisman members may use to protect them from having to ask intimate questions, to wait, to make commitments or, for that matter, to use condoms. They promise to protect pockets of promiscuity. Save the seventies.

All this would be nothing worse than sleazy and exploitative business if it were not also dangerously wrong. The AIDS test itself doesn't say what's happened in the past three weeks, or perhaps three months. It takes time for antibodies to appear.

More to the point, it doesn't protect a person from what a partner did the day after the test. A club may test every six months, even four, but unless it tracks members and draws blood with the vigilance of the FBI, it's no more risk-proof than the rest of the world. Indeed, whatever anxiety people have about the promise of one partner to remain monogamous can only be multiplied about the pledge of an entire membership to be true to the club.

In the end, the promise of an AIDS-free zone is intrinsically dishonest. The most enterprising entrepreneur cannot create a risk-free club any more than the most committed bureaucrat could create an AIDS-free community or country.

continued ▶

What we can do involves a more fundamental and individual change. We can only stop the spread of AIDS at the border of our private lives.

It is far safer to maintain our own admissions standard. Call it responsible behavior. Membership in that club is absolutely free.

QUESTIONS

1. This article dates from 1987. Many things have happened in the past decade in the AIDS issue. What things are different now? What things remain the same?

2. Ms. Goodman stops short of spelling out her solution to the problem. She hints at it broadly in the last paragraph. Write what you think she means. Or, write what solution you'd put there at the end.

THE PARTY'S OVER AT "PARTY SCHOOLS"

At first it looked like just another jolly episode of fun-filled campus high jinks. Then it turned deadly.

It was "bid day," the festive annual event when Louisiana State University's 38 fraternities and sororities select their new members. A couple of hours after a dozen Sigma Alpha Epsilon fraternity pledges got so drunk they had to be wheeled out of a bar in shopping carts, police found them passed out on the frat house floor. One of them, Benjamin Wynn, 20, of Covington, La., was dead. Three others were sick enough to be hospitalized.

How tragic—and ironic, considering that a week earlier LSU had been named the nation's 10th best "party school" by a college guide published for high school seniors.

Fortunately, the "honor" of being considered a great campus for drinking appears to be fading for many college students. The more it fades, the better.

College-aged youths—particularly, but hardly exclusively, males—consume more alcoholic beverages per capita than any other age bracket does. Since the national drinking age is 21, much of this drinking is illegal. Legal or not, it is often excessive to the point that binge drinking becomes an unofficial sport with disastrous results.

But there's hope. Students increasingly are viewing the "party school" image as more of a liability than an asset, particularly when a degree from such a school might hamper career prospects. Many campus organizations, seeing nothing attractive in sloppy drunkenness, have dumped beer in favor of non-alcoholic beverages at campus events. Some schools have gone so far as to shut down the campus on traditional party weekends.

College administrators traditionally play down the "party" aspects of campus life in favor of more serious pursuits. But many of today's students are joining them as potent allies in the battle to stop binge drinking. To borrow a phrase from an earlier generation, the lives they save may be their own.

QUESTIONS

1. In a group, discuss drinking. Divide up drinkers and nondrinkers and have a reasonable and relaxed conversation about each group's choice.
2. What kind of college do you attend? Does it have a reputation as a party school? Regardless of what this article may hint at, do you think a party school reputation like that hurts a college?

A TOWN TAKES ON ROAD RAGE (AN EDITORIAL)

Just about everyone on the road at some time has been a witness to—or worse—committed an act of aggressive driving, so-called road rage.

It's a growing national problem as the highways get more crowded, drivers get more impatient and society in general seems to be taking a turn for the rude.

It finally got the official attention it needed in July when the National Highway Traffic Safety Administration released statistics indicating that road rage is a factor in two-thirds of all highway deaths. In short, it can be as deadly as it is uncivil, but so far no one has figured out how to stop it.

At least one community—Crystal Lake—is giving it a try, and ought to be applauded for the effort.

The police department has a two-pronged approach to combat aggressive driving. The first—and likely the most effective—is old-fashioned law enforcement. Officers are being assigned to work in unmarked cars at unexpected times to specifically look for the morons who excessively speed, weave in and out of traffic, tailgate, cut off or block other drivers, drive on the shoulder, flash their lights and obscene gestures and in general turn the highways into a battleground.

Those who are caught will get a date in court with the arresting officer, who will back up the charge.

continued ▶

Victims of road rage also will get a chance to fight back, and the satisfaction of sanctioned retaliation.

Drivers who see aggressiveness in action are being invited to report the incidents to the Crystal Lake police, providing an account of what happened along with the license number and description of the offending vehicle. They can do so anonymously.

Police in turn will contact or pay the accused driver a visit—in effect politely reading the riot act with details of the dangerous behavior and a lecture on the consequences of aggressive driving. In the most serious cases— especially when the accuser is willing to testify in court—a ticket may be issued, though police must be exceedingly judicious about that when they have not actually witnessed the offense.

Will it make a difference? In some cases, it probably will. If more police departments made the same effort, it almost certainly would. In that sense, Crystal Lake's experiment deserves to be watched closely as a guideline to imitate if it works. It isn't enough to fret about bad behavior, because without some kind of punishment or retribution it will continue. With this program, people fed up with aggressive drivers will have a place to take their complaint, and the jerks just might get the message.

QUESTIONS

1. "Road rage" is not as serious a problem in rural areas of this country as it is in and around cities. Do you think the author has adequately defined it?

2. Write an outline for this essay, showing the "job" of each paragraph. In a good essay, each paragraph does something to move the essay along to its logical conclusion. Is this essay effective?

The Creed Essay

Something to think about

Something exists in people that keeps us from killing each other, robbing banks, and going through red lights all of the time. Somewhere, enough of us were taught something about acting right in polite society. Most of us don't steal our neighbor's lawn mower or try to scam a date with our friend's boyfriend or girlfriend. Many times we smile at unsuspecting restaurant employees, help a friend, or pat a dog's head. Some folks claim that we act good because of religion or morality or a set of philosophical beliefs. Some people think we act good simply because it makes it easier to get through life.

Regardless, there are things that each of us see as being right or wrong. We live our lives by principles. When you find a wallet sitting on a shelf at the local Wal-Mart store, you make a decision about what to do with it. You open it and see whose it is, or you pull the money out and stick it in your pocket, or you leave the wallet there for someone else to worry about, or you take it to lost and found. Each of those decisions marks you as some kind of person. And each of those decisions is made by you, not randomly, but as a result of a lifetime of other choices.

If you found out at a young age that it was easy to put a candy bar in your pocket and sneak out without paying, you'll have different adult moral choices than someone who got caught the one and only time he or she tried to take some powdered donuts out of the grocery story. (My weakness for powdered donuts has not changed, however.)

As we move through the world, we have to make little moral decisions. Perhaps we aren't aware that we're constantly putting our morality to the test, but unavoidably we're weighing right and wrong all the time. Let's say you've just settled down to watch your favorite TV show and a friend calls with a lame crisis. You know she's exaggerating, but she swears she needs someone to talk to. Do you go ahead and talk to her and miss your show, or do you tell her that you were just on your way out the door to take your mother to the hospital? One way you help her. The other way you help yourself.

If you're driving along the highway and see a family broken down in their car, you are again faced with making a decision. Usually, it just takes a half-second, because our moral nature already knows what we're going to do, faced with a situation like this. What would you do?

- Stop and get out of your car and offer help.
- Stop and offer to give someone a ride to a phone.
- Stop, roll down your window partway, and ask if you can drive ahead and call someone.
- Drive by while thinking "They'll be all right."
- Drive by while thinking "That looks too dangerous; I'm going to keep going."
- Drive by while thinking "Nobody would stop and help me. I'm not going to stop either."
- Drive by while not even noticing.

Where do you fit on the list? Are you comfortable with that placement? I'm not judging you, but by offering that list and finding out your answer, I bet I know a little bit about your background. Those of you who picked one of the top three choices have probably been helped by someone somewhere. Maybe not with a flat tire on the side of the road, but by some stranger for something. Perhaps you saw your dad stop and help someone some time. You admired or respected that, and it became a part of your creed or your moral philosophy. If you selected one of the bottom choices, perhaps you've not been helped in those situations and you've decided that your moral philosophy doesn't have to include that kind of action.

We really shouldn't care where *others* fit on the scale. What should be important is where *we* fit. Knowing what we believe and accepting it is the key to having a moral philosophy. If you know your choices and are comfortable with them, then you should be happy. I know mine, but only because I'm interested enough to examine what I believe, where those beliefs come from, and how they affect me on a daily basis.

I'm interested in having a good, successful, and happy life. I want to know my choices and I want to live by some sort of standard that brings me peace and happiness. I can do very little about your choices. I can tell you mine and let you decide if my creed is a good one or a bad one for you.

We have to live somehow, in some way. We have to make choices about doing good and bad. We've all learned our creed from some set of experiences. In this paper we examine them. You've got to look in the mirror in the morning and be happy with the person staring out at you.

Getting started

Your identity as a writer is important, but your identity as a human being supercedes that. During this semester you've been exploring different facets of yourself. The writing in this class, for example, is designed to encourage you to find your voice in lots of different ways. This essay, usually the last one I like to offer my writers, will force you to examine yourself more closely than you might have before. Go into it with that warning!

INNER SELF / OUTER SELF

As you develop during this semester, you move from writing about yourself (personal) to writing about things (observational) to writing about issues (argumentative). I consider this essay to be a culmination of this process, since it involves both your "inner self" (what you think and believe on the inside) and your "outer self" (how you act and react in the rest of the world). You are being asked to discuss your beliefs. Many writers use this essay opportunity to talk about their own particular religious background. But more often than not writers simply try to quantify why they believe what they do.

Here are some questions that need to be answered in this creed essay. You can think of them as "parts" of the essay.

WHERE DID YOU RECEIVE YOUR MORAL TEACHING?

We all get our creed from somewhere. We see others act in society, usually beginning with our parents and family. Then when we become mobile, we begin to interact with acquaintances and friends (who have learned their creeds from their own families). We begin to observe and learn from strangers on the street, not to mention people in movies and television, and so on. At this point in your life you have tens of thousands of moral examples.

In addition to simply observing others, we often also get some kind of moral teaching or instruction. This comes from traditional places such as churches, synagogues, or mosques. But we also get instruction from our parents and families, friends, and even teachers.

Here's a brief example from a student of mine. I asked him to find a moment in which someone he knew taught him a moral lesson he never forgot.

> ▶ I'll never forget Mr. Moore, my 8th grade home room teacher. One day after school a school bus backed into his car, denting the side of the passenger door and breaking a window. The school administrator had the car picked up the next day and when it was returned the door and window had been fixed, plus the repair people had fixed a bad dent in the trunk that no one had noticed before.
>
> I was walking past the principal's office and saw Mr. Moore writing out a check. "What's that for, Mr, Moore?" I said when he was done.
>
> "Oh, that trunk was dented by me a couple of months ago. I backed into my garage one day."
>
> "But the school fixed it for free, didn't they?" I asked.
>
> "Not for free," he said. "It cost *somebody something*."
>
> I told my buddies about it and they just laughed at how stupid old Mr. Moore was. "He could've gotten away with it," one pal said.
>
> I guess Mr. Moore knew he could have gotten away with it, too, but he didn't. Later I asked him about it again.
>
> "Sure, I could have gotten away with it. But that's not the point. There's right and there's wrong. It's not about what you can 'get away with.' It's about what you can *live* with." ◀

In your own essay, you'll be expected to recall some bit of moral teaching. It's difficult, not just to pick a good one but to tell it so that the details of the story don't overshadow or get in the way of the moral message. Our writer here skips nonessential details, like the names of his friends or the details of the accident, so he can focus on the two dialogues with Mr. Moore. That's an example of good, selective storytelling.

WHAT IS A SINGLE, REPRESENTATIVE MORAL ACT IN YOUR LIFE?

This part of your essay definitely draws on the skills you learned and practiced in the personal narrative essay in Chapter 5. You're being asked in this essay to show your reader a representative act, an act that portrays or exemplifies or depicts your moral philosophy in action in the real world.

It's easy to claim you're a good "God-fearing Christian," or a "dedicated humanist," or a "giving Jew," or a "respectful Buddhist," but it's quite another thing to prove that by showing yourself in action.

Think of this section as the proof or the delivery. If you tell me you learned from your grandparents the value of helping those less fortunate, then I want to see that the teaching had an impact. Show me where you, too, helped someone. Tell the story just like you would in any kind of personal essay. Make it real; re-create it so that we can see it and experience it just like it happened. It will be hard for us to believe you otherwise. Also, I think generally this is the largest section of the creed essay, so take your time.

Like the example shown in the section above, this is a storytelling portion of your essay when you must focus on the "message" of the story and not so much on the details. Make sure we see you facing a dilemma of "right" and "wrong" or "good" and "bad."

HOW HAVE YOUR ACTIONS AND EXPERIENCES MOLDED YOU FOR THE FUTURE?

You already know that I love *Hawaii Five 0*. One of my favorite parts is the "epilogue," where we find out what happened after the main story is over. It's always nice to find out how things turned out. When we write about ourselves, we sometimes forget that our readers don't know us, and so can't know anything other than what we tell them.

In this section of your essay, I want you to close with your own epilogue. By now you've given us a thesis (some moral lesson you've learned) and shown us your own morality in action (support or proof of your morality). Now it's time to send us on our way with a conclusion.

In this creed essay it's even more important because what you cover for us is your way of life: how you live and why you live that way. If you tell us a big story through which you learn some crucial lesson of life, we'll be interested to know if this new "philosophy" or creed worked for you. We'll be eager to see how things turned out.

In closing the essay, make sure you provide for us some sense of completion, some sense of at least being ready for future decisions. If the paper expresses your creed, your closing should show us how you're ready and well-armed for moral and philosophical decisions in the future.

Warmups

RELIGIONS

- Nearly everyone has experience with an organized religion: Christianity, Judaism, Buddhism, etc. Free-write on each of the following:
  - If someone asked you what was the "main" lesson of the religion, what would you tell them? Give an example of this lesson in practical application. If you can, recall a moment when you were younger when you first understood this.
  - Write about a place of "worship." Sometimes this is a church or a synagogue or a mosque; sometimes it's a favorite place where your grandparents taught you to "pray." Write about this special place, describing it, recalling it, and explaining its value and purpose to you.
  - Think of the most important "holy" person you've ever known. This may be someone with a traditional religious background or it may be your crazy uncle. Tell a story about discovering the moral or religious wisdom of this great person.

RELIGIOUS AND MORAL TERMS

- In one of the essays below, a writer talks about a moral lesson he learned while working his first job. First jobs and first times living away from home are periods of life ripe with new decisions and moral dilemmas. Make a list of those kinds of firsts for you, and write about a couple of instances when you found yourself alone for the first time with a "right" or "wrong" choice.

- It might be appropriate to include one or two very brief definitions in this paper. While we are a little ways away from doing a research paper, you get the chance to use some kind of reference book or material in this essay as you try to define or describe your own personal philosophy.

> When I was young, one of my uncles used to call me a little "hedonist." I used to eat cookies and brownies when I was a kid, and not in the normal way. I showed no restraint, felt no remorse. If I felt like a brownie, I ate it. I was after pleasure. For a 5-year-old, the brownies were the very definition of happiness. I put my own needs in front of all others. If my little cousins hadn't had their brownies yet, I just kept eating; I was a hedonist. As a grownup, I *hope* I have more restraint. ◄

But the point is, we all have philosophies and creeds that we may not even understand or have names for. Below is a list of some terms that may or may not apply to you. (Some of them may be interesting to you even if they're the exact opposite of what you believe.) You'll need some library time for this, so do it on your own, or ask your professor to take you there. Write a definition for five of the terms below; additionally, write a paragraph about each of those five selected terms, using your own words, understanding, and so forth.

- existentialism
- Zen
- humanism
- hedonism
- altruism
- Christianity
- Buddhism
- Islam
- nihilism

Remember, you're doing two things for each of the five selected terms: a dictionary or encyclopedia definition, and your own version, worded in your own way. Feel free to write a whole paragraph for each, if you have a good understanding.

The essay assignment

We all live our lives in different ways. We all value right and wrong differently. We all have different standards for what's right or wrong. Is telling a little white lie okay if it protects someone's feelings? Is taking a towel from a hotel okay? If a cashier at the diner gives you back an extra dollar, is it okay to keep it?

These are all daily dilemmas that we might face. And whether we stop and really think these decisions over or not, we still make them, and we still make them based on ideas and teachings and events from our past.

Write an essay that expresses your creed or belief system.

Part of your paper should examine your moral teaching, wherever it may have come from. You should attempt to find and explain essential teachings that came to you from your parents, family members, friends, and so on, and show how these teachings have had an effect on you. You certainly may also tell us ways some kind of "organized" religion or philosophical mentor had an impact on how you make your life choices.

Part of your paper should relate a single, representative moral act in your life. For example, recall a moment where you faced the difficult choice of doing right or wrong. You should obviously try to find an exact moment that you think is representative of the kinds of moral choices you're proud of making.

Another portion of your paper may be used to define a moral idea or notion or term, such as truth, love, right, wrong, character, goodness, hate, greed, and so on.

As we've discussed in other papers, your closing should give us some sense of how things turned out for you, an epilogue, if you will. We will likely be interested in your story and eager to find out how the moral decisions you faced affected you in the future.

Sample essays

We'll start with a neat little sample essay. In addition to his television work with *60 Minutes*, Andy Rooney has also written numerous books, often collections of his TV reporting. Because he has worked almost all of his career (in newspapers and on TV) with some kind of space limitations, he's a master at using his time wisely. Each of his essays is a little gem, perfectly made, perfectly rendered. He writes concise, pointed essays that have a point. It's rare that someone is so sure of himself or herself.

Like our other professional essays, Rooney didn't write this essay with our assignment in mind. He was simply thinking about some of the same ideas of "right" and "wrong."

TRUST

BY ANDY ROONEY

Last night I was driving from Harrisburg to Lewisburg, PA, a distance of about eighty miles. It was late, I was late and if anyone asked me how fast I was driving, I'd have to plead the Fifth Amendment to avoid self-incrimination. Several times I got stuck behind a slow-moving truck on a narrow road with a solid white line on my left, and I was clenching my fists with impatience.

At one point along an open highway, I came to a crossroads with a traffic light. I was alone on the road by now, but as I approached the light, it turned red and I braked to a halt. I looked left, right, and behind me. Nothing. Not a car, no suggestion of headlights, but there I sat, waiting for the light to change, the only human being for at least a mile in any direction.

I started wondering why I refused to run the light. I was not afraid of being arrested, because there was obviously no cop anywhere around, and there certainly would have been no danger in going through it.

Much later that night, after I'd met with a group in Lewisburg and had climbed into bed near midnight, the question of why I'd stopped for that light came back to me. I think I stopped because it's part of a contract we all have with each other. It's not only the law, but it's an agreement we have, and we trust each other to honor it: we don't go through red lights. Like most of us, I'm more apt to be restrained from doing something bad by the social convention that disapproves of it than by any law against it.

It's amazing that we ever trust each other to do the right thing, isn't it? And we do, too. Trust is our first inclination. We have to make a deliberate decision to mistrust someone or to be suspicious or skeptical. Those attitudes don't come naturally to us.

We do what we say we'll do; we show up when we say we will show up; we deliver when we say we'll deliver, and we pay when we say we'll pay. We trust each other in these matters, and when we don't do what we've promised, it's a deviation from the normal. It happens often that we don't act in good faith and in a trustworthy manner, but we still consider it unusual, and we're angry or disappointed with the person or organization that violates the trust we have in them. (I'm looking for something good to say about mankind today.)

I hate to see a story about a bank swindler who has jiggered the books to his own advantage, because I trust banks. I don't "like" banks, but I trust them. I don't go in and demand they show me my money all the time just to make sure they still have it.

continued ▶

It's the same buying a can of coffee or a quart of milk. You don't take the coffee home and weigh it to make sure it's a pound. There isn't time in life to distrust every person you meet or every company you do business with. I hated the company that started selling beer in eleven-ounce bottles years ago. One of the million things we take on trust is that a beer bottle contains twelve ounces.

It's interesting to look around at people and compare their faith or lack of faith in other people with their success or lack of success in life. The patsies, the suckers, the people who always assume everything else is as honest as they are, make out better in the long run than the people who distrust everyone—and they're a lot happier even if they get taken once in a while.

I was so proud of myself for stopping at that red light, and inasmuch as no one would have known what a good person I was on the road from Harrisburg to Lewisburg, I had to tell someone.

QUESTIONS

1. Rooney's article supposes that most people trust each other. Do you see that to be true in your world? Or do you think our time is more cynical than that? Show examples of what you believe to be true.
2. The "car at the red light" example is a really neat one. Can you think of five similar real-world ethical dilemmas you face regularly?

Student sample essay

Here's our second essay in this section. It's by a writer named Tod who was quite a good student of mine a few years ago. I think above all else this essay shows the structure of the creed essay perfectly. It is a terrific model for you to use as you compose your own essay.

THE EMPTY BOX

Money made my family's world go around. Some of my earliest memories revolve around allowances and money for chores. I had to "be good" during the week to receive the highest level of three possible allowances that I was eligible for. If I was "good" all week, I got the highest level, $5. If I was good for part of the week, then I got $3. If I "acted up," or "got in trouble" at all during the week, the maximum was $1.

So I worked hard. I made my bed, didn't complain about the food my mom made at dinner, didn't gripe when Dad was late to pick me up after baseball practice. And on Saturdays we'd get in the car and go down to the store to spend my money.

The world made sense to me. If I did good things the rewards would come to me. And the rewards were always the same, money. Cash. You could spend it and it felt great.

I got a job when I turned 15 at the Drive-In theater. I felt very grown up the day my dad took me out to meet Mr. Dobbins, an old friend of his. Mr. Dobbins showed me around the ticket booth and the snack bar and let me pick where I worked. I told him the ticket booth, because the snack bar seemed smelly and dirty. At the ticket booth I figured I'd be able to play my tapes and talk on the phone and then when the cars had all come in I could drift outside and watch the movie, too. It would be easy money!

I started on a Friday night and Mr. Dobbins helped. He explained how much to charge and how to direct people to the open spots, and to watch that no one tried to sneak in through a broken old gate. After a while he left me alone and went to help the others at the snack bar.

That night seemed to last forever. It was a double feature so cars came in for hours. Whenever I'd try to pick up the phone to call a friend someone would need to be let in. If I had my cassette player playing too loud, I wouldn't hear the cars, or hear what the customers said when they talked. I felt like I'd been cheated out of a good deal. I hated that Drive-In.

At the end of the night I counted the cash carefully, stacking the 10s and the 5s and the 20s in their own piles. $460. It was a huge wad of bills and I was excited. I ran to the snack bar and handed it to Mr. Dobbins. He grabbed a five dollar bill off the top and handed it to me and stuffed the wad of cash in his pocket. "There ya go; see you tomorrow night. Saturday's always busiest."

My dad came around to pick me up and I got in with him. I couldn't believe I'd done all that work, a real man's job for only $5. My dad saw that I was disappointed, but he just laughed.

The next night after I counted the money out, I pulled a single twenty dollar bill out for myself. I had worked hard. I deserved the money. I deserved more than the lousy $5 Mr. Dobbins was paying me. I was nervous when I handed him the stack of money, minus the $20 bill I had hidden down the front of my pants, but he just peeled another $5 off and stuck the rest of the wad in his pocket.

During that summer I kept peeling off money for myself, a twenty most nights, on busy nights forty, and once late in the summer I took sixty.

continued ▶

When winter had come, Mr. Dobbins closed the theater for the season. All of us who had worked there, myself and four others in the snack bar, were invited to the projection room after the last car left, and Dobbins started handing out big boxes. I watched the girl on my left open hers; inside was a new gold watch, a gift certificate to a nearby pizza place, and a big silver picture frame. The next girl opened hers and she had a watch, too, and a gift certificate to a pet store. The other two boys opened theirs and found new baseball gloves, a silver watch for each, and a free lifetime pass to the Drive-In. Everyone was laughing and thanking Mr. Dobbins and no one even noticed that I hadn't opened mine yet. It felt light and I was afraid.

I ran outside and stood in the dark, afraid to go find my dad's car out front, and afraid to go back in. Finally I couldn't stand the waiting. I opened the box and pulled from it a single piece of paper that Mr. Dobbins had written on. I held it up to a dim light and read: "The measure of a man's character is what he would do if he knew he would never be found out."

When I got home I hid the empty box and looked up "character" in the dictionary. The first thing I read was: "moral excellence, goodness, trust-worthiness and firmness; a man of sound character." I knew that was not me.

I got a different job the next summer, and the next. The year I graduated high school Mr. Dobbins had to close down the old Drive-In, but Mr. Dobbins got all of his money back. I saved some up every month or so and would drop it by at night at his house. It wasn't much money each time, and I always went late so I wouldn't have to see him. When I went away to college I wrote down Mr. Dobbins' address and kept sending an envelope every once in a while when I thought of it.

After a year or so a box arrived in the mail at my dorm room from him. Inside was a boy's baseball glove, a nice silver watch, and a free lifetime pass to a Drive-In that wasn't there any longer.

I don't know why I thought it was all right to steal from Mr. Dobbins. I know my parents wouldn't have wanted me to learn that lesson, but my allowance and my fascination with cash and what it could do for me was unhealthy. As a child it didn't matter much. As a grownup, with my first real job, it did. I also wonder why Mr. Dobbins let me steal all that summer, never saying a word. Clearly he knew; maybe he knew all along. Even at the end there was no real punishment. He knew that I could walk out of that Drive-In and never return; his money would be gone forever.

Whatever his reasons were for giving me that empty box and that slip of paper, they worked on me. I pay my bills. I owe nobody. I would not steal a nickel or a dollar or a twenty dollar bill today, regardless of whether I thought I could get away with it. I would always know. I sense that somehow

I'd be letting myself down, and Mr. Dobbins, too. I don't want to judge who I was then or what I am now. But I hope that if I see Mr. Dobbins again some day that I can look him in the face, as a man of character.

QUESTIONS

1. Go back through "The Empty Box" and find each of these creed paper elements.

   - **an explanation of the writer's moral background**
     Is there background information given about the writer's formative learning?
   - **a representative moral act(s)**
     Is there a story, or a series of stories, in which moral decisions must be made?
   - **a corresponding religious or moral notion**
     Is there an outside, definable concept that helps make sense of the actions of the writer?
   - **an explanation or proclamation of the ongoing moral belief**
     Does the writer tell us what he believes now and how he lives his life?

2. I think the case could be made that "The Empty Box" contains some unnecessary material. One of my favorite kinds of editing is simply cutting out some sections. You don't want to wreck your book by drawing lines in it, but make notes on a sheet of paper instructing the writer which sections of text you think he could cut without losing the essence of his paper. Ask yourself especially about the information early in the paper.

3. Ask yourself about information that may be lacking. Is Mr. Dobbins explained and shown well enough? If something seems to be missing, what is it?

Another sample

Okay, let's finish with an extraordinary writing sample from a student of mine named John. John was an adult student when he wrote this, and so it benefits from his added experience and slightly nontraditional age.

But what's best about this essay is that it does not sacrifice simplicity in order to be powerful. Many times we assume wrongly that "heavy" or meaningful essays need to be complicated or unnecessarily complex. John wrote a stunning essay that is completely based around common themes and ideas that are recognizable to most people. Let's look at it completely, and then we'll look at a few select pieces later.

FAST CAR

When I was fifteen years old, the State of Mississippi issued me a driver's license. I'd already been driving quite a bit, since at that time in Mississippi you could get a learner's permit when you reached the ripe old age of fourteen. Jim and Scotty, my best friends, were already fifteen when I nabbed the learner's permit, which meant I was a completely legal driver when one of my licensed pals was along for the ride.

The 1967 Chevy Malibu I shared with my older sister was a car of formidable ugliness. Some of the hubcaps were missing. The windshield had a significant crack. The seats were torn and squeaky. The Malibu's paint job—it was once purple, I think—had given up the ghost years before it reached me. There was only one thing worse than driving an ugly, ten-year-old car, and that was driving a slow one. But the compact Malibu had a huge V-8 engine. A tap on the accelerator was almost enough to send it airborne.

I was a suburban kid. My father was a college professor, and my mother counseled students in the public school system. It was understood in our family that my siblings and I would make good grades, go to college, and eventually settle into respectable middle-class lives. A dutiful selflessness was high on the list of qualities we were expected to display.

All of that changed for me when I turned fifteen. The Malibu was my ticket to another life, an escape I'd been dreaming of for years. I became a supremely selfish teenager. My agenda was simple: leave the plodding squares in the dust. I made new and dangerous friends, and my contempt for anything normal or traditional rocketed to staggering heights. Even Jim and Scotty started giving me strange looks.

As far as I was concerned, the future was a toy I could play with indefinitely. The number of stupid, reckless chances I took multiplied with every passing year. By the time my sister had been accepted at Yale Law School, I was a college dropout who'd lived to be nineteen only through sheer luck. Any chance I might have had to accomplish something great seemed utterly lost.

Most teenagers are rebellious, of course. But my crusade, the long, blurred episode that began behind the wheel of the Malibu, went far beyond reason or explanation. Eventually, I went back to school and made peace with my estranged family, but the price I paid in disappointment and regret was terrible.

I often wonder who I'd be now if my parents had allowed me a little less freedom, if they'd taken my car keys and forced me to behave "sensibly" in high school. Perhaps my reaction would have been even more self-destructive. It's entirely possible my mother and father sensed this, and chose the lesser of two evils.

One thing I do know now is that freedom, far from being an absolute end in itself, is a complex state of being. Freedom is worthwhile only in relation to the benefits it grants the individual. Most adolescents and young adults are ill-prepared to deal with the consequences of rapid change, whether it comes as the result of driving privileges or leaving home for college.

My first car was a fast car, and it took me a long way from home. Twenty years later, I remember how it handled on those country roads I drove late at night to escape the frustrations of growing up, and how I felt when I finally realized that I would never be able to outrun myself.

Let's move through this essay a bit and let me draw out some especially useful and instructive sections. We begin with a perfect opening:

LOOKING AT FAST CAR

▶ When I was fifteen years old, the State of Mississippi issued me a driver's license. I'd already been driving quite a bit, since at that time in Mississippi you could get a learner's permit when you reached the ripe old age of fourteen. ◀

First of all it's a good, evocative title. It makes you wonder about the car—how fast? whose car? And in the opening sentences our writer introduces himself and places himself. Additionally, the topic he's dealing with—getting a driver's license—is a universal one, one that all of us can relate to. We're instantly interested because we identify with the writer.

▶ The 1967 Chevy Malibu I shared with my older sister was a car of formidable ugliness. Some of the hubcaps were missing. The windshield had a significant crack. The seats were torn and squeaky. . . . ◀

The entire second paragraph is beautifully done; the car (mentioned in the title) becomes a character here, too. The description sounds real and honest and the writer's love of the car is evident. We always must describe things as carefully as John does here. Our reader never knows what we know, and has never seen things like we've seen them. We must re-create the scene through our words so that the reader becomes really and vitally involved in our world. After all, readers shouldn't be thinking about their own cars and their own licenses. This must be your story, and you must involve readers in a real, personal, and vigorous way.

> ▶ I was a suburban kid. My father was a college professor, and my mother counseled students in the public school system. It was understood in our family that my siblings and I would make good grades, go to college, and eventually settle into respectable middle-class lives. A dutiful selflessness was high on the list of qualities we were expected to display.
> All of that changed for me when I turned fifteen . . . ◀

Here's one paragraph and then the transition sentence into the next. John describes his family life for us, because of course we can't know what it was like. He must show it to us in his own way so that we don't assume that we understand it on our own. The transition is powerful because change or conflict is always a key in good writing. The paragraphs above show how things used to be, and the following paragraphs describe how things changed.

> ▶ The Malibu was my ticket to another life, an escape I'd been dreaming of for years. I became a supremely selfish teenager. My agenda was simple: leave the plodding squares in the dust.
> As far as I was concerned, the future was a toy I could play with indefinitely. The number of stupid, reckless chances I took multiplied with every passing year.
> Most teenagers are rebellious, of course. But my crusade, the long, blurred episode that began behind the wheel of the Malibu, went far beyond reason or explanation. ◀

John uses this section, comprising a number of paragraphs, to show what became of his life once he got his driver's license. It's instantly powerful because the paper had started out so "nicely," with a momentous, but not disastrous, passage into adulthood with the obtaining of the driver's license. How John reacted to that, though, is extreme. We're almost taken along for the ride, along on his "long, blurred episode."

> ▶ Eventually, I went back to school and made peace with my estranged family, but the price I paid in disappointment and regret was terrible.
> One thing I do know now is that freedom, far from being an absolute end in itself, is a complex state of being. Freedom is worthwhile only in relation to the benefits it grants the individual. Most adolescents and young adults are ill-prepared to deal with the consequences of rapid change, whether it comes as the result of driving privileges or leaving home for college. ◀

Here are two sections from the latter part of John's essay. Starting with "Eventually," John moves to the last part of his essay. He's showing us the results of the "blurred episode," and tells us that the price was high for his actions.

And then in the full paragraph that begins "One thing . . . ," he is speaking to us not as the 15- or 16-year old with the driver's license but as a mature adult, able to look back at past events and bring sense and order to them.

In this paper that is an essential ability you will have to find. Whatever story or stories you choose to relate to us, you will have to have enough emotional distance from them so you can look back and make sense of what happened in your life at that time.

As for the last paragraph, I will just reprint it here again. Ask yourself if the writer has found his own "truth" or his own "creed." In the end, that's the key to this essay. We as readers have to feel as though we know ourselves inside and out, and that our actions and philosophy are something that will help us in the future when tough times come around again.

> ▶ My first car was a fast car, and it took me a long way from home.
> Twenty years later, I remember how it handled on those country roads
> I drove late at night to escape the frustrations of growing up, and how I
> felt when I finally realized that I would never be able to outrun myself. ◀

WHILE YOU'RE WRITING

While the essay is in progress, seek help from other writers, your instructor, and other readers whose opinion you trust. These are some of the issues you should address.

- Start early. Many writers have difficulty finding their "moral" teaching. Too many people think that only happens in church. If you can call upon a strong church or synagogue or mosque background where you were taught right and wrong, that's great. But just as many of us learn about right and wrong in less formal ways. We learn right and wrong from friends and peers and parents and siblings. To really get this list going, ask yourself when was the first time you knew you did something "wrong" and the first time you knew you did something "right." Make a list.

- Finding that representative story may be hard, but it likely will come from the list we discussed in the point above. Don't forget to talk to friends and family; oftentimes, their collective memory is better than our single one.

■ We haven't talked much about purpose, have we? Well, I'd guess the simplest way to say it is this way: Your purpose is to teach us something about living in the world. You are holding your own life up in front of us and suggesting that it works for you and that it might work for others. You also must convince us that your system is sound and that you are prepared to make right and good choices in the future.

WORKSHOP QUESTIONS

■ Does the title make you interested in the essay?

■ Does the first paragraph hook you with something fascinating or exciting?

■ Does the writer give us sufficient background information so we see and understand him or her clearly? Are you confused by anything?

■ Are you able to find the representative story? It should be fairly large and should be told as a good narrative story. Remember some of our lessons from Chapter 4: setting, character, background, high point, and lesson.

■ Has the writer tried to make his or her creed or philosophy clear to us through examples and explanation? If you're confused by the writer's creed, then it's likely it hasn't been given to you well enough.

■ Do you believe the writer's creed is one that he or she can or should live with? Do you think the creed is something that others, even you, might admire or wish to emulate? If so, what do you like about it? If not, what parts of it would you avoid?

Paragraphs, Sentences, and Words

During the course of your semester I hope you stop by this chapter whenever you need to. In it are some collected thoughts about the smaller parts of an essay—those words, sentences, and paragraphs that form the bricks and mortar of any well-built essay. It shouldn't, however, be a replacement for a good grammar handbook. Any good writer keeps one of those around. I'd bet your instructor knows a couple of good ones that he or she would like you to use. Check that out.

Paragraphs

There are different kinds of paragraphs. One of the things developing writers must learn, however, is that paragraphs are a means of getting somewhere, of accomplishing something. A good paragraph in an essay does a *job*, it doesn't just exist. Paragraphs must "do" something. Below are a number of ideas about dealing with paragraphs.

OPENINGS

I can't stress enough the importance of your paper's opening paragraph. While you may sweat and strain over all parts of your essay for weeks, many readers will judge the worthiness of your text simply by how you start the essay. Research shows us that if a reader is going to stop reading your essay at some point, it is most likely to happen during or at the end of that first paragraph. That's a lot of pressure to put on a few words at the beginning of an essay.

In fact, we've been calling the opening paragraph our "mindset paragraph." That's because we must get our reader ready to go, up to speed. We must prepare them for the information that's coming next. "Mindset" is the perfect word, I think, because one of the major problems with communication is that our listener or reader doesn't "know" what we know. We must get our minds together.

Here's a really simple example. About a week ago a friend of mine called and said "What was the name of that crazy guy from New York we used to hang out with in Hattiesburg?" I couldn't think of it and neither could my pal. Well, I spent the next day or two thinking about it, wondering about those times, remembering details. Finally, I thought of the name. When I met my friend at a bar the next night, I ran up to him and said "Bob Praino!"

My friend asked "What are you talking about?"

"Bob Praino," I said. "The guy whose name we couldn't think of the other night."

"Oh," my friend said. "I had forgotten all about that."

Forgotten? Was he kidding? The idea stuck in my head and I worked on it. In my mind, the Bob Praino name problem was first and foremost among my jobs of the week. My friend asked me the initial question on the phone, but then just let it slip out of his mind. He didn't care any more. My mind kept working on its own. When I did come up with the name, what I should have said was "Hey, do you remember a couple of days ago when you called me? We were talking about old friends whose names we couldn't remember?"

He would have said, "Oh yeah, I remember. What was the name of the guy from New York? Did you ever think of it?"

"Sure," I could have said. "Bob Praino."

The problem I just described is exactly the problem writers face every time a reader starts a piece of text. They don't know what we've been thinking or worrying about. They don't know we care about the environment, or that for the past week we've been doing nothing but thinking and writing about recycling.

We have to "set" the mind of the reader to ours. Think of it like synchronizing someone's watch to "your" time. If we care about recycling, then we'll have to make sure we help the reader understand that recycling is on our mind. That way when we blurt out our good info and ideas, our reader will be ready for it.

Check this out.

> ▶ Do you ever wonder what makes a car go? Sure, we all get in them and turn on the key. Most of us fill them up with gas. Some of us can change tires and change oil. Maybe some of us even could repair a headlight or taillight. But really most of us don't know what's happening. We're usually happy if we can find a good station on the radio. But I decided I was tired of not knowing. It's my car after all. I decided to get down and dirty. I started by simply opening the hood. Here's what I found. ◀

That's a pretty good paragraph, right? The writer wants to talk about how cars run. To do that, he must get us ready. That paragraph, his opening or mindset paragraph, accomplishes that task.

And just as essays have to open, they also have to close.

CLOSINGS

If you want your essay to mean something to the reader, you must strive to close in a way that will stay on the reader's mind. Let's use the essay example from the "openings" section earlier, the paper written by the guy who wanted to know more about how his car worked.

> ▶ As I closed the hood and put the tools away, I began to wonder how much money I had spent on unnecessary repairs. How many times did mechanics turn a couple of bolts and charge me a hundred dollars? How many more miles could I have gotten on that great Chevy Malibu if I'd just tuned it up once in a while? I no longer have to ask those questions; I'm getting the maximum value out of my cars now because I know what makes them go. Do you? Are you throwing money away? Are you going to be stuck on a dark, deserted road one night soon, because you don't know what lurks beneath the hood? ◀

It's a great closing. It's powerful for a couple of reasons, the easiest one being the use of questions directed right at the reader. The reader has to answer them, and that gets the reader involved. When the paragraph is finished, the reader will still be thinking. That's the goal.

PARAGRAPHING AND TRANSITIONS

Paragraphing, simply put, is the art of separating your text into manageable chunks. The traditional rule of "one idea per paragraph" is not bad, but lots of factors go into paragraphing.

Not only do the paragraphs contain separate ideas, the visual presentation of paragraphs allows readers' eyes a break as they read. Imagine if your essay was a long, unbroken paragraph. A reader would never know where one idea ended or where the next one started. It's less daunting to see reasonably sized paragraphs than one big block.

Think of your essay as a big turkey dinner. (I'm fond of food metaphors.) You *could* take the turkey and mashed potatoes and cranberry sauce and pumpkin pie and put all of it in a big blender. You could hit the puree button and reduce the entire meal to a nice thick shake. (Who knows what color it would be? I'd guess gray.) You could try to swallow the shake, and it's true that you'd get some of the flavors of the foods in the shake, but I don't think many of us would think of it as a rewarding and effective presentation of the meal.

Ideally, a big meal is an event. You start with the good aroma of the food and its presentation on the plate. On the left some nice thick slabs of turkey. On the back edge a bunch of peas. On the right a heaping portion of potatoes. You haven't even eaten yet, but the presentation is good and it pleases you. You eat a little turkey—you don't jam all of your turkey in your mouth at one time, you take just a mouthful, chew it, talk to your friends and family at the table. Have a drink of milk. Then you go for some potatoes. You're chewing. You fill your mouth up, then you take a break. Any good meal goes something like that. Of course, we often stuff our faces at fast-food places or driving in our car or at a party, but then those aren't usually our great dining experiences. A great dining experience is a series of correctly portioned helpings.

An essay must have the same kind of pacing. You can't give your reader a big chunk of "unparagraphed" prose because the reader can't take it all in at one time. Even the simplest of essays has multiple ideas and is built with many pieces (or many side dishes, keeping with the food metaphor). So, you've got to feed that essay to the reader in helpings or chunks. Paragraphs are the chunks.

A PARAGRAPHING ASSIGNMENT

Here's a short observation essay, like the ones discussed in Chapter 6, that has been combined into one long paragraph. Proper paragraphing is an exceptional help to the reader. It allows them to answer the question "Where does one idea stop and the next begin?" Use that question yourself as you read the following essay.

LIFE IN THE LADIES' ROOM

The room is shaped somewhat like a backwards L, with subdued pink lighting glowing from fixtures recessed in the ceiling. There is a subtle scent in the air reminiscent of baby powder. At first, there is no noise; then the sound of Muzak barely becomes audible. As I enter, to the left there is a low gray leather loveseat facing three vanities, with two more vanities to the left of the loveseat. The vanity mirrors are surrounded with mahogany trim, and each vanity has a mauve or hunter green cushioned chair in front of it. Upon each vanity countertop is a silver and marble tray bearing perfumes, hair spray, tissues, and lotion. Each set of vanities is separated by a full length mirror. The floor is covered with a luxurious soft gray carpet that your heels sink into. The walls are covered with a gray satiny wallpaper with a small pattern of burgundy and hunter green threads shot through it. As I enter the tall part of the L, there is an empty chair in the corner, with the matron's "box of tricks" beside it. A blow dryer, a sewing kit, and pairs of stockings are visible from the top. But she's nowhere to be seen. On the right side of the room, six gray marble pedestal sinks stand gracefully, each stocked with a small floral scented soap. Three shelves are stacked with tiny burgundy and green hand towels. Along the left side of the room there are three green marble hampers, each about 2 1/2 feet tall, awaiting the deposit of soiled towels. At the end of the room, there are six green doors, one pair on the west wall, one pair on the north wall, and another on the east wall. Each pair of stall doors has a pen and ink print between the two doors. I've got the place to myself and I breathe easier. The wedding reception is loud and chaotic. I'm glad to have a moment alone. Three young girls (eight or nine years old) enter. They talk to each other while using the stalls, and discover that the commodes are equipped with infra-red sensors for flushing, and that they make almost no sound as they flush. "Oh cool!" "I can't turn it off!" After playing with the flushing mechanisms for a while, they congregate at two of the sinks and wash their hands while talking about handing out confetti. They investigate the contents of the missing matron's box of tricks, they look in the hampers, and then head for the vanities. While they are sniffing lotion and spraying perfume, I get ready to return to the noisy reception, washing my hands and checking my own reflection in the mirror. I gather my purse, toss the towel into the hamper, and as I walk through the door, I take one last look to make sure I have left nothing behind.

While knowing when to break your ideas into paragraphs is important, there's another step that must be taken care of, too, and many developing writers struggle with this: namely, the writing of transitions.

TRANSITIONS

Transitions are a critical part of a paper's progress or flow. Think of transitions as little bridges between ideas or paragraphs. Even though your essay is usually about one thing, you state a number of small ideas during even a short essay as you make your point.

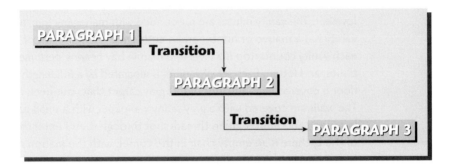

If you intend to tell us that paragraphs 1, 2, and 3 all belong in the same essay, then you'd better have a way of connecting the ideas so they make sense to us. A paper that doesn't have the necessary transitions from paragraph to paragraph is often called "choppy." The paragraphs may be fine on their own, but they are too much on their own, and the paper feels chopped up.

Paragraph 1 has to lead to paragraph 2, which must lead to 3. As the writer, you should be prepared to write words, sentences, and sometimes whole paragraphs to connect your paragraphs one to the next.

THE TEN-SENTENCE ESSAY

Let's use an example. Here's one of my special tricks, a ten-sentence essay! I love doing these, because I can show you a concept quickly without having to take you through a full essay. Below is just a bare-bones structure of an essay. Each small section represents what might one day become an entire paragraph.

What each section really is right now is a topic sentence and a transition. Then another. Then another. Then another. Let's read. See if you can spot where I'm writing a sentence or a phrase designed to bring you along to the next part of the paper.

> ▶ Money is evil. It's a bad way to keep score of a person's success or happiness. Personal satisfaction and doing "good" for others are much deeper and more genuine rewards. However, we all need money to survive. ◀

"However" is a great transition word. In this case, I've raised one idea: Money is evil. But in the next breath I've said "However, we all need money," which means money is not always evil. The transition leads us into a new section of the paper.

▶ How should we balance our financial needs and our right to be free of the sins of greed?

One of the ways to live a balanced life of moral and financial responsibility is to work in a field that is both personally and financially rewarding. ◀

In the first paragraph above, I ask the question "How can we balance our needs and our desire to not be greedy?" When I go to the next paragraph, I want to make sure my reader is hanging with me, not getting lost or confused. So, I restate the idea from the previous paragraph: "One of the ways to live a balanced life . . ." That phrase reminds my readers what I was just talking about, keeping their thought process right up with mine. I'm helping them make the transition from one idea to the next.

Now, look one more time at that sentence: "One of the ways . . . is to work in a field that is both personally and financially rewarding." Can you already sense that a transition should be on its way? Of course. Do you know why? If I say to you there are five ways to make fudge brownies, you're probably going to ask me "What are they?" What do I respond? "One way of making brownies is . . . " In the paragraph above I say "One of the ways . . . ," and you know what to expect next. Here's the transition.

▶ One example is the Red Cross of America. Their employees are paid solid wages, comparable to wages at larger business corporations. Still, their mission toward helping people provides a sense of satisfaction and well-being to their employees.

You don't have to chase money at the expense of your soul. It is possible to have it all! ◀

I promised you one example, and in the first paragraph above I deliver on that promise. The sentence that begins "One example of this is the Red Cross . . . " connects us to the earlier paragraph.

Transitions keep the reader with you. Each paragraph that passes provides another opportunity for your reader to take a break, so we must make an essay that has natural bridges from paragraph to paragraph. Drag your reader along with you by making it impossible for them to turn away.

A SAMPLE TRANSITION

Here's an example of a transition in action. These are two paragraphs that come from an essay about corporations and sports-star endorsers. These two paragraphs do different things and address different parts of the overall topic. However, the writer knows he must make them fit together. As you read the first paragraph and get near the bottom of it, the writer should begin preparing you for that leap over the white space in his essay; he'd better be working on a transition. Watch out for good cue words: *however* (which we've already seen), *but, for example*, and so on.

> ▶ When a sports-star like Michael Jordan or Tiger Woods endorses a product, their face becomes the face of the company. Despite horrific abuses of child labor in some Third World countries, the Nike corporation continues to sell shoes as fast as ever. Why? Because we all want to be like Mike. And we all love Tiger. They look like nice guys on TV, so the actual corporate greed and avarice doesn't enter our mind. Nike's face is Mike's face. But just because these players endorse the products, does that make them in any way responsible for the corporation's actions?
>
> If the corporate sponsors are aware of what their corporations do, well, then of course they are responsible. Let's say for example, you take a job at a car dealership, and you discover that the cars you're selling are stolen from another dealership across town. When the cops come, you're not going to be able to play dumb. ◀

Where's the transition in that first paragraph? How about that last sentence. In fact, a question happens to be a very effective way of moving your reader on to the next paragraph. (Our writer here even uses a good marking transition word, "But.") The first paragraph of his essay raises an idea. At the end of the paragraph, he has a plan to move on to a new idea (the fact that these sports endorsers need to be responsible). He asks the question hoping that you'll want to answer it and in turn find out the writer's answer. If you read on to that second paragraph, then the transition works.

Sentences

TOPIC SENTENCES

Paragraphs, of course, are made up of sentences. Just as there are no hard and fast rules about how many paragraphs make up an essay, there are no hard and fast rules about how many sentences make up a paragraph. A wise guy will tell you that it takes as many as you need.

However, there's one easy thing to agree on: A topic sentence's relationship to a paragraph is the same as a thesis statement's is to a whole essay. The topic sentence is the central, controlling idea of a paragraph.

Each paragraph is like a mini-essay. It needs to have the same kind of care that a full essay does, except it does its job in a much shorter period of time. Let's look at a couple of decent paragraphs.

▶ But Barry and I had trouble. We had differences of opinion about religion and children and family. When we fought, we fought hard and loudly. Even the fortune teller at the state fair one year said we were doomed. We had laughed then, but as we walked around the fair that night I thought about it a lot. She was right. My mom had been right. It would be over soon between us. ◀

In this paragraph, the very first sentence is the topic sentence. Everything else that is in the paragraph is in support of that first one. It's the same concept as the "promise and delivery" model we use when talking about an essay. If you tell me that you and Barry were not meant to be, then you better deliver on that promise you make and support your idea.

In the paragraph below, see if you can spot where the topic sentence is.

▶ Barry's eyes never focused on me. Whenever we went to the mall together or grocery shopping, he'd walk a little ahead or a little behind. I can remember him striding ahead of me at the movies, picking a seat and sitting down. He was already eating popcorn by the time I got there. When I sat down he didn't even acknowledge me. He stopped calling if he was going to be late from work. In the old days he had always done that. He had always been compassionate. He had held my hand for as long as I could remember. But now it was like a stranger lived in the house. One day as we ate breakfast I looked at him while he stared out into the backyard. I might as well not even have been there. I knew what was wrong. He had stopped loving me. ◀

If you think it's the last one, you're right. As in the previous paragraph, this is a paragraph that has a good topic sentence. It just happens to be the last one. Go back and look at this paragraph again. Do you see how the items in it all support the notion of the topic sentence "He had stopped loving me"? In this case, the writer saved the topic sentence for last for effect. It's a powerful last line.

Regardless of where you place the topic sentence, each paragraph has to have one. Think of the topic sentence as a paragraph's raison d'etre, its reason to be. No topic sentence = no paragraph. Think of it also as something to hold every other sentence up to, to see if they match. If you can't match a sentence back to the topic sentence, then you might already be on to a new idea, and thus a different paragraph.

SENTENCE PROBLEMS

As I've mentioned, grammar problems are beyond the scope of this book. I really recommend that all of my writers get a good, recent grammar handbook to help them through the inevitable problems that will arise during constant writing and rewriting. However, during my teaching career I've stumbled across a handful of common sentence errors that usually aren't too hard to fix. I thought I'd show them to you here. Consider this your first line of defense for sentence problems. I'll even use some of the typical "editing marks" teachers use to point out these things. If your teacher notes a problem other than these, find out what he or she means, and then go to your handbook. Here we go.

COMMA SPLICE (CS)

If you have a comma between two complete sentences, that's a comma splice. Here's one:

> ▷ I was waiting for Karen to pick me up, she had my car that week. ◁

There are two parts of that sentence, and we call those "clauses." But both of them are independent clauses (they can stand alone as their own sentences). There are three ways to fix this.

Put a period in place of the current comma, and you have two sentences.

> ▷ I was waiting for Karen to pick me up. She had my car that week. ◁

Use a semi-colon instead of a comma.

> ▷ I was waiting for Karen to pick me up; she had my car that week. ◁

Keep the comma, but add a conjunction; the conjunction will make one part of the sentence dependent on the other.

> ▷ I was waiting for Karen to pick me up, because she had my car that week. ◁

FUSED SENTENCE (FUSED OR RUN-ON)

Similar to the above example, this sentence contains two independent clauses, but with no punctuation.

> ▷ I can't decide which truck to buy they're both beauties. ◁

The same fixes apply as in the earlier example.

Two sentences:

> ▷ I can't decide which truck to buy. They're both beauties. ◁

Semi-colon:

> ▷ I can't decide which truck to buy; they're both beauties. ◁

Add a conjunction:

> I can't decide which truck to buy, because they're both beauties. ◁

FRAGMENT (FRAG)

Fragments are incomplete sentences. Writers almost always make this mistake by letting a dependent clause stand all by itself as a sentence. I'll have to show you a good sentence first, then the fragment that follows.

> We knew there was something wrong with Mary. Something we couldn't fix. ◁

How to fix it? Well, how about a comma after Mary, thus attaching the fragment sentence (a dependent clause) to the earlier, complete sentence (an independent clause).

> We knew there was something wrong with Mary, something we couldn't fix. ◁

PRONOUN REFERENCE (PRON REF)

This is another common error that can be solved by simply paying closer attention to your sentences. Here's a problem.

> Each student knows that they're going to have to work hard. ◁

Here we have a problem of "number." "Each student" is singular, just like "he," for example. The pronoun used later on is "they're," a plural pronoun. One fix is easy.

> Students know that they're going to have to work hard. ◁

We took "each student" and made it the plural "students," to match the plural pronoun "they're." There's another fix that's a little messier.

> Each student knows that he or she will have to work hard. ◁

Here we leave "each student" singular and change the pronoun to a singular. We should also be aware of avoiding a bad fix, such as this one.

> Each student knows that he's going to have to work hard. ◁

What's wrong with that? Well, not all students are male. "He" is a male pronoun only.

VAGUE PRONOUN REFERENT (VAGUE)

> "George had Mike in a headlock before they fell down the stairs. He was really hurt." ◁

Who's the "he" in that sentence? We need to do a little rewriting to fix this.

▷ George had Mike in a headlock before they fell down the stairs. Mike was okay, but George got a big bruise on the forehead. ◁

VERB TENSE AGREEMENT (TENSE)

What's wrong here?

▷ I walked up the sidewalk to confront him. 'What are you doing?" I said. He looks me over good and then he reaches out and smacks my face! ◁

Interesting story, sure, and I'd like to know more, but there's a problem with tense. The writer has "walked" and "I said," both in the past. The past tense is a perfectly reasonable tense for telling a story, since that's usually when stories happen. However, in his excitement at re-telling the story, the writer slips into the present tense.

▷ He looks me over good and then he reaches out and smacks my face! ◁

We've got to make sure our sentences stay in the same tense: past or present. Let's fix it by putting everything in the past.

▷ I walked up the sidewalk to confront him. 'What are you doing?" I said. He looked me over good and then he reached out and smacked my face! ◁

Now the story reads as if it all took place at the same time.

PRONOUN CASE (PRON)

Here are some common pronoun problems.

▷ He is fatter than me. ◁

That doesn't sound like a bad sentence. But what that sentence really means is

▷ He is fatter than me am fat. ◁

Is "me" right? No. Try this instead.

▷ He is fatter than I. ◁

Here is another sort of pronoun problem.

▷ Mom made William and I go to the party. ◁

Pretend William didn't go to the party. Can you say

▶ Mom made I go to the party? ◀

Nope. The correct original sentence will be

▶ Mom made William and me go to the party. ◀

Words

Words, of course, are the smallest building blocks we use as we construct essays. They form the sentences that form the paragraphs that form the entire document. And even though they are tiny in comparison to the total project, missteps made with words oftentimes can control much of the effect your writing has on a reader.

There are a handful of word problem categories I want to talk about here.

VOCABULARY

Like an ice cream sundae, you can never have too big a vocabulary. (That's a little joke.) Seriously, though, it stands to reason that if you've got a large vocabulary, you'll be better prepared to choose just the right words at the right time in any writing or communication situation. It's the same situation a painter faces when he or she is painting a picture. If the artist only has blue and green and yellow paint, then the finished product can only show those colors and their mixtures. And, indeed, a terrific painting may result if the artist is skilled enough.

But an artist with a wider palette (more colors) has more options, more opportunities, and a wider range of feelings and emotions with which to complete his or her painting. Sometimes blue and green and yellow simply aren't enough.

READ WIDELY

How do you improve your vocabulary? Reading a variety of books and magazines is a great place to start. If you only read *Time* magazine, for example (a pretty great magazine), that would be a start. But *Time*, like any publication, has a certain style and a certain vocabulary. You'd benefit more from reading *Time* and *Newsweek*, and *The Nation* and *USA Today*, and some books from different fields written for a variety of reading levels.

How does that help? Simply by bringing you into contact with more words than you'd normally get on a steady diet of watching television and listening to the radio. When you come across a new word in your reading, you have several options.

1. Skip it and hope it's not important.
2. Try to figure out the meaning in the context of the sentence.
3. Look up the word in a dictionary, and then reread the sentence and the paragraph with your new knowledge, thus cementing the word into your vocabulary.

Obviously, option 1 is a bad choice. Numbers 2 and 3 are both good, and even using option 2 only (reading in context) is going to help you move to a bigger, wider vocabulary. I think a combination of reading in context and looking things up is best.

For example, here's a sentence.

> The Texas Rangers suffered a particularly mephitic defeat last night. ◄

Okay, reading the sentence, even with that weird word "mephitic" in there is not so hard. After all, the sentence basically says the Texas Rangers lost a game last night. If we wanted to, we could carry on with our reading of the sports page in this instance. But I always think that if a writer uses a word, he or she probably used it on purpose and that it has some crucial or essential reason for being there.

Contextually, I know what the sentence says: The Rangers lost. But "mephitic" adds something, and as a good reader I want to get the full story, the full meaning. I open my dictionary and I find that *mephitic* means "stinky, malodorous, or smelly."

Well, that's a much harsher sentence than I ever imagined. The loss of the game suddenly is more real and more vital to me. They didn't lose "gallantly," nor did they fight "bravely" to a close defeat. They "stunk" up the joint. Their loss was so bad that it was smelly.

Now, mephitic is not a word I'm going to use every day, but you know what? Now I can, if I ever want to. If it ever gets used again, I'm prepared to deal with it.

SEXIST, RACIST, AND BIASED LANGUAGE

Mankind is currently struggling with the problem of sexist language. Whoops. See, I did it right there. "Mankind" is an example of a sexist term. So are words like "chairman," "cleaning lady," and "postman."

There are plenty of great women who are "chairpersons," and lots of neat and tidy "custodians" who happen to be men.

A broad movement toward a correct and unbiased way of speaking has been sweeping this country over the past thirty years, and we're reaching a sort of equality with language that we've never had before. I know that my letter carrier Joyce doesn't like to be called a postman. It'd be the same sort of thing if she called me a girl, or a lady, or a skunk, for all that matters.

Many out-of-date terms like those already mentioned are being replaced. Additionally, it's no longer proper to use the male pronouns "he" and/or "him" as all-purpose pronouns. Look at this old example and its newer, better versions.

Wrong: Everyone should do his own homework.
Right: Everyone should do his or her own homework.
Also Right: All students should do their own homework.

There are also terms and language relating to race, age, and sexual orientation that you should avoid. As I've stressed countless times in this book, it's incumbent upon the writer to "reach" the audience. Obviously, insulting the audience will make an effective essay impossible.

While terms such as "black," "homosexual," and "elderly" still get used, you may offend a "gay African-American man in his seventies" with any or all of them. Make sure the reader feels comfortable with language by using the most current, acceptable terms. You can usually get a good sense of this simply by keeping up on current reading in newspapers and magazines.

The trend is toward a more specific set of terms. For example, "homosexual," an old term that encompassed both men and women, is now out of date, replaced by "gay" (mostly for men) and "lesbian" (always for women). "Hispanic" used to be a term for all Spanish-speaking people, but now it's correct to use country-specific terms such as "Mexican," "Puerto Rican," and others.

It's important to ask yourself why you would use categorical or stereotyping terms that would point out a person's race, gender, class, sexual orientation, or age anyway. Oftentimes, people use these terms even when they're not relevant. If you're using these terms, make sure you're using them for a reason.

INFORMAL AND FORMAL LANGUAGE

I'll get in trouble with some of my friends for a lot of the language in this book. I know that they'll disapprove of me using words like "neat" and "cool" as substitutes for more formal terms such as "good" and "well done."

How we choose our words often depends on the audience we're trying to reach. I have written about some of the ideas in this textbook to different audiences. This book is for you, students, developing writers, often in a first-year college course. However, I've written about the same ideas to my colleagues in academia, and my language in that case is very different. For example, look at this idea below, expressed first for you and then for my colleagues.

> ▶ Being able to communicate well is the best thing we can do as human beings. It helps us get along in the world. And besides, words are cool. I love stringing words together in a sentence that really says what I mean. How many times do I get to tell it like I see it? ◀

Or,

> ▶ Being able to communicate well is an essential human practice. It enables us to interact with, and succeed in, the world. Additionally, words are valuable and exciting commodities. We all know the power and the pleasure of creating an effective and exemplary sentence. How often do we get the freedom to interpret our experience as we see fit? ◀

Both paragraphs are good. Both say what I mean. But the language is clearly more "relaxed" or informal in the first example.

I don't want to suggest that either one is better than the other. I've chosen to structure this book mostly like the first example. I'm not talking "down" to you, either. In my "real" life, with friends and family, I talk a lot more like the first example, the cool one.

But in my professional life, and in situations where my audience expects something different, I use different language. It's not a cop-out; it's simply another case of the audience dictating what we do.

For example, I'd bet that if you read the sample essay in the research essay chapter, you'd discover that writer's language to be rather different from the language used by the writers in the personal essay chapter.

The writers are all the same age and have mostly the same backgrounds. In class, or with me in conference, they all speak with about the same level of formality. But they all understood that their essays (or any writing) require different kinds of approaches when it comes to language, word choices, formality, slang, and so on.

The key is to let the situation guide you. Don't be informal just because "that's the kinda cat you are." Be informal when it serves the needs of your essay. Be formal when *that* is right.

13

The Support Group

It's hard to get along in the world without friends, family, and colleagues. From the time we're born we rely on people around us for a multitude of things: companionship, love, food, fun. Our parents nurture us as we grow. As soon as we're walking and mobile, we venture out of the house and find a friend. (I used to play G.I. Joes with the kid who lived next door.) When we get into school we're surrounded by others who share something of our interests. Some of these people become life-long friends; some we know for a short time only. Regardless, during the time we know them, some of them are our best friends, friends we trust with our secrets and our ideas. "Don't tell Suzie I like her," we whisper. Or, "Do these pants make me look fat?"

During school we come into contact with some great teachers. We've all had great teachers who are interesting, interested in their jobs, interested in us as people and learners, and just plain fun. Teachers introduce us for the first time to special worlds, often influencing our career choices. Mr. Dibski, the great chemistry teacher, shows you how perfume and lipstick are made. Ms. Landers recites lines from a Sam Shepard play that makes you want to major in drama. Mr. Joly tells you about the first time he taught a class, and you decide to become a teacher.

If we work part- or full-time, we have a squadron of fellow workers who help us. Whether we're washing cars, serving up those delicious Slurpees, or renting movies down at the video store, we learn to work together with others. Sometimes our co-workers stay behind to close up when we have a date or a dentist appointment. Sometimes they just listen when we've got something to gripe about.

When we hit college we sometimes get a roommate or a whole suite of them. We expand our horizons widely past the high school crowd we used to hang with, and now there are new folks to tell our stories to. "Wow, when I was a junior in high school, you won't believe what happened to me!" "You're from Oregon? Wow, what's it like there?" "Hey, do *you* think these pants make me look fat?"

We bump around through life from group to group, with friends, buddies, pals, girlfriends, boyfriends, and family mixed in there too. This is our support group. These are the folks we turn to when we need a favor or fifty bucks or just some french fries. We rely on them partially because of their proximity. Sometimes our bond is formed because of blood ties. Sometimes it's love. Sometimes it's just a shared interest.

If you go down to the public tennis courts every morning and see a guy serving tennis balls by himself every day, you eventually say "Hey, I come down here, too. Do you wanna play a couple of times a week? We both could use the practice." That guy isn't your friend; you don't even know him. But because of where he is and where you are at that time, you suddenly have a connection. You are each other's support group. He serves some and you return them. Or you just pick them up until it's your turn. Then he picks up for you.

In our class this semester, we'll use two different support groups. I want you to make use of your peers in this classroom, and I want you to make use of your instructor.

Workshopping and conferencing

The time will come during your first essay when you'll be looking for some outside guidance. During this stage of the writing process, you open yourself up to your fellow writers and your instructor in a "workshop" and in a "conference." The workshop will likely take place in your classroom. Maybe you'll arrange your tables or desks in a circle. If you're in computer class, you may meet at a central table. If your class is completely online, you might meet while all connected to your computers. However they happen, workshops are gatherings of all the writers in class.

If you get a chance to conference, you'll likely do that in your instructor's office, or in the faculty lounge, or at the student union, or just on the hood of someone's car. (That's one of my favorite kinds of conferences.)

This part of the writing process is hard for some developing writers. We get a little nervous about turning our work over to the class and our instructor. After all, it's not finished yet, it's just a rough draft. But our peers will be struggling with and defeating the same devils and demons we face, so it makes sense to ask for their support. And our instructor has helped countless writers through these tasks before, so he or she makes a perfect target for our questions.

Let's look at these two valuable parts of the writing process.

THE WORKSHOP

Artists have used "workshop theory" for decades. The same is true for poets and fiction writers. Because workshop members have similar goals, they can often see and understand the work of others as well as their own. Poets read each other their poems and allow their fellow poets or peers a chance to respond and give suggestions. "I really like that opening, but some of the language in the middle was dull and ordinary." The poet writes that down, or listens and remembers, and then tries to decide if the advice is good or not. If three people say "Yeah, Doug's right. That middle stuff is dull. Ditch that," then the poet has a pretty good response that suggests he should at least think about changing that middle part.

An essay workshop works in the same way for us. We look outside ourselves for help. However, the neat thing is we're still in charge. This is an important first rule: Even though we are going to open ourselves up to our peer readers and fellow writers, we're still in charge. Listen and give them some trust. But in the end, you have to live with the essay. It's still your call.

Our workshop is simple in principle. A handful of writers will volunteer to read their essays aloud. We're all working on the same type of essay right now, so we all have similar ideas of what this kind of essay should do. Ideally, the workshop will get you some much-needed feedback.

Remember our story earlier about falling off the slide? If we read that out loud, someone might say "That's a cool story. I remember breaking my leg once. Your story reminded me of how stupid I felt." Someone else might offer "I liked it. But I couldn't tell what was going on in the first paragraph; you didn't have enough detail. Were there a lot of people there? How come you lay on the ground so long before someone helped you? Didn't people like you?"

You sit in the workshop and listen carefully to the questions and comments. Write them all down; they're all important. After the workshop is over and you've had time to relax a little (because the first time is a little bit stressful for most folks), look over the comments. Be reasonable and remember that what you have received is honest reader response. You wrote that paper wanting to communicate, remember? If you didn't get your message through, the questions and concerns raised by your audience will help you make the paper better. "Hmm, maybe I didn't really explain that I was playing with a bunch of older kids that day. That's why people let me lie there so long before telling my teacher. They didn't know me and they weren't really my friends." You begin answering the questions and the needs of your audience and next time you show that paper to them, those questions shouldn't come up again. The workshop helps train you to understand the kinds of questions readers might have. The more you workshop, the better you'll get at knowing ahead of time what questions readers ask.

There are typically two kinds of workshop meetings, big group and small group. They are set up differently, work differently, and provide different kinds of feedback. Let's look at each.

BIG GROUP

▪ **Class meets in a circle.** This is a nice way to make sure everyone can see and hear, and be seen and heard. Too many times if we sit in traditional rows, there's a student-to-teacher dynamic only rather than what we like to have, which is a complete class dialogue, students and teacher together.

▪ **Writers read portions of their drafts.** In a big-group workshop, in which there might be as many as 20–30 people listening, we try to read short sections. I've found there's plenty to discuss after hearing only a paragraph or two of an essay. For example, after one paragraph our listeners could reflect back to the writer whether or not they would keep reading. (That is, after all one of the essential goals of an opening paragraph.)

Regardless of the number of paragraphs, each writer who reads should read enough, and only enough, so that listeners get "involved" in the essay. Keep in mind this warning about the length of readings. Whenever 20 people gather in a circle, there's a combined amount of fidgeting and shuffling and clearing of throats that culminates in a lack of attention. We come from the television age and beyond, and our attention spans aren't what they used to be!

It's hard for only one person to focus for many minutes on someone else's essay. It's more difficult for a large group to do the same thing. Find a small but complete section of text to read. It also helps to let the readers know how much is coming: "Here's the opening paragraph of my essay." If we know how much is coming, we can focus in for that.

It's the same reason a good dentist says "Okay, you're going to feel some pain in your gums for about ten seconds, then it's going to be over."

■ **Listeners make note of places in the draft that work well and moments that sound confusing/awkward/boring, and so on.** One of the neat things about the workshop is that we know we're going to be doing something good for the writer. The writer has worked on his or her essay alone. He or she has probably never read the thing to anyone. Even if the writer has told someone about the essay, he or she has probably never sat someone down and actually asked for help. So we're in a prime position. We get to interact in the process and help the writer.

One of the simplest and most important things we can do is simply "react" to the text. Just giving our first reaction to it helps the writer. If you think the paper sounds "neat," then say it! That's a vote of confidence that oftentimes will leave a positive and lasting impression on a writer for months or years. I've sat in these writing workshops for over fifteen years, and I always get a kick out of seeing someone get positive feedback. Just a little—"Wow, you did a neat job of describing your dad"—often gives that writer confidence to keep going. If you like something, definitely say so.

Now, for things that don't work we have an even greater responsibility. The warning I always give is "This isn't personal!" It's hard for any writer to set this notion aside. We closely align ourselves with our ideas and our writing. Sometimes we think that our rough draft somehow really is us. If we write about something, and someone doesn't like the essay, we think that they don't really like us either. Well, that's silly, right? If I don't like that red shirt you've got on, I'm not impugning you personally. I just don't like the shirt. The shirt is something you're wearing; it's not in your soul! Your essay is something you're writing. Even if it is a personal essay with all of your ideas and feelings and hopes and dreams in it, it still isn't your soul or your spirit.

Your essay is just scratches and marks and dots and lines on a sheet of paper. Don't take it personally. As readers, we can help this process by focusing on the work. Don't address the problem by saying "I don't like the way you did that!" Say instead "That paragraph about the party confused me." Don't say "You haven't interested me in your essay yet." Say instead "I need some more details in the opening paragraph to interest me in the paper."

■ **Group determines if the draft meets criteria.** Each of the essays that we write during the semester is different. They have different purposes, different audiences, different goals, different shapes, sizes, and so on.

As you move through the semester you'll be experiencing very different kinds of writing. For example, a letter of complaint to a business is rather different from an observation essay. A research paper about your favorite activity has different kinds of goals from a personal narrative. Each time we take on a new essay we're attempting to understand what the essay *really* is about. In this book I'll talk about the goals of the essay. You'll read that and think about it. Your instructor will likely have his or her own ideas of how the essay can benefit you the most. Your friend next to you will have her opinion. Your roommate will tell you something else. And all of it is likely to be right!

You spend a good amount of time in any essay process figuring out the overall nature of the essay. A perfect time to confirm this process is during the workshop. Use this time to test your understanding. If your classmate Lisa reads a position paper that has a long personal story about her uncle in the opening paragraph, the workshop should decide if that personal opening is appropriate for her position paper. Use the workshop to help yourself find out if you're on the "right track." Have you written an essay that "fits" the assignment?

■ **Writer takes notes as big group discusses the draft, but stays out of conversation until the end, when he or she may ask direct questions as to how to improve the text.** This is always a tough step for writers. We feel vulnerable whenever we turn our ideas or words over to someone else. It's a little moment when we feel naked, but it's important that we stay out of the fray for three good reasons.

1. If we jump in and address people's questions quickly, we give the impression that we don't need help. After all, we're acting like we have all the answers.

2. We want to encourage a free discussion of the paper among our colleagues, our fellow writers. It's as if we're all trying to bake a nice cake. We're not experts or anything, but we've got a bunch of friends who are also busy like us, trying to learn how to bake a cake. They're going to come into our kitchen and look at our first attempt. They're going to dip a finger in the icing and cut a little slice for themselves and talk about things we've done well and poorly. Why listen to them? Because we're doing the same job as them! They're doing the same job as we are!

3. Written communication, unlike verbal communication, lacks the opportunity to respond immediately to listener feedback. For the workshop to be valuable to the writer, he or she needs to listen to feedback as it would be given by a reader who is not worried that the writer will jump in to defend or explain his or her essay. After

all, you're not going to have that chance in the future. You won't be able to drive around to all of your readers' houses and say "What I meant to say was . . ." If the reader doesn't get it from the essay, it's not there.

After the class has discussed the work and come up with a number of different ideas, suggestions, and places to go next, the writer will be invited into the conversation. This is not your time to "apologize" for your essay, or to merely smile at the people who said nice things about it. This is a time for clarification. If Janet said "The first paragraph needs more detail," it's time for you to ask "Do you mean I need more physical description about the horseback riding, or do you mean I should give more detailed dialogue with my brother?" That kind of pointed and direct question will help you come to an understanding of what you should be doing next.

Now here's the good part: This is still your essay. By opening up to the workshop, you've solicited free advice. These readers, your colleagues, have likely given you the best advice they have, based on this single experience of hearing the essay. However, you're still in charge. You still know the essay better than anyone else, and you should still feel like you've got the best handle on things. If you just don't agree with the two students who said your opening wasn't dramatic enough, there's no law that says you have to change your essay. Think of the information you gain from a workshop meeting as a set of suggestions.

While I give you that good news, I should also warn you not to automatically discredit any of the advice you get either. The suggestions you heard are likely fresh, and freshness is one thing writers often lose as they work on an essay for a protracted period of time.

SMALL GROUP

■ **Three to five writers meet together in a group.** In this smaller meeting, each participant bears a little more responsibility. There will not be a chance for feedback from twenty or so, just from the two to four other writers! Everyone needs to pay particular attention. Because we're all a little closer, physically, it's usually easier to concentrate and hear what the writer is saying. If the class is broken into several groups, you might want to find some other classrooms for you to "spill over" into. Check with your instructor.

■ **Each writer reads some of his or her draft while listeners take notes on a sheet of paper, attempting to refer to very specific parts of the draft in order to give the writer feedback.** One neat idea that can really help is for the writer to bring multiple copies of his or her draft. This is a pretty inexpensive proposition when you only need three or four copies. It also makes the job of the readers much easier. Being able to hear the essay being read while reading along at the same time is a terrific way of taking in the information. Also, it provides a neat and easy place for each reader to make notes and comments and suggestions. At the end of the workshop, not only have you had the chance to say: "I think the second paragraph is way too long. You should cut it." You've also been able to draw a line across the page on the writer's draft, where you think that cut needs to be.

■ **Listeners come up with a one- or two-sentence overall response to the draft.** This overall response should focus on positive aspects of the draft. As in any endeavor, we feel vulnerable to criticism. Even though we come into the workshop knowing that we're opening ourselves up to comments and suggestions, it doesn't make the actual process any easier. In a small, concentrated group like the small-group workshop, sometimes there's even more tension. (We are more tightly packed, after all.) As readers we should be aware of how exposed the writer is and respond appropriately. Remember, our job as readers and workshop members is *not* to merely provide negative criticism of the work in progress. Ideally, we're here to help move the essay along, to make it better, and to provide perspective that will help the writer more clearly and completely get his or her point across to desired readers. That's why we gather: To help! So, as you make your comments and suggestions known to the writer, keep that in mind. You are part of the process. Your job is to help the writer make that essay better!

■ **Listeners also respond to any problem areas of the draft, pointing if possible to specific areas of the text and offering a suggestion for how the problem area can be improved.** In the same way that we work on the positive aspects, we must also deal with problem areas. By this point in the process we've earned a little goodwill. We've pointed out some good stuff; the writer and readers are all a little at ease. I hope that very soon in the process of reading and responding you'll realize that when we gather like this, it's always about helping the writer. That's a key thing to keep in mind. We're not getting together to bug you. We're here to help; When we voice our concerns about things that are or aren't working; we're trying to help you with direction and tasks for the future of this essay.

■ **Writer responds with his or her plan for the future.** This is not the time to say "Uh, I know it's a rough draft. I've really meant to fix it. I'm sorry it's so bad." That's silly. It's also how we feel when someone has just spent some time evaluating and judging us. It's almost unavoidable, but it's not particularly helpful. The number one thing to do at this point is say "Thanks." You are going to need the help of your peers as you go along during the course of a long semester. Remember the extra pressure that has been put on them as well. They are helping you on their own time, so to speak. If you are ungrateful and dismissive of their ideas and thoughts, they might not be very eager to help you next time. So, say thanks, and then talk about what you're planning to do next.

If some of the suggestions that were made sound pretty cool, then say so. "I think what Doug suggested is good. I want to try and write a longer introduction. Doug, would you think that I need more description there?"

See what happened there? The writer acknowledged that Doug's remarks were helpful and the writer also went on to get some clarification. Excellent workshop behavior. The next time you're in a workshop with this group of people, they'll be even more willing to offer suggestions that can help your essay.

A SAMPLE WORKSHOP

The most helpful workshop is one in which you get good readings and good responses from a variety of your peers. As mentioned before, it helps to bring a few extra copies of your essay for your peer readers. If they have a clean copy of the text in front of them, and they are told to comment on the paper, they are much more likely to give you feedback. It's sometimes tempting not to take part in the verbal discussion. Some readers may just say "Yeah, I agree with what John said earlier." But with an essay of their own in front of them, readers can make written comments that will be helpful. After all, they have the same option to bring you an essay to read one day, and they'll want your goodwill.

Let's take a look at a short essay from a writer and then at the written comments that were collected afterward. This writer gave copies of her essay to four other people in her group. That's a pretty good number for a small-group workshop, and I think you'll find that four readers' responses will be plenty to get you started on a revision. Sometimes when writers get responses from twenty readers at once (especially if they're all lengthy ideas), they become too paralyzed to actually do anything.

This is a rough draft of an evaluation essay. You may have seen it in its finished version in Chapter 7. Here we get to work on it in its rough draft state. Take it easy as you read, maybe make some notes yourself as you go along and see what you'd have to say to this writer.

DATING

Okay, girls, I just wanted to let you know that I am officially an expert on dating. Actually, any girl who has ever been on a date with a man, or a boy, can be considered an expert as well. One simple evening with a member of the opposite sex can leave a girl feeling so confused that she may never want to associate with a member of the opposite sex again, even if he does look like JFK, Jr. On the other hand, one evening with a member of the opposite sex could leave a girl so intrigued that she only wants more and more contact with males in order to figure out their mystique, to find out what makes their devious little minds tick. Therefore, I have come up with a few guidelines to help my fellow single females weave their way through the jungle out there known as the dating scene.

Countless awkward dates with boring men, and even a few intriguing and enjoyable evenings, have helped me create a framework upon which to build some guidelines to simplify the dating scene for all of you. These guidelines are not complicated, anyone who has suffered through a few horrid blind dates and oafish men could have thought them up.

First things first, there is no such thing as the perfect male. If this is what you are searching for, you are bound to be single for the rest of your life. Don't worry, though, this is where a lot of us go wrong in our dating lives. As some famous person once said, "To err is human, to forgive divine." No person is perfect, regardless of sex. Of course, we as females do not ever have to admit that we are even a smidgen away from achieving perfection. We just need to have a little room in our hearts to forgive the mistakes that we all make, male and female alike.

Since you know that there is no such thing as the perfect male, your criterion for a date should be reworked to accommodate this factor. I do not mean to suggest that you lower your standards by any means. No woman should ever do that. I just mean that when that cute guy (you know, the one that was in your marketing class last semester) strikes up a conversation with you at the bar, do not turn away just because his eyebrows are not perfectly even. Give the guy a chance if he seems nice, nice guys are better than nice looking guys any day.

The second criterion for a good date is to make sure that the guy pursues you, and not the other way around. Your obvious conclusion should be not to go on dates with guys who leave all the work of dating up to you. If you call him all the time, and the plans are always up to you, the guy is not worth it. A guy that is worth dating will pursue you with phone calls and romantic plans.

Finally, remember that when you are single, the perfect guy for you is not necessarily going to be the next one that you meet. Most likely, you will end up going on many dates before you connect with a guy that is compatible with you. Do not let this simple fact discourage you. Dating does not have to be a quest for a husband. It can be a fun hobby. After all, what's wrong with going to dinner and expanding your conversational skills with enjoyable (or maybe not so enjoyable) company for a couple of hours on a Saturday night.

This leads me to my third criterion for a good date. If the guy seems like an acceptable date, go out with him. Do not inspect each prospective date under a magnifying glass as though you expect him to be your future husband and partner for life. Lighten up and go out with guys that might not be acceptable to you as a life partner.

Girls, dating can be very trying if you approach it with the wrong attitude. Remember, dating can be very fun and enjoyable, you might even come up with a few friends along the way. As long as you follow these expert guidelines and criteria for dating, you can have a good time as well. There is no such thing as the perfect male, make sure that the guy pursues you, and accept dates with not-so-perfect men just for fun and your dating experiences can be devoid of the useless and awkward evenings that I have suffered through in order to come to these conclusions. Good luck and happy dating!

Okay, now let's look at responses from her readers. As we said earlier in the writing process chapter, essays are always in progress. Making evaluative comments about an essay that is still being built is not always very helpful. Saying the paper is "good" or "bad" won't help the writer very much.

Whenever you read or hear a rough draft, remember that caution. Point your comments and suggestions toward things to be done next. Let's see how these peer readers did. As you read these responses, ask yourself if the peer reader is helping the writer. Would comments like these help your own work on the essays you might do for this class? If not, what kinds of comments would be helpful?

Peer Response 1

▶ I think that your conclusion says one thing and means another. You say that by doing what your criteria says that you won't have awkward evenings, but your criteria then leads to these awkward evenings.

You say that you are trying to help people from not going on many dates and yet you tell them to go on many dates.

You also say that there is no such thing as a perfect man and yet you tell your audience to go out with the not so perfect men. Does this mean that everyone is still fair game to date? You didn't narrow the field of possible dates at all. ◀

This writer has focused on one concept: the essay's contradictory quality, as he sees it. He points out three separate moments when the essay or the writer makes a contradiction. This is very valuable for the writer. It allows the writer to see the text through someone else's eyes. Now she can go back and look at three separate places in her text to decide if she agrees with the response.

Peer Response 2

▶ Good, honest essay! Your audience is very clear—single girls. I was glad that this wasn't a male-bashing essay, but a truly informative essay about guidelines for dating.

You could use personal examples to explain each of your criteria, however. In the first couple of paragraphs of your essay, there seem to be a few too many introductory phrases (e.g. Of course, ladies, first things first, on the other hand, either way, however, etc.). One way to vary the length of your sentences would be to cut out some of these phrases. Be very direct with some of your sentences. The first two paragraphs are introductory, right? Maybe you could condense. ◀

Another great response, but rather different from the first. I like the positive feedback in the first line. In addition the reader does a simple task and gives his guess as to the desired audience. The reason that's useful is that it reflects back to the writer what an unbiased outsider thinks. If the writer reads this response and says "That's NOT my audience," she'll know that some changes have to be made.

The second paragraph of the response is even better than the first because the reader recognizes that what he should be doing in a peer response is making suggestions for the continuing writing of the essay. All of us in the support group must remember that these essays are not done. They are all in progress, all moving forward. Our comments should reflect ways we think the essays can move more smoothly along in the process.

Peer Response 3

▶ What is this an evaluation of exactly? The various criteria you use seem to be about whether or not you should date a variety of men. Is that right? What about evaluating dates, period? That is, evaluating the experience. "You know a date is good if a guy calls you for it." "You know a date is good if the guy acts relaxed." "You know a date is good if he offers to pay your way." "You know a date is good if the guy lets you decide how much physical contact you're going to share."

That way the criteria moves through the actual sequence of a date, rather than the sequence of the moments leading up to a date . . . ◀

This is a fairly ambitious response. Reader 3 has actually rethought the entire essay, keeping the subject the same, but modifying greatly what parts of the dating process the writer should deal with. This approach (a complete re-do on the topic) commonly comes from an instructor rather than a peer. Peer readers are often shy about sending the writer back to the drawing board, remaking the essay totally.

But you should try to keep the best interests of the writer in mind at all times. If you really think the paper needs to be remade, then it's your duty to say it. Remember, your comments are only accepted as suggestions. Better to offer an ambitious response that pinpoints a problem than to hold back and offer no direction for the writer who is in need.

Peer Response 4

▶ Yeah, it's fine. ◀

This is among the more common types of peer response. But you recognize that it's not very valuable, right? If you wrote an essay that you wanted some real help with, would you be excited about getting this response? I didn't think so. We have to remember that we're all in this battle together and that we all have special abilities to help each other. When Sarah wrote this essay and brought it to her class, she did it because she was looking for assistance. She knew that her classmates, her fellow writers and peers, were working on a similar paper. They had likely struggled with the same kinds of problems she had and therefore would be able to assist her in her endeavor.

Don't feel like the peer response period is something that is infringing on your time and energy. Responding to other writers is definitely part of this or any good writing class. You may not recognize it at first but you're learning about your own essay and the essay type even when you're reading someone else's paper. That's the beauty of the workshop. As you're reading Sarah's paper, you may be thinking "Wow, this is funny; everyone seems to like it; the teacher likes it. I had no idea you could be funny." Then you say out loud "Sarah, this is neat. I like that it's funny. You've done a good job of keeping the topic light; I didn't know if we could do that in this paper, but now I know. Good job!"

You're learning about your own essay all the time: when you're reading about it, when your instructor is assigning it, when you begin doing small free writing and brainstorming, when you talk to people about it, when you show your work to your peers and your instructor, when you talk about other writer's essays, and when you read other writer's essays. It's an ongoing thing. It's all part of the same process. All those activities feed different parts of your brain.

When you're hungry, you probably don't just eat a big plate of mashed potatoes. You may love mashed potatoes; I know I do. But you need to feed different parts of your body: meat or protein, vegetables, some bread maybe, and a big dish of ice cream and a piece of pie. A variety of different flavors. Use the same thinking when you're writing your essay; open yourself up to a buffet of ideas and skills and steps and options.

THE CONFERENCE

Conferencing as a composition concept is certainly as old as composition theory itself. We've been using that word, however, and making it a part of contemporary pedagogy only since the great composition renaissance of the 1960s.

By the time you've gone through a workshop and worked on some revisions, you'll have a new draft. You'll be further along in the process, closer to the deadline. It's time for a conference with your instructor. A conference is much like a workshop, except you get a response from only one reader. But because it's your teacher, your reader happens to be a pretty good one, one who has likely seen a tremendous variety of essays on this same assignment, making him or her aware of some possibilities that might never occur to you or to your peer respondents.

Conferencing is without a doubt the single most beneficial thing I can do for my writers. I can teach all day long. I have enough wind in my big barrel chest to lecture for days about the concepts of writing. My memory is long, and I can recall hundreds of good and bad essays. I've got assignments for every occasion.

But I'm at my best when I just shut up and let your essay be the focus of our time together.

So I'm a big fan of conferencing. Let's break it down into its parts and look at it as a process.

A conference is any meeting between a writer and his or her instructor. These meetings may not even be called "conferences" by your instructor. You may be asked to "stop by the office and bring your paper." That's a conference. You may have a five-minute chat at your desk during class one day. That's a conference. If you're walking across campus and ask your teacher a question about that first paragraph and the trouble you're having, that's a conference, too.

All instructors have office hours, or at least let you know when you can find them to ask questions, and that's primarily how and where you can get your conference help. Even if your instructor hasn't offered "conferences" by using that term, you still have the same access. All you have to do to get your instructor to meet with you and look at and discuss your essay is ask!

You may be lucky and have one of the many instructors around the country who have a formal and established procedure for conferencing. In fact, I sometimes cancel a whole day of classes and replace that very general meeting with a series of 10- or 15-minute conferences with students. Much more gets accomplished when the writer and I can sit down with no interruptions and actually look at the paper together.

It's far different than the conversation we can have during a regular class. If I'm up front doing a lecture and a student says "I'm having trouble with my opening paragraph," the response I give will be something like "Well, in any good opening paragraph, you're expected to grab the reader's attention. Some of the typical things we try are, blah blah blah."

That's good, general information for the whole class. However, what my student really wanted to know was about his "own" first paragraph. He's not looking for the general. He's got a bad first paragraph and he wants help. But in the scope of a general class meeting, I can't say "Everyone, go get a Pepsi; I have to help John for a minute."

That's why I meet students individually whenever I can. Then when the student says "I'm having trouble with my opening paragraph," I can look at his essay and say "Well, John, let's start by cutting this first sentence. You see how the same information is in the second sentence, too? Now, let me draw an arrow here and move this other stuff." I can't do that in class. I can only do it one on one.

We must open our writing up to others in order to learn.

Let's look at some of the responsibilities that go on around the time of our conference.

BEFORE THE CONFERENCE

The time between getting a writing assignment and having a conference or meeting with an instructor is what I consider "free" time. I tell my writers to go wild with ideas. I tell them to experiment and do as much thinking and creative stumbling around as they can. The point of the writing assignment is to get you on your way. It should be a stimulating moment that opens up a world of possibilities to you. If your instructor is going to offer conferences for you, then he or she is already expecting to see a rough draft from you somewhere in between the assignment and the actual due date. Take advantage of that great opportunity to give your draft all that you've got: time, energy, and creativity.

Why? Because a conference is a bit like a safety net. You're the guy or the gal on the high wire, the trapeze artist, but you get to make some mistakes without crashing. The whole writing process as I designed it for this book allows you, in fact almost commands you, to experiment, to grow, to go wild. Of course, it means work, too, but you already know that.

Having the conference in your future means you've got room to stretch out. So, get a clear understanding of the assignment by asking for clarification, if needed, and then get on the job. If you're following the steps and warmups in this book, then you'll always have a little "teacher" right there with you. But nothing makes up for getting to work right away.

As you write and invent and draft, keep to a schedule. I've found that my very best writers actually block out time each day or each week just to work on my class. This proves to be a pretty good idea. Just having a vague notion of "I think I'll work on my essay today," doesn't always equate with actually doing it. Make it definite: "Between 4 and 6 PM today I'm going to close my door, get my computer up and running (or your notebook), and I'm going to get this first draft on the way!"

While I want you to feel comfortable experimenting *before* the conference, keep in mind that you want to bring something fairly complete *to* the conference. Sure, it's still a rough draft, but that's no reason for showing up with a haphazard collection of notes and ideas. It's also your job to shape that collection of notes and ideas into a real essay—and I mean paragraphs and everything—for your instructor to look at in your conference. The more detailed and polished the rough draft, the better the comments and suggestions that your instructor can make for you.

I'm always very impressed when a writer comes to one of my conferences with a rough draft that at least "looks" like an essay: typed, with a title, with real paragraphs, with an opening and a closing. It allows me to see the essay's shape. Sure, I expect there will be things within the essay that we will have to fix, but I'm much more excited about fixing something that looks good and that has been taken care of by the writer, rather than a bunch of scribbles that could have been done in the hallway outside my office minutes before the conference.

Remember, an instructor usually cares as much for your essay as you do. If you show a lackadaisical attitude, he or she might, too. It's human nature.

Your last step before a conference is to really read your own essay and come up with questions of your own about it. This is a step that even well-meaning writers sometimes leave out. They feel they've worked so hard already that it's not necessary to go through the essay one more time, very carefully. There's the belief among some writers that their conference is going to be a magical experience where the teacher is going to rewrite their entire essay for them. This is a fantasy, folks. When my students come in with their essays, I'm not correcting their papers. That's not what the conference is for. It is your paper from start to finish. The conference is there so a good reader will help you understand

1. things that a reader needs you to do, and

2. things that a writer might do to address those needs.

DURING THE CONFERENCE

Many writers come to a conference with very little to say or ask. Don't be shy. It's very likely this is your only undisturbed time to ask specifically about your essay. You're always able to get general questions answered in class, but this is your best chance during the entire writing process to get help with your essay.

So, ask questions. Be involved. Talk and listen. Don't look around the office. Don't space out. Don't think about places you'd rather be. Pay attention. (Sorry; I love conferences and want to make sure you get your money's worth.)

Here is a transcribed conversation between myself and one of my good writers from a couple of years ago.

Me: Hey, Amber, how have you been?
Amber: Okay. Got my essay here. *(Hands it to me. It's typed, clean, and it looks good.)*
Me: Okay, so how is the paper going?
Amber: Well, at first I had trouble with the opening, so I'm not sure about it. Could you take a look at it for me?
Me: Sure. What else?
Amber: Hmm, I don't know. Maybe I'm worried about the closing, too.
Me: What's new? Closings are hard for everyone. We'll look at it.

(I read for a while, just the opening paragraph.)

Me: Now, what do you think the goal of your opening paragraph is?
Amber: I don't know. To get the reader interested?
Me: Yeah, that's part of it. Have you done that? *(I hand her essay back to her. She reads a little.)*
Amber: Well, I announced the topic at least.
Me: Yeah, and that's good. We know what the topic is, but what have you done to make it exciting?
Amber: Well, everyone knows scuba diving is exciting. Ha ha.
Me: Not me; you wouldn't catch me dead scuba diving.
Amber: Well, then you're not the audience.
Me: Nope. Don't let me off the hook that easy. Don't let readers have the chance to just bail out. Think of maximizing your audience whenever you can.

Amber: How?

Me: Well, first of all, why do you like scuba diving?

Amber: Because it's neat.

Me: Ha ha. Sure. Neat. But what about it?

Amber: Well, it's quiet and peaceful and when you see fish and stuff, it's beautiful.

Me: See, that sounds cool to me. I might read this paper if you told me that in the opening.

Amber: Really?

Me: Yeah, really. Let's put that in there somewhere in the opening. I mean, you said it.

Amber: Yeah, okay. Right now?

Me: Yeah, write it in. Got a pen?

Amber: Yeah. *(She writes for about thirty seconds.)*

Me: Okay, read the new opening.

Amber: "Scuba diving is a fun sport that takes you deep into the ocean and away from the troubles of the world. You can float quietly away from the dry world and live among the beautiful, multi-colored fish and sea life."

Me: See, that's already better.

Amber: Really?

Me: Sure, don't you think so?

Amber: Well, I say something like that later on.

Me: Yeah, but your reader may not get to "later on," right?

Amber: Yeah, yeah, I know. You have to hook them. You're always yelling about that. Ha ha.

Me: Me? Yell. Right? Okay, so that's a much better opening. You told me you were worried about the closing. What about? *(I flip to it and start reading.)*

Amber: Well, I just can't think of anything to do at the end except say that scuba is cool.

Me: Nah, that's not enough. You know what you want, right?

Amber: No, what do you mean?

Me: Why tell us about scuba diving at all?

Amber: Because it's cool?

Me: Nope. *(Long pause. I finish reading the last paragraph and just set the paper down between us. Thirty seconds pass.)*

Amber: I don't get it.

Me: Remember we sometimes say that a good essay makes the reader want to "do" something at the end?

Amber: Yeah! I want them to go scuba diving.

Me: Even me?

Amber: Yeah, so instead of just saying scuba is cool, I tell them to go.
Me: Go where?
Amber: Go diving?
Me: How? Where? Where do I get the stuff? Where can I get trained?
Amber: Okay, okay, I get it. I have to finish with, like, a phone number
          of the dive shop, tell them the hours, like that?
Me: There ya go! That's it.
Amber: Cool. I think I can do the rest now.
Me: Okay, so what are you going to do?
Amber: I'm going to look up contact information for the dive shop. I'm
          going to rewrite that last paragraph to be more forceful.
Me: All right; see you in class. Let me know if you need more help.
Amber: Okay, thanks.

That took a total of three minutes and fifty seconds Not ten minutes, not even five. Less than four minutes. And in that time Amber fixed two of the most important parts of her essay. And that's pretty normal. And it didn't happen because I'm a genius (you can tell that, can't you?); it happened because I reacted like a reader and told Amber what it was I needed from the essay that she wasn't giving me yet. She thought of the stuff to add, not me. She's still in charge of her essay; I just helped her realize some things.

That's the value of a good conference. Just this amount of contact helps reassure both you and your instructor that things are happening. Even the worst conference is better than nothing. This is what a "worst" conference goes like.

Me: Hi, Matt. How's it going?
Matt: Okay, I guess.
Me: So, do you have a draft with you?
Matt: It's not due yet, right?
Me: No, but today is conference day and we're going to talk about
         how the paper is developing.
Matt: Well, I don't have anything yet.
Me: Have you got any ideas?
Matt: Uh, yeah, I'd like to write about the Beatles.
Me: What about?
Matt: Uh, just their music and stuff.
Me: What about their music?
Matt: I don't know. How their music is still cool.
Me: What do you mean?
Matt: I mean one guy's dead and the others are old, but we still play
         their music.

Me:	And what kind of paper is that?
Matt:	Uh, it's a paper that says I think the Beatles are the best band. They're better than bands out right now.
Me:	Can you prove that?
Matt:	Sure! I mean I've got all their CDs and I know all about them.
Me:	Okay, well get going then.

I really can't do much in a situation like this except to keep asking questions. This particular conference at least got the writer around to a topic he liked and helped me help him discover what he wanted to say about the topic. That's not the ideal situation, though. You are wasting valuable time (yours and the instructor's) when you come to a conference ill-prepared.

AFTER THE CONFERENCE

After you've received help of the kind Amber got above, you should be energized or, at least, clear about what's the next thing to do. Don't leave a conference until you have a plan for the next few steps of the paper.

Then the work again falls to you. Sorry, but that's the way it is. As I always say to my students when I'm feeling like getting into a fight, "I've already passed this class. If *you* want the grade, *you* have to do the work."

I always think of the conference as a giant revolving door. You're on the outside, stumbling around on your own. You're picking up ideas and holding them in your hands, trying to have them all make sense. You stumble toward the door with a little bit of momentum and I'm waiting on the inside of the building. As you flash past, I check out what you've got, help you re-arrange some of it, maybe slip you a phrase or an idea that hadn't occurred to you yet, and then push you back outside, giving the door a little extra push as you hurtle away on your own again.

No matter how wholeheartedly you take to the workshop and/or the conference, the paper still rests mostly on you. This troubles some writers, especially ones who feel as though they struggle mightily with writing. I see it differently, however. I see it as a wild and wonderful opportunity.

When you come and spin through my door, I'm always smiling. I like seeing you show up, and I like seeing you head out again.

Good luck!

The writing center

The last piece in the support group puzzle doesn't even involve your instructor or the rest of your class.

The college or university writing center has radically changed over the past years. In fact, the kind of writing center you have on your campus may be rather different from those of other colleges or universities in your area.

Generally, writing centers fall into one of two categories.

SCENARIO ONE

- Dictionaries, workspace, computers with word-processing software, all monitored by a student worker who signs people in and out

Many teachers might simply make an assignment of logging in at the writing center a certain number of times a semester or of spending a set amount of time there each week. Chances are this kind of writing center or lab is primarily used as a workspace for the writers who do go there.

I find even this, the most rudimentary of centers, a helpful place for many writers, especially those who don't have their own workspace to really block out time for their essays. If you've got a roommate who parties all day and night, or just snores too loud, or if you just spend more time watching TV in your dorm room than working, then head to the lab. There's not much "fun" to be had there, and having some basic tools around you—paper, ink, computers, software—will give you the opportunity to get working.

You can make this place work for you, but you have to be a little dedicated. You might have to find out what kind of software they have in advance, what kind of disks you need. You might have to bring your own paper or perhaps buy some at the bookstore. You might not have any editing help available, but if you are there to work anyway, you'll be able to make the best of it for yourself.

SCENARIO TWO

- Computers, software, printers, grammar/diagnostic software, tutoring help

This may be the most common type of writing center in existence right now. Most colleges and universities that I'm familiar with have something resembling this setup. The computers are usually in decent enough shape; and even if there aren't a bunch of great laser printers, the printers are good enough to create "grade-ready" work.

In addition, the computer software may be advanced enough so that you can get some rudimentary computer help with your work. Be forewarned, however, about the dangers of "spell check" and "grammar check." Spell checking is one of the most wonderful tools ever invented, and is a helpful thing to run on your text as you're working on it. However, the flaws of spell checkers are common and famous. This sentence, while quite badly spelled, would not be caught by most spell checkers.

▶ Their are better weighs too do this. Eye can't belief that I trusted this spell checker. There no dam good. ◀

Still, if you're prepared to spell check on your own as well, a good piece of software can help you along the way.

Grammar checkers, such as *Grammatik,* or the built-in checkers that come with the most current version of Microsoft Word and Word Perfect, are vaguely helpful, sometimes catching stylistic problems of wordy sentences or misplaced verbs, but for the most part I don't find them to be helpful enough to even spend the few minutes it takes to run them. Your best bet is to grammar check the old-fashioned, human way.

And that takes us to the best part of this scenario—a tutor. Again, the kind of tutor you have access to varies widely. Tutors typically range from upper division (junior or senior) English majors to part-time faculty from the English department to actual full-time staff or faculty who work in the center all of the time.

You should be enthused about any of these options. Any good reader is helpful, as you have been learning during all of your essay assignments. The writing-center reader is not likely to be in your class or to be aware of the special nature of your writing assignment, so make sure you explain your assignment and any steps that have already occurred.

▶ This was assigned by my writing instructor. She wants me to write an argument paper in which I state my opinion. I wrote a draft already, and read it out loud in my class in a workshop meeting. Most of the people who heard it thought I was being way too controversial with my language. They told me to tone it down. I tried some of that but don't know if I did the right thing. That's why I came here today. ◀

By saying all that, you assure that the reader is aware of what you've done and what you need. It's very helpful for the tutor or writing-center helper to know exactly what you need, as they see dozens of writers every day with a wide variety of assignments, needs, and problems. If your instructor has given you an assignment sheet, bring that with you to show the tutor.

A last word about help

One of the best things about being in a writing class surrounded by peers and an instructor is the sense that you are not alone. Improving our writing is not an easy process; it involves us trying, failing, and revealing things about ourselves and our minds. Facing those challenges alone are difficult and confusing. Sharing the hard work with others either in the same place or a little ahead of you in experience makes the job easier to handle and understand.

Don't be shy about asking for help, whether it be of your peers, your instructor, or a tutor at the writing center. Our process is designed the way it is so you don't have to face your difficulties alone.

Additional Academic Writing

While the book so far has detailed several essential and interesting essay assignments, the truth is that during your college career you'll be asked to complete a wide variety of writing tasks. This chapter aims at discussing some of these, showing you how the principles learned elsewhere in the book (hopefully) relate to these new tasks or assignments.

Whether you face an essay test, a semester-long writing project in your history class, or a four-page research paper in your philosophy class, I'll try to open up the process to you in some different ways so you can face those challenges as they come to you.

The essay exam

Without a doubt, I get more concerned students who want to know about essay exams than any other single writing task they face. I even hear less moaning and wheezing about research papers! The problems with the essay exam are enormous, and I don't intend to mislead you otherwise. But all of the problems tend to stem from the element of "time."

TIME

There's no getting around this one. You face a time limit on in-class essay exams. It creates problems in two primary ways. First, you have less time to work on your essay than you would in an out-of-class essay. Second, the realization of this time pressure often brings about an undue amount of stress for any writer, even the best of them.

So, what to do about time?

I think the first thing to do is relax. Sure it sounds insane, but getting upset or nervous or jumpy about the time constraints is definitely not going to help you perform better. I've taught lots of classes where my students took timed, in-class essays tests—in all of my literature classes, for example. After the first couple of years of teaching I recognized that the level of writing I get from an in-class prompt is different from an out-of-class essay with virtually unlimited time.

So have some faith in your instructor. He or she is very aware of effects created by the restraint of time. Chances are that any experienced instructor will realize that only a certain level or quality is possible given the constraints of the timed test.

What is the best thing you can do? Make the most of your time.

If you're given an hour to write, segment that hour into some kind of reasonable schedule of events. Look at some of our essay assignments for the semester in this book. You might be given one or two weeks to work on an essay. Ideally, you should be using that time doing different things: some thinking, some initial drafting, some revision, some final copying, and so on. This book attempts to provide a writing process that will be useful to you outside of this class, even outside of your college days.

Let's then transfer the concepts of a regular writing experience to this timed test/essay exam experience.

Let's say you've got an hour.

FIRST 5 MINUTES (55 MINUTES LEFT): READ THE QUESTION

Really read the question. Try to understand what's being asked. Many times when I give a poor grade to an essay exam, it's almost entirely because the writer didn't answer what was being asked. This is a tough notion for us, because we've been trying to spend our writing time on topics and ideas of our own choice. Suddenly, on an essay exam, we may be forced to talk about something we don't have much interest in, or we may even be asked to defend or support a belief or point of view we don't agree with. You must try to get inside the question, to understand the thought process of the instructor. The question is probably a good one and probably one you've talked about during your class. Think. Try to find a memory of that topic.

Here's an example from a history class.

> Question: What are two essential flaws with a capitalistic society, and how do they manifest themselves?

Okay, you're in luck with this question. It's pretty simple and straightforward. However, I see writers every semester get questions like this and freeze. They don't see all the words. They fixate on a few and miss the rest. For me, as a teacher of writing, I'm not even thinking about the answer; I'm thinking *how* I'm going to answer. Forget "capitalism." Forget "flaw." Concentrate on "What are two . . . and how do they manifest themselves." Your answer must have two parts to it. That happens to be two flaws of capitalism. And you aren't just being asked to identify them ("What are two . . .), you're also being asked to explain or show them (" . . . and how do they manifest themselves"). Two flaws, and each has to be shown clearly. That's four things, right? $2+2=4$. My goodness, you had no idea we were going to do math, too, did you?

But seriously. This is crucial. So many writers panic and start answering questions that aren't there. For example, some writers would answer this question as if it said

> Question: Discuss generally, all of the flaws of capitalism you can
>   possibly think of.

An answer to this is definitely not what is being asked for in the real question.

So your question says, "Identify two flaws of capitalism." (I'll leave this up to you; after all it's not my class.) And the question also says, "Show how each flaw manifests itself."

Like I said, four things. Add an opening and a closing because all essays have those, and you've got six mini-paragraphs. That's an essay exam.

NEXT 5 MINUTES (50 MINUTES LEFT): FREE-WRITE

Gather your information. Of course, this will be a lot easier if you actually know your subject well. Contrary to what most students believe, bluffing or B.S.ing your way around an answer will NOT work. Instructors know their subjects and questions and what they expect for an answer. They're trying to read through your answer as quickly as possible, checking off whenever they see a required element. B.S.ing might even make it more likely that the instructor will actually miss the correct answer if you do give it.

But what if you only know one flaw of capitalism? Then you'd better do a whale of a job talking about it and perhaps explain two ways it manifests itself. Beyond that I can't help you. You should try to remember that one of the reasons your instructor has offered you this test is to find out if you've actually learned anything. These tests can reveal if you've done some *thinking* about the subjects covered in the course (just as writing an out-of-class essay can only be successful if you've actually thought about your topic enough to come up with a thesis). If students haven't done that, no system for taking an exam will be all that helpful.

Ideally, you're a good student and you know two flaws of capitalism from your class, your instructor, your lectures, and your textbook. If the instructor has asked for two, there are probably more. Make a list of all of them you can think of.

Class war
Egotism
Greed
Lack of care for others?

Then, for each of the ones you can think of, write a couple of sentences, even phrases, to help you to see what you actually know about the topic and to find out if you have anything to say about it.

Class war: Professor Burris told us that capitalism builds the classes. Lower class, middle class, etc. He said that when you have classes, you have class envy. And that can lead to war, or violence.

Egotism: The book had the chapter about "egotism," and it explained how we could be out of control or something. That egotism ran wild and that was bad. Something like that.

Greed: I can remember the movie "Wall Street" that Professor Burris told us to rent. The idea was that greed overtakes those who get a taste for it and no longer are they capitalists; they become dictatorial, like a monarch. Once a capitalist reaches his peak, he begins to horde the money and capitalism stops. Now he wants a monarchy where he can keep what's his.

Lack of care for others? Something about the welfare system and the difference in socialistic countries like Canada and England.

Even if you don't know much about this topic, you must be able to see which of those four concepts our writer is most familiar and comfortable with. You can physically see that he knows more about "class war" and "greed" because he writes more about those topics. He'll be able to tell that he even writes more coherently about those. On a quick reread of these notes, our writer should be able to know instantly which two he's going to be able to spend the most time on.

NEXT 10 MINUTES (40 MINUTES LEFT): TRUST THE PROCESS

Because of our compressed time, we can't rely on our ability to revise in as leisurely a manner as we might in a full essay process. We have to try to foresee how the essay will go, and where it must go in order to answer the question, and then to set some goals or guidelines. Think of an outline as a sort of first draft. We know from the previous step that the writer has some good ideas. Let's shape them.

I. Opening statement (restate the question as a thesis and forecast answer).

II. First flaw—class war/struggle/conflict (identify by name and define it).

III. First flaw (as it manifests itself).

IV. Second flaw—capitalistic greed (identify by name and define it).

V. Second flaw (as it manifests itself).

VI. Closing (what this all adds up to).

Excellent work. The writer has now taken two things he figured out and put them together to form his outline: 1) how many parts and 2) what the parts are. Having this outline will make up for the fantastic rush he's going to be in.

Now here's a critical question that students always ask me. "What about those people not using the system? They've been writing for ten minutes; they're way ahead of me!" I know that. But what have they written? Clearly you recognize that it's not as well-ordered as yours is going to be, right? I mean, it took you ten minutes to get your outline. They have no outline; they're simply filling up pages. It's not a contest for the most words; it's a contest for the best answer. Additionally, those folks who are in movement, filling pages, are not likely to be willing to start scratching out stuff that doesn't work, or getting rid of ideas that don't make the grade, because those bad, false starts (like the one we had earlier about "lack of care for others?") are going to be right in the middle of this essay they're so hurriedly writing. We've weeded the bad stuff out already. Our fast friends are going to have to include their bad ideas in their finished answer.

NEXT 30 MINUTES (10 MINUTES LEFT): DRAFT

Okay, here's the work. But in our case we're just filling in blanks a bit. We're writing six little parts of an essay that we already know go together well; they fit in the outline, right? All we do now is write each of our smaller sections. Again, this is a timed event, so you have to be smart. Many of your peers will be stressing out and losing track of time. You're playing it cool. You're relaxed. You have thirty minutes to write six little mini-paragraphs, five minutes apiece in this example.

Let's try the "opening statement." That's the first step from our outline above. We already know some of the stuff we want to say. We want to restate the question as our thesis. That will help keep us on track, right? How's this?

> ▶ While capitalism is commonly understood as this country's accepted form of ideology, there are in fact flaws in the system. One flaw involves the serious division that results between ensuing classes. Another flaw involves greed and its inevitable rise amongst capitalists. ◀

We're merely following the steps set out in the outline. We've restated the question into our own thesis, and forecasted our answer by declaring two flaws. This essay is on its way to a good grade, and much of that is simply because the essay has begun in an ordered and clear fashion, something that most timed essay exams cannot claim.

> ▶ Let's begin with what I see as the most serious flaw in capitalism. Capitalism encourages a division of classes. When classes develop: upper, middle and lower, for example, tension is sure to increase . . . ◀

That's the beginning of our second paragraph; it addresses the second and third steps of our outline. We've stated the first flaw, defined it, and are now beginning the explanation.

Once we finish this, we simply keep moving through our outline, writing each section in turn.

It's going well, but here's one more thing we must do with our essay to give it the best chance possible.

LAST 10 MINUTES (0 MINUTES LEFT): FINISH

What do we do with this time? Well, like any essay experience, we're going to make sure we've said something worthwhile. We're going to read the whole thing again and watch for simple things. Have you connected the paragraphs so that they make sense? Have you written legibly (if you're doing it longhand); have you formatted it cleanly, and is the printer ready (if you're doing it on computer.) Even with only ten minutes, you can do some scribbling out and marking in new words. It's a fantastic idea to double-space your longhand drafts just for that reason; it will give you room to correct some things that didn't go right the first time. It's not too hard even to replace whole sentences. Draw an arrow if you have to lead your reader to a new, better sentence.

Also, with that thought in mind, it's nice to know what your instructor thinks about the presentation of this essay. Are cross-outs okay? If not, then you might need more than ten minutes at the end to simply re-copy the whole thing. If he or she allows cross-outs and corrections, then maybe five minutes is all you need at the end.

The point is, planning and structure can help you overcome a normally stressful assignment. All we've done is adapt the writing process from this book to fit this test's schedule. Instead of two weeks or so, you've got an hour or two. Simply trust the process (it's worked for you so far, right?), and you'll be in good shape.

Essays in other disciplines

It's extremely likely that once or twice a semester one of your other classes will require that you write an essay. The concept of "writing across the curriculum," a phrase you might have heard, is all about encouraging students in all fields to spend part of their education writing within that field. Many instructors and professors—of history, philosophy, the sciences, and even mathematics—around the country are being urged to include some kind of essay in their classes.

The reason many instructors in other disciplines require students to compose essays is that testing someone's ability to write on a topic is directly equivalent to testing their ability to *think* about the subject. This change in the academic world is tremendous validation of what I've been saying. The widespread acceptance of "writing across the curriculum" makes me pretty happy to be a writing instructor. Becoming a better thinker and communicator is essential to your success, academically and otherwise.

With these "other discipline" essays looming, let's specify two problems you will face when confronted with them.

PROBLEM ONE

Unlike an English class, your instructor is a well-trained professional only in his or her own field. It's rare that you'll find your sociology teacher also has a degree in English, for example. That worries some writers, but it shouldn't. College-level instructors and professors have usually spent a good portion of their careers writing, and likely publishing, papers and articles in their own fields. While they may come at the job of reading your writing in a different way than your English teacher will, they are qualified and exacting in their own way.

As in any essay assignment, make sure you understand the requirements of the assignment. You must ask questions about the topic assigned, or if you are to supply your own topic, you should brainstorm or free-write your way to a couple of possibilities to try out on your teacher. You must ask questions about style and length. (Your teacher may want you to follow something other than the MLA style that I show you in our research paper chapter; your teacher may even have a special format for your typing.) You must ask questions about the length of the paper and about the number of sources.

PROBLEM TWO

It's more than likely that your essay for this other class will not take up nearly as much regular class time and focus as an essay you might write in a composition or "writing" class. Your instructor in this other discipline usually has tests and reports and/or lab work that also make up crucial parts of your class. You will probably not get much class time to talk about the essay, and almost assuredly you won't have the benefits of a workshop or individual conference. Writing in other courses will require you to assume even more of the natural individual burden of composing an essay, without the direct support you might have gotten used to in your comp class.

Even without the accustomed (maybe even mandatory) support of your English class, you must deal with subject-area essays in the same manner as we've been developing in this class: find and develop the topic; brainstorm and free-write to a plan; write a discovery draft; seek help and assistance from good readers (don't forget the teacher who assigned the paper!). It's even possible that you and your fellow English classmates might be able to share concerns and help each other on these other "academic" papers you'll face.

Writing about literature

Chances are you'll be involved at some collegiate level with writing about literature. At one time in American colleges and universities, the second part of freshman composition (often called ENG 102 or ENG 1302) was a class that dealt with composition and literature. Over the past 20 years or so, that second class has become more of an argumentative writing class, and more of a simple continuation of ENG 101 or 1301. There are still schools and courses which still ask the student to read and write about literature, however, even if it's only a small component of a semester.

Beyond your freshman year you will probably be asked to take some kind of literature class, perhaps an introductory course, or a "sophomore survey" course in American, British, or World Literature. Of course, if you have a major in humanities, you may take a number of literature courses. And if you're really crazy, you might end up being an English major; in which case, you'll be reading and writing about literature a lot.

CRITICISM

Criticism sounds like it's a bad word, but don't get hung up on that single meaning. We've let the word "criticism" become a one-dimensional word that means we're going to say something negative. In academic writing, we don't use it that way at all. To write criticism is to write commentary and analysis and to pass judgment (both good and bad) about a piece of text.

Here are some general typical responses that a writer will make when writing about a poem or a short story. It is possible to write an essay using any one, or two, or all three of these, depending on your confidence, your abilities, and your desires or goals with the essay.

RESPOND IN AN EVALUATIVE WAY

In much the same way that we evaluated things in Chapter 7, the opportunity exists to evaluate a poem and/or a story. Of course, as for any evaluation, we have to be able to play the role of "expert." Again, that simply means we have special interest and experience with the topic to be evaluated. If you've read poetry and/or short stories for a while, and feel that you have an understanding of what separates good ones from bad, then you should have no hesitation about taking on a piece of text in this way.

> ▶ Henry Taylor's poem "At the Swings" is a wonderful, moving piece of text that seems to emote far more than most contemporary poems. ◀

Evaluative criticism concerns itself with the "goodness" and "badness" of the work.

RESPOND IN A STYLISTIC WAY

This type of response requires that you have some experience with the language and theory of poetry and/or fiction. Those things are beyond the scope of this book, but following the two long writing samples to come, you'll see questions that lead you to think about stylistic concerns.

> ▶ Barthelme's story relies on a sort of "snappy" language. The characters, Minor especially, speak in a sort of shorthand that shows them to be intimate or friendly. A different kind of ongoing conversation would change drastically the overall tone of the piece, making Minor less threatening and Ben more unaware. ◀

Stylistic criticism concerns itself with the mechanics and the form of the literature.

RESPOND IN A CRITICAL WAY

Earlier we were talking about the definition of the word criticism. Well, be careful here because "critical" is used the same way. Critical reading of a poem or story does not imply a negative view. A critical view is one in which the text's meaning is examined carefully. Unlike "evaluative"—which is a personal value judgment of the work—or "stylistic"—which is an examination of the form and structure of the work—a "critical" examination concerns itself with the message and the underlying point of the work.

It is in this type of response or paper that you bring us the meaning of the work through your eyes. It's very much an opinion paper in that sense.

> ▶ Taylor's poem examines the very structure of life and death and time. The speaker's trip to the playground is mere action; the true journey involves the speaker's trip through his own memory of life-affirming and life-ending experiences. It's a poem about time, a poem in which the speaker hopes to stop time. ◀

Short story

The short story "Fish" comes from the acclaimed story collection *Moon Deluxe* by the writer Frederick Barthelme. His more recent work is brilliant and breathtaking, including the novels *Bob the Gambler*, *Painted Desert*, and *The Brothers*.

Read the story below slowly and carefully. When reading literature, you're not simply getting the facts and moving on, you should be experiencing the small world the writer creates. You need to listen carefully to what characters say and keep track of what they do. If something seems odd or confusing, read it again. It's not a race to the end of the story. It should be an experience. Many good readers of literature read the same stories and novels many times, because they enjoy the feeling of being swept away into a world not their own.

This story centers around an uncomfortable evening that Ben spends with a long-time ex-girlfriend Sally and her younger brother Minor. Tension or conflict is often an integral part of any story, and the tension here is real, but sometimes quiet. There are no fistfights. Instead, the intensity comes out in small moments. Watch for that. Here we go.

FISH

BY FREDERICK BARTHELME

Sally meets me in the driveway. "It's great you're back," she says. She's tall, willowy, tailored. "I'm going to a German movie at the university, but I'll be home right after. Will you be here?"

"Sure," I say. "You look great." I watch her get into her car, a red Audi four-door.

I've just rented a house from her younger brother and he's invited me to dinner. He comes out waving a rolled-up newsmagazine. "Already?" he says to her. "He hasn't even moved in yet, Sally." He kisses the magazine and waves it at her, and she gives him a drop-dead smile.

He comes down the concrete steps and stands alongside me in the drive. When she pulls away he puts an arm on my shoulder and pokes me in the stomach with the magazine. "There's a thing about elephants in here. You want to read it?"

"Sure. What's it say?"

It's cool for October, but Minor's wearing shorts. He insists we eat on the deck behind his house. His legs are bony and pink. "Go on and wear your coat if you're chilly," he says. "Sally's got everything set. All I've got to do is pop it in the microwave. I want to have a drink first, though." I follow him into the house and then out onto the deck. He puts a wedge of lime on the rim of his glass and points to the white director's chair next to his. "Check out the natural beauty," he says, waving toward the backyard.

A bug twice the size of my thumb is skittering up the side of the swimming pool. He hasn't filled the pool since last year, he tells me. He stares straight across the yard. There are pads of fat under his eyes. "So what do you think of the color?"

"Terrific," I say.

The walls of the pool are dark blue. He had it drained and painted by some kids from the junior high school, friends of a friend's daughter, he tells me. They worked a long time to get the color just the way Minor wanted it. They even built a model and painted it, then filled it with water to be sure of the color. "Sally can't pass up a movie. She says I should go with her." He sticks a couple of fingers in the waistband of the shorts. "You like elephants? You ought to take that article home with you. It's incredible what's happening to elephants."

"I want to read it," I say, pouring myself a glass of tonic. We sit on the redwood deck for a few minutes looking out into the yard.

"So, Ben, we haven't had a chance to talk. What've you been up to? What is it—ten years? Fifteen?"

"Seems longer," I say.

"Know what you mean," he says, nodding seriously. "Same here. I bought this place originally for Mama and Dad, but they moved to Tampa in seventy- eight, so I took it over. I had a restaurant and a shop, but I quit that—figured I could do better. I've sold a lot of glass animals, Ben. I started buying property in seventy-five. Sally lived in the yellow bungalow next to you there, after I bought it, but then she married this guy Paul, an art director, and they moved to Atlanta. She came back after the divorce."

"She looks good," I say.

Minor laughs and pulls at the leg of his shorts. "Always did."

I finish my tonic and pour another half glass. "So, how many houses do you have?"

"Six," he says. "You know, she wanted to marry you. Everybody got crazy about that—what were you, seventeen? So Sally threatens to quit school and get an apartment." He picks at the fly of his pants. "After you went to college there was this guy named Frank. He did better than you."

"What do you mean?" I stick my hands into my coat pockets, but I can't stop myself from shivering.

"You know what I mean," Minor says. "He got her right there in the garage. First time out." Minor squeezes his neck. "You chilly? It's cold out here, isn't it?"

"I'm freezing, as a matter of fact."

He snorts and stands up, tossing the ice from his drink out into the pool. "I felt bad for you when I saw that," he says. "Really."

The kitchen is a narrow room with a four-bulb fluorescent light fixture mounted on the ceiling. The wallpaper is marigolds and buttercups. There's a round butcher-block table pushing into one corner of the room. "It's

continued ▶

easier to eat in here, I guess," Minor says. "Anyway, I want to keep an eye on the microwave. You know about microwaves?" He hustles around the kitchen, selecting dishes, checking the food already in the oven. In a couple of minutes he serves two pale steaks and some cut green beans that have golden spots all over them. "Think I overdid these," he says, rolling beans onto my plate. "They should taste O.K. though. See if they're crunchy."

I spear a couple of beans, avoiding the splotched ones. "Good," I say. "What about cable? You get cable out here?"

He picks a bean off my plate and chews thoughtfully. "Crap," he says. "This ain't crunchy." He scrapes my beans back into the casserole. "You go ahead and start. I'll do up something else." He plants a shoe on the garbage can pedal and then dumps the beans into the can.

"Sure," I say, cutting the steak. "We had this great cable TV in Ohio—thirty channels. Incredible stuff. The Playboy channel, three supersta-tions, everything. Twenty-four-hour sports—you get that?"

"Nope." He touches the microwave key pad, setting the oven to defrost and cook frozen broccoli. The oven chirps every time he touches a number.

"I guess I'll get by without it," I say. "I didn't use it all that much."

He points at the microwave. "We're interfering at the molecular level," he says. "You're going to love this broccoli."

The phone rings. Minor takes the receiver off the wall and says hello, bending to look inside the oven. He listens for a minute, then puts his palm over the mouthpiece and says, "It's Sally. She and her friend left the movie and they want us to go eat at Cafe 90."

"Sure," I say, waving my fork. "It's up to you—you haven't eaten yet."

"Forget it," Minor says into the phone. "We're staying put."

By the time he's ready to eat I'm on my second cup of coffee. He puts a sprig of broccoli on a butter plate for me.

"Very nice," I say, trying the broccoli. "Very tender."

"Does anything," he says, his mouth full of steak. "Anything. Bacon, eggs—bake you a potato in five minutes. You want a potato?"

I hold up my hands. "Not tonight, thanks."

"I'm not pressing," Minor says. "You don't want a potato, that's fine with me. I'm just being polite." He finishes the piece of steak he's chewing and cuts the rest of the meat on his plate into bite-size sections. When that's done he looks up and stares at me for a minute as if he's trying to recall who I am. "You probably don't even like broccoli."

"Sure, I do. Broccoli's one of my favorites."

Minor's face is bloated and tight. "Crap. That's crap. You're almost squirming there, you know that? Doesn't make any difference to me. I'm set up. I got my houses, Sally—you're the renter." He wags a hand at me, wiping his mouth with a yellow napkin. He gets a quart of Miller beer from the refrigerator and takes a drink, then points the bottleneck at me. "You want a beer?"

"Yes." I dump the last of my tonic into the sink and start to rinse my glass.

He looks at the ceiling. "Why don't you just get a new glass, huh? We've got glasses. Check the cabinet."

I get a mug out of the cabinet, and he pours the beer.

"You want to sit in here?" he says when I sit down again. "We don't have to sit in here. Why don't we sit in the other room?"

"Sure. Great. Let's sit in there. What the hell. You don't want to go to the bar?"

"No," he says, heading into the den.

The only light in there is green and comes from a twenty-gallon fish tank

under one window. Minor climbs into a recliner and a small footrest pops out from under the seat. He points to the matching sofa. "She'll be home quick enough."

I sit on the sofa arm and look into the aquarium. The filtering system is bubbling, but there aren't any fish. "Hobby?" I say, touching the glass.

"She won't feed 'em. I try, but sometimes I'm late getting home, this and that." He twists his head to look at the aquarium "I've got one angel left, stuck in the castle—see the castle? Went in a month ago and now he can't get out. I drop food on him but I figure he'll go belly-up pretty quick." Minor wipes his forehead and takes another drink from the quart. "Look on the side there, see if you can see in that window in the turret or whatever it's called."

The castle is four shades of green and two of pink. There's an opening as big as a stamp in one side, and through the opening I see the stripes on the fish, which is tilted at about forty-five degrees. The gills flap a little. "He's breathing," I say.

"Look at his eyes."

"I can't see his eyes. All I can see is his side."

"Bang on the glass."

I tick on the glass with my fingernail and the fish jerks a couple of times. Then one eye appears in the hole in the castle wall. "There he is," I say. "He looks sick."

Minor sighs. "I told her to get him out of there last week, but I guess she didn't."

"You want me to do it?"

continued ▶

He squints at me, then shrugs. "I guess you'd better leave him alone. He's probably grown or something." He gets up and comes over to the aquarium. "I don't know why she couldn't just take care of this," he says, sticking a hand into the water. He uproots the castle, and the fish slips out and into a tangle of aquarium grass, its body still leaning.

"Hiya, pal," Minor says, looking down into the tank. He replaces the castle, twisting it into the dirty white rocks to seat it securely. "Looks like a little dead guy, doesn't he?" He pinches some food into the tank above where the angelfish is swimming, then closes the cover and returns to his chair. "He wasn't the pretty one to start with. Really. You know what I'm saying?"

Sally is four years older than Minor, my age. "I'm glad you stayed," she says when she comes in. "He told me you were taking the house, but I thought he was messing around."

"Who's this 'he' you're always talking about?" Minor says.

She ignores him. "Minor says he feels very close to you. He says you might as well be family."

"Not quite what I said, Piggy."

"Oh hush, Minor." She pulls her sweater over head and arranges her hair with her fingers. She's wearing a white T-shirt with "Girl" stitched in red above the small pocket. "He always calls me Piggy when he gets mad," she says, looking at Minor. "It's his way of telling me that I'd better watch out. Anyway, Betty wanted to come back with me, to meet you, but her boy has a fever so she couldn't. I told her we'd have you and she for dinner one night soon,"

"Betty's your class-B divorcee," Minor says.

Sally makes a small ticking sound with her lips and rolls her eyes. "This one," she says, pointing a thumb toward Minor, "wouldn't know a divorcee from a koala bear." She reaches under the shade of a floor lamp and turns on the light. "How come it's so dark in here?"

"I let the fish out," Minor says, motioning toward the aquarium.

"Well thank God for that," she says. She goes to the aquarium and bends to look inside. "Poor baby's nearly dead, it looks like."

She reaches for the fish food but stops when he says, "I already did that."

"Fed him, too?" She looks at me. "He's a take-charge kind of guy, my brother." She waves at the angelfish, then turns around and shakes her head. "I'm getting something to eat before I faint. You want anything? A sandwich?"

"Nope," he says.

I pick up the magazine that has the elephant story in it. "We just ate, thanks."

"He explained the microwave, I bet," she says.

Minor makes a face at her back as she disappears into the kitchen. "How was the movie?"

"The seats were hard and the sound was awful," she says. "The guys behind me were arguing with the guys behind them about smoking grass in the theatre. That's why we left. This one guy leaned over to me and whispered something, and I thought he said he was going to burn my hair off. He must have had a speech defect. What he said was could he borrow a lighter. What's with the beans in the garbage?"

"We had a bean problem," Minor says. "We did broccoli instead."

"It was very tender," I say.

Sally comes out of the kitchen carrying a tiny glass of milk and a plate of crackers, cheese cubes, and apple slices. "I hate broccoli, but my friend Ann makes me eat it because she says it kills cancer. I just love Ann. She's so great even he likes her, don't you?"

Minor crosses the room to look at Sally's plate, then wags his head. "Maybe we should get her and Betty over together and let Ben take his choice, how's that?"

"Maybe he'll want both of them," Sally says. "How come you ate so late?" She balances a cheese cube on a cracker and puts the cracker into her mouth. "Oh, never mind. I don't want to know."

"You," he says. "Ben and you. That's the reason."

"Too bad we didn't stick together," she says to me. "Paul was a lizard."

"She hates her ex-husband," Minor says. "She likes to hate people."

"Uh-huh," Sally says, holding the milk glass close to her lips. "Pete Rose I totally hate."

"That's so easy," Minor says. He's standing in front of the aquarium.

"I'll bet Pete Rose smells funny," she says.

Minor yawns. "I'm real tired."

"Now wait a minute," she says. "I just got here. I haven't had a chance to talk yet."

"I ought to go on," I say, flipping through the magazine. "I've got elephants to do."

Minor squats and leans his forehead against the aquarium. "I hate this fish," he says. "Can we get rid of this fish? He's driving me nuts."

"Maybe we could give him away," Sally says.

Minor rubs his nose on the glass and starts to say something but then stops and swivels around on his heels, looking at me. Sally looks, too. The two of them look at me as if I'm the answer to their prayers.

WRITING ABOUT "FISH"

I won't suggest that there's any one way of writing about literature. Even a deceptively simple and beautiful story like "Fish" has several levels of meaning. But there are some places to start, and there are some questions that should get you started.

The questions that follow do not add up to a single essay; instead, they are like a series of mini-essays. If your instructor intends to spend some time on writing about literature, he or she will be supplementing this part of the chapter with some of his or her own ideas. But this is a great place to start, and you'll be introduced to a variety of starting points in looking at a piece of fiction.

Consider each question or set of questions below separately. Spend time sketching out or free-writing some ideas before actually answering each question. I'd suggest that two paragraphs would answer most of the questions below.

Keep going back to the text as you try to figure out an answer. Use lines or events from the text to support your answer. Don't hesitate to have a point of view. Like any good issue paper, you should believe in your position and state it clearly (with support). There are as many "interpretations" of a short story as there are readers. Don't worry about being wrong! Be as right as you can be, and support your opinion. As in the Rogerian paper, you should be concerned only with making sure your reader "understands" your point of view and respects it.

QUESTIONS

1. The story is called "Fish," and the poor angelfish figures prominently in the story. Why do you think that is? Why does the fish get top billing?

2. Let me suggest that the title "Fish" is not just a title representing the angelfish but is also one of the characters in the story. Who in the story is most like the fish and why? Use several examples of actions and words from the text.

3. Some obvious tension exists between Minor and Ben, and it comes out in the story right after Minor asks Ben about the broccoli. Go through the entire story and catalog all the moments of tension between those characters.

4. What do you think is the "source" of tension between Ben and Minor?

5. Short story writers seldom waste words or space on nonessential items or ideas. Short stories are typically quite compact. If that's the case, what possible reason do you see for the ongoing discussion of the "elephant" story in the newsmagazine. (Be creative and really think about this one.)

6. What do you think about Minor and his fascination with the microwave? What about his fascination about the swimming pool? Do those two things add up to anything in particular? (Don't just say he's wacky, although that's not a horrible answer.) Spend some time looking for a better way to explain his interest in those two things.

7. Sally, although she's rather important to the story, doesn't appear very much in it. Write a "character study" about her. That means, describe what you know about her physically, mentally, and so on. Is she a good person? A bad one? Do you like her? Do people in the story like her and respond well to her? Do you think the author wants us to like or dislike her? Why? Prove it.

8. I'll suggest that the last line has more meaning than simply the fact that Minor and Sally have found someone to give the fish to. I think that last line means a lot more. Open your mind up. Why else would Ben be the answer to Sally and Minor's prayers?

Poem

The poem "At the Swings," comes from the Pulitzer Prize–winning poet Henry Taylor. It is from Taylor's book *The Flying Change,* his most well-known work.

Generally, poems are much more compact and dense than stories. But like short story writers, poets also pack in much meaning and complexity in a few lines and in a few words. Perhaps the reader simply must be more "aware" and more "active" during the reading of literature in general. We're not just looking for the day's high temperature or the score from the basketball game last night. When we read a poem or a story we're involving ourselves in an art, a beautiful structure of words and ideas designed to make us think and respond. So our reading must be as focused and concise as the writer's attention when he or she did the work.

Here's Henry Taylor's poem "At the Swings." It recalls a walk to the park that a father makes with his children, but the real story behind the poem is a flood of memories and thoughts the speaker has about his loved ones and their place in his life.

AT THE SWINGS

BY HENRY TAYLOR

Midafternoon in Norfolk,
late July. I am taking our two sons for a walk
away from their grandparent's house; we have
directions to a miniature playground,
and I have plans to wear them down
toward a nap at five,

when my wife and I
will leave them awhile with her father. A few blocks
south of here, my wife's mother drifts from us
beneath hospital sheets, her small strength bent
to the poisons and the rays they use
against a spreading cancer.

In their house now, deep love
is studying to live with deepening impatience
as each day gives our hope a different form
and household tasks rise like a powdery mist
of restless fatigue. Still, at five,
my wife and I will dress

and take to the boulevard
across the river to a church where two dear friends
will marry; rings will be blessed, promises kept
and made, and while our sons lie down to sleep,
the groom's niece, as the flower girl,
will almost steal the show.

But here the boys have made
an endless procession on the slides, shrieking down
slick steel almost too hot to touch; and now
they charge the swings. I push them from the front,
one with each hand, until at last
the rhythm, and the sunlight

that splashes through live oak
and crape myrtle, dappling dead leaves on the ground,

lull me away from this world toward a state
still and remote as an old photograph
in which I am standing somewhere
I may have been before:

there was this air, this light,
a day of thorough and forgetful happiness;
where was it, or how long ago? I try
to place it, but it has gone for good,
to leave me gazing at these swings,
thinking of something else

I may have recognized—
an irrecoverable certainty that now,
and now, this perfect afternoon, while friends
are struggling to put on their cutaways
or bridal gowns, and my wife's mother,
dearer still, is dozing

after her medicine,
or turning a small thing in her mind, like someone
worrying a ring of keys to make small sounds
against great silence, and while these two boys
swing back and forth against my hand,
time's crosshairs quarter me

no matter where I turn.
Now it is time to go. The boys are tired enough,
and my wife and I must dress and go to church.
Because I love our friends, and ceremony,
the usual words will make me weep;
hearing the human prayers

for holy permanence
will remind me that a life is much to ask
of anyone, yet not too much to give
to love. And once or twice, as I stand there,
that dappled moment at the swings
will rise between the lines,

continued ▶

when I beheld our sons
as, in the way of things, they will not be again,
though even years from now their hair may lift
a little in the breeze, as if they stood
somewhere along their way from us,
poised for a steep return.

QUESTIONS

1. Let's begin with some factual questions, to make sure we've all witnessed the same action. Make a list of all the main characters in the poem and their current state or situation. There are two sons, for example. Make a list of all characters that you can identify as being essential in the poem.

2. Focus on the "wedding" story. What are the key elements of it? Tell us what the speaker thinks of the wedding and why. Prove that your understanding is correct with text from the poem.

3. Focus on the story about the dying grandmother. I believe there are language cues all through the poem that relate to her and her condition. Search the poem for images and words that suggest death.

4. Nature plays a role in the poem. What are the principal appearances of nature: the wind, trees, and so on?

5. Focus on the speaker's relationship with his two sons. Forward a thesis that tells us how he feels about them, and then use the text to prove that it's real. (Be careful; saying he loves his sons is not nearly enough. His feelings for them are far more complex and interesting.)

6. The passing of time appears to be a rather important, overriding theme in the poem. Decide for yourself what kind of relationship the speaker has with "time," and then prove you're right by showing numerous examples from the text.

Real-World Writing

Aside from your regular job as a writer in this class, you will undoubt-edly find other ways in which you'll need or want to communicate. The "letter to the editor" is a traditional and viable form of communication which enables you to interact with your community, large or small, and assert yourself as a member of your society. On a more practical level, the writing of a "job application letter" and "résumé" are essential skills for all of us as we move through the working world.

This chapter provides you with insights into these real-world writing situations.

The letter to the editor

If you're like me, you've got opinions. You get mad when something bad happens and you get happy when something good happens. And because you live in a community of some kind, there are people all around you doing good and bad things all the time.

TOWN SQUARE

I can remember my grandfather telling me about the little town square in the town where he grew up. He was a farmer and the town had no news-paper. Once a week he'd take the family and the cart into town, get an ice cream, and sit on the benches of the town square. Some folks would be talking about an upcoming dance at the legion hall, and some folks would be arguing about the upcoming mayoral election. Some people might be talking about a new family that had come to town and had opened a grocery store. My grandfather would learn the "news" of his town and hear the town's opinions and thoughts about it all at one time.

That happens today in the daily newspaper. And it doesn't matter if it's a traditional ink-on-paper newspaper or a leading-edge electronic-format newspaper or magazine. In our far-flung society, there aren't as many town squares, and there certainly isn't one big enough for all of us to get together and chat about the ideas and the news of the day. So the newspaper remains our best source of information and opinion. There is information spread around in the "news" pages, and there are opinions shared, offered, and debated in the opinion or editorial pages.

What does that mean for us? Well, we live in this town, right? We are affected by the news and the shared opinions and ideas of our fellow "townspeople." It's hard for us to know what Joe Smith of Colleyville thinks, unless Joe Smith writes in to the newspaper and we read it.

But when he does, suddenly we're back in the world of the town square. Joe Smith matters to us because he cares enough about our world to respond to it. We matter to Joe Smith because we have the good sense to be interested in things that matter to us, too. When we write back, we're entering the town square mentality of our ancestors. We live here; we have a right to speak our mind.

The letter to the editor assignment is a neat one that I love to help my writers accomplish. It gives me a special kick because we actually send the finished letters in to the newspapers and wait for the results. Generally, between 20 and 50 percent of my writers get their letters published in the paper. It's a big moment that next week or so as students start bringing the paper in. "Look, I made it!" And it's an even bigger moment another week down the road if one of my students get mentioned in someone else's letter. "Look, someone's talking about my letter."

SOCIETY'S CONVERSATION

The letter to the editor assignment is a vital way of involving yourself in the ongoing conversation that makes up our society. It doesn't matter if your town or city is small or large. The conversation is taking place in the local newspaper, just like the conversation took place in my grandfather's town square.

Start reading the paper for a week or so, every day. Read articles that interest you; read some things that pertain strictly to your town; read the editorial section (that's where the editors of the paper tell you what they think); read the op-ed section or the letters section, where ordinary folks have sent in their letters. Reading those sections will give you a pretty clear idea what sorts of topics are current or "hot" in your area.

Think about talk radio. It's the same format. A host or personality or DJ raises some issues of interest. Then he or she takes calls.

Host: You know I've been thinking about this insane amount of money baseball players are making for playing a game. What do you think of that? We've got a call here from Terry in Grand Rapids. Go ahead, Terry.

Terry: Hey, you're nuts. Those guys work hard. They're the top of their profession. Cut them some slack.

Host: Okay, here's Norma from South Lake.

Norma: Terry's not thinking this through. I'm a teacher and I'm good at my job. I'm at the top of my profession but Ken Griffey, Jr. makes more in one game than I do teaching all year long. How is that fair?

Host: Thanks Norma. Let's go to Stan in Ipswich.

Stan: Hi, I want to respond to what Norma said. I like teachers a lot and think they should get paid well, but Ken Griffey, Jr. isn't just a really great ball player, he's also an entertainer and he makes a lot of money for his employers, and for all of major league baseball. If Norma's excellent teaching brought lots of money into her school district, she'd have a point and she would or should get more money. But sports is not the same as our ordinary professions.

That kind of interaction is one of the most popular ways in which we communicate with one another. If you've ever spent much time listening to talk radio, you of course recognize that the folks in the example above are pretty polite. That's not usually how things go. Terry is the only one who sounds like the people I usually hear when I tune in.

RESPOND

Pick out a particular story, column, editorial, or letter to respond to. I urge you to do this because it will give you a greater chance of catching the interest of the editors. Editors are keeping track of what their readers are interested in, and therefore tend to publish letters that are "on topic."

Once you've got a piece of text to respond to, spend some serious time reading it and thinking about it. Prepare yourself to actually "respond" in some way to the text. Think of it as a conversation. If the writer of your chosen text came up to you and said those things, what would you say in response?

Begin writing your response. But keep in mind that your letter, if it is published, will appear in the paper days or even weeks after the original. You can't assume that the readers of the paper will be able to keep old essays in their memory banks very long. You'll have to remind readers of the original piece so they know what you're talking about. Here's an example of an original letter to the editor (the one you want to respond to), and a neat way of identifying it in your own letter.

> Dear Editors:
>
> It makes me sick to think that professional baseball players make so much money. They're all spoiled brats with little or no ability beyond batting a ball around. We have good folks in all walks of life who work hard and who deserve to make better money than they do. My sister is a teacher and I see her come home every day, tired of the hard job. Why should Ken Griffey, Jr. make so much money? My sister works harder than him, for longer hours, and for a fraction of the salary. Our society is messed up!
>
> Marvin Blass
>
> Arlington, Texas

Okay, that's the letter that got you worked up. You read it and wanted to say something back to Marvin Blass, or at least about Marvin Blass and the things he believes. Your first job in your own letter is to identify what you're talking about.

> Dear Editors:
>
> Recently, Marvin Blass wrote an impassioned letter in your pages showing his concern about the great discrepancy between major league baseball salaries and the salaries of the rest of us.
>
> I sympathize with Mr. Blass, for I'm a teacher just like his sister, but . . .

In two sentences you've been able to announce to the readers exactly what you're writing in response to. You've even had time to get some of your own thoughts in. That's an excellent example. You'll also notice that great word "but" in there. As we discussed earlier, "but" is a transitional word that begins a refutation, just like the one we learned about during our Rogerian essay experience in Chapter 10. "But" lets the reader know that we're headed in a different direction. "I know you want me to clean your car, but . . ." "Sure, I'd like to stay and watch your home videos, but . . ." It's a nice way to change the direction of a conversation or an essay.

Note that most newspapers have guidelines about letters to the editor; those guidelines can be found somewhere in the editorial or op-ed section. (Typically, these refer to the length of the letter being 250 words or less.) Beyond that, check with your instructor for other special features he or she may want.

The job application letter

Not surprisingly, this is another kind of writing that interests my writers. I don't make it a regular part of my classes, but sometimes I'll let a very interested student take a shot at it, especially if it's the kind of writing he or she is really in need of at that time.

Letter writing is usually a pretty formal affair, similar to the call-to-action essay from Chapter 8. Obviously, looking for a job is a pretty formal situation, so it's likely that in your letter you'll be dealing with a reader and a situation where being courteous and dignified is expected.

There are classes at most colleges that teach this skill, oftentimes called Technical or Business Writing. There is also the possibility that your instructor in this course will want you to work on the special challenges of this kind of writing. After all, we all need jobs, right? And in fact, a lot of our preparation in our other essays leads up to this. Think about some of the other essays and skills we've worked on: personal writing, issue writing, stating your position, convincing someone that something is good. If you combine features from some of those essays, you can see that a paper in which we evaluate ourselves as a good worker, and then state the position "You should hire me," is something we should be prepared to accomplish.

When we're looking for a job, we're selling ourselves, right? What other purposes are there?

- **To announce that you're interested in the job.** It may sound silly, but this is a standard part of any job letter. In one way, it's very helpful to the reader because there may be more than one position open at the time. It's also helpful to the reader if you are able to announce where you heard about the job. There may be special consideration given to you if you heard of the job through another employee of the company or through someone who may know the reader.

> ▶ I'd like to apply for the position of "copier" you now have open in your store. An employee of yours, Mark Johnson, told me about the position. Mark and I are long-time friends, and we once worked together at a print shop in Tucson. He's well-acquainted with my abilities and skills. ◀

Or, here's an opening for when you don't have any special connection to the place.

> ▶ I'd like to apply for the position of "copier" you now have open in your store. I found your ad on a bulletin board at Richland College, where I am now a part-time student. ◀

In both of those examples, you've let the reader know what job you're interested in as well as a little about yourself. That identification continues in the next paragraph.

To identify who you are and how you're qualified. Your résumé should probably do most of this, but different readers put different emphases on the letter and résumé package. In my technical and business writing classes our research of companies often reveals that some employers *only* read the letter itself, hoping to draw enough facts out of it to make their decision. If the letter doesn't sell them, they are not going to read the résumé. So, this section has to be your best shot. In essence, it's your thesis.

> ▶ I've read your job description and find that I have all of the skills you are in need of. I have two years of experience with the Ricoh line of professional copiers, and during my previous employment in Tucson at Pro Printing, I routinely received monthly bonuses for efficient work and steady attendance. ◀

Of course, mention anything that makes you sound like a good worker. Some writers are afraid to "toot their own horn" a bit, but often folks make the error of going the other way and do not present themselves strongly enough. It is true you don't want to exaggerate your responsibilities or duties in past positions, but don't short-change yourself, either.

To ask for the interview (a call to action). By the end of your letter you should have given your audience enough reasons to want to call you right away, but it doesn't hurt to remind them of the single most important purpose of any job letter: to get the interview. You'll probably not be hired simply on the strength of the letter. Employers and personnel departments use the letter to weed out ill-prepared candidates from well-prepared ones. They are going to use another step before they give you the job. So, ask for that step.

> By this point I hope you recognize my great desire to work for your company. I hope I've proven my interest and suitability, and I hope you'll give me a chance to discuss the position further with you, in person. I'm available Monday through Friday anytime after 2:00 PM; that's when my classes end for the day. You may reach me at (214) 555-5555 evenings, or leave a message at (214) 777-7777 anytime.
>
> Thanks for your time.

After that, you hope for the best.

The résumé

Think of the résumé as a companion piece to the letter of application discussed above. The variety of résumés that are acceptable and practiced around the country make it nearly impossible to generate a standard form for you to follow. Plus, it's outside the scope of this book. I'd suggest tracking down a specific book about business or technical writing if you're looking for a large array of examples.

However, there are definitely some essential elements that any good résumé includes.

CONTACT INFORMATION

You want any future employers to be able to reach you. To that end, you should be as clear as possible about offering telephone numbers, fax numbers, current work numbers, e-mail addresses, and so forth. Some business experts will tell you that showing too many numbers might contribute to a cluttered look on your résumé. This is easily avoided by offering just one phone number, one fax, and one e-mail if available. (Also, offering an e-mail address can be beneficial to you if the company is online, as more and more of them are these days.) And even though we operate in a fast-paced society of phone calls, faxes, and e-mail messages, there are still companies that like to operate via surface mail (U.S. Mail, UPS, Federal Express, etc.), so a correct mailing address is necessary, too. Here is a very simple example.

Jonas Thompson

9999 Northwest Road
Dallas, TX 77777

ph: (214) 555-5555
fx: (214) 556-5656
e-mail: jonas@internet.com

Let's talk formatting just briefly. You'll notice that this example requires very little computer trickery. I've made the name slightly bigger and then centered everything. Even the most rudimentary of computers and software can do this. Computers have made this sort of thing so easy that employers expect a little sophistication in your presentation. A typewriter-produced résumé doesn't have the same impact.

As for the content, it's fairly simple to extract from this example the address, phone number, fax number, and e-mail address. If an employer needed to contact Jonas, it would be a simple matter to choose one of those contact options.

OBJECTIVE

This has become a fairly standard part of most résumés. Many effective job seekers can use this short objective line to reiterate part of the message of the job letter. Remember, these pieces of paper (résumé and job application letter) can and do become separated during a normal job search. These individual sheets become passed around, copied, and shared. As a veteran of job searches, I can assure you that things get misplaced or separated. It's nobody's fault. You can use the objective line to make sure a crucial bit of information doesn't prevent your résumé from getting the most appropriate attention — state what it is you want!

Jonas Thompson

9999 Northwest Road
Dallas, TX 77777

ph: (214) 555-5555
fx: (214) 556-5656
e-mail: jonas@internet.com

OBJECTIVE: To work in the publishing field at any
editorial level: proofreader to editorial
assistant.

EDUCATION

This section and the next—Employment—can be reversed depending on your preparation for the job in question. If your scholastic past is more relevant to the job you're applying for, then put your education first. If it's your employment background that will help you the most, then place it here.

A crucial thing to remember, though: Don't fabricate anything. It's become more and more frequent that first-time job seekers feel it's acceptable, or even necessary, to "beef" up their résumés with partially phony information and exaggerations of skills and abilities. That's a bad idea. Getting caught in a little white lie is just as bad as saying "I don't want this job."

Stay on the truth.

Jonas Thompson
9999 Northwest Road
Dallas, TX 77777

ph: (214) 555-5555
fx: (214) 556-5656
e-mail: jonas@internet.com

```
OBJECTIVE:   To work in the publishing field at any
             editorial level: proofreader to editorial
             assistant.

EDUCATION:   B.A. in English, May 1997
             Hamline University, St. Paul, MN
             Minor: Journalism
```

In the example above, the information is brief and clear. The university's address is not necessary. City and state will be sufficient. The addition of the applicant's "minor" field of study is helpful here as it applies to the job being sought. If your grade point average is good — 3.0 or better, usually — it's okay to provide it on a separate line at the bottom of the section. If it's lower than that, you definitely don't need to include it.

Unless you went to a very important and well-known high school or prep school, it's unnecessary to include any high school information here.

EMPLOYMENT

In most cases, you can be assured that recent employers will be contacted. In fact, if you're asked to provide references it will be expected that at the very least your two or three most recent employers will be included on your list of references. It is perfectly acceptable to skip short-term, nonapplicable jobs in your employment section, if you feel they aren't pertinent to this job search. Listing three undistinguished months at Hot Dog Haven won't help much.

However, if Hot Dog Haven is all you've got, and you were a good employee, always on time, then there's nothing wrong with listing it. Having a too-short employment section is more off-putting for employers than having a moderate number of short-term but successful jobs.

Jonas Thompson
9999 Northwest Road
Dallas, TX 77777

ph: (214) 555-5555
fx: (214) 556-5656
e-mail: jonas@internet.com

OBJECTIVE: To work in the publishing field at any
              editorial level: proofreader to editorial
              assistant.

EDUCATION: *B.A. in English,* May 1997
              Hamline University, St. Paul, MN
              Minor: Journalism

EMPLO*YMENT:* ST. PAUL GAZETTE — ST. PAUL, MN
              Assistant Proofreader
              Proofread copy for weekly "Weekend Guide"
              edition. Organized reading schedules
              for interns. July-August, 1995; July-
              September 1996.

              HOT DOG HAVEN — MINNEAPOLIS, MN
              Counter Clerk
              Took orders and made change. Opened and
              closed restaurant for weekend shift. Shift
              leader on Sundays. March 1994-March 1997.

I like the choices made by this writer in both of these employment entries. There are lots of places where he could have "beefed" up his duties. Imagine something like "Weekend Manager" for the Hot Dog Haven. That would be a lie. A management position is not so casually given to a counter clerk, and although our writer did have some added responsibility, he was never a manager.

It's also good not to apply too much imagination to job duties. Getting the thesaurus out could boost "Took orders and made change," to something like "Formed company's first line of interface with customer base; negotiated financial terms on hundreds of transactions." Sure, in a way it's right, but any résumé reader knows "résumé-speak" when he or she hears it. Saying it plainly is safer and more honest.

ADDITIONAL AREAS OF INTEREST

You'll find experts are rather divided about this kind of section, formerly called something like "Interests." Use your own judgment about including items such as "Member St. Paul's United Methodist Church" or "triathlete." As in all decisions for your résumé, if the information is truthful and applicable to the job you're asking for, include it. Singing at barbershop quartet festivals nationwide might not be interesting to some employers, but to others it becomes an interesting fact or a "hook." They might remember you and your résumé better. Yet, that's not a green light to include something odd just for its own sake. To a different reader, the barbershop quartet thing might just suggest you won't be around for important weekend work!

My best advice is to avoid using the category unless you have something quite germane to the job. Look what Jonas does below, for example.

Jonas Thompson

9999 Northwest Road
Dallas, TX 77777

ph: (214) 555-5555
fx: (214) 556-5656
e-mail: jonas@internet.com

OBJECTIVE: To work in the publishing field at any
              editorial level: proofreader to editorial
              assistant.

continued ▶

```
EDUCATION:    B.A. in English, May 1997
              Hamline University, St. Paul, MN
              Minor: Journalism


EMPLOYMENT:   ST. PAUL GAZETTE — ST. PAUL, MN
              Assistant Proofreader
              Proofread copy for weekly "Weekend Guide"
              edition. Organized reading schedules
              for interns. July-August, 1995; July-
              September 1996.

              HOT DOG HAVEN — MINNEAPOLIS, MN
              Counter Clerk
              Took orders and made change. Opened and
              closed restaurant for weekend shift. Shift
              leader on Sundays. March 1994-March 1997.


ADDITIONAL AREAS OF INTEREST:
              EDITOR
              Kaylor Park Residents Newsletter—
              St. Paul, MN
              Write and edit 4-page, 4-color, neighborhood
              newsletter, formatted on Photoshop, Quark,
              and PrintMaven software. Distribution:
              155 residents.
```

Jonas happens to have an additional bit of info that clearly isn't a real job, but that has much applicability to his interest in a publishing career. In this case, he's used our "additional" category to showcase some job-appropriate skills and abilities.

REFERENCES

It has become standard over the past twenty years or so for the references line to read "References furnished upon request," or "References supplied upon request." The theory is you'll be able to hand a nicely typed list of references after or at your first interview.

However, with the job market as competitive as it is, there's nothing wrong with including a separate "references" sheet. The contact information for your references needs to be as accurate and easy to use as your own contact information.

Also, you must assume that the references listed will be contacted, so make sure you feel confident about what each person will say, and that each person you list is aware that he or she may be contacted about you. If you know these references well enough, you might even tell them what kind of jobs you're applying for, and who might be contacting them.

THE FINISHED PRODUCT

Jonas Thompson
9999 Northwest Road
Dallas, TX 77777

ph: (214) 555-5555
fx: (214) 556-5656
e-mail: jonas@internet.com

OBJECTIVE: To work in the publishing field at any
editorial level: proofreader to editorial
assistant.

EDUCATION: *B.A. in English,* May 1997
Hamline University, St. Paul, MN
Minor: Journalism

EMPLOYMENT: ST. PAUL GAZETTE — ST. PAUL, MN
Assistant Proofreader
Proofread copy for weekly "Weekend Guide"
edition. Organized reading schedules
for interns. July-August, 1995; July-
September 1996.

HOT DOG HAVEN — MINNEAPOLIS, MN
Counter Clerk
Took orders and made change. Opened and
closed restaurant for weekend shift. Shift
leader on Sundays. March 1994-March 1997.

ADDITIONAL AREAS OF INTEREST:
EDITOR
Kaylor Park Residents Newsletter—
St. Paul, MN

continued ▶

```
                    Write and edit 4-page, 4-color, neighborhood
                    newsletter, formatted on Photoshop, Quark,
                    and PrintMaven software. Distribution:
                    155 residents.

REFERENCES:  On separate sheet.
```

Here's a sample reference sheet. The styles of reference sheets vary, but this one picks up some of the style conventions and same fonts from the résumé, thus making it slightly easier for any reader to recognize it.

Jonas Thompson

```
9999 Northwest Road
Dallas, TX 77777

ph: (214) 555-5555
fx: (214) 556-5656
e-mail: jonas@internet.com
```

```
REFERENCES SHEET:

Carlene Ellerswitch, Weekend Editor
St. Paul Gazette
111 Main Street
St. Paul, MN 56565-6565
(222) 222-2222

Chris Rudolph, Manager
Hot Dog Haven
888 St. Joseph Way
Minneapolis, MN 55555-5555
(555) 575-5555

Carol Bennett
H. P. Lovecraft High School
444 Machinist Avenue
Northridge, MN 44444
(444) 444-4444
```

16

Writing with a Computer

Why use a computer?

Some people don't like technology. They aren't bad people. They're just not ready to catch up yet. There was a time when a lot of people didn't like riding in cars very much. They preferred to go horseback, or in a buggy. Cars didn't seem very safe. They were loud and odd and made up of parts and concepts beyond most regular folks' understanding. Well, my little Chevy Cavalier is beyond my understanding, too. But I sure love getting in it and driving to the post office or the store or just down the block sometimes when I'm lazy.

I've been coaxing writers onto computers for over ten years. It's not because I have any stock in IBM or Apple or anything; it's just that I was lucky and was exposed to computers when I was pretty young. They seemed mysterious and weird to me at first, but I found out they helped me do things better and faster than the old way I used to do things. And I'm talking primarily about writing.

I remember getting a big Sony word processor when I was a sophomore in college. It didn't do anything cool like most modern computers; all it did was process words. It was huge and heavy and awful looking and hard to use. But that screen glowed and my words jumped out of my head, onto the keyboard, and onto the screen every day, and they looked good.

EASIER TO READ AND UNDERSTAND

Having instantly legible and readable prose is, in fact, one of the first benefits that developing writers tell me they appreciate. Most of us don't have very good penmanship. Generations before us actually took classes in "cursive," or handwriting, and that skill used to be valued. It's very rare now that students past first or second grade get that kind of training. So, the first time we type on a keyboard, whether it's the hottest, fastest computer on the block or just on an old portable type-writer, our words look better, more professional, instantly. Legibility, you know?

Imagine if they published the newspaper every day written in long-hand. If every writer just scribbled his or her stories on paper and then someone photocopied it all together, it'd be a mess.

But the reasons to get on a machine go far beyond that.

EASIER TO WORK WITH

My principal reason for urging you to write on the computer (not just for final drafts, but for every draft) has to do with a discovery I've made about writers' attachment to their words. I've been reading student essays for about fifteen years. That's thousands of essays. When a writer's essay is in progress, I act as an editor. I don't write my student's essays for them; I help them along the way. And what I find myself doing the most as I help them through their drafts is cutting and pasting. I cut stuff that's not going very well, and I paste or move stuff that's in the wrong spot.

To see what sort of things I do, and why the computer makes it easier, let's look at two paragraphs one of my students turned in one day.

> ▷ The most important day of my life was graduation. Graduation is a great day for everyone. It really means something. It sure meant a lot to me. I was so proud and happy on graduation day. That's when I really knew I was destined for something big. I will never forget what a great day that was.
>
> The power had been out all night. When six a.m. came and went, my alarm sat next to me, lifeless and dark, just like my mood was going to be. It was graduation day and I was late before I even woke up. ◁

Read that again. That first paragraph isn't very good, is it? But that second paragraph is really quite good. The first paragraph is just taking up space and wasting my time. The only thing I know from the first paragraph is that the paper is in some way about the writer's graduation.

Look at the second paragraph. Even though it's just three sentences, there is life in those three sentences. A story begins; it's interesting. We learn the fact about it being graduation day and we are actually interested in the poor character sleeping peacefully and becoming late already.

Why do I show you that? Because when my student brought me those two paragraphs, she had filled a whole page of a legal pad. The first paragraph had at least ten strikeouts; whole sentences had been tried and discarded. The first paragraph showed that it had been worked on over and over again. I felt horrible. I hated the first paragraph, but the legal pad showed that the writer had spent much time on it.

What did I do? I found the biggest marking pen I could and drew a huge "X" through the whole paragraph. I swear the young writer gasped audibly; her eyes opened wide, and her face clenched tight. Her hands formed little fists. I knew it was coming, but the right thing to do was to get rid of the bad stuff and leave the good stuff there.

My writer didn't see my reasoning though. All she saw was that horrible big "X" with which I destroyed her hard work. It was visual and messy; the evidence was still there, smudged, but still visible through the dark marker.

Of course, I spent a long time that day explaining why the second paragraph was so much better, and in time she forgave me (although it wasn't easy). But once she began writing on the computer, she began to see her words differently. She became less attached to them. It was simple to move stuff, simple to cut stuff, and she began to realize that there was a skill involved in that, too. Like lots of developing writers, she was terrified by the writing process and so clung to the one part of it that was really hers, her words.

When I was able to show her that there were plenty more words in her head, just waiting to jump onto that screen, she began to play with and modify and re-arrange her words like I did.

GETTING ON A COMPUTER

I want to get you on a computer, if you aren't on one now. Your school is likely to have them in the library, or in a computer building, or in labs somewhere on campus. They'll likely be free, ready to go, loaded with software, and maintained by professional computer people. With a little bit of assistance you can begin typing and saving and editing and printing your essays on them.

Usually, you'll need a little bit of help getting started, but schools offer that, too. Ask your instructor who can help you get started; he or she can probably track someone down for you who will show you how to get going if you're worried about those first few days.

Chances are you've already done some work on a computer and I'm going slow in this chapter for no reason. But I still get good students every semester who are petrified by the things.

Let's look at how computers in classrooms and in our lives have changed the landscape of education.

Classrooms

FROM THE OLD MODEL TO THE NEW

Well, if you're here and your instructor wants you to read the following sections, you're one of the lucky ones. You might even be in some kind of computer classroom! Computer assisted instruction (or CAI) has come to the forefront of composition instruction throughout the country over the past ten years or so. In fact, the computer is an essential part of what many educators call "the new model." Some colleges and universities have made tremendous inroads into understanding the special needs and problems of running CAI classrooms. While the computer classrooms may not have spread to every department and every college, their influence is undeniable. And the good news is, if you're in one of the "new model" classrooms, you don't have to feel as if you're a guinea pig; this model is over a decade old already. Many writers have gone before you, and the things that we've learned from them will help make your experience a great one.

The old model still exists, of course, at lots of colleges. The old model has strengths in lots of disciplines, but gradually, writing instructors have found its "one way instruction" is too limiting. Look at the old model diagram. The students are all lined up in straight rows, facing forward at a teacher who stands in front. Most of the instruction or information in the old model goes from teacher to student, with very little coming back to the teacher, and virtually none going back and forth between students.

OLD MODEL CLASSROOM
Arrows Show Informational Flow

For a pure lecture of facts and figures, it's not a bad system. But for writers to share and talk, it's terrible.

The new model diagram, on the other hand, shows a whole different world. Not only are those computers there, all connected to one another, but the students are always arranged in a circle, where they can always see and interact with each other.

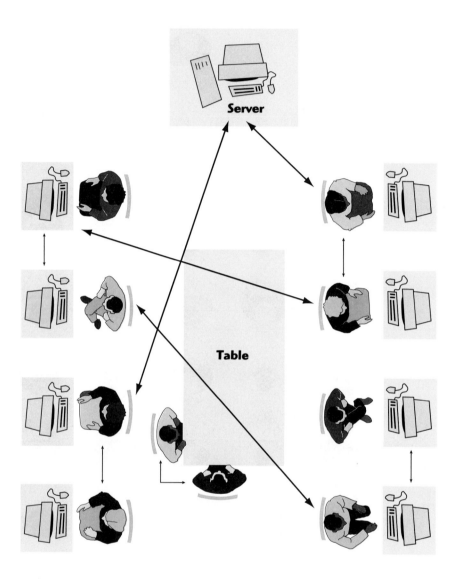

NEW MODEL CLASSROOM
Arrows Show Informational Flow

The middle area is taken up by a table for convenient discussion groups as needed, and open space for the instructor to "float" from writer to writer, sharing and helping in a variety of ways. The instruction/information flow of the new model isn't only in straight lines, it curves and twists and bounces all over between instructor and writer and back, and between writer and writer.

It's partially the concept of the "new model" that this book is based on. I'm assuming that if you're using this textbook, you are either taking this class in a fully networked computer classroom (like many writers all across the country) or are at least connected in some way (via e-mail, etc.) to your instructor and your writing peers, and perhaps to the World Wide Web. If those things aren't true, the assignments in this book still work; you'll just be gaining your help and feedback through the traditional support group (workshopping and conferencing through the "old model") as described in Chapter 12.

You just might not be getting all that you can.

TEXAS TECH

As I prepared this chapter, I spent some time visiting the composition department at Texas Tech University in Lubbock, Texas. I couldn't have completed this section without the hard work and hospitality of all those fine folks. During my research, I was able to interact in their classrooms, working with first-year writers and their instructors. I sat and participated in the writing classrooms just like any new student, and the technology of their system was new to me, just as it often is to incoming writers.

Texas Tech's experiments in networked computer writing labs began in the mid-1980s, and they have on their faculty one of the creators of the influential Daedalus® Integrated Writing Environment program (widely used in labs around the country and discussed later in this chapter).

They teach composition, technical writing, and literature in these lab classes, and the overall response of faculty and students is extraordinarily positive. Even students who have little computer experience going into the process discover that the translation of their writing habits to an online environment is easy and painless. One student told me

> ▶ "I had never used a computer in my life before this class. I was scared out of my mind, but when you're surrounded by others who are learning and when the teacher is right there to ask questions to, it's easy. By the second class, I was helping others learn what I already knew!" ◀

During my research with the program, I corresponded and met with upward of 50 student writers. I became connected into the Texas Tech program in the same way faculty and students are, right there on site. I took part not just as an observer, but as a participant, sending in my suggestions to students' papers as they were discussed among the writers' classmates, peers, and editors.

In fact, it was fun to learn in each class just how many writers had walked into their first day of class to discover that instead of an "old model" classroom with rows of single-file desks, they faced a "new model" room of long tables, covered with gleaming new, top-of-the-line computers. Some students expressed their horror at the scene, since many of them had never worked on computers.

But as I sat there with the students, talking easily now only a couple of weeks into the term, even the former novices were able to show me around the system, clicking their mouses (mice?), moving text around like professionals!

Let me help you understand some of the concepts behind this "new model" and how they can affect you.

THE TEACHER

This person is still a part of the "new model." (Thank goodness! That means I still have a job.) But the role of the writing instructor or teacher has changed in the new model. One of the explanations I've heard recently shows how the teacher's role, while still important, has shifted. No longer is a writing-class teacher the "sage on the stage." Now, he or she is expected to be the "guide on the side." It's a repositioning of your teacher into the role of a helper. Of course, the teacher in the "old model" was your helper, too, but the actual day-to-day operation of the old model teacher was rather different.

In the old model, the teacher would usually lecture or lead a discussion, giving his or her ideas and strategies. The students would follow these guidelines fairly closely, hardly ever questioning them. After all, it was long assumed that the teacher was the sage or the wise one. Why would anyone question his or her position at the front of the class?

However, the study of writing is rather different from other disciplines. For example, the main work that gets done in a history class is "teaching." The teacher is generally better versed and better prepared in the field. He or she, with the help of a textbook, films, and so on, teaches you the story of a period of time often quite distant from ours. The teacher knows more about the subject because he or she has studied it for years. For the most part a student has very little to add. When the teacher says "George Washington had baby blue eyes," it's rare that a student can stand up and say "No, he didn't. They were brown." We don't know as much as the history professor, so we shut up and take notes. At the end of the semester, we take a big test that sees how many of those George Washington stories we remember. If we remember 74 percent of them or so, we get a C+; 87 percent and we get an A–.

But the study of writing doesn't work like that. The main work that gets done is writing, and it's such a subjective skill that each writer requires a different kind of help and "teaching." There's no need for the instructor to be up front, in a spotlight. The teacher needs to be available to offer help and assistance while each writer has his or her own little spotlight.

In the computer classroom, the focus of the room is no longer the front, or the lectern, or the teacher. Some of the time you are facing your computer, and the rest of the time you're facing the assembled class, all in some sort of circle. The focus is on your own work. Your instructor is a part of that, and so are your peers.

THE MACHINE

It's hard to get past the notion that there's a large, humming computer in front of you. Of course, it's a little bit daunting for anyone. Whenever I sit in front of someone else's computer, I immediately begin worrying about breaking the silly thing. Listen, your college or university has bought a bunch of these machines. They are in your classroom because your university and your instructor wants you to experience them and use them. They're tough to break, amazingly helpful, and a lot of fun. Get over the fear quickly simply by messing around on them.

LEARNING CURVE

I don't mean in any way to minimize the learning curve you'll undoubtedly go through. Even those of you who have computer experience will have some stuff to figure out and adapt to. But chances are your classroom has been used before; your teacher has taught with these before. All of the problems and mess-ups and trouble that can happen have probably already happened. You won't be the first one to say "Hey, my screen went blank" or "The printer won't work."

In my conversations with scores of writers who were introduced to computers for the first time in a writing class, I've learned that most folks were up and running and doing all they needed to do on the machines in about a week. Sure, it's different for everyone, but your instructor will know when you're having trouble (like when you're staring at a blank screen, or your head is on the keyboard). If you're confused, ask for help.

You'll make it through the learning curve, and soon you'll be helping others when they have questions.

THE PEERS

Well, you'll notice that you've probably got some friends along for the ride. If you're in a computer classroom (where a number of writers all gather in one place at their own machines) versus a virtual classroom (where there are no other writers with you physically), you'll still benefit from the traditional face-to-face, human interaction that you're probably used to.

It's true, however, that in the old model, sometimes the ideas and comments of your peers were not a great part of the proceedings. In fact, the new model benefits as much from the increased role of the peer (in our case peer writers) as it does from anything else.

The theory behind this is quite simple. You're working on some skills in this writing class. You're being introduced to a process of writing and being turned loose on a series of different writing assignments. At the very same time your peers—the folks all around you in this classroom—are being offered the same challenges and opportunities. Who better to have around to learn from and share with?

One of the best parts of this new model classroom is the added feedback available from peers. There's a feeling among writers and students, left over from the old model of teaching, that the teacher's ideas are the only ones that count. Well, that's not true. I often think of a class as a shared knowledge event. We come into an empty room and begin filling it with our ideas. I say a few things that we all hear. Someone asks a question. I answer it. Someone asks another question; someone else answers it. Someone talks about an essay he's working on. The person sitting next to him says she's read it and she thinks it's good but that it needs some more description.

That's a shared experience. The things being said and the ideas being shared by students become part of the overall event of being in a class together. Get used to the idea that your learning is going to occur all around you. It will come from your instructor; it will come from you and your own work, and it will come from your peers as they work around you.

Virtual classes

It seems like a dream in a way, the virtual class. Some people think it's a nightmare. In the virtual class, students operate in their own private space and are connected to the class only through an online link. The instructor maintains a Web site, a chat site or chat room, perhaps, and a place to exchange papers and messages. Students are required to post a certain number of messages, write a certain amount of pages during the semester, but no one ever actually ends up in the same room. This scares many students (and teachers) because it is so different from the traditional model. It's new, but not untested.

And, of course, it's happening already. Colleges across the country are experimenting with virtual classes, some of them with resounding success. In addition to the good folks at Texas Tech, Creighton University, Michigan State University, and several others have turned at least some classes and instructors loose in the virtual classroom, a sort of cyber-educational experience.

The personal computer becomes the conduit to learning and instruction, and the flow of information doesn't have to be contained by classroom walls. Anthony can log in from home and read Sela's essay, sent earlier from a computer terminal in the library, or the computer lab, or where she works.

There are several things students first think when they hear about this system. Let's try to get rid of any confusion or preconceptions by talking about what really happens.

CAN I WORK IN MY PAJAMAS?

Yes. No problem. Or in your boxers. As long as your roommate, or your parents, or your boss, or the librarian doesn't mind, you can sit at your computer completely nude if you want! But seriously, you will be working outside of the normal space of a classroom. Sometimes this means your own computer, if you're lucky. (Some schools even issue students laptop machines just for this reason.) Some of you will be working in a computer lab on campus. You may work on a computer at work if you have one. But the key is you've got a wider variety of times that you can do your classwork. If it's 2 AM and you feel like reading one of your peer's drafts, then do it. If you want to check your instructor's website to see what assignment is next, do that, too.

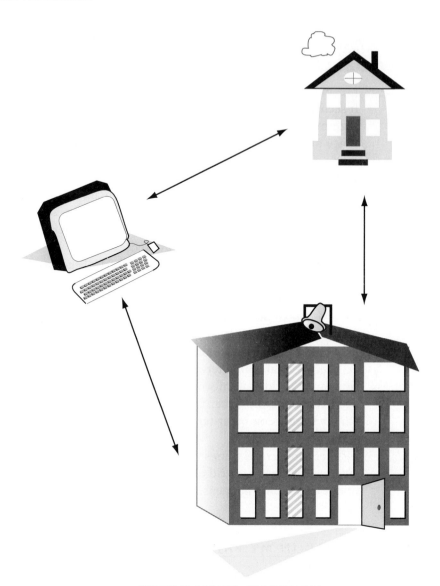

VIRTUAL MODEL CLASSROOM
Arrows Show Informational Flow

It is true that even in the virtual class that your instructor will get everyone together in a chat room sometimes. This does involve some traditional scheduling. But if you want to work on your own schedule, then the virtual class is a big step for you.

IS IT EASIER? IS THERE LESS WORK?

That depends. Many writers tell me they do more work, but that's because time is much more flexible; the process is actually easier.

One contributing factor to the ease or difficulty of the class is how well suited you are to taking responsibility for yourself and your work. If you want to work at 2 AM, you can. But if you don't want to work at 9 AM, there's no one there to force you. Sometimes writers need an outside force (like the old model classroom and class-time meeting) in order to do their work.

Being disciplined about keeping in touch with the instructor and the class through e-mail, chats, and so on is crucial if you want to reap the benefits of the virtual class *and* get your work done. Don't let the "freedom" of the virtual class fool you into not working as much as you should.

WILL I EVER MEET WITH MY CLASS?

Yes and no. In virtual classrooms currently in use, students are held to some kind of minimum standards for being "in touch" with peers and the instructor. Usually, each writer is expected to send a certain number of e-mails or to respond to a certain number of drafts or posts that other writers make. Obviously, you should respond to any question or e-mail generated by your instructor.

Just like a traditional class, you have as many chances for contact as you want to make. I've had lots of students in a traditional class who never meet with me out of class, even though they may have *seen* me in class 45 times a semester. And I've had students in a virtual class who have had contact with me through their notes and writing almost every day of the semester. How much "contact" you want is up to you.

There is not the same kind of physical contact, meaning face-to-face meetings, but even that rule is sometimes bent in some virtual classes. Many virtual classes that are taught within a single location or college will sometimes have a group meeting, often early on in the process. You may in fact have already met with your peers and your instructor, at least to pass out the syllabus, get your e-mail address, or maybe just pass out this textbook. But the rest of the time, you'll likely be out of physical touch with the rest. It's certainly true that you will see a classmate now and then in a computer lab, and you may even see your professor around campus a time or two. But the virtual class works because it's a writing intensive course; don't forget that.

WHAT'S WRITING INTENSIVE OR WRITING IMMERSION?

Joseph Unger, the computer guru who keeps the computers running for the composition program at Texas Tech University, explained it to me this way: "It's a writing intensive course. Everything the student does is writing." If a student wants to let the teacher know his draft is going to be late, he has to write. The teacher writes back for an explanation, and the student has to write back once again. Even the simplest tasks take the form of a writing exercise. If we believe that writing is a skill that you can learn and practice (like swimming or playing the piano), then clearly as much writing as possible is the best. Unger also says "What's the best way to teach someone any language? French, for example. We immerse them in that language; in class they do nothing but speak French. Why not the same for writers of English."

WHAT DOES THE PHRASE "TIME-SHIFTING" MEAN, AND WHY IS IT GOOD FOR ME?

When you tape *ER* on Thursday nights and save it to watch on Saturday afternoons, you've effectively shifted time around to suit your schedule. This is called "time-shifting."

This concept exists in computer and virtual classes, too. And for me, it's one of the best features. A writer who really wants feedback on an essay is able to get it around the clock. Unfailingly, teachers who opt to teach this kind of class are comfortable with computers, check their e-mail often, and are pretty good about getting back to writers on a regular basis. It's not possible to turn in your essay at 3 AM in most traditional circumstances, but with an online hookup to your virtual class, you can turn that thing in whenever it's ready or in need of help. It always blows my writers away when they send e-mail at an odd time and get a return from me shortly. They forget that the virtual class is a virtual class for *all* of us. I'm keeping flexible hours, and I'm in my pajamas, too!

IS THIS DISTANCE EDUCATION?

Well, the precursor of what we know as distance education or distance learning was the correspondence course. Penn State started their renowned correspondence program in 1892. That's 1892, not 1992.

In the 1920s and 1930s, radio technology was sometimes used to broadcast lessons over distances. When television took over in the 1950s and 1960s, lessons began being broadcast live. Of course, in the 1970s until today, videotape has made the TV broadcast easier. An instructor can tape dozens of lessons suitable not just for his or her class but for all the classes at the college or, indeed, anywhere.

Distance education as we understand it today, came into its own in the 1980s, as hundreds of colleges and thousands of courses became available through tele-video presentation around the country. This was distance education's boom period. Many community and junior colleges offered tele-classes over local cable stations. Students bought textbooks and watched live or pre-taped programs once a week. The more advanced kinds of these classes included a "call-in" portion of the class in which students made phone calls to the instructor.

Obviously, connecting through a TV program and the occasional phone call is not nearly as interactive and useful as being online with your whole class and instructor through a chat option, as discussed earlier in this chapter. But in some of the more financially viable institutions, a two-way interactive video hook-up is possible, with students on camera in one location and a teacher on camera in another.

Now distance education exists in a very multifaceted way. The telecourse is still very prominent, but computer or cyberclasses are booming as well. Perhaps Distance Education will one day be completely computer intensive, with students and teachers responding over distance, through video, audio, text, and graphic hookups in their computers. See each other. Talk to each other. Show each other text. Show each other graphics. It sounds a little like the Jetsons, but it's here now.

And the neat thing about distance education and the virtual classroom is that it widens the options for all kinds of students. No longer do you have to be at the college at the time specified to take the class. Computers help us do away with the constraints of time. We can have a terrific class experience when no two people are working at exactly the same time. If Doug likes to write after he gets off work at 11 PM, that's okay. If Jodi wants to work first thing in the morning, that's fine. If Judith never knows when she can work because of her kids and her part-time job, it doesn't matter. Whenever you can make the time to do your work, the computer will be there, the work will be waiting, messages sent to you by your teacher and your peers can be received by you any time you want.

That's a freedom in education that should be exhilarating to you.

Daedalus® Integrated Writing Environment (DIWE)

Daedalus® Integrated Writing Environment software was developed by a group of writing instructors during the mid-1980s. As they watched writers struggle with the transition from the traditional writing methods to the new model methods (writing on a computer), they put together a series of steps or "modules" that would provide writers with some necessary help.

Daedalus is a piece of software in use at over 500 colleges and universities. Its popularity continues to grow, and it seems quite likely that its influence will be felt for years to come.

If you're in a class that will be using Daedalus, let me go through the six modules and give you an idea of what terrific fun you have ahead. If you've gotten this far in the chapter and don't use Daedalus, let me encourage you to read through some of what follows anyway, as many of the Daedalus functions are easily replicated using a variety of easily found online tools.

INVENT

In the early stages of any writing process, it's important to begin generating ideas. You know that already from Chapter 1, which presents a great deal about the pre-writing or creating stage. The Invent module of Daedalus is made up of a series of prompts or questions that are designed to make you think about your possible topic in a variety of ways, thereby forcing you to come up with some ideas you might not have thought of on your own. The neat thing about Invent is that while it comes with a series of standard questions for all types of essays—narrative, persuasive, and so—with the Daedalus function of "prompt maker," your instructor can tailor questions that suit your essay exactly.

Let's look at a sample of this function. When you first get into Invent, you'll be asked to type in your topic; then you'll be given a series of questions or prompts to address about your topic. They come up on the screen as you go, and when you're done writing (ask your instructor how long or how much he or she wants), you go to the next page. Below is a partial peek at that process. Keep in mind as you read each response that the writer has as much space and time as he or she wants to respond to each prompt. Sometimes a prompt will encourage you to go on at length. Sometimes the prompt only gives you a few ideas.

Don't be discouraged if one of the prompts fails to move you to write a big chunk; the prompts are just helpers to get you moving along the way. Just relax and type away on your blank screen. Any invention is good invention.

Topic:
```
Lubbock
```

Prompt #1:
```
How does "Lubbock" "grow"? Use your imagination.
```

Reply:
```
It grows from the inside out, like a spiral. Like a
wheel. It moves like soda pop over gravel. It spreads
like weeds across the desert, one blade at a time. It
grows outwards, not upwards. It grows slowly, creeping
across the scrub brush.
```

Prompt #2:
```
How is your subject like a plant? Describe the seed,
the roots, the blooms, the branches, the leaves ...
```

Reply:
```
It's got roots, and flowers. Flowers are cool places.
Roots are old, established, traditional places. The
seeds are the new suburbs. If the seeds take root then
new flowers will grow. Blooms? That's hard. Blooms are
when pretty things unexpectedly grow up! Blooms are
when Western High School won the girls volleyball. Our
team and town and girls blossomed on a national and
state level.
```

Prompt #3:
```
Imagine enlarging a photograph of "Lubbock." What
features would you bring into focus? Explain.
```

Reply:
```
I'd bring the school into focus, and the restaurants and
the clubs. I'd focus on how pretty the land around
Lubbock is. People think it's dull, but it's full of
life and animals and bushes, etc. I love the oil pumpers
all in a long row outside of Posey, and the deserted
train tracks by Snyder. I'd show the living and the
dying things all around the area.
```

Prompt #4:

"Lubbock" has exploded. Everything is flying around. Describe what you see.

Reply:

First of all there's sand everywhere. Because when the wind even blows a little bit, sand gets in my eyes. Sand and red buildings. The red buildings at the university fly around first. Then the explosion lifts off all the fast food restaurants and cars. Sonic burgers flying like in a tornado. Taco Bell, where I am, uplifts, but surprisingly we're all safe inside. I'm still eating my bean burrito. The whole town lifts off and spins and I can look back down at the ground below us. Everything is flat and getting farther away.

Now, at this point the writer has certainly covered some ideas and ground that he or she would have probably not covered on his or her own. Those four sample prompts above are varied and interesting and certainly require the writer to apply creative ideas to the process.

But those short responses by themselves don't equal an essay! This is a crucial little lesson. This writing that has been going on hasn't been in the middle or drafting stage (remember Chapter 1?). This writing is all part of the creating or pre-writing phase. In fact, I even use the word "invention" in Chapter 1 myself.

WRITE

Write is Daedalus's word processor. It's simple, easy to use, and takes almost no time to get used to. It's perfect for first-time computer users and has all the necessary writing functions for the creation of drafts and essays: copying, cutting, pasting, spell checking, and printing. It may seem simple to more advanced users of computers, but folks who are experienced likely are comfortable with another, more complex and full-featured piece of software, such as Microsoft Word or Word Perfect.

It's also likely that if you've got a computer of your own, you have a word processing program that you like. Or if you're using computers on campus, they'll surely have some word-processing software already loaded for your use. It's really a matter of preference; I won't tell you what I think is the best, because it doesn't matter. People have different preferences, but most of the top software programs all offer the same features and controls.

The simpler the software the better for first-time users, because we don't want you to have to struggle just to get your essay typed in. If you're really new to things, then Write works great.

RESPOND

Respond's functions are very similar to those of Invent, discussed earlier. Using this part of the Daedalus software will be very helpful once a draft has been written (after getting your topic together with Invent, and after writing it with Write!). At this point you're in need of feedback, and by turning your paper over to other readers (your peers, especially) you can see your essay from a whole new vantage point.

Just like the Invent module, your instructor has the chance to modify and write his or her own prompts, thereby giving you the best help possible. Here's an example of one peer reader's work in the Respond module.

```
    I never dreamed that one day I'd live in the big
city. It seemed so far away. It seemed to be a great
dream that would always exceed my grasp. At night if
the moon was hidden we could even see the lights of
the big city in the horizon. They glowed, almost hot
to the touch. They were beckoning to me like a magnet.
    On Sundays sometimes we'd make the long drive up
the highway into the city. We'd sit at traffic lights
and I'd look out at the buildings, all bunched up
together, stacked, one on top of the other. Apart-
ments loomed, tall, imposing. I would see faces in
windows, seemingly millions. When we'd turn around
and head home, the highway away from the city seemed
dull, unexciting, lifeless. Our little town seemed
tiny. Our house seemed lonesome out there by itself.
I yearned to go back.
```

Respond's Prompt:
```
What specific suggestions concerning development do you
have concerning the paper?
```

Peer's Response:
```
I like the paper so far. It sounds like my life, too,
because we used to live out in a suburb and I was always
amazed when we'd go into the city. Since this question
asks about development, I guess I'll point out your
```

second paragraph. I think there are two main ideas in
your second paragraph. (Which probably means you need to
break that into two paragraphs anyway . . . he he . . .
that's a whole other prompt, I bet!)

But I think your first main idea in that paragraph is
that the city is big and overwhelming. You give some
general examples or support of that, like the apartments being "tall." But why not say "The apartments
were tall, at least 30 stories high. They blocked out
the sun and turned the city dark." Maybe that's too
dramatic, but I can see that image better than the one
you've got.

Then you have to develop the second part of the
second paragraph separately. See, it's about going back
home and how dull everything seems. I love that line
about the house being lonesome, but why not expand and
develop the idea of it being dull. "Everything looked
gray and dull. The windows were covered in dirt and
sand and the faces of the men on the park bench were
plain and emotionless." Maybe too dramatic again, but
give it a try.

Good start! Keep going!

Respond works very well because it asks the reader for something
specific and exacting. Remember that a peer response with no direction
matches up a relatively inexperienced reader critically reading the rough
draft of a likewise inexperienced writer. With no direction such as the
prompts in Respond, it's very easy for even a well-intentioned reader to
read an essay and simply say "Hey, it's pretty good. It's funny. I like that
thing about the big apartment." At this point of your development as
writers and readers, the prompts supplied by the Daedalus Respond
module, and/or the ones your instructors write for you, will help you
respond in a more focused and useful way to your peers. (And, of
course, help them respond better to your essays!)

MAIL

The Daedalus Mail feature is a nice, versatile mail program that allows
you to send your essays, drafts, responses, and such to individual members of your class, to your instructor only, or to everyone at once. The
software keeps track of all this communication so when you want to
check something you sent or received earlier, you can simply call it up.

If, for example, you have a simple question of scheduling, and you want to check with your teacher, you can simply select that option. If you've been asked instead to post your rough draft so that all your peers can see it, you'd select the option to send to "all."

INTERCHANGE®

Of all of the modules of Daedalus®, InterChange appears to me to be the most useful. In my time in computer classrooms, it's the one constant that all instructors and all students seem to like.

The practical application of InterChange is much the same as any "chat" function of an online computer service. If you're familiar with America Online (AOL), CompuServe, or Prodigy, these would be the chat rooms. If you're hooked right up to the Internet, then you might be familiar with Internet Relay Chat (IRC) or with some of the newer World Wide Web–based chat areas. InterChange is comparable to these.

One of the key differences of the InterChange system, though, is a seemingly simple one: size. In nearly every other online chat system, the writer is typically limited to a comparatively small area to type into. In AOL, for example, you have room for about 90 characters or letters. That's only enough space for 14–18 words, just a couple of short sentences or one long one. If you have more to say, you have to keep entering text and sending, over and over again. I find that sometimes I lose my train of thought if I've got to keep starting and continuing sentences in between typing and sending.

But on InterChange, the writer's window—the bottom part of the screen—is rather larger. Having that extra room allows the writer a chance to stretch out and say what he or she needs to say, without fear of running out of space.

In the top screen appears the text written by the other folks in the InterChange. Those are likely your peers and perhaps your instructor, too. How much text is there, of course, depends on the number of folks taking part in the InterChange. At times this top screen gets full and you should scroll back often and read what was passing by while you were typing. In fact, it's an excellent idea to save the InterChange as a file so you can look it over again. Whenever I do an InterChange and read it later, I find stuff I missed. (Then I rush to a computer and send some mail to people who said something I want to know more about!)

Let's take a look at a sample InterChange. This one begins, like most, with a prompt from the instructor.

Instructor:
Okay, although we're not all online yet, I'll post the prompt for the day. I'd like everyone to talk about their pre-writing or creating phase. Tell us what you did and what you discovered. After you type a little something, take time to read some of the other posts, okay? Away we go!

Marcia L:
During the creating phase I used the free-writing skills we talked about. I sat at the student union with a new notebook and just wrote about stuff that came to my mind.

Ilena F:
I used free-writing.

Steve P:
Hope I didn't miss anything.

Instructor:
Ilena, how did you use free-writing?
Marcia, did you do focused or unfocused free-writing?

Steve P:
I wrote in my journal in my dorm about as many people from my past that I could remember. Then once I'd done twenty minutes of that, I picked out the most "surprising" name on the list, an old friend of mine who I barely remembered. Then my next free-writing was just about him. I focused on remembering as much stuff as I could about this old friend. I thought up a bunch of stories and then later I wrote one more free-writing about one particular story.

Instructor:
Everyone, read Steve's long post. What type of free-writing is he talking about?

Ilena F:
Sorry. I wrote using the 5 Storyteller Questions. I took my topic idea (the story about my brother I told you about) and I tried to write a little about character, setting, and all the rest.

Nate S:

Steve was looping. Same as I did.

Steve P:

It was looping.

Ronelle B:

I did a character study of my roommate. I wrote for about
an hour about all of her good and bad points. I wrote
long lists. Then I didn't know what do with it.

Instructor:

Terri, are you online?

Terri M:

Yes, just reading right now.

Steve P:

Then when I was done looping, I decided to go ahead and
use the topic of my old friend. Does that sound okay?

Nate S:

But my looping had less steps. I just looped one time.
I wrote one thing about this place I used to always go
and hang at. It was away from the rest of the town.
Then I wrote another looping that described it.

Instructor:

Terri, can you give us an idea of what type of invention
you went through as you got ready for this paper?
Steve and Nate, sounds like you guys are on the right
track.

Steve P:

Hey, Nate . . . are you talking about Lake Leon?
Hahahahahaha.

Ilena F:

Ronelle, I did something similar but then I just had a
list, too. I had to try to connect some of my list
entries so that they made up sections. Like if your
roommate is always making trouble for you, you've gotta
circle all those list entries that relate to her being
a b---h and make a paragraph or something out of that.
That way you've got a bunch of ideas that all fit
together.

Nate S:
You know it, Steve . . . Lake Leon is DA BOMB!

Instructor:
Good advice Ilena. Ronelle, I think Ilena is exactly
right! Nate and Steve, I've been to Lake Leon, too!
When I was your age. Hahahaha.

The first time I saw or took part in an InterChange, I was pretty confused. I spent a lot of time trying to respond to everyone who said something. The advice I hear from students is to just respond to a few things or even one entry at a time. In the example above, the instructor does a pretty good job of getting people started, helping them focus their ideas, and giving positive feedback to those who are doing a good job.

In my experience chatting with students who use the InterChange as part of their regular classes, I found most students had enormous respect for the system. In one way it tends to allow shy folks the chance to say something when perhaps in a loud, traditional classroom, they might clam up. It's easy in a quiet room where the only sound is of keyboards clacking, to type a couple of words in response to something. And then when you hit that "send" button, the thoughts you had look good there on the screen. They're neat, tidy, and usually spelled right. Your words join the dialogue and somebody is bound to say "Yeah, that's right, Todd," or "Sure, Sarah! Me, too."

Many students told me that they liked talking to their peers and even their instructors better this way than the traditional way in the old model classroom. One student told me "Even my instructor is just one of us. Her words on the screen aren't any louder or bigger or anything. She has to type in just like us. If she forgets and starts talking out loud during an InterChange, we don't respond. One of us, or all of us, just types 'TALK TO US ON THE COMPUTER!'"

Another part of the beauty of the InterChange is that there's no waiting around. If you want to type and send, there's no one to stop you. In the old model or traditional classroom, you're always waiting your turn in some kind of way. And if that other person talks long enough, it's easy to lose your train of thought. Not on the computer InterChange. You can type what you're thinking right when it occurs to you.

In fact, these concepts hold true for any kind of chat gathering of fellow writers, not just the Daedalus InterChange software. You can have the same experience in your class if your teacher helps you all get hooked up in an America Online or CompuServe chat room or in one of the thousands of IRC (Internet Relay Chat) rooms on the Internet.

These rooms are used mostly on the Internet as meeting places for people, and when you're trying to get 10–20 writers together at one time—with some of them perhaps working from home on their own computer or some in the library—a common chat room where all can take part at the same time makes perfect sense.

BIBLIOCITE®

BiblioCite® is a useful tool to help writers compose a bibliography, works-cited page, or references page. The proper documentation style for MLA (used in the humanities) and APA (used in psychology and some other physical and social sciences) is built into the software, and all you do to complete the page is fill in the necessary spaces or fields on the screen.

This is a useful, but dangerous tool. After all, one of the purposes of any college course is to teach you skills that you can use again in other situations and classes. It's unlikely that Daedalus's BiblioCite will be available to you for the rest of your college career and beyond.

BiblioCite takes the raw data (name of author, title of book, etc.) and orders them correctly according to MLA or APA guidelines. That's very different than having the writer learn the proper method.

By all means use BiblioCite if it's available to you; you'd be crazy not to. But keep in mind that when you use it, you are letting the machine do work for you that may be left up to you in other classes and situations.

Last thoughts on machinery

Regardless of what you use to write with, or what kind of class you're in, writing is still an activity that mostly involves your heart and your mind. Most of the work still takes place inside of you. Machinery and technology aren't substitutes for good ideas and hard work; they're merely gadgets, devices, and systems by which we may be able to do our thinking more easily.

In the end, you're still likely to be sitting somewhere (in front of a computer, or just a piece of paper), scratching your head and wondering what to say or do next. Technology will never change that.

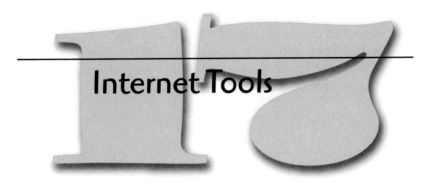

Internet Tools

One of the reasons this book got written at all was the inevitable and unstoppable force of the Internet. The Internet's amazing abilities to move and share information worldwide is too delicious to bypass if you're a writer, thinker, or student. (And of course we are always all three of those.)

Think of the Internet as the largest source of ready information there is. Think of it as the largest collection of "connected" writers, researchers, and experts there is.

Your instructor probably knows something about the Internet, and I bet many of you are knowledgeable about it as well. There's been a glut of books on the market in the last several years about the "Net," so this chapter will focus primarily on some of the principal Internet tools and how you can use them to become better writers and communicators.

By this point you're likely aware that this book has its own Web site at <http://www.prenhall.com/english>. I encourage you to visit it every once in a while, especially when you first get this book, to see what new things have happened and what new things are planned for the future.

Let's look at the principal features of the Internet.

E-mail

E-mail is something of a miracle, nothing less. Every day, I send my thoughts, words, and ideas across the country, around the globe, or just across town to a friend. I type what I want to say on my computer, hit a button, and within seconds (actually sometimes more quickly) my words are there for someone else to read.

It's fast and wonderful and powerful. I'm sure you're convinced how powerful words are; when we add the speed and convenience of electronic mail to that, we have a formidable combination.

Are there dangers? Sure, as with any other kind of communication, there are some things to watch out for. Speed might be one of your biggest enemies. Because it's so easy to send a quick note virtually anywhere (to a friend, a newspaper's editorial page, a major corporation), sometimes we don't spend enough time thinking over what we actually are saying.

I had just been to a concert the night before and was angered when I read in the morning newspaper a review that was clearly wrong and uninformed. The writer of the column listed his e-mail address at the bottom of each of his stories, so within 30 seconds of reading the article, I was typing a response. The eagerness I had for writing was good. But as in any kind of "argumentative" writing, I made a classic mistake. I didn't give myself the chance to cool down or think things over. I teach my writers that lesson every single semester, but here I was committing the same error.

E-mail is easy, and when I was through with the letter, feeling all flushed and excited about setting this guy straight, I just did the easy thing and hit the magic button called "Send."

I felt good all day until his e-mail came back to me. He had copied some of my letter and sent it back to me. I had made some typos. I was mad at him in my letter for spelling the name of a band member incorrectly, and he showed me how I had spelled "his" name wrong as well. What my poorly edited letter had done was sabotage whatever good information I may have had to share with my reader. Why? Because I let "speed" get in my way.

Of course speed and convenience are great things, and e-mail is such a powerful tool because of those things. But in the online world, we must still remember to build in time to think things over. That's the nice thing about sending a letter. You type it. Print it out. Spend time looking it over on a piece of paper. Sign it. Fold it. Go find an envelope. Find a stamp. Address the envelope. Seal it. Get in the car. Go to the post office, and then send it. There's a built-in period of time in which you can reconsider what you've said, think about it some more.

With e-mail, you type it on the screen, never printing it out. No envelope. No stamp. No hard copy to read. Just a glowing screen and that always-tempting SEND button glowing in the corner of your monitor. "Click me," it says.

Resist the temptation. Just as with any essay for class, take your time and don't send that e-mail until you're completely happy with what it says. You wouldn't turn in an essay to your instructor without reading it carefully, weighing your audience and purpose, checking spelling, and so on. Don't allow the convenience of e-mail to trick you into sending before you or your writing are ready to go.

GETTING STARTED

If you're already online, this section won't tell you much. If you've already been on one of the major commercial services (America Online, CompuServe, Prodigy, MSN, etc.) you've likely already sent or received some e-mail. Many of you are probably handling a dozen or more e-mails a day. Typically you're offered a multiwindow screen with space for you to type the address of your recipient, a subject line for your message, and the message itself.

In most cases, when your recipient gets this piece of mail, he or she will see your name and the subject line first. Treat that subject with the same kind of care we've treated essay titles. Make sure it's informative and evocative and that it encourages your reader to read that mail. Busy folks who get lots of e-mail a day are pretty choosy about what gets read and when it gets read.

Depending on your software, you may or may not have a lot of editing functions for your message. Some e-mail programs allow you almost full word processor editing, spell checking, formatting, and so forth. America Online, for example, allows you to change the font, the style, the size, and the color of every word and letter you type.

Once you begin reading a lot of e-mail, however, you'll realize too much formatting has a negative impact. You'll see what I mean the first time you get a goofy piece of e-mail with six colors and four different backgrounds and some BIG letters and some small. There's a place and a time for some neat formatting, but never let gimmicks or formatting get in the way of the purpose of your e-mail.

PRACTICAL APPLICATION

Over the past few years I've done a lot of experimenting with e-mail as a tool for me to help my writers. I don't hesitate to say that it is a miracle, and the most beneficial device I've found yet to be an active participant in my writers' development.

The first remarkable advance that e-mail provides is the fast and simple transport of your essays. Traditionally, students have had to actually find the instructor in person to turn in an essay. The teacher has to take that essay home, transporting it from briefcase to kitchen table, maybe back to his or her office, and then eventually back to class and the student's ready hands.

With e-mail, however, we can condense a process that took a week or more down to minutes or hours. Many times a week, one of my writers sends me an essay via e-mail. I can read it, edit it, write comments wherever I want on it, and send it right back. I can do in ten minutes for my writers what used to take me days. And turning your paper in by e-mail means you can do it at three in the morning. Or at noon. Or on days when you don't even have class, even the weekend.

As I'm writing this part of the book, I'm just finishing up a semester with a composition class like yours. Over these past couple of weeks my students have been sending me e-mail like crazy. A typical morning can go like this.

```
 8 am: Log on and check my e-mail. There's a new draft
        of Lisa's research paper. I read it, find a problem
        on the first page. Correct it and send it back.
 9 am: Walk the dog.
10 am: Log on again. Lisa has gotten my e-mail in between
        her morning classes and has made the change. Now
        I read the whole paper. When I find an MLA problem
        on her Works Cited page, I correct one as an
        example and e-mail that back to her. Before I log
        off this time, she's already gotten it and sent it
        back for a second look. Now it's right.
```

Our old model doesn't have writer and teacher in the same room very often. With e-mail, it's as if we're connected, working together, every day. And that is the goal, isn't it?

Is the system perfect? Well, pretty close, but of course there are problems. If you aren't willing to work, then no matter how many times your instructor sends you back your pages, your essay is not going to get better. What if you're too busy to get logged on? What if your instructor doesn't have time to log on that day? All of those things can break down the system. If you're using this book (or at least reading this chapter), I'm assuming your instructor is going to provide a system in this class that will enable you to have e-mail contact with him or her.

You still have to work; you still have to ask for help. But the new model works better because we can cut down on the time delay between you writing something and your instructor having a chance to read it. If it's true that writing is a skill, like swimming (and I believe it is), then this system is better than the traditional model; if you were learning to swim, would you want to swim every day, or take a week or two off between each half-hour lesson? That's an easy question, right? It's better to keep at something. It's better to keep the essay in your mind as you work on it. It's better to keep swimming.

World Wide Web (WWW)

The World Wide Web is the remarkable and highly visible graphical part of the international network of computers. If you've heard about home pages or Web sites, the WWW is where they "are." Your school probably has a Web site that shows information about admissions, faculty, programs, and so on.

If you like music, your favorite musical artists probably have pages devoted to them (everything from Beck to Bach, from Van Halen to Vivaldi, from Depeche Mode to Debussy to Bob Dylan). If you're a lover of art, you can view paintings by Monet, Van Gogh, Rubens, and Pollock, by linking to art galleries and museums the world over. Sports fan? Watch and/or listen to games live on your computer screen.

Major corporations spend millions on developing an Internet Web presence. Even small companies do the same on a smaller scale. You can buy flowers and groceries and luggage and furniture off the Web. You can find out the temperature in downtown Gstaad or see a live camera shot off the top of the CN Tower in Toronto, Canada.

There's helpful information available; there's useless information available. You can book airplane tickets for yourself to go visit your family. Or you can find out how many cans of Pepsi there are in a soft drink machine on the campus of some university.

Like the real world, the WWW is what you make of it.

Personal pages outnumber corporate ones. Anybody with an Internet hookup, a modem, and some simple software can put together a home page that talks about them! Talk about the ultimate personal writing example! Many of you reading this book likely have knowledge of "surfing the Net." Some of you have your own pages, I bet.

GETTING STARTED

The two principal World Wide Web browsers of choice are the Netscape Navigator or Communicator and the Microsoft Internet Explorer. I do not intend to weigh in on the relative merits of these fine pieces of software. Chances are that if you're online, you'll already have one or both of them available to you. If you're using a computer on your campus, find out from your teacher or from a computer assistant what software you have for WWW browsing and how to get started.

If you already have online capabilities with America Online or CompuServe, you have already access to a browser already, built in to those powerful commercial services.

If you're online and don't have a browser, it's fairly simple to get one. Just ask your Internet Service Provider (ISP) for some software. Whoever got you set up for an online Internet account, e-mail, and so forth will have access to freeware or shareware programs that are fully functional for the new user.

PRACTICAL APPLICATIONS

Our time is not called the information age for nothing. One of the first things I recognized about the WWW when I began surfing was "Look at how much stuff!" And it was true. I literally hopped from page to page to page, hyperlinking from the IBM page to the Netscape page, to a Netscape developer page, to his link about his family, to their link to an ice cream company, from the ice cream company's link to the weather in Gary, Indiana, from there to a link about weather balloons. It's a web of information where almost everything is connected in some kind of way. That's cool, certainly, but it's also messy. There is very little order on the WWW.

It's very likely that if you're online through your school, the WWW will be available to you already. But how you view that wonderful tool matters as well. Older text-based browsers such as Lynx are vastly out of date. Unless you're surfing with the newer browsers, Netscape's Navigator or Communicator or Microsoft's Internet Explorer, you will miss a tremendous amount of graphic material that is often crucial to an understanding of the whole page in question.

Because our discussion of the WWW is strictly about its research value, we'll be brief here.

Accessing Web sites involves knowing at least one crucial bit of information: the site's URL, its universal resource locator or address. Watch most television commercials for large corporations (Toyota, for example), and look for a tiny line of print, something like "www.toyota.com" on the bottom of the screen. That's the URL for the Toyota corporation. If you've got browsing software on your computer, simply typing that URL (with http:// added) will tell your computer to access that page. (In Chapter 18, I'll give you a whole series of URLs, so you'll get some good practice.)

It's entirely possible now to do all of your research online. As machines grow even faster and more powerful, no amount of information will be too large to pull in to your own computer through the telephone lines that connect most of us to a large Internet Service Provider.

Newsgroups

Newsgroups, or more correctly Usenet groups, are bulletin board–like gathering places where people post their thoughts and respond to others on a wide range of interests. Currently, there are over 20,000 Usenet groups, covering every imaginable topic: food, culture, music, movies, politics, scuba-diving, sex, and on and on.

GETTING STARTED

Most Internet users monitor only a handful of groups on a regular basis, but may view others when they're looking for a specific bit of information. I had a student spend a couple of days reading and writing messages on the newsgroup called alt.food.taco-bell on which she found all the information she needed to write her essay.

You may post a message on a newsgroup fairly easily using any one of several Usenet or newsgroup mail readers. Typically, it's a great deal like a piece of e-mail, with a message and subject line. That subject line becomes important. Because ten or a hundred or a thousand people might read your message, there's no telling how many people will respond to it by posting their own thoughts next to yours.

When a series of people write, read, and respond to the same message, that's called a "thread." It's always neat when your topic or message engenders enough interest in other folks on the newsgroup to start and maintain an ongoing conversation or thread.

Because the Net is such an anonymous place, pranksters exist in large numbers. They will do everything from attacking you or your ideas (commonly called "flaming"), to simply unleashing a barrage of annoying messages your way. It's an unfortunate fact of life of the unlimited reach of the online world. However, most of these pranksters are harmless, and only poke at people to get reactions. If flamed, it's best to ignore it. Getting involved in a long flame war solves nothing and usually only adds to your irritation.

Good newsgroups feature lively conversations and good insight into the topic. I happen to be a regular on alt.tv.seinfeld (the name of the newsgroup for the TV show *Seinfeld*), and enjoy reading and writing messages back and forth with a large group of avid fans. We discuss episodes, the history of the show, actors and actresses who have appeared on the show, and such. For the most part, it's a kick.

PRACTICAL APPLICATIONS

In many ways, I do as much writing online in newsgroups as I do in my regular life as a teacher and writer. My newsgroup writing, in fact, is the most frequent writing "practice" I get.

As a resource, it's also unparalleled. When my Taco Bell writer needed information about contacting Taco Bell national corporate headquarters, she posted a simple note on the Taco Bell newsgroup and got more than a dozen responses, giving her addresses, phone numbers, and contact names. She even heard from Taco Bell store managers who had advice for her on her paper.

How she would have gotten that information in one day in a traditional way, I don't know.

MOOs and MUDs

MUDs (multi-user dungeons) have been around since 1979, and they have grown into a widely used educational tool through a newer name, MOOs (MUD object oriented). Simply put, MOOs or MUDs are fantasy lands where users can log in as a character (real or imagined) and interact with other users. At first, MUDs were simply used by folks wanting to escape through a role-playing game into fantasy worlds—typically of the Dungeons and Dragons sort, saving maidens, slaying beasts, and so on.

Quickly, however, more mainstream users began adapting the technology for their own uses, and now education-based MOOs are sweeping computer composition classrooms. Think of them as multi-user, text-based meeting places, where 2 to 50 users can gather.

MOO enthusiasts will tell you that MOOs are rather more useful and interesting than other "chat-like" online options (IRC, AOL Chat, etc.), because each MOO is built a little differently. MOOs are set up, often-times, like buildings or towns in which as a character in the MOO, you can move from room to room, from group to group. You can enter the MOO and, by typing an appropriate command, find what rooms are available and who is in each. Users already online often post their topic of discussion, so you don't "wander" into a group discussing something you have no interest in.

Other enthusiasts will tell you that one of the great features of MOOs (and for that matter most chat options) is that users can maintain some anonymity. A 55-year-old woman taking classes at Texas Tech University told me that she felt far more comfortable when she was connecting with other writers in her class over the MOO rather than in person. Her age, which she perceived as being a hindrance, wasn't a factor there. The fact that she was a woman was also unimportant. She felt "equal" to her younger classmates and had a much richer and more empowered experience because of that.

The anonymity of MOOs in fact helps erase other limitations, real or perceived. People with verbal difficulty or handicaps are equal with their classmates in a way that some of them might not otherwise feel.

GETTING STARTED

It's best to visit an introductory MOO site such as "The Lost Library of MOO" <http://lucien.berkeley.edu/moo.html>. It will provide a list of existing MOOs for you to experiment with, in addition to explaining MOO terminology, commands, and so on.

Once you have some confidence about commands, a neat MOO to start with is the Diversity University MOO, a site originally developed by a grad student at the University of Houston. You can get there by entering the following text in your Web browser: <telnet://moo.du.org: 8888>.

MOOs, if they are to be used by your instructor, will likely be accompanied by a couple of days of instruction and training.

PRACTICAL APPLICATION

Many of the educational MOOs that are currently running exist within college composition programs. They are a little scarce, however, and you may not have a MOO where you're taking this class. That doesn't mean you're locked out of this technology. Most of the MOOs allow you to register or log in regardless of where you may be in school. You simply log in initially as a guest. I've done this a number of times over the past months and have found MOOs across the country to be inviting and exciting places to visit and work in.

One night this past week, I was able to take part in discussions with a class of writers at a state university in New York, a group of writing lab tutors in Oregon, and another class of students at a large college in Texas. Our conversations ranged from the best way to write a personal essay, to methods of revision for an issue paper. I did it all from a computer on the campus of my college, but for a while my thoughts and ideas were out there in cyberspace, mixing and mingling with minds distant from me only physically.

World Wide Web Resources: 50 Hot Links

A world of information

I remember the first time I went to a library. I was a sports geek, so I went straight to where the sports books were. I stumbled around for hours, picking things off the shelves, sitting on the floor right between the stacks, reading parts of each book, looking at the photos, then putting them back and moving on to the next book. Time passed, and soon my mom came after me and told me we had to go. "You can only check out one," she said. I looked at the great wall of books, about baseball, hockey, football, and basketball, and like any good boy, started to cry. Mom hauled me out of that place, and I never got a book that day.

I was overwhelmed by it all. There was too much information to sort through; too many options. I couldn't take it all in. In fact, I feared that there were so many good books there that if we ever got to go back again, they'd all be gone.

But by the next time we went back to that library, I was prepared. I ran through the place to the sports section again and to my surprise, all the books were there. They were all lined up and ready to go, so I started pulling books out again. I knew I could only have one book to take home. (I still don't know if this was a library policy for new cardholders or just my mom's evil ways!!) I stacked baseball books together and hockey books together and narrowed my choices. "Too long. Not enough pictures. Not enough statistics. Too heavy." And when she came around the corner this time to retrieve me, I had one book in front of me. We marched to the front desk, handed over my card, and I was out of that place with my very own library book. And the neatest thing about it was that I knew the other books weren't going anywhere. I knew that the library was going to be there the next time I wanted a book.

Now of course, the World Wide Web is like a library. Except there are no fluorescent lights, no long stacks, no drinking fountains, and no pretty librarians to flirt with. (That's another story.) And it's not as orderly. It's huge. It's huger than huge. It's more huge than you're ever going to need. It's a messy place, but there is lots of great material to be found.

When I first started "surfing the Web" (which is the goofy but most accepted phrase for this activity), I became very discouraged about ever finding anything worthwhile. The first couple of days were terrible. I just kept bouncing around from page to page, never finding anything worthwhile. I didn't need to find "Wendy's Wild World of Cats" or a hundred photos of all the different clocks this one guy had. Most of what I found seemed silly or useless. Luckily, I stuck with it though, and the WWW began to make some sense. At the time I became immersed in the WWW, a pal of mine and I were working on a book about music. We were using the vast resources of the Web to help us track down information for our book. We started sharing addresses. He'd look all day and find four or five really great and useful resources; I'd do the same. We'd pass these pieces of paper back and forth and after a couple of months, we had found a large, useful, and well-organized set of music sites. (This work eventually led to a book I wrote with my pal Ted Gurley, *Plug In: The Guide to Music on the Net*, available from Prentice Hall and in good book stores everywhere.)

I'm trying to help you in this chapter by giving you some starting places. This chapter will contain a number of WWW resources where you can find some stuff to get you started. That first day I went to the library, I needed help. I asked the librarian at the front desk where the sports books were. She pointed. That's all I needed. I'm going to point you toward some stuff here to help you along.

However, be assured that this is only a tiny fraction of neat things to be found. I will also show you some tools to help you along on your own search toward the end of this chapter. Look at the section on "search engines" especially. Once you get used to the WWW, you'll find that they are your greatest allies.

The list below will be duplicated at this book's Web site, but here you'll find longer and more useful descriptions. If you find that a link is no longer active (a very common thing in the quickly changing WWW), check the Web site for an updated WWW address.

Above all, don't get discouraged. The Web is overwhelming and difficult. But it's a mass of information that we all can use.

Sources: 50 hot links

Any kind of "complete" list of interesting and relevant WWW sources is beyond this or really any single book. As the Web increases by literally thousands of pages a day, there is no easy way to keep track of things. The landscape of resources literally changes hour by hour.

So, instead, I've prepared a rudimentary, basic, but pretty sensible group of sites. This is the best list of 50 that I can put together at the time of this writing.

I've tended to give you sites that are sturdy, long-lasting, and not prone to closing down overnight. Indeed, that may be the principal problem with WWW resources. Even established companies with sites tend to move around from server to server as they solidify their Web presence. Smaller sites may go up and down daily, depending on the reliability of the Web masters (the operators) and/or their Internet Service Providers (ISPs).

These are some basic places to stop whenever you're looking for information about the world: news, entertainment, computers, writing, culture, and so on. The information available is vast and at times complex, but most of these sites have good search functions (or search engines) and that makes the job easier.

You have to be a little bit of an explorer. You have to get out there and surf with the rest of us. These 50 places are great sites to start with, but be prepared to go much further on your own.

SEARCH ENGINES

When in doubt, search engines are the lifesavers. They each have their own little tricks and gimmicks and interfaces, but they're also all very intuitive. Try them all and see which one seems to work the way you like it best. Even the most expert of WWW surfers devote a lot of time to using search engines to help them find what they're looking for.

1. AltaVista
```
http://www.altavista.digital.com
```
The best, most comprehensive overall search engine, but it's geared to more advanced WWW users.

2. Excite
```
http://www.excite.com/
```
Another excellent search engine.

3. Yahoo

`http://www.yahoo.com/`

Category-driven search engine. If you know a general area of interest—magazines, pollution, crime, for example—this is a good place. For online novices, the best place to start.

ONLINE INDICES: BOOKS, MAGAZINES, AND NEWSPAPERS

4. Project Gutenberg

`http://www.cs.cmu.edu/books.html`

This is the wonderful Carnegie Mellon University site that houses over 7000 books online. You can find, browse, search, and read everything from Louisa May Alcott to Émile Zola. This is an amazing site and one of the most formidable additions to online research.

5. Electronic Newsstand

`http://www.enews.com`

An easy to use and graphical site that showcases magazines and their online sites.

6. Internet Public Library

`http://www.ipl.org/reading/news/`

A terrific and extensive worldwide guide to online newspapers.

NEWS, POLITICS, CURRENT EVENTS

NEWSMAGAZINES

7. *Time*

`http://pathfinder.com/time/`

The popular newsmagazine's online home.

8. *Newsweek*

`http://www.newsweek.com`

Once housed only on America Online, *Newsweek* has now joined the cyberworld with its own developing WWW site.

9. *U.S. News and World Report*

`http://www.usnews.com/usnews/home.htm`

The most education-friendly of the big newsmagazines.

10. *The Nation*
http://www.thenation.com/
A highly respected and well-written political journal.

11. *The National Review*
http://www.nationalreview.com/
Ditto above.

TELEVISION NEWS

12. MSNBC
http://www.msnbc.com/news/
The NBC/Microsoft team does the news.

13. ABC News
http://www.abcnews.com/
ABC's version.

14. CBS News
http://www.cbsnews.com
CBS' version.

15. CNN News
http://www.cnn.com/US/index.html
CNN's version.

MAJOR NEWSPAPERS

16. The *New York Times*
http://www.nytimes.com/
All the news that fits on the Web.

17. The *LA Times*
http://www.latimes.com/
Los Angeles' paper.

18. Reuters
http://www.reuters.com/news/
The well-respected news service's news page.

19. The *Nando Times*
http://www2.nando.net/nt/nando.cgi
The Web's first paper.

20. *USA Today*
http://www.usatoday.com/
The graphically wonderful daily's online home.

BUSINESS AND MONEY JOURNALS

21. The *Financial Times*
    http://www.usa.ft.com/
    FT's online location.

22. *Wall Street Journal Interactive Edition*
    http://www.wsj.com/
    The fine newspaper's online site.

POPULAR CULTURE AND ENTERTAINMENT

This is a highly selective list. The WWW has thousands of sites that would fit this category, and several of the search engines discussed above can help you find them all based on your interests.

MAGAZINES AND JOURNALS: TRADITIONAL AND ONLINE

23. *Wired*
    http://www.wired.com/news/
    Wired is a premier online guide to all that's excellent and electronic.

24. *Boston Review*
    http://www-polisci.mit.edu/BostonReview/
    A fine political and cultural journal.

25. The *Atlantic Monthly*
    http://www.theatlantic.com
    A terrific magazine that has an even better online site. Fast, easy to use, and full of great current and archived information.

26. *George*
    http://www.georgemag.com/
    John F. Kennedy, Jr.'s hip political magazine.

27. *People* Weekly
    http://www.pathfinder.com/people/
    For research on the cult of celebrity.

28. *Rolling Stone*
    http://www.rollingstone.com/
    The venerable rock & roll, entertainment, and politics magazine.

29. *TV Guide*
    http://www.tvguide.com/
    A helpful archive for television topics.

30. *Sports Illustrated*
   http://CNNSI.com/
   A joint venture between the Cable News Network and *Sports Illustrated.*

31. *Harper's*
   http://www.harpers.org/
   An eclectic and well-written magazine that covers all aspects of American culture.

COMPUTERS AND WRITING

This category contains sites devoted to the field of computers and composition. Some are geared toward students, some are geared toward writing instructors, but all have some benefits to make this list. Be warned that sites at universities (those that end in .edu) tend to move from time to time, so you may find the occasional dead link as you go. However, this book's Web site will update essential links as they move around.

UNIVERSITY RESOURCES AND LINKS

32. **Purdue Online Writing Lab**
   http://owl.english.purdue.edu/
   The well-respected and innovative Purdue University site. Excellent source of sites.

33. **The Alliance for Computers and Writing**
   http://english.ttu.edu/acw/acw.html
   More of a teacher's resource, but good source material on how schools nationwide are using computers in writing classes.

34. *The Electronic Journal for Computer Writing, Rhetoric and Literature*
   http://www.cwrl.utexas.edu/
   This is a fairly advanced online journal out of the University of Texas.

35. **World-Wide Web Resources for Rhetoric and Composition**
   http://www.ihets.org/information/internet/comp.html
   Maintained by the Indiana Higher Education Telecommunication System, this is an excellent starting point to sites that involve university and writing-related links.

36. Research and Educational Resources—University of Texas
`http://uwc-server.fac.utexas.edu/resource/resrch.html`
A concise general list of useful research resources for writers, online and otherwise.

37. Creighton University Composition Program
`http://mockingbird.creighton.edu/english/comp.htm`
A fun and useful page from the influential Creighton (NE) University composition program. Useful links to other university online programs.

38. Carnegie Mellon's "Advice on Research and Writing"
`http://www.cs.cmu.edu/afs/cs.cmu.edu/user/mleone/web/how-to.html`
A terrific collection of helpful writing and researching links from all over the WWW.

39. Rochester Institute of Technology's "Point of View Journals"
`http://wally.rit.edu/pubs/guides/pov.html`
This is only a guide to traditional magazines and journals, so you won't find the magazines themselves at this site. Most of the issue-oriented magazines and journals that this site indexes will be in your own college's library.

40. Selected Bibliography: Computers and Composition
`http://www.louisville.edu/groups/english-www/cai/bibliography.html`
A University of Louisville site that provides a number of traditional (non-online) articles and essays about writing and computers.

41. Composition in Cyberspace—Diversity University
`http://www.du.org/cybercomp.html`
An excellent starting point for writers and instructors of composition. Terrific links, updated regularly.

GRAMMAR, STYLE, DOCUMENTATION, AND MISCELLANEOUS

42. Guide to Grammar and Writing
`http://webster.commnet.edu/HP/pages/darling/grammar.htm`
It might appear to be a little elementary (and too much fun!), but it's a fine, interactive grammar stop for when you're struggling. It's based on a community college campus in Hartford, Connecticut, and maintained by Charles Darling.

43. Grammar and Style Notes

http://www.english.upenn.edu/~jlynch/Grammar/

Jack Lynch at the University of Pennsylvania has compiled a wide-ranging and helpful grammar companion.

44. Beyond the MLA Handbook: Documenting Electronic Sources on the Internet

http://english.ttu.edu/kairos/1.2/inbox/
mla_archive.html

An excellent primer to MLA electronic source documentation. Be fore-warned, though, the final word should always come from the MLA's own site, www.mla.org, discussed in Chapter 9, and listed below.

45. The Merriam-Webster WWW Dictionary

http://www.m-w.com/netdict.htm

Excellent search function.

46. Paradigm Online Writing Assistant

http://www.spaceland.org/paradigm/

In the site's own words, Paradigm Online Writing Assistant is "an interactive, menu-driven, online writer's guide and handbook written in HTML and distributed freely over the WWW." Its usefulness to developing writers is limitless. I urge you to spend some time here.

47. MLA

http://www.mla.org

The last word in MLA documentation. Oh, first word, too.

48. *The Elements of Style*

http://www.cc.columbia.edu:80/acis/bartleby/strunk/

The influential grammar text online.

49. Daedalus® Integrated Writing Environment

http://kairos.daedalus.com/info/overtext.html

The main site for Daedalus questions and information.

50. The Lost Library of Moo

http://lucien.berkeley.edu/moo.html

The starting point for all matters concerning MOOs and MUDs. Excellent historical info and updated links.

51. Writing That Matters: The Website

http://www.prenhall.com/english

Prentice Hall's English Central Web site, through which you can reach this book's Web site.

Index